W9-BBS-418

The Catholic Church and the Holocaust, 1930–1965

The Catholic Church and the Holocaust, 1930–1965

Michael Phayer

INDIANA UNIVERSITY PRESS
Bloomington and Indianapolis

This book is a publication of

Indiana University Press
601 North Morton Street
Bloomington, IN 47404-3797 USA

http://www.indiana.edu/~iupress

Telephone orders 800-842-6796
Fax orders 812-855-7931
Orders by e-mail iuporder@indiana.edu

The paper used in this publication meets the minimum requirements of American National Standard for Information Sciences—Permanence of Paper for Printed Library Materials, ANSI Z39.48-1984.

Manufactured in the United States of America

Library of Congress Cataloging-in-Publication Data

Phayer, Michael, date.
  The Catholic Church and the Holocaust, 1930–1965 / Michael Phayer.
    p. cm.
  Includes bibliographical references and index.
  ISBN 0-253-33725-9 (alk. paper)
  1. Pius XII, Pope, 1876–1958—Relations with Jews. 2. Judaism —Relations—Catholic Church. 3. Catholic Church—Relations— Judaism. 4. Holocaust, Jewish (1939–1945) 5. World War, 1939– 1945—Religious aspects—Catholic Church. 6. Christianity and antisemitism—History—20th century. I. Title.

  BX1378 .P49 2000
  282'.09'044—dc21
                                                            99-087415

  1 2 3 4 5 05 04 03 02 01 00

Take heed lest you forget
the things which your eyes
have seen and teach them to
your children and to your children's children.

—Deuteronomy 4:9, Yom Hashoah, Milwaukee, 1988

ACKNOWLEDGMENTS

It is not possible to write a book such as this without borrowing extensively from other historians' studies. Often I refer by name in the text to those to whom I am indebted. I have learned much from them and many others, and can only hope that in using their research I have not misused data or taken ideas out of context.

Other scholars have contributed even more directly to my efforts. John Conway and Doris Bergen read parts of the manuscript and generously provided me with many corrections and alternative points of view. Ronald Modras offered many improvements for the first two chapters, as did Eva Fleischner for the last two. Although I benefited a great deal from the suggestions of these reviewers, mistakes of fact or interpretation are mine alone. I want to thank Derek Ciemniewski for translations from Polish; my brother, Richard Phayer, for translating Italian passages; and John Patrick Donnelly, S.J., for help with a difficult Latin document. I also want to acknowledge the work of a dozen or more graduate students from whose research and historical interpretations I have learned a great deal over the years.

Historical research is expensive, especially in Europe. Had I not been awarded a Senior Fulbright Research Fellowship in 1992–93, I could not have gone forward with this study. The fellowship allowed me to spend the better part of a year at the Institut für Zeitgeschichte in Munich and in other German and European archives. Munich's famous institute afforded me both a hospitable and superior workplace. In January of 1993 I visited Auschwitz and Treblinka alone in the cold. I want to thank the Holocaust Educational Foundation and its president, Theodore Z. Weiss, for providing funds for this momentous experience. Marquette University also generously underwrote my research project in the form of two faculty fellowships and two research fellowships, one of which came from the Bradley Institute for the Study of Democracy and

Public Values. This assistance provided me with travel funds to work in archives in the United States and time to work on the manuscript.

Working in German church archives is profitable to the extent of the helpfulness of their archivists. For this reason I must pay special thanks to Wolfgang Strecker of the Deutscher Caritasverband and to archivist Gotthard Klein in Berlin. Kolbsheim, France, is a difficult place to get to, but René Mougel of the Maritain Archives made my trip well worth while. I very much want to thank Dietrich Goldschmidt for making a tape-recorded interview of Gertrud Luckner available to me. In January 1993, Cardinal John Willebrands and his associate, Stjepan Schmidt, S.J., graciously afforded me a very valuable two-hour interview. State-side, Martin McGann of the National Archives in College Park, Maryland, was a knowledgeable and ready guide. Special thanks to Stephen Feinstein, Director of the Center for Holocaust and Genocide Studies at the University of Minnesota, for locating the jacket illustration, created by Fritz Hirschberger, a survivor who exhibits widely in the U.S. My fellow student at the University of Munich during the 1960s, Helmut Rankl, now a Privatdozent at our alma mater, made my year of research in Germany go by quickly and enjoyably with his hospitality. Finally, I owe a special debt of gratitude to my wife, Pat, and my late father-in-law, Peter Katsune. During my research trips both kept the home fires burning and both were very much missed.

INTRODUCTION

The Mosaic law of Hebrew Scripture, "Thou shalt not kill," became part of the moral code of all Christian churches. Why is it, then, that when prominent scholars write books about the murder of the Jews, church leaders receive scant mention? Contrariwise, those who have written about rescue of Jews during the Holocaust often deal at length with ordinary Christians. Why are the names of these rescuers obscure to us?

This book deals specifically with the Catholic response to the Holocaust. True to form, I found that Pope Pius XII did relatively little for Jews in their hour of greatest need, and that ordinary Catholics did a great deal more. It was never my intention to write a book solely about Pius XII's response to the Holocaust, yet the pope stands center stage or in the wings of nearly every chapter of this study, overshadowing ordinary men and women who acted heroically but had little or no authority in their church.

If the Catholic response to the Holocaust was somehow backward or upside down, how is this to be explained? Catholics in modern times had grown accustomed to the leadership of their pope, especially since the promulgation of the dogma of infallibility in 1870. During the Holocaust the table was reversed. Instead of leading, Pope Pius XII said that the church's bishops spoke for him when the Nazis came for the Jews. But the bishops, not used to acting independently, said nothing or very little. In the end, when it came down to actual rescue work, a few Catholics, people in the pulpits and pews, left to their own devices, acted courageously.

This explanation, while essentially valid, generalizes too much and analyzes too little. There were highly placed churchmen who participated in rescue; I refer to the Vatican's diplomatic corps operating in eastern Europe near the fulcrum of the Holocaust. This select group included Angelo Roncalli, the future pope. Even if the impetus to intervene for Jews was limited and usually came from the papal diplomats rather than from Rome, the diplomatic corps worked under the direct supervision of the pope. For this reason we may assert that through his diplomatic corps Pope Pius XII intervened at times to save Jews.

It was all well and good, of course, that the pope used diplomatic channels to save Jews. In the matter of genocide, however, diplomacy proved more of a weakness than a strength. Diplomacy functions within the boundaries of civilized behavior. The Holocaust ruptured those bounds beyond all measure. Hitler did not know or care to know the language of diplomacy. Pius XII's greatest failure, both during and after the Holocaust, lay in his attempt to use a diplomatic remedy for a moral outrage.

Fear of communism was a thread that ran through Pius XII's papacy. Filled with anxiety about communism's spread into central Europe during the war and its successes in western Europe after the war, Pius engaged the Vatican in no-holds-barred diplomatic solutions to the Red threat. Defying international efforts to bring Holocaust perpetrators to judicial accountability, the Vatican allowed fascist war criminals and fugitives from justice to become engaged in the postwar struggle against communism. The ethical credibility of the papacy fell to its lowest level in modern times.

Those who have debated Pius XII's response to the Holocaust—and they are numerous—either condemn him for cowardice for not speaking out or praise him for a gallant prudence for keeping silent so as not to endanger more Jewish lives. It is useless to debate what would have happened if Pope Pius had spoken out in language that directly challenged Hitler. Historians unanimously agree that Hitler would not on that account have curtailed the Holocaust. But beyond that, we simply do not know exactly what effect such a pronouncement might have had.

Actually, Pope Pius had options other than speaking out or being silent. The most important of these, especially for those making the "gallant reticence" argument, would have been to support individuals and groups who were rescuing Jews. Both moral support and financial assistance lay entirely within the pope's reach. Assistance of either kind would have resulted in the rescue of many more Jews.

Three decades ago Rolf Hochhuth, introducing Pius XII in his famous play *The Deputy*, instructed the actor to capture the pope's "aristocratic coldness" and the "icy glint" of his eyes. Hochhuth's Pius was a person incapable of compassion for human suffering. In his 1999 biography of Pius, *Hitler's Pope*, John Cornwell pinned an even uglier face on Pius—that of an antisemite. Cornwell's Pius was the perfect pope for Hitler, because the pontiff's antisemitism allowed the dictator to carry out genocide while he kept silent.

These images of Pius XII miss the mark. Jews and Gentiles alike who had audiences with the pope recalled his warm personality, and documents record a number of occasions when the pope wept openly. He was not a cold, unemotional human being. If Pius was tainted with antisemitism, it did not keep him from aiding Jews during and after the Holocaust. I have found that in deciding whether to intercede or not for Jews the pope responded to concrete circumstances and developments of the war. To hold that the pope always acted negatively toward Jews is to close one's eyes to the historical record.

This study differs from other works about Pope Pius in two additional respects. A historical portrait of Pius XII lacks a clear focus if his record during the Cold War era is ignored. Nearly half of this book takes up that record. Second, the pope was not a lone player in the drama of the church and the Holocaust. Shining the spotlight on Pius alone has diverted attention from the actions of other Catholics. The choices that confronted Pope Pius during the Holocaust often confronted the individual churchgoer.

What was the record of the whole Catholic church, not just the papacy, during the Holocaust? The 1998 Vatican statement on the Holocaust, "We Remember: A Reflection on the Shoah," indicates that individual Catholics committed wrongdoing but that the church itself incurred no responsibility.[1] No one would accuse the bishops or the pope of murdering Jews, but did they not have the duty or mission to urge Catholics to protect, not harm, Jews? Rather than individual "straying" Catholics, was it not the church itself, including especially its leaders, who bear the burden of guilt?

The question is relevant for both theoretical and practical reasons. Judaism and Christianity are intimately linked historically, and the physical extermination of the Jews took place on the largely Catholic continent of Europe. We are faced with the plain, appalling fact that many of the world's greatest mass murderers were born and raised Catholic— Adolf Hitler, Heinrich Himmler, and Rudolf Höss, to mention only a few. The small number of Catholic rescuers are obscured by the mountain of evil cast over them by these perpetrators.

Rescuers and perpetrators were but a slight minority of Europe's Catholic population. Whether adversely or kindly disposed toward Jews, most Catholics played no role at all during the Holocaust. Their church was a sleeping giant that awoke too late to exploit its organizational potential to save Jews in a concerted effort. Within twenty years of the Holocaust, that same church hastened to rid itself of the age-old poison of antisemitism. Progress was too dearly purchased.

Between 1930 and 1965, the Catholic church completely reversed its position relative to Jews. The centuries-old teaching of contempt gave way to a recognition of the ongoing vitality of Judaism. This reversal indicates that the church recognized that it was unprepared for the Holocaust, and that, subsequently, it found itself compelled to rethink its relationship to Jews and Judaism. By dealing with both the Holocaust and post-Holocaust years, I have tried to indicate why the church was unprepared to save Jews in a concerted effort and why it suddenly reversed its teaching.

Along the way an unexpected and surprising discovery greets us— the role that women played during and after the Holocaust. Although women had no place in the authority structure of the church, they were vocal in urging church leaders, including Pope Pius, to speak out. Reflecting on the cowardice of church leaders, French Catholic Germaine Ribière made reference in her diary to their "ridiculous prudence." Urging Hungarian bishops to intervene on behalf of Jews, Margit Slachta warned prophetically that if they were not willing to take such a risk, "the cause of the church, its possessions and schools will be lost."[2] During and after the Holocaust, Gertrud Luckner worked tirelessly to cleanse German Catholicism of antisemitism.

Although Catholic women were prominent in rescue work, they were not alone. It is significant that Catholics at every level of the church hierarchy, including the pope, became involved in the rescue of Jews. However, "We Remember" exaggerates not a little when it asserts that the pope personally or through his representatives saved "hundreds of thousands of Jewish lives." Although the number of rescuers was small, their work carried enormous consequence. It is difficult to imagine that the reversal of Catholic teaching toward Jews would ever have occurred had not at least a few members of the church seen fit to challenge the Holocaust.

When the historic moment of the church's definitive rejection of antisemitism finally came, it was not during Pope Pius's reign but immediately after it. Pius was elected months before the beginning of the Second World War, and he remained in office until 1958. Clearly, the dozen post-Holocaust years provided ample opportunity for Pope Pius to take the lead in rethinking Christian-Jewish relations. The need to address Catholic antisemitism became apparent when some forty Jews were murdered in Kielce, Poland, in 1946. Immediately, French Catholic

Jacques Maritain and American rabbi Philip S. Bernstein urged Pius to take steps to suppress European antisemitism. A few years later, French survivor and educator Jules Isaac prodded Pius to uproot the antisemitism embedded in Catholic teaching and worship. But during the Cold War, Pius showed more interest in clemency for Nazi criminals than in the problem of antisemitism.

Is it correct to speak of Pius's silence? Yes, if we take it to mean that the pope did not speak out unequivocally against the murder of the Jews. No, if we take it to mean that the pope failed to use the Vatican's offices to help in the rescue of Jews. In the three chapters on Pope Pius in this study, I argue that the pontiff was concerned about the Jews, but that his limited intervention on their behalf was measured and calculated for very specific reasons that he adopted to guide, or at least to explain, his actions. The image that emerges of Pope Pius is that of a pontiff whose deep concern about communism and the intact physical survival of the city of Rome kept him from exploring options on behalf of the Jewish people.

Contemporaries, both Catholic and non-Catholic and within and without the Vatican, urged Pope Pius to denounce forthrightly the murder of the Jews. He considered their advice but chose an alternative path. It is possible, of course, that Pius was psychologically and temperamentally incapable of decisive action. Some close observers or associates of the pope have suggested this. The fact that he did not or could not address the problem of genocide when it involved Catholics in Poland and Croatia before the Holocaust began gives further weight to this perception. Shortly thereafter, when the Holocaust itself occurred, it became even more difficult for Pius to speak out, because Germany was a country that the pope both feared and admired. Understanding Pius's disposition toward Germany is the key to understanding the serpentine course he consistently charted for himself during the Holocaust, sometimes intervening on behalf of Jews and sometimes ignoring their plight.

Would the history of the Catholic church and the Holocaust have been different had Pius XI lived five more years? Yes. Pius XI was quick-tempered, and he had become deeply concerned about fascist racism late in his life. Would church history read differently if Angelo Roncalli had been elected pope in 1939 instead of 1959? Again, yes. Roncalli involved himself directly in saving Jews, even if that meant their passage to Palestine, the Holy Land. Would either Roncalli or Pius XI have been able to prevent the Holocaust? No. The church had no power over Hitler.

What characterized Catholic behavior toward Jews most during the Holocaust was diversity. Some bishops participated in rescue efforts;

between the moral and political spheres."[3] I have attempted to hold Pius XII and other church leaders to no standard other than their own and that of their peers. Finally, we must heed historian Michael Marrus's wise admonition not to fantasize that we today would act any more courageously than people of faith of another time. The reader will judge to what extent I have succeeded or failed.

The Catholic Church and the Holocaust, 1930–1965

1. Catholic Attitudes toward Jews before the Holocaust

Beliefs and feelings of European Catholics toward Jews varied considerably on the eve of the Holocaust. Antisemitism, it is true, was prevalent everywhere. But the kinds and degrees of antisemitism differed widely from east to west and from north to south. Scholars have pointed to the vehement antisemitism of the Church Fathers and have drawn up concordances comparing antisemitic policies of medieval Christian rulers with those of the Nazis. Although these facts cannot be contested, traditional Christian antisemitism did not cause the Holocaust.[1] However, along with more modern varieties of antisemitism, it conditioned some European Catholics to become part of Hitler's murderous machinery.

The Vatican itself was a principal reason why Catholic attitudes toward Jews lacked uniformity. Although the church had defined the dogma of papal infallibility in matters of faith and morals at the First Vatican Council (1870), the popes did not speak officially about Jews. In fact, the Holy See's attitude appeared to be changing under Pope Pius XI (1922–1939), but under Pius XII (1939–1958) this trend reversed. This shift meant that even if the Vatican had possessed the influence to dictate Catholic feelings toward Jews (which it did not), little attitudinal change would have occurred. Still, the promising direction that Catholic-Jewish issues had taken under Pius XI (only to end abruptly under Pius XII) had positive and negative effects on how Catholics responded to the Holocaust.

Just what was the "new direction" of Pius XI, and what evidence is there for it? Perhaps anticipating fascist antisemitism, the Vatican issued an important statement on antisemitism in 1928. The directive broke no ground theologically, referring as it did to the Jews as blind for rejecting their messiah and as the former people of God, but it condemned all antisemitic hatred and stated that the Vatican wished to protect Jews from unjust treatment.[2] Acting consistently with the 1928 directive, Pius XI published his famous encyclical in 1937, *Mit brennender Sorge,* which condemned racism (but not Hitler or National Socialism, as some have erroneously asserted). Consistent with the directive of the previous decade, the encyclical affirmed Christianity's roots in the Old Testament but called attention to the crucifixion of the Savior by the Jews.

A number of events took place in 1938 which indicate an increasingly confrontational attitude on the part of Pope Pius XI toward fascist racism. The Anschluss, or Nazi seizure of Austria, occurred in the spring, in conjunction with which Hitler made a triumphant entry into his former city of residence, Vienna. To welcome him, the reigning prelate of that country, Cardinal Theodore Innitzer, rang the bells of the city's churches and flew the Nazi flag from them. Furious at this, Pius ordered Innitzer to Rome for a dressing down, which was communicated in detail through diplomatic channels to the United States so that world governments would know where the Vatican stood regarding Hitler's Germany.[3] Shortly thereafter, when Benito Mussolini decked out Rome's streets with Nazi swastikas on the occasion of Hitler's state visit in May, the pope snubbed the dictators by leaving the city. While Hitler was still in Rome, the Vatican newspaper *L'Osservatore Romano* carried a front-page article roundly condemning Nazi racist ideas about the purity of blood and forbidding Catholics to teach such notions.[4]

By summertime Pius was warming even more to the task. After the Italian government put out a racist declaration in July, Pius XI pointed out the contradiction between Catholicism and racism to two audiences. To one group he said that "catholic" means universal, not racist and separatist; a week later, Pius told a group of 200 seminarians that there is only one human race and that Catholic Action, a religious activist group, should oppose racism. Both addresses were published in *L'Osservatore Romano.*[5] Pius then resolved to speak authoritatively about the problem of antisemitism and racism. We know this because in August Pius XI asked American Jesuit John LaFarge to start work immediately on a draft of an encyclical on racism.

Pius XI's words to a group of Belgian pilgrims in September 1938 were of great significance for many Catholics during the Holocaust. Speaking more positively and theologically than the 1928 directive had, Pius XI began to build a bridge between Christians and Jews when he told the Belgian Catholics that Christians are children of Abraham, which should make antisemitism abhorrent to them. Instead, Christians should learn from Abraham faith, reliance on God, and obedience to his will. Jewish leader Ernst Ludwig Ehrlich believes that had this attitude struck root in the Christian west before the Holocaust, it might have been prevented or diminished in its fury.[6]

Historian Ronald Modras has pointed out the unique circumstances surrounding Pius's words "Spiritually we are Semites," spoken to the Belgian pilgrims. Pope Pius spoke spontaneously after reading a text in a Mass book about Abraham, who he referred to as "our Father, our Ancestor." "Antisemitism," the pope went on, "is not compatible with the sublime thought and reality which are expressed in this text." The pope then paused, overcome with emotion, before continuing. "It is not possible for Christians to participate in antisemitism."[7] Pius's identification of Christians and Jews as belonging to the same tradition became widely known among Catholics in western Europe.

The spontaneity with which the pope spoke was remarkable. Equally remarkable were the circumstances surrounding the publication of his words. Realizing that since he had spoken to the Belgian group before the beginning of a general audience his statement would not be printed in the official publication *Acta Apostolicae Sedis* or in the Vatican's newspaper, Pius asked that the Belgian Catholics, who were in the communication field, see to its publication. Because of this, Pius's phrase—"we are Semites"—provided inspiration for Catholic rescuers during the Holocaust.

Pope Pius XI's repeated denunciations of racism in 1938 were inconsistent with his silence toward the end of the year in connection with the great destruction of German Jewish life and property that took place during the November pogrom of 1938, or "Kristallnacht." Undoubtedly, the pope's previous utterances against fascist racism led many churchmen, including some of the most prominent—Cardinals Schuster of Milan, Van Roey of Belgium, Verdier of Paris, and the Patriarch of Lisbon—to condemn stringently the Nazi violence of November.[8] But why would the pope have kept silent after speaking out with much less provocation during the preceding months? It has been suggested that Pius was dissuaded by the caution of his secretary of state and successor, Eugenio Pacelli.[9] This is a possible explanation, since the pope was nearing the end of his life—he would suffer a debilitating heart attack within a fortnight—and Pacelli was viewed as his probable successor. Still, when Italy's racial laws were decreed almost simultaneously with the November events in Germany, Pius XI reacted negatively, asking why "Italy was disgracefully imitating Germany."[10]

A more likely explanation for Pius's uncharacteristic silence would be that he intended to speak to the outrages of the November pogrom

definitively in an encyclical. The pope was expecting the draft of an encyclical on racism which he had commissioned in August (*Humani Generis Unitas*—The Unity of Humankind). Unbeknownst to the pope, one
of the draft's authors, American Jesuit John LaFarge, had already delivered it to the general of the Jesuit Society, Wladimir Ledóchowski. When
the co-author of the draft, German Jesuit Gustav Gundlach, attempted
to find out why the draft had not been forwarded to the pope, Ledóchowski gave him no explanation and told him that he need not concern
himself with the matter any further![11] Nonplussed and disillusioned,
Gundlach wrote to LaFarge expressing his fear that the draft had fallen
victim to Vatican intrigue occasioned by Pius XI's approaching death,
adding that his deep trust in General Ledóchowski had turned out to be
misplaced.

LaFarge and Gundlach decided finally to bypass their superior, Ledóchowski.[12] This strategy worked, but the manuscript evidently did
not reach the pope's desk until weeks or days before his death in February 1939. With Pius too ill to make whatever changes he felt necessary
before publishing the encyclical, it ended up as unfinished business. Immediately after the pope died, the manuscript disappeared.

Copies of the draft, discovered years later, revealed that its views on
antisemitism were quite unexceptional culturally and theologically. But,
despite its weaknesses, it did condemn both racism and racial antisemitism explicitly. One draft likened German antisemitic racism to American anti-Negro racism, and bemoaned the fact that this prevented the
church from becoming "a house of God . . . for all races."[13] We have no
idea, of course, how the pope might have changed the encyclical so that
it would express his reaction to the November pogrom, his oft-repeated
warnings about racism, or his "Spiritually we are Semites" assertion of
September. Gundlach knew that the death of Pius XI closed the door on
the ill-fated encyclical draft. He wrote to LaFarge that the election of
Pacelli to succeed Pius XI meant that diplomacy would now take precedence over justice.[14]

Fascism, Antisemitism, and Pius XII

A clue signaling that Pius XII would not share his predecessor's vocal
opposition to racism and antisemitism occurred in Hungary in 1938
on the occasion of the International Eucharistic Congress held in Budapest. The congress met in the spring at a time of increased antisemitism
in Hungary, whose first antisemitic laws were at that moment being
passed by the legislature. The Vatican secretary of state, Eugenio Pacel-

li, addressed the congress, making reference to Jews "whose lips curse [Christ] and whose hearts reject him even today."[15] Such a statement given in Hungary at the time of the new legislation would have fed the country's antisemitic inclinations. Certainly it ran counter to Pius XI's September statement urging Catholics to honor their spiritual father Abraham.

Soon after Pacelli became pope, a situation arose in Vichy France which illustrated the Vatican's lassitude regarding fascist antisemitism. In 1940 the first antisemitic decrees took place, eliminating Jews as public employees. Catholic reaction was ambiguous: two bishops and some priests endorsed the law; others opposed it.[16] In the summer of the following year, the Vichy government issued a second antisemitic decree. This time Catholic reaction against it was sharp enough to cause the conservative rightist government to inquire about the Holy See's views.

Vichy's ambassador to the Vatican, Léon Bérard, reported back to his government that he had spoken with very competent authorities, and that the Holy See had no insurmountable difficulties with the statute and did not intend to become involved in the matter. The Vatican's nuncio to France, Valerio Valeri, became embarrassed when Marshal Henri Philippe Pétain presented him with this information at a public gathering. Thinking that Bérard had probably oversimplified the Vatican's position, Valeri checked the accuracy of the report through Cardinal Secretary of State Maglione.[17] Valeri learned that Bérard had consulted with top Vatican personnel, Monsignors Domenico Tardini (Secretary of the Sacred Congregation for Extraordinary Affairs) and Giovanni Montini (who became Pope Paul VI in 1963). Although Maglione told Valeri that he thought the statute was unfortunate, the Vatican did not choose to change its position or overrule the report given by Bérard to Pétain.[18]

Shortly after the episode in France, new antisemitic laws—a Jewish Code—were promulgated in Catholic Slovakia in September 1941. The code differed from France's law in that it disallowed marriage between Jews and non-Jews. This time the Holy See disapproved.[19] The Vichy law, racist though it was, lacked the marital proscription and got past the pope without remonstrance. The Vichy incident underscored the low priority the new pope gave to racism. With the Holocaust about to begin, the Vatican, invited by the French government to provide direction regarding treatment of Jews, failed to do so.

Two early pioneers who sought to improve Catholic-Jewish relations in the 1930s, Austrian John Oesterreicher and German Karl Thieme, thought they detected a sharp break in papal policy when Pius XII succeeded Pius XI.[20] In the face of Nazi antisemitism, the Austrian and German wanted to put together a pro-Jewish statement for European dignitaries to underwrite. But Thieme doubted Pius XII would sign on. The new pope seemed too fearful of Nazism. Oesterreicher wrote in June 1939 that it was inconceivable why Pius XII, after all his concordatory work as secretary of state had been violated by the Nazis, "would stick with diplomatic approaches instead of speaking out truthfully."[21] Oesterreicher referred disdainfully to the new pontiff's feckless flattering of Hitler and remarked that if he was still trying to get the Führer to abide by the Concordat, it was time to either laugh or cry.[22]

For centuries, dating back to medieval times, the Catholic church has attempted to regularize relations between itself and other states through treaties known as Concordats. They serve the purpose of safeguarding the rights of the church in a foreign country. As secretary of state under Pope Pius XI from 1930 to 1939, Eugenio Pacelli forged several Concordats. The most important one for our purposes linked the Vatican in 1933 with the new Nazi regime in Germany under Adolf Hitler. In addition, Pacelli played an important role in the negotiations leading to the Lateran Treaty in 1929 between the Vatican and Mussolini's fascist Italian government. The treaty is also of great importance for this study because it settled the "Roman Question" by creating Vatican City as an independent and sovereign state in the center of the city of Rome. During the Second World War Pacelli, as Pope Pius XII, became preoccupied with preserving his state, Vatican City, from bombardment.

Cardinal Eugene Tisserant, a Vatican insider, spoke critically of the new pope in 1940, revealing his perception of the disappointing difference between Pius XI and his successor. Tisserant told his fellow countryman Cardinal Suhard of Paris that Pius XII's policies in diplomacy were self-serving, "and this is extremely sad—particularly for one who has lived in the reign of Pius XI."[23] When Germany invaded Poland and proceeded to terrorize the Polish people, the English minister to the Vatican, Francis Osborne, made the same disadvantageous comparison of Pius XII to his predecessor. "The Holy Father appears to be . . . adopting an ostrich-like policy toward these notorious atrocities. It is felt that as a consequence of this exasperating attitude, the great moral authority enjoyed by the Papacy throughout the world under Pius XI has today been notably diminished."[24]

Catholic Attitudes about Jews beyond the Vatican

In Catholic Europe beyond Rome, attitudes toward Jews differed considerably. The exception to this general statement concerns naturalized

Jews, the outsiders in every country. These were the hapless Jews who had emigrated from one state to another after the Great War or who found themselves stateless as a result of Nazi-sponsored border changes at the beginning of the Second World War. In France, Germany, Poland, Slovakia, Rumania, and Hungary, these Jews experienced greater hostility from indigenous nationals than did native Jews.

In Germany itself, an influx of Jewish immigrants after the Great War stirred up antisemitism.[25] In Austria, the young ne'er-do-well Hitler reacted strongly, some would say neurotically, when he encountered Orthodox or Chassidic Jews in Vienna before the Great War. Later, when Germany invaded Poland in 1939, many Jews fled into Ukraine. The leader of the Greek Catholic church wrote to the Vatican that the Jews gave "the activities of the [Russian or Soviet] authorities a character of sordid avarice which one is accustomed to seeing only among Jewish petty merchants."[26] Romanian Jews, who were culturally Hungarian and former Hungarian nationals, found they were unwelcome in their one-time home country after being returned as a result of a border revision with Romania. More than 100,000 former Transylvanian Jews— branded as aliens—found themselves in a similar position.[27] After Vichy passed antisemitic legislation, French bishops affirmed the natural rights of Jews, but many of those who reacted against the law made a distinction between the rights of French Jews and those of immigrant Jews.[28]

Attitudes toward sedentary Jews, on the other hand, varied from country to country. The ambiguity of the Vatican's own position regarding antisemitism accounts for some of this diversity. Even in Italy, in closest proximity to the Vatican, variations were commonplace. Some priests gladly sought to "aryanize" Jews by providing them with baptismal certificates, even back-dating them if necessary. Other priests did not.[29] Of course, in the church each bishop oversees the spiritual affairs of his own flock, but from time to time the Holy See has attempted to assert greater influence locally. This was especially the case after the First Vatican Council in 1870, which had increased papal authority substantially. But this remained without effect on Catholic-Jewish relations throughout the Catholic world, simply because the Vatican itself had not given the matter of antisemitism a high priority.

The countries of eastern Europe, newly established after the Great War, vibrated with a national Catholic identity that excluded Jews. Nowhere was this more in evidence than in Poland, whose government even failed to fulfill its obligations, stipulated by the Paris Peace Conference, toward minorities. The print media of the church and the private sector built up a laundry list of grievances against Jews. Readers learned

to equate the word "Jew" with "Bolshevik," "Freemason," "liberal,"
and "international capitalist."[30] Consequently, Jews took the blame for
prostitution and pornography or whatever other woes plagued the country. The Franciscan press—above all their *Maly dziennik,* Poland's largest circulating daily—identified Jews with Communists.[31] Catholic priest
Stanislaw Trzeciak wrote obsessively about the Protocols of the Elders
of Zion, and his ideas were widely circulated in the Catholic press.[32]
Even after the Protocols were exposed as fabricated plagiarism, they
continued to be popular in Poland.

In both Poland and Hungary, the belief that Jews were "Christ-killers" was common. Less common, but widespread, was the accusation of
blood libel. Catholic newspapers nurtured both myths.[33] The particulars
of the blood libel myth varied, but the basic notion was that Jews engaged in ritual murder of Christian infants or children to use their blood
to make unleavened bread or Passover wine.[34] In 1882, Hungarian Jew-
ess Tisza Eszlar was accused of murdering a Christian child. Courts of
law found her innocent, but Catholics believed in her guilt and kept the
libel story circulating.[35] The Vatican had held no truck with this non-
sense for several centuries, but it did nothing to disabuse Catholics in
eastern Europe of the hateful tales. In fact, the Jesuit journal *Cività
Catholica,* published at the Vatican, accused the Jews of being "Christ-
killers" and of ritual murder as late as 1941 and 1942.[36] As in Poland,
Hungarian Jews were identified with Marxists and liberals. Newspapers
such as the *National Journal* and the *New Generation* made them the
scapegoat for Hungary's misfortunes during the Great War.[37]

Religious antisemitism of the sort associated with the ritual murder myth no longer had currency in Germany. Religious antisemitism
and Nazi racial antisemitism are clearly distinct, but this does not mean
that historically the two could not be linked. In May of 1943, at which
time Hungarian Jews had not yet been molested by Germany, the two
Nazis most responsible for the implementation of the Holocaust, Heinrich Himmler and Ernst Kaltenbrunner, plotted to use the ritual murder
myth to their advantage to exterminate eastern European Jews. Himmler, Reich Führer for the Establishment of the German People, wrote to
Kaltenbrunner, chief of the Reich Main Office for Security, instructing
him to spread ritual murder propaganda in Hungary so that it would be
easier to extract their Jews.[38]

The ritual murder myth was beginning to decline in Austria, but the
Anderl von Rhinn shrine in the Tyrol, which depicted Jews siphoning off
the blood of the slain youth, was still popular.[39] Unofficial religious devotion still pilloried Jews as "Christ-killers," as in the *Oberammergau*

Heinrich Himmler, who was in charge of carrying out the Holocaust,
exploited the myth of blood libel, or the ritual murder of Christian children
by Jews, to incite anger among eastern European Catholics against Jews.
(Courtesy of the United States Holocaust Memorial Museum Photo Archives)

Passion Play in Bavaria, but these events did not bestir deep antisemitic
feeling.[40] In interwar Germany, "assimilated Jew" was a negative term
referring to secular, educated, deracinated people of Jewish heritage. The
idea that such Jews threatened civilization found its way into influential
Catholic journals such as the Jesuit organ *Stimmen der Zeit.*[41] But the
same journal also published articles proclaiming the religious nature of
Judaism and denouncing antisemitism.[42] Other Catholic journals, including *Junge Front,* also supported Jews.[43] In Germany, in contrast to
eastern European countries, there was no obsession with Jewish issues.
On the contrary, the German Catholic press took little interest in such
questions.[44]

Hitler's *Mein Kampf* was also ignored by the German Catholic press.
The Nazi brand of antisemitism was rejected in no uncertain terms, and
Nazi violence toward Jews when Hitler finally achieved power in Jan-
uary 1933 was not supported in Germany, although some Austrian

Catholic newspapers did. Unlike the Polish Catholic press, which generally reported that the national pogrom of 1938 was wrong but "understandable," German Catholic papers did not give the event coverage. Readers would understand this as being tacitly negative, because the press supported religious Jews.[45] Before the Concordat between the Vatican and Germany was signed, Catholic newspapers had predicted that the church and National Socialism would be enemies if Hitler came to power.[46]

Nazism fared better among Austrians, for whom a certain measure of hatred toward Jews was more or less part and parcel of the believing Catholic.[47] At least three Catholic churches in the country had stained-glass window depictions of Jews carrying out ritual murder. By the time of the Anschluss (1938), many Austrian priests were outspokenly antisemitic; others, only moderately so.[48] This prejudice was mirrored in the Christian Socialist party and in newspapers that showed some tolerance for Nazi violence toward Jews. In commenting on Hungarian antisemitic laws and on Jacques Maritain's book *The Impossibility of Antisemitism*, the Catholic weekly *Schönere Zukunft* warned that conversion to Christianity did not expunge the Jew's race. Christian nations had to be on guard, because even good Jewish converts could ruin a country's social and economic life.[49] Still, the overall position of the Catholic press held that Nazi racism was inconsistent with Catholic teaching.[50] A young Catholic priest and Jewish convert, John Oesterreicher, combated antisemitism in Austria, whose church leader, Cardinal Innitzer, approved of his work.[51] But Oesterreicher found that there were limits to what he could realistically try to accomplish because of the great number of "brown Catholics" or "Nazikatholiken" in Austria.[52] Eugon Kogon wrote that it was precisely antisemitism that attracted Austrians to Nazism.

After Cardinal Innitzer's 1938 papal dressing down, he opposed compromises with Nazism more forthrightly than did his counterpart in Germany, Cardinal Bertram. The star decree illustrates this. Wishing to further stigmatize Jews, Hitler ordered them to wear the Star of David in public, beginning in the fall of 1941. This meant that Catholics would worship at services alongside Jewish converts who would be clearly marked by the star. Some Catholics refused to kneel next to a converted "Jew" to take the Eucharist at the communion rail.[53] (Prior to 1965, the sanctuaries of Catholic churches were partitioned off from the laity by a railing at which communicants knelt side by side to receive the Eucharist during mass.)

Cardinals Innitzer and Bertram responded differently to the dilemma that the star decree created among Catholics. The German prelate directed priests to avoid any announcements that would be embarrassing for converted "Jews," such as declaring a portion of the communion rail off-limits for them. However, should Nazi party members create a scene in church to protest the presence of Jews, the latter were to be directed to attend an early morning mass which would not be frequented by Nazis.[54] Thus, in case of a confrontation, Nazis would be accommodated at the expense of Catholics of Jewish descent. At the time of the decree, there were still about 8,000 Jews living in Vienna, many of them converts or married to Catholics. Innitzer ordered that no distinction based on race should be allowed in prayers or liturgy, and he told parish personnel not to make distinctions based on race.[55]

The following year, 1942, another crisis arose when the Nazis threatened to dissolve by decree all Jewish-Gentile marriages. Marriages between Jews and Catholics and between converted "Jews" and Catholics were considered valid by the church, that is, sacramental. Both Bertram and Innitzer reacted strongly. A protest from Cardinal Bertram, together with planned simultaneous local protests on the part of both Protestant and Catholic churches, forestalled the divorce decree.[56] Innitzer went so far as to request that Pope Pius intervene in the matter by contacting Hitler himself.[57]

In spite of such conflicts between Nazism and the church, one Austrian bishop stood out conspicuously for his adulation of Hitler. Alois Hudal, who by his own admission harbored Nazi war criminals—including the most infamous ones such as Adolf Eichmann—after the Second World War, was obsessed with Jews. Hudal accused the Jews of undermining European society in general and German society in particular. Hudal defended the Nazi movement and the Nuremberg racial laws as well.[58] In 1936 Hudal published a booklet, *The Foundations of National Socialism,* and in 1942 a second pro-Nazi pamphlet, *Europe's Religious Future.* The latter piece was in answer to an Italian publication written by Francesco Orestano which appeared in *Gerarchia,* a fascist journal founded by Mussolini. The Italian asserted that after the German conquest of Europe, Teutonic culture would have to integrate itself with European culture, meaning, among other things, that Nazi antisemitism would have to be mitigated. Hudal responded that Jews inspired both liberalism and Bolshevism, and that Christianity must use Nazism to fight these corrupting elements.[59]

In spite of his appreciation of Nazism, Hudal won an appointment as the rector of the Collegia del Anima in Rome, the school of theology for Austrian seminarians. There he remained throughout the Nazi era, acting on occasion as an intermediary between Pius XII and Nazi occupational forces, and, after the war, helping Holocaust perpetrators to escape justice.

French Catholics no longer believed in blood libel stories, but, like other Europeans, they were antisemitic for religious or social reasons, as distinct from racial antisemitism. French church leaders, both bishops and cardinals, condemned Nazi racism as it developed during the 1930s. This, together with the Vatican's own denunciation of racism in 1937, had considerable impact on French Catholics, except for the radical right.

In addition, there was a layer of secular antisemitism in France, which especially targeted post–World War I immigrants. This bias fed on newly published editions of the Protocols of the Elders of Zion which accused Jews of sedition and treason.[60] Both kinds of antisemitism were fanned by radical right-wing Catholics, who had nurtured a dominant strain of antisemitism dating back to the previous century, when Eduard Drumont published *La France Juive*. In the 1930s Action Française, along with individuals like Charles Maurras, perpetuated antisemitism with great effect, particularly among the older clergy.[61] Articles in the journal *Études* were consistently antisemitic but lacked the strident tone of the Catholic right.[62] A middle-of-the-road Catholic publication was mildly antisemitic. Another journal, the *Semaine religieuse* of Evreux, published an article under SS duress justifying Nazi antisemitic measures in France.[63] These journals were balanced, to a much greater extent than in eastern European countries, by other prominent Catholic writers and intellectuals such as those on the theological faculty of the university of Lille. Jacques Maritain published *The Impossibility of Antisemitism* in 1937, and a French-speaking Belgian Jesuit wrote a book that discredited the Protocols.

The same balance characterized the English-language Catholic press. Although the American Catholic press largely ignored the torment of the Jews, two leading weekly journals, *Commonweal* and *America,* took notice of Nazi antisemitism from the beginning of Hitler's rise to power in 1933 to the end of the Holocaust. After describing accurately the November pogrom of 1938, *America* editorialized that "We have no words to express our horror and detestation of the barbarous and un-Christian treatment of the Jews by Nazi Germany."[64] *America's* continuous coverage of Nazi antisemitism and the Holocaust—fifty-six articles and forty editorials—resulted, no doubt, from the influence of John LaFarge, one of its editors.[65]

On the eve of the Holocaust, no one was as farsighted as Maritain regarding Judaism. The French philosopher broke entirely new ground by insisting on the permanence of Yahweh's covenant with Israel and on the necessity of Christian-Jewish reconciliation for the survival of western civilization.[66] In *The Impossibility of Antisemitism,* Maritain condemned the prejudice of Maurras and even rejected his own views of 1921, which had justified antisemitic legislation.[67]

Maritain was not content to remain on a theological level in his fight against antisemitism. In 1939 he published *A Christian Looks at the Jewish Question,* a scathing attack on antisemitism as it was found in various European countries. He pointed out the stupidity of stereotyping Jews as bankers or financiers when they numbered some 16 million, many of whom lived in poverty. Drawing on information in the American journal *Catholic Worker,* Maritain alluded to the fact that various U.S. rabbinical associations had condemned Russia's persecution of Christians. Unfortunately, the reverse was not true: the influence of Nazism in eastern Europe, in countries which were largely Catholic, was bringing about an increase of antisemitism.[68]

Antisemitic Legislation in Catholic Fascist Countries

After Germany's 1935 Nuremberg Laws were promulgated, copycat legislation became the order of the day in much of Europe. As we have seen, Maritain's own countrymen were party to it in Vichy France, as was Hungary, starting in 1938 at the time of the World Eucharistic Congress. There was an essential difference between Catholics in eastern and western Europe in this regard, however. Catholic priests and bishops in the west were not active in political circles or parliaments that adopted antisemitic legislation, but in the east they were.[69]

The Arrow Cross, Hungary's very antisemitic far-right political organization, was supported by individual priests and even bishops such as Jozsef Grosz, who was promoted in 1943 by Pius XII to the bishopric of Kalocsa, the second most important bishopric in the country.[70] Clergymen such as Cardinal Justinian Serédi and Bishop Gyula Glattfelder, who served in Hungary's Upper Chamber of Parliament, voted in favor of antisemitic legislation first passed in 1938.[71] These laws began with economic and social restrictions on Jews, and culminated during World War II with a government initiative to expel Jews from Hungary. When

Russia occupied the Baltic countries in 1939, Lithuanian Jews asked Bishop V. Brizgys to issue a pastoral letter forbidding Catholics from participating in pogroms. "The church cannot help you," the bishop replied; "I personally can only weep and pray."[72]

Slovakia, a new Nazi rump state formed by Hitler when Germany annexed the western half of federated Czechoslovakia, exhibited many of the same problems for Jews. Pronounced antisemitism existed well before the state fell under the Nazi shadow. During the interwar period, antisemitism characterized the Catholicism of the Slovak people. Catholic Action sought to exclude Jewish influence in business and social matters.[73] A leading political party, the Slovak People's Party, founded and dominated by Catholic clergymen, used antisemitism to win public favor. American diplomat George F. Kennan was a witness to the antisemitic terror practiced by the party's vigilante wing, the Hlinka Guard.[74] In 1939 a Jesuit wrote that Jews should be segregated in ghettos and marked by a badge. "The church," he wrote, "advocates the elimination of the Jews," which most likely meant their expulsion, not extermination.[75]

With the People's Party ruling Slovakia, Monsignor Jozef Tiso, the president, promulgated the first antisemitic legislation in 1939 and 1940. It had the distinction of placing race over grace by declaring that those people who were baptized after 1918 were to be treated as Jews.[76] Up to this point in time, the Vatican was not concerned about the events in Slovakia. It was pleased to see a new Catholic state in eastern Europe. Pope Pius XII extended an apostolic blessing to President Tiso.

The Vatican found the next year's antisemitic steps less to its liking. The Codex Judaicum, passed in September of 1941, was based on the Nuremberg Laws; the legal rights of Jews were ended.[77] The Vatican's concern was for the rights of Jewish converts. Restrictions on marriages between Jews and Catholics upset Rome because of the principle of sacramental grace.[78] The Slovakian bishops also deplored the Jewish Code on this score, but went further, telling Tiso that he acted against the principles of religion by persecuting people on the basis of their race. As a result of this disagreement, the Vatican "retired" Tiso's title of monsignor, thereby demoting him.[79]

In Poland the attitude toward Jews by church authorities of the dominant Catholic culture aggravated Jewish life. Church leaders, including the titular head of the bishops, Cardinal August Hlond, believed that at best, Polish Jews could not be assimilated into the country's life, and that at worst, they poisoned it.[80] Church leaders therefore believed that

Jews should emigrate or, failing this, that their influence on domestic life should be strictly limited by law.[81]

Polish Catholic elites followed the same pattern. Catholic students in all major universities succeeded in getting "ghetto benches" established for Jews in classrooms.[82] Although the Catholic press fed its readers a steady diet of antisemitism, church pronouncements and literature were explicitly nonviolent regarding Jewish policy. Nevertheless, church authorities tended to overlook street violence against Jews, which became more frequent after 1935, and the Polish church did not denounce the attack on Jewish life and property that took place in Germany in November 1938. In fact, several church papers, including that of one of Poland's most important churchmen, Prince Adam Sapieha of Cracow, condoned the violence.[83]

The German Catholic Church and Nazi Antisemitism

Unlike many churchmen in Croatia, Hungary, and other eastern European countries, most German bishops were not mean-spirited toward Jews. Cardinal Faulhaber gave a series of Advent sermons in 1933 that affirmed that God had entrusted his Word to the Chosen People, in this way preserving a cultural bond between Judaism and Christianity, which the nazified German Christians were at that time attacking.[84] Munich rabbi Leo Baerwald was encouraged by Faulhaber's sermons, even though the cardinal had neither commented on Nazi antisemitism nor broken with the ancient Christian idea of a curse on the Jewish people. From the time the Chosen People rejected their messiah, Faulhaber had said, "Ahasueris wanders, forever restless, over the face of the earth."[85] This was typical Christian antisemitism, but it was not Nazi antisemitism. The assertion that Faulhaber sanctioned Nazi racism during his three-hour Obersalzburg discussion with Hitler in 1936 cannot be substantiated, and it overlooks the fact that the cardinal played a leading role the following year in formulating the encyclical *Mit brennender Sorge*, which condemned racism.[86] After reviewing Faulhaber's private correspondence, historian Theodore Hamerow concluded that the cardinal "disapproved of the regime's racial policy, particularly regarding 'non-Aryan' Catholics," but also "for those who remained loyal to their ancestral religion and tradition."[87] Faulhaber believed, like Nazis, that there could be a "community of blood," but for the cardinal such a community should not lead to "hatred of other peoples."[88]

Not all German bishops were free of antisemitism by any means, but Nazi racism held no attraction for them. Distinguished theologians such as Michael Schmaus, Joseph Lortz, and Karl Adam spoke warmly of the Nazi movement, but their attraction to it was cultural, not racist.[89] Bishops such as Hilfrich of Limburg and Gröber of Freiburg, who had said earlier in the 1930s that Jews hated "Jesus and that their murderous hatred has continued in later centuries," would later disapprove of Nazi violence against Jews.[90] It was Gröber who appointed Gertrud Luckner to work on behalf of Jews through the national Catholic charity organization Caritas.[91] When deportations began in Gröber's diocese, he was very upset: "Their misery is great; it has led to suicides here. I have already turned to the nuncio for help."[92] Several German bishops, in addition to Faulhaber of Munich, had a hand in formulating the 1937 encyclical *Mit brennender Sorge*.[93]

Although church leaders had failed to speak out against the Nuremberg Laws in 1935, they had no hand in formulating antisemitic legislation, as did clergymen in neighboring lands east of Germany. Only one Catholic newspaper, the *Klerusblatt*, justified the legislation.[94] Churchmen failed to speak out against the national pogrom of November 1938, but privately they opposed it, and they certainly did not urge Catholics to participate in harming the Jews.[95] Nor did they make statements hinting that the Jews themselves had provoked the violence through their immoral or seditious behavior. The church in Germany opposed racial antisemitism, but Catholics were socially antisemitic, just as Jews were socially anti-Catholic. This intolerance of each other broke down during the Third Reich because both groups were persecuted by the Nazis.[96] One Berlin priest, canon Bernhard Lichtenberg, led his congregation, as usual, in evening prayer on November tenth, the day after the beginning of the national pogrom, adding the following supplication: "I pray for the priests in concentration camps, for the Jews, for the non-Aryans. . . . What happened yesterday we know. What will happen tomorrow we don't but what happened today we lived through. Outside the synagogue is burning. It is also a house of God."[97]

Hitler himself, the born Catholic, developed a neurotic or psychopathic hatred of Jews that had nothing to do with his religious background. The earliest traces of Hitler's antisemitic obsession were rooted in the *Ostara* magazine, published by Lanz von Liebenfels, a hallucinatory Austrian. Liebenfels attacked both Jews and Catholics. One issue featured pictures of two people with the caption "The Jewish and Jesuit Popes as Representatives of Anti-Aryan World Policy."[98] As Hitler came of age, living as a would-be artist and then as a virtual street person in Vienna, he became passionately attracted to the music of Richard Wagner, the German antisemitic composer whose operas feted pre-Christian Teutonic culture. Nothing about the rich Catholic culture of Vienna, or later Munich, attracted the brooding, anxiety-ridden, pessimistic Hitler.[99] After becoming chancellor of Germany, Hitler told Bishop Berning of Osnabrück in 1933 that he was going to do to the Jews what the Catholic church had tried to do for 1,500 years, namely, eliminate them.[100] If the dictator, long a fallen-away Catholic, thought he could win favor among German Catholics in this manner, he was mistaken.

Jewish-Catholic relations had become cordial, and to some extent friendly, in Germany prior to the Holocaust. In Munich, Cardinal Faulhaber and Rabbi Leo Baerwald were on excellent terms before and after the Holocaust.[101] After the November 1938 pogrom, Bishop Galen inquired personally about the well-being of Rabbi Fritz L. Steinthal of Münster. In 1966 Steinthal wrote that the Jews had felt spiritually strengthened by the bishop's conduct and by those he influenced.[102] On the occasion of the death of Bishop Konrad Preysing in 1952, the president of the Jewish community of Berlin recalled that "he had especially thrown himself into the battle against the hatred and poisoning of our community. He was for our people a protector and certain refuge with whom many of us found security and hiding during the time of persecution."[103] In the Catholic Ermland region of old East Prussia, Jewish and Christian religious leaders and their flocks maintained good relations before and during Nazi occupation.[104] In Bamberg, a very Catholic region, Bishop Jacobus von Hauk spoke in 1934 against the idea of an Aryan Christ, and against the notion that the Apostle Paul, a converted "Jew," had poisoned Christ's religion.[105] Jews attended the bishop's New Year sermon. Förtsch von Hohengüssbach, also in Bamberg, spoke positively of Jews, as did pastor of the Eichstätt cathedral, who even attacked Julius Streicher's vicious antisemitic journal, *Der Stürmmer.*

There were exceptions to this trend. Jesuit Hermann Muckermann, who preached in the Frauenkirche in Munich to large congregations, said that Christ's teachings did not have Jewish origins but stood in opposition to them.[106] But neither Muckermann nor any other German priest had a following that could begin to compare with that of the American antisemitic priest, Father Charles Coughlin, who attacked Jews vehemently two weeks after the November pogrom of 1938. Like Hitler, the Detroit radio priest thought that "Jew" and "Communist" could be used interchangeably.[107] Like the Nazi newspaper, the *Völkische Beobachter,* Coughlin reprinted the Protocols of the Elders of Zion in his journal, *Social Justice.*

While the pope could speak against racism, as Pius XI demonstrated,

German bishops believed they could not. Ever since Germany and the Vatican had signed the Concordat at the beginning of the Hitler era, Catholic leaders had accommodated themselves again and again to the new regime. A number of bishops, such as Preysing and Maximillian Kaller, came to realize that the Concordat had been a mistake. Kaller later blamed instructions given him by the papal nuncio to Germany, Orsenigo, for his early cooperation with the Nazi regime.[108] By 1935 the Nazis had singled out Kaller, alone among German bishops, as an enemy of the state. After the simultaneous announcement in Catholic churches throughout Germany of Pius XI's anti-racist encyclical *Mit brennender Sorge* in 1937, church and state were in open conflict in Germany.[109] In this climate of confrontation, Karl Thieme developed a theory of Catholic resistance to Nazism.[110] Pius XI, who had kept silent when Germany's racial laws were passed in 1935 because of the Concordat, wanted to break ties with Hitler after the national pogrom of 1938, but was dissuaded from doing so by his secretary of state and successor, Pius XII, whose pro-German proclivities dismayed the Vatican's Cardinal Eugene Tisserant.[111]

The Concordat remained in place. John Cornwell argues in *Hitler's Pope* that the Concordat was the result of a deal that delivered the parliamentary votes of the Catholic Center Party to Hitler, thereby giving him dictatorial power (the Enabling Act of March 1933). This is historically inaccurate.[112] But there is no question about Pius XII's tenacious insistence on the Concordat's retention before, during, and after the Second World War. From the beginning to the end of the Third Reich, the agreement inhibited bishops from speaking about matters not directly related to the Catholic church. The idea that the Concordat itself could be a vehicle of resistance, a notion that German church historians have bandied about, is questionable and certainly does not apply to the Jews' predicament.[113]

Neither the Catholic church nor any other institution was prepared for the abominations that came to be known as the Holocaust. Pioneer Holocaust historian Raul Hilberg maintains that on the eve of the Holocaust, the Christian churches had become nothing more than the clock keepers of Europe, marking the milestones of the lives of their followers with sacraments but having no power to control events.[114] In a similar vein, historian Lucy Dawidowitz asserts that the Holocaust could have occurred only because of the collapse of the two pillars of western civilization—law and religion.[115] The judgments of Hilberg and Dawidowitz cannot be gainsaid. Antisemitism as an ingredient of socio-religious culture, especially in eastern Europe, was a controlling factor negating church-led resistance to the Holocaust.

But much of the response of the church and of Catholics cannot be explained by antisemitism. Just as there were many German Holocaust perpetrators who were not antisemitic, so also there were many Polish rescuers of Jews who, like Zofia Kossak-Sczcucka, were antisemitic. Pope Pius XI, who by the time of his death had orchestrated "a swelling chorus of Church protests against the immorality of Axis racial legislation," would have condemned the murder of innocent people, be they Christian or Jew, in "language of outraged conscience."[116] Had he not died the year the Second World War began, the encyclical *Humani Generis Unitas* would have condemned fascist racism and antisemitism on the eve of the Holocaust.

Unlike his predecessor, who had come to see Nazism as the greatest threat to Christianity, Pius XII believed that Russian communism posed that threat.[117] Soon after his elevation to the papacy, the new pope saw fit in April 1939 to lift the ban on the fiercely anticommunist Action Française movement in France.[118] In doing so, Pius XII showed that he was willing to accept the rabid antisemitism of Action Française in the balance. It marked a turning point in Vatican policy and introduced the first of many such tradeoffs on the part of the new pontiff that would follow in the years to come. Had Pius XII shared his predecessor's concern about racism, he would not have allowed *Cività Catholica,* published at the Vatican, to spread grisly slander about Jews even while they were being murdered en masse by German mobile killing squads. The papal succession of 1939 was the critical event shaping the Catholic church's response to the Holocaust.

2. Genocide before the Holocaust
Poland, 1939

When Germany invaded Poland in the fall of 1939, Hitler's objective was to create new "living space" or, in Nazi ideological terms, *Lebensraum,* for the German master race. This meant, quite simply, the end of Poland.[1]

The country was predominantly Catholic, and Polish nationalism was embedded in its Catholicism. Since Jews were a minority and had not been integrated into the Polish national self-image, they posed a smaller, secondary problem to the Germans, who had not yet determined their ultimate fate. Thus, when the time came to transform Nazi Lebensraum theory into practice, Christian Poles would be targeted in greater numbers than Jews, at least until such time as the latter's fate had been decided. Of course, when that time came, the severity and extent of the genocide against the Jews knew no parallel.

For the purpose of this study, it is necessary to establish Nazi policy in Poland. The Polish church and the papacy were confronted by genocidal acts against Catholics, and then, subsequently, by the Holocaust itself. It is not the intent here to compare degrees of victimization, contrasting, as it were, Polish Gentiles with Polish Jews. It is critical to realize that the Nazis did not yet have a concrete plan to exterminate all Jews in 1939. When that plan emerged in 1941 and was put into execution in 1942, the systematic extermination of the Jewish people exceeded anything experienced by Polish Gentiles. In fact, the lot of the Gentiles improved after the campaign in Russia stalled and Polish labor and conscription potential became a German imperative. The goal in this chapter is to review events in Poland that occurred prior to the Holocaust itself, and to discuss the Vatican's reaction to these developments.[2]

Top Nazi and army personnel discussed how Hitler's Lebensraum would become reality in Poland. The decision was made to divide Poland into two parts. One part would be annexed to the German Reich outright; the second part, called the General Government, would be used as a dumping ground for dispossessed Poles and as a ghetto area for Jews. The Polish elite, be they Christian or Jewish, would be liquidated or imprisoned.[3] Hitler instructed Martin Bormann and Hans Frank that "all representatives of the Polish intelligentsia are to be killed."[4] The non-elite, or "primitive Poles," would become a migrant workforce living on starvation diets.

As originally planned, then, genocide was to embrace all of Poland. Hitler made this clear to the commanders of the German army in August 1939: "I have put my death-head formations in place with the command relentlessly and without compassion to send into death many women and children of Polish origin and language. Only thus can we gain the living space that we need."[5] Heinrich Himmler, who had been appointed to the key position of Reich Führer for the Establishment of the German People, echoed Hitler's words: "For us, the end of this war will mean an open road to the East. . . . It means that we shall push the borders of our German race 500 kilometers to the east."[6] "All Poles," Himmler asserted, "will disappear from the world."[7]

Hitler's and Himmler's subordinates understood the explicit meaning of these words. In September 1939, Security Police Chief Heydrich met with General Eduard Wagner of the army high command and agreed upon a "cleanup once and for all of Jews, intelligentsia, clergy, nobility."[8] Jews, it is true, ranked even lower than Poles in Himmler's absurd racial classifications, but non-Jewish Poles posed the greater problem because of their number and cultural dominance. During the period from the beginning of the war in the fall of 1939 through 1941, a reign of terror ensued for the Polish people which exposed Christians more than Jews to arrest, deportation, and death.[9] In the words of historian Yehuda Bauer, "German policy in Poland was radically genocidal, aiming at the elimination of the Polish nation as such."[10]

During the course of the war, more than 2,000 concentration camps dotted the Polish countryside. There Poles died from overwork and starvation. Until 1942 there were more Gentile Poles in Auschwitz than Jews, and Poles were deported to slave labor camps elsewhere, such as Dachau, Sachsenhausen, and the infamous Mauthausen camp in Austria. Altogether Poland lost about 6 million citizens during the war years. These Poles fell victim to "prisons, death camps, raids, executions, annihilation of ghettos, epidemics, starvation, excessive work and ill treatment."[11] Of the approximately 3 million Polish Gentiles who died during Poland's occupation, only about 600,000 died while in combat against Germany.[12] Many—it would be impossible to say exactly how many—of the Gentile deaths occurred between 1939 and 1941. Germans murdered 10,000 of the city of Bydgoszcz's 140,000 citizens during the first four months after the invasion.[13]

Polish Church Leaders Protest to Pope Pius XII

To suppress the Polish people and their culture, the Nazis knew that they would have to eradicate Catholicism. A Franciscan priest, whose parishioners were ethnic Germans or Volksdeutsch residing in one of the areas incorporated into the Reich, wrote to Pius XII to tell him that the Nazis had as their goal the complete suppression and uprooting of religion, and that they were using the Warthegau region, where he administered the sacraments, as a laboratory. Polish Catholics were of course much worse off than Volksdeutsch Catholics. The Germans, Pope Pius learned, allowed only seventy to eighty priests for the 3.5 million Poles in the Warthegau, and they were allowed to go to church only on Sunday between 9 and 10 a.m.[14] In Danzig, Gauleiter Arthur Greiser suppressed religion totally. Deprived of their churches, Poles actually had to rent buildings for the celebration of mass.[15] Bishop Karol Radonski reported similar conditions throughout Poland.[16]

Along with politicians, doctors, lawyers, and teachers, the Nazis targeted Catholic priests for extermination. In June 1940, the security police reported that the clergy led the opposition to German occupational authorities and that they were the hub of resistance activity.[17] "In Wroclaw 49 percent of [the] clergy died; in Chelmno 48 percent; in Lódz 37 percent; and in Poznan, 31 percent."[18] About 2,600, or 20 percent, of the all Polish clergy died at the hands of the Nazis; a much larger percentage were imprisoned.[19] Five of the six bishops of the Warthegau province were imprisoned, and 500 of its priests were in concentration camps by 1941.[20] Germans targeted the clergy because of their resistance activity and their cultural importance.

The atrocities to which Polish Catholics were subjected led to an outcry for papal intercession. The bishop of Cracow, Adam Sapieha, wrote Pope Pius saying that the situation "is tragic in the extreme. We are robbed of all human rights. We are exposed to atrocities at the hands of people who lack any notion of human feeling. We live in constant, terrible fear . . . of going to concentration camps from which only a few will ever return."[21] The Polish clergy, even the Volksdeutsch, desperately wanted Pope Pius to speak out against Nazi atrocities. Bishop Sapieha requested this explicitly in November 1941. Bishop Radonski, exasperated with papal silence, wrote that "the churches are profaned or closed, religion is scorned, worship ceases, bishops are driven [from their sees], hundreds of priests are dead or imprisoned, nuns are in the hands of spoiled depraved thieves, innocent hostages are murdered almost daily before the eyes of children, people are dying of hunger, and the pope keeps silent as if what happens to his flock doesn't concern him."[22]

After writing to the Holy See several times seeking his intervention, the apostolic administrator of the Warthegau province told the pope that "Catholics ask repeatedly if the pope could not alleviate [their plight] and why he keeps silent." Even members of the Gestapo, in conversation with the Volksdeutsch, were surprised that the pope had not yet spoken out.[23] Because of the pope's silence, it seemed to Polish Catholics that the Vatican was either in league with Hitler or unconcerned about their suffering. There was even talk of cutting off allegiance to Rome.[24]

Cardinal Hlond, in self-imposed exile, told Pope Pius that his silence was playing into the hands of the Germans, and that it could have the disastrous effect of alienating Poles from the Vatican. Hlond said that the pope's prestige would be great in Poland, and in the whole world, if he would speak out.[25] When his promptings had no effect, Hlond too became exasperated, telling the Vatican that he doubted "that it was the will of God that the atrocities and anti-Christian programs [of the Nazis] be passed over in silence."[26] The Polish president in exile, Wladislas Raczkiewicz, was of the same opinion as Hlond.

Kazimierz Papée, the Polish ambassador to the Vatican, continuously pressured the Vatican to speak out. In May 1942, he complained to the secretary of state that the pope had failed to condemn the latest wave of German terror in Poland. (Undoubtedly there were earlier complaints; this one was relayed to the U.S. State Department by Harold H. Tittman, the assistant to Myron Taylor, President Franklin Roosevelt's personal representative to the Vatican.) Cardinal Maglione replied that it was impossible for the Vatican to document each atrocity, to which Papée retorted that "there was sufficient proof and, besides, when something becomes notorious, proof is not required."[27]

During the following month Tittman reported, again from information given him by the Polish ambassador, that "in Poland the attitude of the population toward the Holy See is reported to be reserved, even openly hostile. . . . The Polish people apparently have no patience with arguments to the effect that intervention by the Holy See would only worsen their plight." The same attitude was spreading to other European Catholics outside Germany, where people lost faith in the Vatican because the pope did not speak out against Nazi terror.[28]

The Holy See Vacillates

The coming of the Second World War had put the Vatican in a dreadful diplomatic dilemma. If Russia sided with England and France against Germany, the Vatican would be allied with the world's leading Communist power should it oppose Germany. On the other hand, if the Vatican sided with Germany, Catholic Poland would be expendable. This dilemma was resolved in the most unfortunate way, as far as the Holy See was concerned, when the Hitler-Stalin pact was announced in August 1939. The continent's two principal anti-Catholic powers were now allied.[29] Depressed by this turn of events, Pius nevertheless bit his tongue, choosing to remain diplomatically uncommitted.[30]

Although the Vatican knew that the German invasion of Poland was likely and that war in Europe would follow, it could not have been prepared for the news of Nazi atrocities against Catholic Poles. During the first months of the war, the Holy See sought to address the issues of the war and the atrocities separately. Pius's message about the invasion of Finland by Russia and of Poland by Germany was so vague that neither of the aggressors were mentioned by name.[31] In his 1939 encyclical, *Summi Pontificatus,* Pius XII condemned the war but not the German invasion. The French urged Pius to condemn Germany's aggression but he declined "out of consideration for repercussions on Roman Catholics of the Reich."[32] Cardinal Hlond naturally also wanted the pope to condemn Germany's invasion. Hlond and two other Poles, the General of the Jesuits, Wladimir Ledóchowski, and Ambassador Papée, met with Pius on September 30, 1940, but were profoundly disappointed when he sympathized with Poland but did not condemn Russia and Germany for destroying their country.[33] Pius refused to do so, because he did not want the Vatican to become a platform for Polish objections against Germany. Instead of a radio broadcast, an article appeared in the official Vatican newspaper, *L'Osservatore Romano,* saying vaguely that the pope suffered because of the destiny of a Catholic nation, but that the Holy See would remain impartial and speak in the name of truth and justice. Loyal Catholic Poland, which had expected the Vatican to curse the German invaders, "felt abandoned and left to its fate."[34]

On the other hand, Pope Pius spoke about atrocities against the elderly, women, and children in an address to the College of Cardinals in December of 1939.[35] The Vatican also used its radio and press to inform the world in January 1940 of terrorization of the Polish people. Part of Poland had been organized into a General Government, the January broadcast continued, into which Poles were being forced "in the depth of one of Europe's severest winters, on principles and by methods that can be described only as brutal." This was a reference to the Poles of the Warthegau area and the 750,000 Poles of the Polish Corridor area, both of whom were dispossessed of house and home and driven into the General Government region. Once there, the Vatican reported, "Jews and Poles are being herded into separate ghettos, hermetically sealed where they face starvation while Polish grain is shipped to Germany."[36] The broadcasts, given in several languages, accused the Germans of wanton larceny and of depriving the people of their religious freedom by sending their priests to concentration camps.

There was an additional broadcast by Vatican radio in November 1940, but it lacked the specific detail of the January statement. Its purpose was to deny reports that religious conditions in Poland had improved during the latter half of the year.[37] Thereafter Vatican radio fell silent regarding Poland and the decimation of its populace. Pope Pius himself alluded only vaguely to atrocities at Easter 1941, when he said that how a country treats civilians during wartime is an index of its level of civilization. Seeking to placate the Polish ambassador to the Holy See, Cardinal Secretary of State Luigi Maglione explained to him that when the pope spoke in veiled words about atrocities, he actually had Poland in mind, even if he never mentioned the country by name.

Why had the Vatican changed course? According to the Holy See, silence spared Poles from greater atrocities. In May 1940, Pope Pius learned of "unbelievable atrocities" against Poles from an Italian consul who had had to leave Poland. Three days later, the pope told another visitor of his decision to spare Poles from worse punishment.[38] Such a justification seems preposterous, considering the tone of the supplications that Pope Pius had received from church leaders in Poland. In fact, word came later from Poland objecting to this excuse, but the Holy See continued to use it later on, during the Holocaust itself. It is possible that the original protest broadcasts were sanctioned by Hlond's fellow countryman Jesuit Wladamir Ledóchowski, rather than the pope, and that Pius then withdrew authorization later on.[39] But this view seems unlikely given Pope Pius's hands-on control of foreign policy, especially when Germany was concerned.

A more probable reason for Pius's silence was fear of German retaliation against the Vatican rather than retaliation against Poles, which apparently never took place.[40] In a conversation with Italian minister of state Roberto Farinacci, Hitler threatened to go so far as to destroy the Vatican if it spoke out against the "battle of the German Volk."[41] Hitler apparently meant the dispossessing of Poles and the resettlement of Volksdeutsch from the Baltic Sea region into Polish homes and onto Polish properties. Sometime after the January broadcast, the German ambassador to Chile requested that the nuncio there ask the Vatican to stop the broadcasts of "Bishop Hlond" [*sic*] about the disastrous conditions of Catholics in Poland.[42] Three days later, Cardinal Secretary of State Maglione told the nuncio that the Vatican was disposed to stop the broadcasts in order not to make the situation of Catholics in Poland more grave. When Polish bishop Leon Wetmanski died in October 1941, the Vatican newspaper *L'Osservatore Romano* took note of the death but failed to report that he was a prisoner in Auschwitz at the time.

For the remainder of the war, the Holy See tried to salvage the situation in Poland through charity and diplomacy. Pope Pius asked the United States to publicize as widely as possible, both at home and in Poland, its donation of $50,000 to the American Committee for Polish Relief.[43] This attempt to win favor with the Polish people, who were angered by the pope's silence, failed when the Americans declined to associate themselves with the pope's plan. The Vatican also sought to ameliorate Poland's situation by negotiating with Nazi Germany to coax it into honoring the Concordat between Poland and the Vatican. This effort would prove utterly futile. Finally, the Vatican followed a circuitous route, acting as a middleman in negotiations between England and German resisters of Nazism to overthrow Hitler.

Surprisingly, the alternative route proved somewhat realistic. While genocide proceeded in Poland, Pius allowed his close confidants, Germans Monsignor Ludwig Kaas and Father Leiber, to meet secretly in Rome with Dr. Josef Müller, a Bavarian involved in the resistance movement against Hitler. To some extent the objectives of the anti-Nazi Germans, the English, and the Vatican coincided: in return for peace in the west, Poland and most of Czechoslovakia would be restored after Hitler was dispatched.[44] Pope Pius wanted both an independent Poland and a strong postwar Germany. In 1940, Pius gave an allocution in which he stated that the European order established by Versailles after the Great War was not a necessary basis for peace, and he spoke on a number of occasions about Germany's "vital necessities."[45] The negotiations eventually broke down, possibly because the Germans feared that they would

terminate in a Carthaginian peace for Germany, but the Vatican ex-
changes had "brought about an unprecedented degree of understanding
between the British authorities and the German conspirators."[46]

Pius put high stakes on the table when he gambled to end Nazi aggression through covert diplomatic activity. Such a venture broke all
the rules of the diplomatic neutrality the Vatican claimed for itself. The
chances of success were not great, partly because of Pius's own hopes
for a stronger Germany, and partly because he badly underestimated
the territorial ambitions of the anti-Hitler conspirators.[47] The risk, had
Hitler discovered the plot—and he nearly did—would have been grave
for the Vatican and for Pius himself.[48] Paradoxically, had Pope Pius been
exposed and in some manner severely dealt with by Germany, he would
likely be the recipient today of historians' adulation rather than, as is
frequently the case, their suspicion or censure.

Meanwhile, the Vatican's attempts to soften Germany's terrorism in
Poland got nowhere. Pope Pius approached the Nazi regime repeatedly,
using papal nuncio to Germany Cesare Orsenigo as an intermediary.
Three times during the latter half of 1941, the Vatican instructed its
nuncio to Nazi Germany to plead for better treatment of Polish priests
and laypeople.[49] The nuncio accomplished nothing for the Poles, not
even religious freedom. Orsenigo, a pro-German fascist, was accused by
the Poles of downplaying German terror in his reports to Rome. Polish
pressure led the Vatican to press Hitler more intently to intervene. In
January of 1942, the Vatican secretariat sent the Nazi government a
long, detailed note about religious conditions in Poland. The Holy See
did not even get the courtesy of a response. Finally, when the Vatican
hinted at papal retaliation if Germany did not comply, von Ribbentrop
returned the threat: "The Vatican has to be brought to understand that
aggravating ties between Germany and the Vatican will certainly not
result in one-sided disadvantages for Germany."[50] Thereafter, the Vatican timidly backed off.[51]

In 1942, Pope Pius also came under heavy pressure from other countries to let his voice be heard as a moral leader about atrocities in Poland.[52] The English minister to the Holy See, Francis d'Arcy Osborne,
noted that the "continued silence of the Pope on the moral issues of the
day, especially in the face of one notorious Nazi atrocity after another,
has alarmed many loyal Catholics."[53] Checking the record, Osborne
brought it to the attention of the secretary of state that Pope Pius had
not referred explicitly and publicly to Poland since June of 1940.

In the fall of 1942, six countries—the United States, Great Britain,

Brazil, Uruguay, Belgium, and Poland—presented Pius XII with simultaneous démarches which, although the wording differed, warned him
about loss of papal moral authority: "A policy of silence in regard to
such offenses [in Poland] against the conscience of the world must necessarily involve a renunciation of moral leadership and a consequent
atrophy of the influence and authority of the Vatican."[54] Although the
Holocaust itself was under way by the time of the démarches, and would
soon become the reason for additional pressure on Pope Pius, the démarches did not refer to Jews but to atrocities in general in Poland.

Hardly had the démarches been presented when the new secretary
of the British legation to the Holy See arrived from England and was
formally presented to the pope. During the exchange of greetings, the
legate "happened to mention to the Holy Father that the Poles in London were unable to understand the continued silence of the Holy See in
the face of the horrors being committed by the Nazis in their country."
Upon hearing this, an agitated Pius XII defended himself, speaking so
rapidly that the legate could not understand everything that the pope
said.[55] As to the démarches themselves, Secretary of State Maglione said,
inscrutably, that so many countries had filed them that the Vatican could
not accede without the Axis accusing it of giving in to Allied pressure.

Monsignor Domenico Tardini explained in the summer of 1942 that
the Holy See had two reasons for not speaking out: fear of greater punishment of Poles and an end to the Vatican's attempted charitable work
for the Poles, which, he admitted, the Nazis had not allowed anyway
up to that time.[56] Ambassador Osborne believed that the real reason
lay in the pope's determination to act as an intermediary in a negotiated
peace between the Axis and Allied powers. Trying to win some sympathy from his home office for Pius's position, Osborne wrote that "the
pope's ambition [was] to play his part in ensuring a just and lasting
peace based upon Christian morality supplanting egotistic materialism."
In fact, however, Osborne thought the pope's approach misdirected. "By
desiring to be [a] mediator, Pope Pius XII has given up moral leadership.
Thus he has jeopardized his chances of being listened to as the peace
advocate."[57]

No matter how insistently or frequently various diplomats to the
Vatican made this point, Pius stayed his course. Late in 1942, word came
from Poland of better conditions. Earlier, Bishop Sapieha of Cracow
had wanted the pope to speak out publicly against Nazi terror. When
Pius refused, Sapieha managed to convince the pope to write a private

letter in support of the Poles. Five thousand copies of the statement were made and circulated underground to the church in Poland. Bishop Sapieha wrote that the strategy was at last paying off.[58] After Pius's Christmas address of 1942, in which neither Poles nor Jews were mentioned by name, Sapieha wrote the pope to tell him that the Polish people liked his message and knew that he was referring to them.[59] (It is unclear about whom the pope spoke—Polish Gentiles or Polish Jews.) The Franciscan Father Breitinger, also formerly disenchanted with Pius, wrote him much more optimistically early in 1943. Most Poles now understand, Breitinger avowed, that His Holiness's silence was a "heroic silence" that would "create the foundation for a new peaceful order in the world."[60] Actually, the change that had come over Poland had nothing to do with Pius's diplomacy but with the momentous events of the war that took place during the winter of 1942–43, culminating in the battles of Stalingrad and Kursk.[61]

It is necessary, then, to distinguish between two phases of Nazi policy in Poland—before Stalingrad, when Poles were suppressed, and, afterward, when Germany tried to utilize the church to mobilize the Polish people against Communist Russia.[62] March of 1943 marked the last strong letter of protest to the Holy See from a bishop residing in Poland, that of Stanislaus Adamski.[63] After Stalingrad, the Germans, forgetting about "their pompous pretensions to racial purity," started to harness the Poles for the war effort against Russia.[64] In 1942, Poles began to be recruited into the German army. The occupational forces in Germany ended their suppression of Polish culture. It was time to patch things up with the Polish Catholic church. When the Germans captured Cardinal Hlond in 1943 as he tried to make his way from France back to Poland, they promised to free him if he would inspire the Polish people to join Germany in the fight against the common enemy, Bolshevist Russia.

The Holocaust is understood to be the systematic extermination of European Jewry. Before it occurred or had even been planned, genocide occurred against the Polish people at large (including some Jews). Polish Catholics, shepherds and flock, waited in vain for their pope to condemn German genocide. The Holy See claimed that to have spoken out would have worsened the situation for the Poles. Until after the battle of Stalingrad, the excuse made no sense to the Polish people.

Instead of condemning German genocide in Poland, Pius XII sought to derail the Nazi regime through clandestine diplomacy. Thus, even before the Holocaust itself had commenced, the Holy See responded to genocide in a way that would evolve into a pattern throughout the war years. Soon after the invasion of Poland in 1939, Pope Pius, speaking through *L'Osservatore Romano,* denounced German atrocities, but then abruptly abandoned the moral approach. Engaging German resistance elements, Pius sought to negotiate a peace between England and Germany that would eliminate Nazism but preserve Germany's strength in central Europe. Disregarding the pleas of Polish church leaders, Pius XII chose a diplomatic rather than a moral approach.

3. Genocide before the Holocaust
Croatia, 1941

The murder of east European Jewry by Nazi Germany began in late June 1941 with Hitler's decision to invade the Soviet Union. What came to be known as the Holocaust—the decision to murder all European Jewry in six death camps—did not begin until the spring of 1942. Before either of these events took place, genocide occurred in Croatia.

Historians cannot fix precisely the date of the Nazi decision to kill all European Jewry. Careful scholarly research suggests that the decision was made sometime during the latter half of the year 1941.[1] If this estimate is correct, then genocide in Croatia, as in Poland, began even before the Nazi decision to kill all of Europe's Jews. According to historian Jonathan Steinberg, the murder of the Serbs was the "earliest total genocide to be attempted during the Second World War."[2]

Establishing the fact of genocide in Croatia prior to the Holocaust carries great historical weight for our study because Catholics were the perpetrators and not, as in Poland, the victims. In this case Orthodox Serbs were the victims, along with a much smaller number of Jews. One other important circumstance distinguished genocidal events in Poland from those in Croatia: in the case of Poland, Vatican knowledge about the murder of the people was limited and sketchy in comparison to the Croatian case, in which both the nuncio and the head of the church, Bishop Alojzije Stepinac, were in continuous contact with the Holy See while genocide was being committed. Would these circumstances matter? Would the Holy See condemn the genocide of an avowedly Catholic country?

Fascism in Catholic Croatia

Croatia came into existence when Germany occupied Yugoslavia in the spring of 1941 and immediately dismembered it. Most of the former country fell to the new state of Croatia. This represented a great triumph for the Croat fascist movement, the Ustasha. Ante Pavelic headed this fascist organization, which both resembled Nazism and differed from it. The Ustasha was antisemitic, anti-modern, anti-Communist, and genocidal. But unlike Hitler, Pavelic was anti-Serb and pro-Catholic because Catholicism was part of the Croat heritage.[3]

The Ustasha overlapped ideologically with Nazism sufficiently to allow easy cooperation between Pavelic and Hitler. Exiled from Yugoslavia, the terrorist Pavelic had plotted with Nazis for the overthrow of the Yugoslav state.[4] After this occurred, Pavelic and Hitler met in the Führer's Alpine resort, the Berghof, in the summer of 1941. There the only two genocidal fascist leaders in Europe ironed out the arrangements that would govern relations between Germany and the puppet state of Croatia. These included Germany's right to almost unlimited raw materials, special privileges for the Volksdeutsch of Croatia, and an understanding regarding Jews.[5]

For the Ustashi and Pavelic, relations with the Vatican were as important as relations with Germany. "Croat" and "Ustasha" were far from synonymous. The hook that Pavelic needed to win Croat popular support for his fascist state was religion in the form of Vatican recognition. Croatian church leaders favored an alliance with the Ustasha because of its promise as an anti-Communist, Catholic state that might very well succeed in reconverting the 200,000 souls who had switched their allegiance from Roman Catholic to Serbian Orthodox since the end of the Great War. Bishop Stepinac rejoiced at the prospect of a Catholic Croatia that would replace the religiously and ethnically diverse creation of the Treaty of Paris that was the Yugoslav state—"the jail of the Croatian nation."

Bishop Stepinac arranged an audience in May with Pope Pius XII for Ante Pavelic. Pius and Stepinac both saw communism as the greatest menace facing Christianity. That the Vatican would favor a Croatian state is not surprising; after the First World War, the Holy See had regretted the Paris Peace Treaty's dissolution of the Austro-Hungarian dual monarchy, a predominantly Catholic force dominating southeast Europe. Fascism represented an opportunity to reestablish Catholic influence.[6] The Vatican, however, stopped short of formal recognition of Croatia. Pope Pius sent Giuseppe Ramiro Marcone, a Benedictine abbot, to the new country as his apostolic visitor.[7] This served Pavelic's purposes well enough, because Marcone acted like a nuncio. Stepinac, too, was satisfied, feeling that the Vatican had de facto recognized the new state.

Thus, in a timely manner and within just a matter of weeks, the Ustasha leader had solidified Croatian ties with Hitler and Pope Pius XII. By April 1941, the German army had routed the Yugoslav forces. Pavelic and the Ustashi now governed the new state of Croatia, although the word "govern" belies the chaos in which the country found itself. In April the Ustashi decreed that "all those who in any way offend the honor and vital interests of the Croatian people" would be subject to capital punishment.[8] This vague "law" made it possible for the Ustasha terrorists to kill anyone they wished. During their first weeks in power, thousands of Serbs were murdered. Genocide was under way in Croatia.[9]

Yugoslav Jews, a small minority, experienced similar treatment. In April and May 1941, the Ustashi issued Nazi copycat edicts eliminating Jewish citizenship and forcing Jews to wear the Star of David. Soon thereafter, about 25,000 Jews were put into detention camps, from which they were deported to Lithuania in July of 1941. This was precisely the time when Hitler remarked to Pavelic that "if there were no Jews left in Europe, the unity of the European states would be disturbed no longer. It does not matter to where the Jews are deported."[10] In this way it happened that one of the very first Jewish colonies to be deported from its homeland took place in a Catholic country as a result of cooperation between the Ustashi and the Nazis.

Genocide in Croatia began in earnest after the German army pulled out of the country in June 1941 to participate in Operation Barbarossa, Germany's surprise attack on Russia. With the Ustashi in complete control of Croatia, large-scale massacres took place in July and August. Historian Jonathan Steinberg describes the bloodletting:

> Serbian and Jewish men, women and children were literally hacked to death. Whole villages were razed to the ground and the people driven into barns to which the Ustashi set fire. There is in the Italian Foreign Ministry archive a collection of photographs of the butcher knives, hooks, and axes used to chop up Serbian victims. There are photographs of Serb women with breasts hacked off by pocket knives, men with eyes gouged out, emasculated and mutilated.[11]

Tens, if not hundreds of thousands, were murdered during these first months of Ustasha power.[12]

Pavelic's plan was to kill half of the Serb population and force the other half to convert to Catholicism or emigrate. Unlike the Nazis, the Ustashi made no secret of their genocide. By broadcasting their murders, they hoped to terrorize the remaining Serbs into fleeing for their lives or converting. The Ustasha's nonsensical racial ideas allowed that the Serbs, while less pure than the Croats, were not "non-Aryans." Once they converted, they could be assimilated into the Croatian population as long as there were not too many of them.

While allowing the Ustasha fascists to go about their business against the Serbs, the few remaining German authorities in Croatia co-ordinated their Jewish policy with Berlin. Foreign Office Plenipotentiary Felix Benzler sought permission to have Croatian Jews deported to Poland or to Russia. If they went to Russia later, they would be shot by mobile killing squads; if they went to Poland, they would be ghettoized, since death camps in Poland did not yet exist. The top Nazi bureaucrat of the Holocaust, Adolf Eichmann, refused permission for this deportation and gave instructions over the telephone to shoot the Jews where they were.[13] As a result, an additional 4,000 to 5,000 Jewish men were murdered in the fall of 1941, and their families—wives, children, and the elderly—were placed in ghettos.

Croatian Church Leaders and the Ustasha Regime

The events of the first months of Ustasha rule caused consternation for the relatively youthful head of the Croatian Catholic church. When Bishop Stepinac was raised to the episcopacy by Rome in 1934, he was the youngest Catholic bishop in the world. Only a few years later, while still in his thirties, Stepinac was chosen by the Holy See to head the national church. His position was unenviable. While Rome apparently offered him very little direction about what policy he should adopt re-garding the Ustasha government, he found that not a few bishops and priests in his homeland disregarded his authority.

This became apparent when, after Stepinac denounced Ustasha ter-ror, priests and even a few bishops collaborated with Pavelic. Some Catholic priests even served in the dictator's body guard. Ivan Guberina, the leader of Catholic Action, was among them. Another priest, Mate Mugos, wrote in a newspaper that previously the clergy had worked with a prayer book, but now was the time for the revolver. Most mur-derous were the Franciscan Miroslav Filipovic-Majstorovic, known as the devil of the Jasenovac, a concentration camp where 20,000 Jews perished; Bozidas Bralo, who was the chief of the security police in Sara-jevo and initiator of antisemitic actions there; and Dyonisy Juricev, who wrote in the newspaper *Novi List* in July that it was no longer a sin to kill seven-year-olds.[14] Many other clergymen were involved both directly and indirectly. There is independent verification from Italian Corrado

Zoli and Englishman Evelyn Waugh that clergy participated in genocide.[15]

Of the bishops who supported Pavelic, the worst is said to have been Ivan Saric. In the midst of the initial Ustasha terror against Jews, his diocesan newspaper carried the message that "there is a limit to love. The movement of liberation of the world from the Jews is a movement for the renewal of human dignity. Omniscient and omnipotent God stands behind this movement."[16] Bishop Saric was also accused of appropriating Jewish property for his own use.

Other Croat bishops recognized immediately after the Ustashi came to power that their authority would be based on murder and terror. The first to realize this was the bishop of Mostar, Aloysius Misic. Seeing that any short-term gain the church experienced under the Ustashi would be reversed in the long run, Misic warned Stepinac that the fascists' atrocities could not be ignored.

For his part, Bishop Alojzije Stepinac began to distance himself from the Ustashi in May 1941, just a month after Pavelic came to power. He objected publicly to the fascist's racial laws, complained about converted "Jews" having to wear the Star of David, and then extended his concern to all Jews.[17] Stepinac appealed to the Ustashi to moderate the decree: "We . . . appeal to you to issue regulations so that even in the framework of antisemitic legislation, and similar legislation concerning Serbs, the principles of their human dignity be preserved."[18] In July of 1941, when the first deportations of Jews and Serbs were taking place, Stepinac wrote to Pavelic objecting to the conditions of deportation; he asked that deportees be allowed contact with families at home, medical care, and decent transportation. Later that month, he sent the government a memorandum asking that deportation of Serbs who had not converted be stopped. Realizing that what he had urged earlier—namely, that Serbs not be coerced into conversion—could be their death sentence, Stepinac instructed the clergy to baptize people upon demand without the usual period of waiting and instruction. "Do not require any special religious knowledge, for Orthodox are Christians like us and the Jewish faith is the one from which Christianity originated."[19] In comparison with other eastern European church leaders, especially those in neighboring Hungary, Bishop Stepinac showed courage and insight in his actions.

Instead of abating, Ustasha murders increased exponentially during the summer and fall of 1941. The atrocities became so obnoxious that Muslim and Italian allies of the Ustashi criticized Pavelic's government. Even the Germans, who were pleased with Ustasha treatment of Jews, found the mass expulsion of Serbs so economically disruptive that they considered replacing Pavelic. Bishop Stepinac began to fall under heavy criticism for the church's support of the fascists. Croat members of the former Yugoslav government contacted Stepinac, objecting to the fact that clergymen were accomplices in the Ustasha murders of women, children, and the elderly, and demanding that Stepinac publicly condemn such atrocities.

But Stepinac was not yet prepared to break with the Ustashi. It was not clear in the first weeks of Ustasha rule whether the murders and atrocities had been planned or were spontaneous. Even Serbs, the chief victims, thought that the violence was unauthorized. On this assumption, some Serbs, reconciled to the inevitability of fascism in a nazified Europe, appealed to Ustasha authorities for suppression of the violence. Stepinac, a strong supporter of the Ustashi initially, probably gave them the benefit of the doubt, assuming that the bloodshed resulted from Pavelic's suppression of partisan opponents whether they were Yugoslav, Chetnik, or even Croat non-fascist dissidents. But as the bloodletting continued and increased, Stepinac decided on a limited response; in November he called for a national meeting, or synod, of Croatian bishops.

The meeting served the purpose of coordinating church policy toward the fascist government, and, no doubt, of reining in many of the lower clergy who had been carried away with "baptism-or-the-sword" missionary activity. Stepinac attempted to set a correct policy for Croatian clergy, but it is doubtful that they followed it with much uniformity. In a letter to Pavelic, the bishops objected to forced mass conversions of Serbs and to Ustasha atrocities. The synod also appealed to Pavelic to treat Jews "as humanely as possible, considering that there were German troops in the country."[20] Pope Pius's representative in Croatia, Abbot Marcone, reported this to Vatican secretary of state Cardinal Luigi Maglione, who in reply praised what the bishops had done for "citizens of Jewish origin." There is some question, however, regarding which Jews the synod sought to protect. According to Israeli historian Menachem Shelah, the synod singled out converted "Jews" in their appeal to Pavelic, whereas Marcone reported that the appeal had been for all Jews.[21] Pavelic, in either event, ignored the bishops.

Why had Stepinac waited until November? Why was he not prepared to object publicly to Ustasha crimes? The Holy See and Stepinac wanted to see a Catholic state succeed in Croatia. After learning in August 1941 about oppressive conditions for Jews, Maglione notified Abbot Marcone that "if your eminence can find a suitable occasion, he should recommend in a discreet manner, that would not be interpreted as an official appeal, that moderation be employed with regard to Jews on Croatian territory. Your Eminence should see to it that . . . the impression of loyal cooperation with the civil authorities be always preserved."[22] The language of the Holy See's secretary of state clearly indicated that the Vatican did not wish to cut its ties to Pavelic's government. Neither, then, could Stepinac, who, after all, had used his good offices only a few months earlier to recommend the Catholic dictator to the Holy See. For its part, the Vatican found the bishops' November synod perfectly satisfactory. After receiving a report on it from Bishop Stepinac, Pius responded to him, praising the "courage and decisiveness" of the bishops in confronting the Ustashi regarding their treatment of Serbs.[23]

The Ustasha genocide continued. Estimates regarding its extent vary immensely. Some have put it as high as 1 million, others as low as 100,000. The most reliable figure, that of a Serb scholar, places the mortality between 300,000 and 400,000.[24] To this figure we must add the approximately 50,000 Jews whom the Ustashi murdered or turned over to their German allies to dispose of. Many of these Jews and Serbs perished during the first year of Ustasha rule, although it would be impossible to determine exactly how many.

The Vatican and Ustasha Genocide

The extent of the murders and the fact that the Ustashi made no secret of them meant that the world outside Croatia would soon hear of the genocide. The Vatican got wind of them from several different sources. Undersecretary of State Monsignor Giovanni Battista Montini (later Pope Paul VI) was involved with day-to-day matters concerning Croatia and Poland. Late in 1941 he had heard of the Ustasha atrocities, as did Pope Pius, since Montini reported to him on a daily basis.[25] In March 1942, Montini confronted the Ustasha representative to the Vatican with the rumors that alarmed western Europe, asking explicitly about Pavelic's extermination of Serbs. "Is it possible," he asked, "that these atrocities have taken place?"[26] "Lies and propaganda," said the Ustasha representative, to which Montini replied that he had viewed the accusations with "considerable reserve."

Montini's colleague Monsignor Domenico Tardini also interviewed Pavelic's representative to Pope Pius. Tardini let the Croat know that the Vatican was willing to treat the Ustasha excesses indulgently: "Croatia is a young state. . . . Youngsters often err because of their age. It is therefore not surprising that Croatia has also erred."[27] Tardini's words, if quoted accurately, indicated the Holy See's policy of wanting to believe that Croatia was the Catholic state it had promised to be or that it would become that in time.

Further evidence suggesting this interpretation comes from Bishop Stepinac, who was himself summoned in April of 1942 to Rome. The Croatian bishop reportedly gave the Holy See a nine-page document detailing his account of Pavelic's misdeeds. This document, omitted from the Vatican's collection of World War II materials, evidently enabled the Holy See to believe that the Ustasha movement's massacres were anomalies that Pavelic did not know about or at least had not authorized. But upon his return to Croatia, Stepinac strongly criticized the Ustashi, saying that "it is forbidden to exterminate Gypsies and Jews because they are said to belong to an inferior race."[28] This indicates that in the spring of 1942 the Vatican saw the seriousness of Ustasha crimes and preferred to have Stepinac try to rein the fascists in rather than risk the effect that a papal denunciation would have had on the unstable Croatian state. After Croatian rabbi Miroslav Shalom Freiberger wrote in August to Pope Pius asking for his help to save Jews, Apostolic Visitator Marcone was instructed by the Holy See to thank him for his letter, but to do so prudently and tactfully.[29] In other words, Pavelic's fascist government was not to be impugned.

It is impossible to believe that Stepinac and the Vatican did not know that the Ustasha murders amounted to genocide. Historian Jonathan Steinberg writes that "the repression and terrorism of the Ustasha regime" were "without parallel in the history of southeastern Europe."[30] The Croat fascists had made no secret of their intention to murder or convert the Serbs and Jews. As early as 1941, the Italian army turned on the Ustasha regime and engaged militarily in support of the Serbian Orthodox Christians. In 1942, when Franciscan Miroslav Filipovic-Majstorovic ran the infamous Jasenovac concentration camp, 40,000 Jewish and Serbian prisoners perished there. Among the captives were 24,000 children, half of whom were murdered.[31] Soon after the war, a Vatican official acknowledged that the Holy See had a "list of all the clergymen who participated in [the] atrocities and we shall punish them at the right time to cleanse our conscience of the stain with which they spotted us."[32] In 1943, after the German military became active once again in Croatia, between 6,000 and 7,000 Jews were deported to Auschwitz, of whom only two dozen survived. Rabbi Freiberger, who had appealed for papal intervention a few months earlier, was not among the survivors.[33] Hundreds, perhaps thousands, of additional Jews were murdered in gas vans in Croatia itself.[34]

Rather than jeopardize the Ustasha government of Croatia by diplomatic wrangling, the Vatican chose to help Jews privately. But there was
little the Holy See or anyone else could do under the chaotic conditions
that prevailed in the country. When the bishop of Ljubljana in Slovenia
wrote Cardinal Secretary Maglione requesting that Croatian Jews who
had fled into his diocese be allowed to remain there under the protection
of Italian civil authority, Maglione sent Jesuit Pietro Tacchi-Venturi to
government offices in Rome to make the necessary arrangements.[35] Of
course, the Jews in question here were converts to Catholicism. In 1942
two additional similar situations arose, which Maglione tried, albeit
unsuccessfully, to resolve. Marginal charitable efforts such as these did
not begin to address the core issue of genocide.

Clearly, the Vatican's response to genocide in Croatia gave preference to diplomacy. The wording of Secretary Maglione's instructions to
Apostolic Visitor Marcone regarding the misery of the Jews makes this
clear: "If your eminence can find a suitable occasion, he should recommend in a discreet manner, that would not be interpreted as an official
appeal." In the words of historian John Morley, the Vatican record is
"particularly shameful" because Croatia "was a state that proudly proclaimed its Catholic tradition and whose leaders depicted themselves as
loyal to the Church and to the Pope."[36]

The Croatian genocide is significant historically because of its tim-
ing and the circumstances surrounding it. By failing to speak out publicly against genocide in Croatia, the Holy See lost an opportunity to
condemn it in 1941, just months before the Holocaust began. The circumstances are equally important. Since the main victims of the Ustasha
genocide were Orthodox Serbs, Pius XII forfeited an opportunity to denounce a genocide that did not primarily involve Hitler's plans for Jews,
which had not yet been worked out in detail. Among the Axis powers,
the Italians found the brutality of the Ustasha murderers horrifying, and
the Germans saw it as economically disruptive. The summer of 1941
would have been the right moment in time for the Holy See to exercise
moral leadership.

Why, then, did Pope Pius not address this moral issue? It was not
because it did not occur to him. Cardinal Eugene Tisserant had smelled
genocide in the air at the beginning of World War II and had suggested
to Pius at that time that he address the issue in an encyclical.[37] Rather, it
was because the Holy See preferred to bring diplomatic pressure on the
Ustasha government instead of challenging the fascists publicly on the
immorality of genocide. Pavelic's diplomatic emissaries to the Holy See
were merely scolded gently by Monsignors Tardini and Montini. The

implication was that the Vatican intended to make formal diplomatic recognition of the Croatian state dependent on proper conduct on the part of the Ustasha government. But in the meantime, Orthodox Christians were being slaughtered.

The Vatican gambled, putting its moral authority at stake for the sake of a favorable diplomatic position. What Bishop Stepinac and the Holy See sought was a Catholic state in place of the former pluralistic Yugoslav state. But by failing to condemn the Ustasha murders, the Holy See unwittingly helped create an even less desirable entity: Communist Yugoslavia. Historian Aleksa Djilas has pointed out that Ustasha brutality caused a "black revolution" that destroyed the delicate balance of the old Yugoslav state. The resulting chaos spawned Tito's Red revolutionary movement when the war turned against Germany and Hitler was no longer able to prop up Pavelic's government.[38] In 1943, Marshal Josip Tito's Communist-dominated National Liberation Movement emerged as the actual power in Croatia. At the end of the war, the leaders of the Ustasha movement, including its clerical supporters such as Bishop Saric, fled the country, taking gold looted from massacred Jews and Serbs with them to Rome—possibly even to the Vatican.

4. The Holocaust and the Priorities of Pope Pius XII

Between 1939 and 1941, genocides occurred in occupied Poland, claiming mostly Catholic victims, and in Croatia, where Catholics were the perpetrators rather than the victims. In 1942 and 1943, the world became aware of yet another genocide that came to be known as the Holocaust. Everyone knew that the principal perpetrators were Nazis and that the victims were Jews. With the exception of the two statements made at the onset of the Polish genocide, the Holy See had kept silent. It may seem unlikely that Pius would then change course and condemn the killing of the Jews. But the circumstances surrounding the Holocaust differed altogether from the two previous localized genocides. The Nazi dragnet blanketed the continent and continued for a much longer period of time. As a result, the Holy See found itself subject to extraordinary pressure to speak out. It is well known that Pius XII refrained from doing so. In this chapter we take up Pius XII's reaction to the Holocaust and explore the reasons for his continued silence.

The initial phase of the Holocaust began with the murder of somewhere between 1 and 1.5 million Jews, starting in the summer of 1941, when Germany launched Operation Barbarossa, the invasion of Russia. Four *Einsatzgruppen,* or mobile killing squads, were organized under Reinhard Heydrich, Heinrich Himmler's next in command. Careful, explicit coordination between the mobile killing squads and the German High Command of the Army was devised to facilitate the work of the four mobile killing squads. Their murderous mission consisted of killing all Jews—men, women, and children—as Germany's army pushed eastward along a thousand-mile front that stretched from the Baltic Sea to the Black Sea.

The second phase of the Holocaust began with the decision to murder all European Jewry in specially constructed gas and crematorium facilities located in or near the General Government area of Poland. According to the Nazi plan, Jews would be transported from Europe's far corners to six death camps, where, upon arrival, they would be immediately gassed in four of the camps. In two others, Majdanek and Auschwitz, some Jews would be used for slave labor, but others—at Auschwitz the majority—would go immediately to their deaths.

Between 1942 and 1945, about 3 million Jews were murdered in the death camps: according to Raul Hilberg's analysis, 750,000 died at Treblinka; at Sobibor, about 200,000; at Chelmo, about 150,000; at Belzec, about 550,000; at Majdanek, about 50,000; and at Auschwitz, about 1 million.[1] Altogether the mobile killing squads and death camps killed between 5 and 6 million human beings, the overwhelming majority of whom were Jews.

As historian Walter Laqueur has pointed out, it is not possible to kill so many people and keep it a secret.[2] Word about the murder of the Jews spread with startling quickness throughout Europe and even across the Atlantic Ocean to the United States. Vatican officials, including the pope, were the first—or among the first—to learn about the Holocaust.

There is a difference between learning about German atrocities and learning about the Holocaust. Many people heard about atrocities. Sometimes participants bragged about them; onlookers regaled others with hair-raising accounts of unimaginable scenes of brutality. But knowing about the Holocaust means that the information concerns more than isolated accounts of atrocities. Rather, the information had to come from a number of different and reliable sources, from a number of different countries, and it had to concern vast numbers of victims. The Holy See did not seek information on such a scale, but it became privy to it.

When Polish underground courier Jan Karski told American Supreme Court justice Felix Frankfurter about the Holocaust, the justice said he could not believe it.[3] The Holocaust was beyond the pale of human understanding. This chapter takes stock of the Vatican's accumulation of information bearing on the murder of the Jews, in order to focus in on that point in time when the Holy See could be said to have understood that the Holocaust was occurring. At what point in time were Vatican officials able to overcome their skepticism about tales of horror, a skepticism that was rooted in false claims of German atrocities during World War I? The second half of the chapter seeks to discern, from among the many explanations the Vatican offered for its policy, what considerations actually governed its interventions on behalf of Jews and its silence about what was happening to them.

Information about mobile killing squads and death camps was accumulated piecemeal and gradually, both within and outside the Vatican. Only a compilation of information would lead to the conclusion of genocide. The Vatican was capable of such a compilation. By drawing disparate accounts together from its diplomats stationed throughout Europe and by soliciting information from them, the Holy See could have played a vital role in accelerating the process of Holocaust knowledge. It chose instead to decelerate the dissemination of this knowledge. The Vatican had "no wish to give publicity to the issue." This had mortal consequences because the public at large, including Jews, found it difficult to "accept the ample evidence about the 'final solution' and did so only with considerable delay."[4]

In 1942 the Holy See, or spokesmen for the pope in the office of secretary of state, said that rumors about mass murder could not be verified. Later, when the Holocaust could no longer be denied, Vatican personnel said that the crimes of one World War II combatant could not be condemned without condemning the crimes of another. There were other explanations for the pope's silence as well, but one, which was not given, was the most important—Pius XII's fear that Rome and Vatican City would suffer extensive destruction from aerial bombing either by the Germans or by the Allies.

It is important to note at the outset that the picture, as it develops, will not be black and white. We will see here and again in chapter 6 that in certain situations and under certain conditions, Pius XII intervened on behalf of Jews. This concern is not addressed by John Cornwell, who characterizes Pius as "Hitler's pope" because of his antisemitism. Clearly, then, Pius was mindful of the Jewish predicament. But at other times and under different circumstances, Pius did not intervene. Our goal is to discover what fears and hopes led the pope to act with studied caution.

When Did the Holy See Learn about the Murder of the Jews?

Between July and October of 1941, a mobile killing squad murdered more than 18,000 Kovno Jews, including more than 5,000 children, with the help of Lithuanian Christian partisans. Before this tragedy occurred, the Jews had appealed for help to the Catholic archbishop of the city without success. The doomed Jews were walked from a ghetto of the city of Kovno to pits located about three miles out in the country, where they were shot in groups of about 500.[5] Unimaginable brutality took place. In an attempt to save her baby while en route to the killing pits, a mother tried to throw "her child over the fence [to safety], but missed her aim and the child remained hanging on the barbed wire [enclosing the ghetto]. Its screams were quickly silenced by bullets [of the guards]."[6]

Just slightly more than three months after the Kovno massacre, a member of the Berlin Catholic resistance circle, Margarete Sommer, filed this timely and accurate report:

> The Jews had to undress (it could have been eighteen degrees below freezing), then climb into "graves" previously dug by Russian prisoners of war. They were then shot with a machine gun; then grenades were tossed in. Without checking to see if all were dead, the Kommando ordered the grave filled in.[7]

Sommer's report circulated among German bishops.

Konrad Preysing, Sommer's collaborator and the bishop of Berlin, would have seen to it that Nuncio Eugenio Orsenigo became privy to the information about the work of the mobile killing squad. Preysing, the leader of those bishops who wanted the church to take a stronger stand against Hitler, also wanted the pope to know about the atrocity at Kovno. But the report never reached the Vatican. The explanation for this breakdown in communication is to be found in the special relationship between Pope Pius and Germany.

At the outset of his reign, Pius told Vatican officials that "to me the German question is the most important; I will reserve handling it to myself." He added, "Naturally I will follow German matters closer than all others."[8] The new pope appointed Luigi Maglione, a specialist in French affairs, as his secretary of state, and kept Orsenigo in Berlin as his nuncio. For the Berlin appointment, the pope wanted a person who would not undo the work he had done as nuncio and later as secretary of state, namely, maintaining the Concordat and German-Vatican relations. In Orsenigo, Pius had the right man for the job. A pro-German, pro-Nazi, antisemitic fascist, Orsenigo would have no trouble adjusting to the Nazi regime in Berlin.[9] In addition, Orsenigo, who hankered after a cardinal's hat, could be trusted not to interfere with Pius's own well-known intention to deal with Germany himself. Although the pope was well aware of Orsenigo's limitations and would hear more about them during the Holocaust from Bishop Konrad Preysing, he could be sure that in matters concerning Jews the nuncio would not rashly overstep Vatican policy.

[handwritten margin note at top: pope claims Orsenigo kept from him but he appointed to begin with knowing he was pro-Nazi!]

Ensconced in his Berlin residence, Orsenigo took on a priest-assistant who was, secretly, a member of the Nazi party.[10] After the Concordat was signed in 1933, the nuncio urged German bishops to support Hitler's regime. Bishop Kaller (Ermland) later complained that the nuncio had "put the skids under me" by telling him to patch things up with the Nazis. Kaller, assuming that the nuncio spoke for the pope, did as he was told.[11] Later, when Bishop Clemens August von Galen publicly confronted the Nazis regarding their illegal euthanasia program, Orsenigo's report to Rome was critical of him, and when the war began, the nuncio complained that Catholics did not support it as strongly as Protestants.[12] On the occasion of Hitler's fiftieth birthday, Pope Pius told Orsenigo to congratulate the Führer warmly and publicly.[13]

[handwritten margin note: when ... to intervene he was embarrassed ?????!]

Under the circumstances, it was unlikely that Nuncio Orsenigo would relay unfavorable information to Rome, especially if the information was not common knowledge. The nuncio seldom intervened on behalf of Jews.[14] Sommer's report on the Kovno massacre, which did not find its way to the Vatican, was no exception. Orsenigo became impassioned on one occasion about Nazi treatment of Jews, when a plan developed to "resettle" Jews married to Christians, but his concern actually extended more to the Christian spouses, especially if they were the wives, because of the likely impoverishment of their families.[15] At other times, when the nuncio was directed by the Holy See to discuss incidents concerning Jewish victims with Nazi officials, he did so timidly and with embarrassment.[16]

A few months after the news about the Kovno massacre, SS officer Kurt Gerstein paid a surprise visit to Nuncio Orsenigo. Gerstein had just come from Belzec, where he had observed firsthand how a death camp functioned. He watched as 700 to 800 Jews were squeezed into four rooms of the Belzec gas chamber, into which the exhaust from a diesel engine was vented. Before the fumes could do their work, the motor malfunctioned and stopped. "For two hours and forty-nine minutes" (Gerstein used a stopwatch), the victims "were kept standing naked in the four chambers measuring five square yards each. When the motor was finally activated, it took thirty-two minutes to kill all of the victims."[17]

Gerstein was a man with a troubled conscience. Although he served in the apparatus of the Holocaust, he wanted to end it. This is why he sought out the papal nuncio in Berlin to tell him about the Holocaust so that he could tell the pope. Not wanting to hear what Gerstein had to say about the murder of the Jews, Nuncio Orsenigo refused to see him.

Officer Gerstein turned next to the auxiliary bishop of Berlin, a member of the city's anti-Nazi clique, who received him warmly and heard him out.[18] The bishop found Gerstein's report entirely credible, as did others with whom he communicated, such as Protestant bishop Otto Dibelius. Gerstein's request that his report be sent on to Rome was fulfilled, but not, of course, by the nuncio's office. The Vatican, however, allowed Gerstein's information about the Holocaust to die; that is, it was not relayed to other countries, such as France, whose Jews had not yet been "resettled."[19] The Vatican was a dead end for information about genocide.

The lack of communication about the Holocaust between the Berlin nuncio and the Holy See also characterized the Vatican secretariat's dispatches to its nuncios and the European hierarchy. Father Josef Tiso, president of the Slovakian government when his People's Party persecuted Jews in 1941 and again in 1944, serves as an example. When the Jewish community reacted to imminent deportations by appealing to Tiso as a priest and civic leader to intervene, his reply was to launch an investigation into how the Jews had found out about the plan.[20] The Vatican disapproved of Tiso and, as we have seen, demoted him. Monsignor Tardini of the secretariat of state remarked that although everyone understands that the Holy See cannot displace Hitler, that it is unable to restrain a priest, no one will understand.[21]

But the Vatican never informed other European bishops of Tiso's involvement in the Holocaust. Cardinal Michael Faulhaber of Munich embarrassed himself after the war by pleading for Tiso, who had fled to Germany, to the American occupational forces: "I feel duty bound to notify the Holy Father of [your] arrest of Dr. Tiso, since as a prelate in good standing he is a member of the papal family."[22] When Tiso was returned to Slovakia, tried, and hanged, Vatican radio refused to defend him, saying, "There are certain laws that must be obeyed no matter how much one loves his country."[23] The world learned too late of the Holy See's disapproval of Tiso's involvement in the Holocaust.

Bishop Alojzije Stepinac of Zagreb provides the opposite type of illustration. The Vatican was constantly in touch with him and with Pope Pius's representative to the fascist Ustasha government in Croatia, Abbot Marcone. For the most part, the Holy See left it to the bishop to figure out how to censure the Ustasha genocide and still remain on good terms with its fascist leader, Ante Pavelic. In July and October of 1943, Stepinac condemned racial killing explicitly and bluntly. His denunciation was read from pulpits across the land. German authorities in Croatia, who took Stepinac's words as a condemnation of their Jewish pol-

icy as well as of Ustasha's anti-Serb policy, arrested thirty-one priests.[24]
No leader of a national church ever spoke about genocide as pointedly
as Stepinac. His words were courageous and principled, because he—a
Croat—denounced Croatian nationals at a time when Germany's war
fortunes suggested that they would soon no longer be able to prop up
the murderous Ustashi. Stepinac had no illusions about his fate should
Marshal Josip Tito's Communists come to power.

Unfortunately, the Holy See let no one know that Archbishop Stepinac had dared to speak out against racism and genocide or whether it
approved of his conduct. Based on Stepinac's words, the Holy See might
have established guidelines for the bishops to follow regarding genocide, and based on Stepinac's actions—he gave refuge to endangered
Jews and Serbs—the papacy might have held him up as a model for
Catholics to emulate. But until the Cold War era, the world never heard
of Stepinac.

Tiso's and Stepinac's actions were directly related to the Holocaust,
but their original involvement with fascist racism antedated it. When
exactly did Vatican personnel become aware of the Holocaust itself?

- In October of 1941, the Vatican got reports from Chargé d'Affaires Giuseppe Burzio, Slovakia, about Jews being immediately
shot by Germans.[25]
- In March of 1942, Burzio informed Secretary of State Maglione
that 80,000 Jews were likely to be deported to a certain death, and
in May he reported that they had been deported.[26]
- Gerhart Riegner of the World Jewish Congress sent a memo in
March 1942 to the nuncio in Bern, Monsignor Filippi Bernardini, stating that there was sufficient information from a number of
sources to verify Jewish extermination.[27] (Document omitted from
Vatican collection *Actes et Documents*.)
- On May 12, 1942, Italian priest Pirro Scavizzi wrote to Pope Pius
informing him of the mass murder of Jews; some details were inaccurate.[28]
- In the summer of 1942, Abbot Ramiro Marcone wrote to Maglione telling him that Croatian Jews were to be deported to Germany and killed, and that 2 million Jews had already met this fate.[29]
- Bishop Szeptyckyj of Lwow, Poland, notified the Holy See that
"the number of Jews killed in this small region has certainly passed
two hundred thousand."[30]
- Memos of Ambassador Kazimierz Papée (Poland) and Envoy My-

ron C. Taylor to Secretary of State Maglione dated September 26, 1942, reported on the liquidation of the Warsaw ghetto, mass executions at special killing centers, and mass deportations of Jews from various European countries.[31]

• On October 3, 1942, the Polish ambassador to the Vatican reported that all over Poland Jews were being put in camps to be murdered.[32]

• Sometime in mid- to late 1942, SS officer Gerstein's eyewitness report on the Belzec death camp operation became known in the Vatican. (Document omitted from the *Actes et Documents*.)

• Chargé d'Affaires Tittman filed a memo on November 23, 1942, reporting on mass extermination of Jews in occupied Poland by poison gas in chambers especially prepared for that purpose and by machine-gun fire.[33]

• In December of 1942, the British minister to the Vatican, Francis d'Arcy Osborne, had an audience with Pius XII in which he gave the pope the English-American-Soviet report on the systematic starvation and massacre of Jews.

• Archbishop Anthony Springovics wrote Pius XII on December 12, 1942, that most of the Jews of Riga, Latvia, had been killed.[34]

An estimate of the quality of the information that flowed into the Vatican may be deduced from reports on the fate of some 80,000 Slovak Jews. In the spring of 1942, the Vatican heard from three sources—Nuncio Rotta (Hungary), Nuncio Bernardini (Switzerland), and Chargé d'Affaires Burzio (Slovakia)—that these Jews would be deported and killed. In June, confirmation of these reports came from the Polish government in exile in London.[35] By the end of 1942, the Holy See had received accounts about the ongoing murder of Jews from at least nine different countries where the Holocaust took place, including occupied Poland itself.

Yet the Vatican avoided coming to the conclusion that genocide was occurring in Europe. In response to Taylor's September genocide memo, Secretary Maglione responded that the papacy had also heard of "reports of severe measures taken against non-Aryans" from sources other than Taylor, "but that up to the present time it has not been possible to verify the accuracy" of the reports.[36] What kind of confirmation, beyond the tracking of Slovak Jews, was Cardinal Maglione looking for? In fact, Taylor's memo verified a report that the secretariat had received just a few days previously from an Italian source: "The massacres of the Jews have reached proportions and forms which are horribly frightful.

Incredible killings take place every day."[37] Secretary Maglione's response to Taylor appears to have been less than truthful. The fact was that the Holy See did not make public the reliable Holocaust reports of church leaders or members of its diplomatic corps; nor did it circulate them privately among Vatican diplomats and church leaders in Europe.

In the final months of 1942, President Roosevelt's personal envoy to the Vatican, Myron C. Taylor, and England's Minister Francis d'Arcy Osborne put considerable pressure on the pope to denounce the Holocaust. Osborne was outraged: "Is there not a moral issue at stake which does not admit of neutrality?"[38] After his audience with the Holy Father, Taylor had a more explicit discussion with Monsignor Tardini, during which Taylor said, "I'm not asking the pope to speak out against Hitler, just about the atrocities." Tardini wrote in his diary, "I could not but agree."[39]

The failure of the Vatican to exchange atrocity information with Taylor was critical because it came at a time when England and the United States were attempting to verify what turned out to be very reliable information about ongoing ethnic cleansing and about Nazi plans to exterminate all Jews. U.S. Undersecretary of State Sumner Welles and Rabbi Stephen S. Wise worked intensely to verify rumors about the atrocities, but, as historian Richard Breitman has noted, Myron Taylor "was unable to gather much information" at the Vatican.[40]

The pressure on the Holy See from the United States, England, and a host of other countries to break out of its silence about the Holocaust led Secretary Maglione to promise that the pope would speak about the issue. This he did in his 1942 Christmas address. Pope Pius's radio talk contained twenty-seven words about the Holocaust out of twenty-six pages of text. The part about the Holocaust, buried in a sea of verbosity, did not mention Jews. A few months later, Pius wrote to Bishop Preysing in Berlin saying that his address was well understood. In reality, very few people understood him, and no one, certainly not the Germans, took it as a protest against their slaughter of the Jews.[41]

In the following year, 1943, more Holocaust news and events came into the Vatican.

- In January, Pius XII received a letter from Wladislas Raczkiewicz, president of the Polish government in exile, detailing Nazi horrors in Poland.[42]
- Bishop Preysing wrote to Pope Pius on March 6, 1943, to tell him of the roundup of Jews in Berlin that had taken place from February 27th to March 1st. Preysing indicated that their deportation prob-

ably meant their death. They were in fact sent directly from their workplaces in Berlin to Auschwitz and gassed immediately, without even being registered.

• Just as Pius received Preysing's appeal for intervention regarding Berlin Jews, Hungarian Catholic activist Margit Slachta asked him in a personal audience to intervene to save Slovakian Jews.[43]

• On July 16, 1943, Father Marie-Benoit Peteul of Marseilles had an audience with the pope to plead for his help in rescuing Jews in the Italian-occupied part of France.

• The Holy See was itself a witness to the October 1943 roundup of the Jews of Rome.[44]

• From April to June 1944, the nuncio to Hungary, Angelo Rotta, notified the Holy See of the deportations of Jews to Auschwitz.[45]

By the end of 1943, it was simply no longer possible for the Vatican to deny that Germany was perpetrating a genocide. Already in the spring of that year, Secretary Maglione himself wrote that of the 4.5 million Polish Jews (his figure) living in Poland before the war, only 100,000 remained:

> After months and months of transports of thousands and thousands of persons about whom nothing more is known, this can be explained in no other way than death. . . . Special death camps near Lublin and near Brest Litovsk. It is told that they are locked up several hundred at a time in chambers where they are finished off with gas.[46]

At approximately the same time that Maglione made this admission, Monsignor Antoni Czarnecki, pastor of a Warsaw parish, sent the Vatican details concerning the mass deportations and gassings at nearby Treblinka and of the ghetto uprising.[47]

The realization that genocide was taking place did not spur the Vatican to change its policies regarding the Holy Land. It was Catholics and their rights that Pius thought about when the question of Jewish escape to Palestine arose. Historian John Conway has pointed out that the Vatican never wavered from its path regarding Palestine, even in the middle of the Holocaust, when that land offered Jews one of the last hopes of escape. In May of 1943, Cardinal Secretary of State Maglione said that Catholics had a right to the holy places, and that their "religious feel-ings would be injured and they would justly feel for their rights if Palestine belonged exclusively to the Jews."[48] The Vatican repeated this position even when the failure of the Allies at the Bermuda conference to deal specifically with the rescue of Jews at the height of the Holocaust doomed them.

The Silence of the Holy See

Secretary Maglione did not share his terrible knowledge about the murder of the Jews with anyone outside the Vatican; nor were any of the other details about the Holocaust made known to the world. Thus, the policy to conceal information about genocide, which began in Croatia and Slovakia, continued when all European Jews began to be murdered. The reports about the Holocaust that the Vatican would continue to receive from the middle of 1943 to the end of 1944 it kept to itself. The German ambassador to the Vatican wrote that although Rome had always been considered a good listening post for diplomats, there was actually little current information. This was true; an absence of communication characterized the highest levels of the hierarchy. A German bishop complained in 1941 that the country's bishops had heard nothing from Rome, nothing from Nuncio Orsenigo, and little from each other.[49] In the same year, two other German bishops, having heard that 10,000 Jews would be sent from Austria to the General Government in Poland, asked each other "whether the episcopacy should intervene for them out of humanitarian concern or whether this must be left up to Rome to do."[50] Catholic bishops felt the need of a coordinated policy.

It was not as if Germany's bishops were out of touch with the Holy See. Pius's letters to individual prelates during the war years number well over a hundred. He wrote eighteen times to Bishop Preysing alone, eleven times to Cardinal Bertram, and nine times to Cardinal Faulhaber.[51] But Pius never divulged to them the horrible news that the Vatican had learned in 1942 and confirmed in 1943, namely, that Germany had built extermination centers in occupied Poland where millions were being murdered. Rather, Pius commiserated with German bishops about their bombed-out cities and churches, recalling with fondness his years in Germany and the particular churches, now in ruins, where he had celebrated this or that holy day liturgy.[52] When the war turned against Germany, Pius assured its church leaders that he was praying daily, almost hourly, for peace.

But he almost never said a word about the Jews. Writing to Bishop Preysing, Pius said in April of 1943 that he was heartened to hear that Berlin Catholics were showing empathy for the city's Jews. To fend off Preysing, who pressured him more than any other Catholic bishop to speak out about the Holocaust, Pius adroitly put the blame on the United States. Recalling that a few years earlier in 1939 Bishop Preysing had urged him to assist emigrating Jews, Pius said that he "didn't want to mention all the difficulties the United States made for Jewish immigration."[53] Of course, it is true that the United States had been painfully negligent in the matter, not even admitting the allowed quota of Jews. But the difference between disallowing immigration of foreign nationals and persecuting and killing one's own citizens need not be belabored. The pope used the United States as a dodge for failing in what Bishop Preysing believed was his responsibility.

At times, lack of communication became miscommunication. In November 1943, Cardinal Bertram of Breslau wrote the Vatican secretary of state asking what could be done to provide the last sacraments for those being condemned to death and summarily executed in occupied Poland. Instead of telling Bertram that it would be impossible to get permission to provide the last sacraments for the victims because Germans were murdering them by the tens and hundreds of thousands, Maglione assured him that the Vatican was doing everything it could through local church officials (in Poland) to get permission to spend the sacraments.[54] There was clear intent here to conceal the facts about genocide.

Nor did the Holy See share its information about the Holocaust with Catholic resistance movements that were trying to save Jews. Volume eight of the Vatican's World War II documents contains numerous reports from French bishops and Nuncio Valerio Valeri that briefed the Holy See on their statements opposing Vichy antisemitic policies, made known the courageous rescue work of the Témoignage Chrétien group, and gave voice to their fears for the Jews. But one looks in vain in this and subsequent volumes of the documents for any kind of response from the Vatican regarding Jews.[55] It would have been quite possible to share information about the Holocaust with Zegota in Poland, with Catholic resistance movements in greater Germany that were centered in Berlin and Vienna, and with the Témoignage Chrétien circle in France. Historian Gerhard Weinberg believes that had Pope Pius spoken out about the murder of the Jews, many more Catholics would have had the courage to hide them.[56] Such encouragement, even given privately, would certainly have bolstered the work of the four groups mentioned here and those that are discussed in chapter 7.

How could the Holy See have supported the work of these groups? Rescue work required organization and numbers as much as courage. Because of food rationing and the frequent relocation of refugees, rescue work was more of a group than an individual activity. The French newsletter *Cahiers du Témoignage Chrétien* sought to inspire people to become active by reminding readers of Pius XI's "Spiritually we are Semites" statement and by urging action. "The church cannot disinter-

est itself in the fate of man, wherever his inviolable rights are unjust-
ly threatened."[57] The *Cahiers* was clandestinely delivered to all French
bishops and to thousands of priests and laypeople—even Pétainists read
it. As early as the end of 1942 the *Cahiers* affirmed, based on information from Cardinal Hlond, that hundreds of thousands of Jews had been
murdered in gas chambers; in 1943, it reported that Hitler intended to
exterminate all the Jews of Europe. Had the newsletter received confirmation of this information from the Holy See, or had it received encouragement from Pius XII similar to that of his predecessor, some
French bishops would have continued after 1942 to protest the deportation of Jews, and more French Catholics would have become involved in
rescue work. No, the Holocaust would not have been stopped, but as
Elie Wiesel has written, "the trains rolling toward [Auschwitz] would
have been less crowded."[58]

The Zegota rescue circle in Poland had no need of Holocaust information; they had firsthand knowledge of the gruesome details. But the
papacy could have assisted them with money. Since Polish Catholics had
been the first victims of Nazi aggression and had felt totally abandoned
by the papacy, any Vatican support of Jews, when their hour of despera-
tion came, may have angered Poles. As we have seen, however, after the
battle of Stalingrad, Polish church leaders became reconciled to Pius's
ways. Certainly, more Poles would have been swayed to help rescue Jews
if they had known the work had Rome's blessing. Zegota had need of
money because Polish Catholics would not always harbor a Jew altruis-
tically, and even if they would, they often did not have the money needed
to feed extra mouths.

Could the Vatican have given financial support to resistance groups
such as Zegota and Témoignage Chrétien? Early in the war, the Vatican
transferred all or nearly all of its liquid assets to the Chase Manhattan
Bank of New York and converted them to dollars. The Holy See then
requested that some of the money be used to buy Swiss currency to allow it to carry out its work in various European countries. The U.S.
Treasury Department hesitated to allow this, since some of the countries
in question were occupied by Germany. Permission was nevertheless
given, because the money would be used for charitable purposes and
would not benefit the Nazi regime to any significant degree. During the
war years, the Vatican budget for its operations in Europe fluctuated
between 1.3 and 2.2 million dollars. By converting some of the dollars
into Swiss francs, the Vatican could finance its work in Nazi-occupied
Europe.[59] Clearly, the Holy See could have supported rescue operations.
As it was, Zegota and Témoignage Chrétien depended solely on the Po-

lish government-in-exile and on American Jewish organizations for infusions of cash.

Pius XII's Hope for a Diplomatic Role

A second important theme to consider is the reasons that the Holy See gave for not speaking out about the Holocaust. One such explanation was that it was unnecessary because whenever and wherever cardinals and bishops denounced Nazi crimes, or other crimes throughout the world, they spoke for the pope. This is precisely what American Chargé d'Affaires Tittman was told in September of 1942.[60] On this occasion the Holy See specified France and Germany, among other countries, but as we have seen, Pope Pius failed to tell German bishops what their country was doing to the Jews. It was disingenuous for the Holy See to make the claim that bishops spoke for the Vatican when the pope withheld the very information from them that would have disposed them to speak out more explicitly. This was particularly true of France, because of the Témoignage Chrétien circle, but was even more critical in Germany's case, for reasons that will be taken up in the following chapter.

With the exception of the very guarded terms of the 1942 Christmas message, Pope Pius did not speak out publicly about the Holocaust; nor did he disseminate information about it privately through the Vatican's effective network of nuncios. At various times the Holy See gave different reasons for papal silence, some of which ring true and some of which ring hollow. Pius XII often repeated what he had told the Italian ambassador to the Vatican in 1940: "We would like to utter words of fire against such actions [German atrocities] and the only thing restraining Us from speaking is the fear of making the plight of the victims even worse."[61] This justification cannot be taken seriously. The statement made to the Italian ambassador referred to Polish Catholic victims whose church leaders—both those in occupied Poland and those in exile—repeatedly begged the pope to condemn German aggression. Pius reiterated the argument that he had given the Italian ambassador in an address to the College of Cardinals in June 1943. By this time—post-Stalingrad—church leaders in Poland had reversed themselves and agreed that it was better for the pope not to speak out.

Taking this argument seriously, apologists for Pope Pius point to the Dutch case. After Archbishop of Utrecht Johannes de Jong publicly protested against Nazi treatment of Jews in July 1942, the Germans retaliated by seizing Catholics of Jewish descent, including Edith Stein (Sister Benedicta).[62] The Vatican often reverted to Holland's experience to explain its own silence during the years of the Holocaust. Pius XII's house-keeper and sometime confidante, Sister M. Pasqualina Lehnert, recalled after the war that after the pope found out about the roundup of Catho-lic Jews in Holland, he quickly formulated a sharp protest condemning the Nazi action on two large sheets of paper. Then, almost immediately, the pope had second thoughts. Fearing further Nazi retaliation against the Dutch, Pius destroyed his statements, burning them in the kitchen of the Vatican's papal quarters (and, Sister Pasqualina emphasized, remain-ing there until the flames had completely consumed the document).[63]

Is this story credible? Even assuming that Sister Pasqualina's mem-ory served her correctly (her memoirs were not published until 1983), several problems or questions arise in connection with the Dutch pre-text. Earlier, during the Croatian genocide, when Pius might have as-sumed that he could have restrained the country's Catholic regime from slaughtering Jews and Orthodox Serbs, he said nothing. After January 1940, Pius said nothing about atrocities against Poles even when the victims themselves begged him to, thereby relieving him of his concern about worsening their plight. About the October 1943 roundup of Ro-man Jews—much closer to home than the roundup in Holland—Sister Pasqualina has no recollection at all of her beloved mentor's reaction. Finally, if Pope Pius refrained from speaking out so as not to endanger Christians of Jewish descent in Europe, why did he not speak out after the Nazis murdered them? In short, although the Vatican frequently used the Dutch case to explain papal silence, we must look elsewhere for the actual explanations.

A second reason for not condemning the Holocaust—one more im-puted than asserted—concerns Pius XII's fondness for Germans. That Pius was a Germanophile there can be no doubt. He had made his mark as a young diplomat in Germany by skillfully concluding concordats with several states. As we have seen, when he became pope, he insisted on having hands-on control when it came to German matters. Pope Pi-us chose German nationals as his closest advisers, and he delighted in charming Germans with his facility with their language and knowledge of minutiae about their country.[64]

But it is difficult to conclude that Pius's love of Germany weighed heavily in his consideration not to speak out about the Holocaust. Al-though both Belgian and German historians have accused Pius of letting his attitude toward Germany lead to bias in his diplomacy, the pope retained sufficient impartiality to send messages of sympathy to Belgium, Luxembourg, and Holland when Germany invaded them, even if he did not condemn Hitler's aggression.[65] Pius also knew, as did German bishops, that if Hitler won the war and succeeded in nazifying Europe, a final and decisive showdown would be launched against Christianity and the Catholic church. Pius was pro-German, not pro-Hitler.

Two other facets of the question of the pope's love of Germany deserve mention. Pius apparently expressed his apprehension that by denouncing exterminations in occupied Poland he would bring German Catholics into a conflict of conscience, since they served in Hitler's army or supported the war effort on the home front.[66] If this is to be taken seriously, it would mean, first, that the pope was prepared to sacrifice Polish Catholics for German Catholics and, second, that Pius feared that Germans, forced to choose between Hitler and their church, would follow their Führer. Pope Pius is in fact on record as telling Chargé d'Affaires Tittman that he could not speak out at that point in time—early fall 1942—because the "German people, in the bitterness of their defeat, will reproach him later on for having contributed, if only indirectly, to this defeat."[67] The statement is surprising and disconcerting—surprising because in the fall of 1942 Germany's ultimate defeat could not be predicted, and disconcerting because of the warped standard that is implied—German disappointment with the pope as opposed to millions of innocently murdered Jews.

While these statements are not to be denied, we should beware of placing too much value on isolated individual remarks. From time to time Pope Pius or his secretary of state would, under pressure, respond variously about why the Holy See had not spoken out. It is clear from Pius's correspondence with German bishops that he would not have objected to their challenging Hitler about the Holocaust, although he did not advise them to do this.[68] Thus, the remark made to Tittman cannot be taken as the entire reason for the pope's silence or as the sum total of the Vatican's position on the question of the murder of the Jews.

Pius XII's assertion to Tittman in December of 1942 can be viewed similarly. Pius said that he could not condemn Nazi atrocities without also condemning Soviet atrocities, "which might not be wholly pleasing to the Allies."[69] It is completely unclear to what Soviet atrocities Pius was referring. Was it to the Stalin purges? They had occurred five years earlier, well before the beginning of the Second World War and were already well known. Was it to the Katyn Forest massacre of German officers? Germany had not yet even charged the Soviets with this atrocity. Thus, the remark appears to be a temporizing exercise. Tittman was put off for the time being.

To find the actual reasons for Pius XII's silence about the Holocaust, we must look beyond these occasional stopgap statements and objections toward two concerns of utmost importance to the pope: his desire to play the role of a diplomatic peacemaker, savior of western Europe from communism, and his fear that Rome and the Vatican, entirely defenseless, would be obliterated by aerial attacks before the war came to an end.

Years after the end of the war, Robert Leiber, the German Jesuit who was one of Pius's closest confidants, made clear the connection between the pope's silence about the Holocaust and his diplomacy. The reason that Pius XII did not speak out about the murder of the Jews, Leiber confided to the Dutch historian Ger van Roon, was that he wanted to play the peacemaker during the war.[70] To safeguard his credentials for such a role, the Holy See had to preserve Vatican City's status as an independent state and neutral government. Pius's role model in this respect was Pope Benedict XV, whose efforts to negotiate a European peace during World War I had impressed a younger Eugenio Pacelli.[71] There would have been nothing negligent about this policy had it not kept Pius from dealing adequately with the Holocaust. In his postwar report to the British Home Office, Minister Francis Osborne said that Pius had at his disposal two strong weapons against Nazi criminality— "excommunication and martyrdom."[72] Pius did not use these, Osborne said, because he wanted to be the mediator of a negotiated peace. Thus, the Englishman, Osborne, a close observer of Pius, and the German, Leiber, his trusted adviser, are in full agreement on this point.

An effort to explain Pius's preoccupation with diplomacy would be somewhat speculative, but the consistency of this preoccupation lies beyond doubt. Because Pius wanted to see a Catholic state in place of Yugoslavia, he did not condemn the Catholic fascists in Croatia when they perpetrated genocide against Orthodox Christians. The Vatican secretariat of state actually treated the murderous Ustashi like children who "make mistakes" and who would have to learn to behave if they wanted the pope to recognize their state. As we have seen in an earlier chapter, Croatian bishop Stepinac's tardy condemnation of the Ustasha genocide may be explained by the priority the Holy See gave to diplomatic negotiations. Nor did Pius condemn the Nazis for murdering Catholic Poles. Rather, his preference was to have Nuncio Orsenigo press Hitler to recognize the Polish-Vatican Concordat. The next major genocidal victims during the war years were the Jews. Bishop Konrad Preysing of Berlin wanted Pope Pius to recall his nuncio to Germany, break off diplomatic relations with the murderous Nazi regime, and condemn the Holocaust. Acting with consistency, Pius declined to do so.

In the latter case there were additional reasons for Pius XII's reluctance to part company diplomatically with Germany. The pontiff viewed Germany as the key to the European chessboard that pitted bolshevism against Christianity. In his mind, Germany was and would remain the European bulwark against Russian communism; he wished, therefore, to preserve the country intact. From the beginning of the war to its very end, Pius sought to undo the consequences of the First World War by enlarging Germany. Even as Germany's fate became clear late in the war, Pius wrote to Cardinal Michael Faulhaber of Munich in 1944 indicating that in a negotiated peace Germany should not have to give up Austria and the Sudeten province of Czechoslovakia![73]

Historian Klemens von Klemperer has reviewed the Holy See's contacts with German anti-Nazi resistance and Pius's efforts to negotiate between them and England to overthrow Hitler. Although both sides were unclear about the details of a possible understanding, the status quo following the Munich Conference, which had awarded the Sudetenland to Germany, was the point of departure.[74] Pius wanted a powerful Germany without Hitler, and he seriously underestimated German ambitions, even of those Germans who opposed their dictator.[75]

Pius's concentration on diplomacy persisted. When the United States and Germany became World War II belligerents in 1941, Pius was disappointed. He had hoped to team up with President Roosevelt to negotiate a peace.[76] But a negotiated peace was precisely what the Allies did not want. The American president made the mistake of sending his envoy to the pope in 1942 to ask him not to seek a negotiated peace, and to tell him that the Allies would win the war as a moral crusade against evil. Pope Pius would naturally have taken exception to this, because in his mind the "moral crusade" should be directed against Communist Russia, and because he wanted to display world leadership himself by negotiating a peace. When President Roosevelt and Prime Minister Winston Churchill called for an unconditional surrender in their 1942 declaration at Casablanca, Pope Pius found himself cut out of the picture altogether.

A negotiated peace became an overriding concern for the Holy See. Before Stalingrad, Pius believed that the Americans should help the Russians, but with reservations, so that hostilities on the eastern front remained far from Germany. After the battle of Stalingrad and the successful Allied invasion of southern Italy in July 1943, Pius hoped that England and the United States would abandon the Russians so that Germany could deal with the Communist threat. Ideally, he hoped England would recognize the danger to the Christian west that communism posed, and conclude a separate peace with the Axis powers.[77] This would pay a second dividend: Rome would no longer be threatened with air raids.

When Germany switched ambassadors to the Vatican in 1943, Pius tried to impress the departing Diego von Bergen and the newly appointed Ernst von Weizsäcker with his belief in a powerful Germany to withstand the Marxist threat from the east. If the Nazis would just live up to the terms of the Concordat, Pope Pius could support a German mission against Russia.[78] After his first private audience with the pope, Weizsäcker reported to Berlin that "hostility to Bolshevism is, in fact, the most stable component of Vatican foreign policy," and that "the Anglo-American link with the Soviet Russia is detested by the [Holy See]."[79]

The combination of Russian successes on the eastern front, the invasion of Italy by Anglo-American forces, and the fall of Mussolini (July 1943) led to a very noticeable increase in Communist activity in Rome and northern Italy, where a number of Catholic priests were murdered by Communist guerrillas. This disturbed Pope Pius, particularly because of vehement anti-church Communist propaganda. Still, the Vatican refrained from promoting a separate Italian peace with the Allies, because it would necessarily weaken Germany. The radical cure for Italian communism lay in the defeat of Communist Russia.

But Communist agitation in Rome was close to home, and it rested uneasily on Pius's mind. It would necessarily have reminded him of the tumultuous days in Munich at the end of the Great War when he had himself faced down a gun-toting Red revolutionary. Pius's concern over Italian Communist activity coincided with Germany's concern about Rome's Jews, whom they wished to "resettle." When the roundup of hundreds of Jews took place in October 1943 just outside Vatican city, Ambassador Weizsäcker and other Germans held their breath to see if the pope would protest. He did not, but three days later he requested that Germany increase its police manpower in Rome in order to cut down on Communist agitation.[80]

The same priority of concerns was reflected several months later, in December 1943, when a Vatican consultation about Germany was intercepted by Berlin or allowed to leak out by the Holy See. Reichssicherheitshauptamt (Reich Security Main Office) chief Ernst Kaltenbrunner sent a memorandum to Joachim von Ribbentrop, German minister for foreign affairs, which reported that the main obstacles to a loyal relationship between the church and National Socialism lay in the latter's euthanasia and sterilization policies. The murder of the Jews was left out of the equation.[81]

Pius XII's response to the Allies' Casablanca ultimatum for an unconditional surrender was to call for a peace of justice rather than a peace of force in his 1943 Christmas address.[82] Sitting on the diplomatic sidelines, Pius referred derisively to the "Big Three" in conversation with Germany's Ambassador Weizsäcker.[83] Pius had been upset with Germany when Hitler negotiated a non-aggression pact with Russia and invaded western Europe, but when the dictator returned to his quest for Lebensraum and invaded Russia in 1941, the pope became visibly emotional in conversation with the Spanish ambassador about what appeared to be the German defeat of the Communist menace.[84] Because in Pius's mind Germany remained the last line of defense against Russian communism, the pope frequently discussed schemes for a negotiated peace with Weizsäcker.[85]

The troubling aspect of Pius's preoccupation with diplomacy was that Jews would continue to be murdered as peace negotiations were under way. Hundreds of thousands of Jews were murdered during the time period between the battle of Stalingrad and the end of the war. Instead of confronting Weizsäcker with these crimes, Pius discussed peace negotiations with him. The subject of the Jews and their fate never came up. During 1943, Pius's attention remained riveted on his church and the potential danger to it from aerial attacks and from communism. Historian Saul Friedlander asks,

> How is it conceivable that at the end of 1943 the pope and the highest dignitaries of the church were still wishing for victorious resistance by the Nazis in the east and therefore seemingly accepted by implication the maintenance, however temporary, of the entire nazi extermination machine?[86]

Pius would necessarily have been aware of the ongoing murder of the Jews because of reports about it to the Holy See and appeals for him to intervene. This continued almost to the end of the war, when international efforts, which involved the Holy See, got under way to save Hungarian Jews from deportation to Auschwitz.[87] A high-ranking official in the secretariat of state, Monsignor Domenico Tardini, told the German ambassador that the United States would probably object to his (latest) proposal for negotiations because of the Holocaust (the "Jewish matter").[88] While Weizsäcker fished Vatican waters for negotiations, the Allies pressed Pius to speak out about the Holocaust.

Although Catholics and non-Catholics inside and outside the diplomatic corps reminded Pius of his role as a moral leader with reference to the Holocaust, he concentrated on diplomacy, often to the exclusion of genocide. The pope allowed the Vatican to become involved with German resistance in an attempt to overthrow Hitler. Later, when Italy wearied of the war, Pius again violated the Vatican's neutrality by allowing England's minister to the Holy See to be an intermediary between England and Italy.[89] But when it came to the Holocaust, strict diplomatic rules were adhered to. The Holy See did not allow its diplomatic offices to involve themselves in the negotiations with England and the United States that were necessary to ensure safe passage across the Mediterranean for the Jews in the Italian zone of France, who were desperately seeking to avoid deportation to Auschwitz.[90]

As the Holocaust lingered on into the latter years of the war, Pius wearied of hearing about the Jews. "I remember," Polish ambassador to the Vatican Kazimierz Papée recalled, "when I came to see the Holy Father for . . . perhaps the tenth time in 1944; he was angry. When he saw me as I entered the room and stood at the door awaiting permission to approach, he raised both his arms in a gesture of exasperation. 'I have listened again and again to your representations about Our unhappy children in Poland,' he said. 'Must I be given the same story yet again?'"[91] Even though ambassador Papée and western diplomats repeatedly pressed Pius about the Holocaust, the pope omitted time and again to discuss it with Germany's Ambassador Weizsäcker, who would later be found guilty of war crimes against Jews at the Nuremberg Trials.

Pope Pius's Concern about the Possible Bombardment of Rome

The correspondence and dispatches of the German ambassador and the American envoy to the Vatican make it clear that Pope Pius's second great concern was the possible bombing of Rome, not the murder of the Jews. With the Holocaust in full force, the Vatican's diplomatic staff and the pope himself devoted most of their energy to ensuring that neither Germany nor the Allies would bomb Rome. This became possible for the Allies after General Erwin Rommel's Panzerkorps had been pushed out of northern Africa, allowing English and American troops to cross the Mediterranean and occupy Sicily. Driving German forces from mountainous southern Italy proved a more difficult task, one that lasted from the summer of 1943 to the summer of 1944. During these months of acute danger, the Holy See communicated directly with Envoy Taylor or Chargé d'Affaires Tittman no fewer than thirty-four times in an effort to forestall the bombing of Rome.[92]

The problem facing Pius XII was that he had failed to condemn the German bombing of England during 1940 and 1941, but then spoke out against the bombing of civilians when the Allies gained aerial superiority. Perhaps Pius's words of affection for German air-raid victims resulted from the ferocity and duration of allied attacks after Marshal Hermann Göring's air force had become totally defenseless. Still, by expressing sympathy and concern for Germany's bombed-out churches after not having regretted the Nazi destruction of Coventry Cathedral in England, the pope had made a serious tactical mistake.[93]

In October 1942, when Taylor attempted to extract a promise from Winston Churchill not to bomb Rome, the prime minister refused to commit himself. Pius continued to hope that he could get the Americans to persuade the English not to bomb Rome, but Myron Taylor delicately pointed out that this might be difficult: "I am not clear," he told Monsignor Montini, "whether the Holy See has condemned the bombing of London, Warsaw, Rotterdam, Belgrade, Coventry, Manila, Pearl Harbor, and places in the South Pacific."[94] Early in 1943, Foreign Secretary Anthony Eden, addressing Parliament, stoked Pope Pius's anxiety when he said that "we have as much right to bomb Rome as the Italians had to bomb London. We shall not hesitate to do so to the best of our ability and as heavily as possible if the course of the war should render such bombing convenient and helpful."[95]

President Roosevelt tried to be more conciliatory. He promised that no American aircraft would drop bombs over the Vatican. The Holy See continued to press the issue relentlessly, both through Envoy Taylor and through the apostolic delegate to the United States, trying to exact promises that Vatican property outside Vatican City would also not be harmed. Roosevelt, somewhat exasperated, finally gave instructions that the apostolic delegate should be informed that "war is war," and that with the Germans in charge of the city of Rome, no further promises would be forthcoming.[96] The Holy See responded that if Vatican property were indeed bombed, the pope would protest publicly.[97] No such threat was ever made regarding the murder of the Jews.

It exasperated observers, both inside and outside the Vatican, that the pope would be so concerned over what had not yet taken place and so little concerned over the ongoing murder of the Jews. Cardinal Tisserant remarked as early as 1940 that the pope dwelt too much on the danger of Rome's being bombed and not enough on the affairs of the church.[98] In September, Myron Taylor told Montini that the "deplorable inhumanities in Germany against civilian populations are even more reprehensible than the attacks on all her neighbors whom she invaded."[99] Minister Osborne put it to the Vatican secretary of state more bluntly on December 14, 1942: "Instead of thinking of nothing but the bombing of

Rome, [the Holy See] should consider [its] duties in respect to the un-precedented crime against humanity of Hitler's campaign of extermina-tion of the Jews."[100]

Bishop Preysing, writing to Pius from heavily bombed Berlin, adopt-ed the perspective that Minister Osborne found lacking in the pope. "Even more bitter [events than the air raids] face us here in Berlin with the new wave of Jewish deportations that were put in motion just before the first of March [1943]." Preysing then asked the pope to speak out again about the Holocaust.[101] Six months later, in October 1943, Pope Pius was confronted with the precise choice that Bishop Preysing had put to him so pointedly—deportation of Jews versus aerial bombard-ment. It was at that time that the Reich Security Main Office moved to deport the Jews of Rome to Auschwitz.[102]

When the catastrophe struck the Roman Jews, the bombing of the Basilica of San Lorenzo, which took place in July, still weighed heavily on the pope's mind. Although President Roosevelt had assured Pope Pius in May 1943 that no American planes would drop bombs over the Vat-ican, the city of Rome was hit on numerous occasions. The Basilica of San Lorenzo was badly damaged. Pius wrote President Roosevelt ex-pressing his anguish: "In person We have visited and with sorrow con-templated the gaping ruins of that ancient and priceless Papal Basilica of St. Laurence."[103] Later, Undersecretary Montini called Taylor's assistant, Tittmann, on the carpet for not expressing promptly enough his regrets about the bombing to the Holy Father.

In November, bombs fell on Vatican City itself, slightly damaging St. Peter's Basilica and other structures. These attacks, together with the unnecessary destruction by the Allies of the Abbey of Montecassino south of Rome, chagrined Vatican personnel. Pope Pius visited the dam-aged churches of Rome, commiserated with the Romans, and took the unprecedented step of granting a plenary indulgence for victims of air raids.[104] The evening of the day on which San Lorenzo was bombed, Pope Pius wept as he prayed the rosary while looking out over the city of Rome from his Vatican quarters.[105] When Vatican City itself became the victim of an air raid, the Holy See assumed, incorrectly as it turned out, that an American plane was to blame.[106] Because of all of the destruction by the Allies, Ambassador Weizsäcker could report to Berlin that Ger-many was winning the propaganda war.[107] How could this be, survivor and historian Saul Friedlander has asked, at a time when the pope was aware of the nature of Hitler's regime?[108]

In his correspondence with Bishop Preysing, Pope Pius made no se-cret of his priorities. Responding to the Berlin prelate, who had urged the pope to address the Holocaust, Pius asserted that the most pressing problem facing him lay in maintaining the absolute trust of Catholics, regardless of which side they fought for, so as to ensure the church's unity. Pius felt that if Rome became contested by Germans on one side and Anglo-Americans on the other, this trust would be in jeopardy.[109] Pius also defended his policy by saying that he was conscience bound to bring all the pressure he could muster on the Allies not to bomb Rome. Catholics the world over, he said, saw the Eternal City as the center of Christendom and the birthplace of the church. As such, Rome symbolized the universal nature of the church. Should this symbol be destroyed, Pius affirmed, faith and hope among Catholics would be shaken.

What Pope Pius told Bishop Preysing, he could not tell the rest of the world. The fortunes of the war made the threat of Allied bombardment greater than bombardment by Germany so long as Pius remained silent about the murder of the Jews. The Holy See dared not link its concern over the possible bombing of Rome to its silence about the Holocaust because of the implication that the murder of Europe's Jews was a lesser priority.

Earlier Pius had assured Bishop Preysing that he was doing all that he could for the persecuted Jews, that he deeply sympathized with them, and that he prayed for them. The pontiff asserted that what he had said about the persecution of the Jews in his 1942 Christmas address "was short but well understood," and he said that he intended to speak out again when the circumstances were right.[110] Whatever circumstances the pope had in mind evidently never came to pass.

The inconsistencies of papal policy relative to the Holocaust may best be understood in the light of Pius's assumptions and priorities. These were, first, that the welfare of Catholic states took precedence over the interests of Jews. The Holy See used diplomacy rather than (public) moral strictures to attempt to curtail the involvement of Slovakia and Croatia in genocide. Pius XII did not want to undercut popular support for the fledgling governments of these new Catholic countries by threatening their leaders with excommunication. The same policy held in western Europe for Catholic Vichy France. The Vatican avoided interfering with the "resettlement" of Jews after a sharp government warning following the courageous statements of a number of French bishops.[111]

Second, the long-term danger that communism potentially held for the church preoccupied Pope Pius.[112] His assumption that Germany would be the west's defense against bolshevism ensured that Pius's diplomatic course would be rocky, since Hitler instigated both the Second World War and the Holocaust. But Pius stayed his course inflexibly. The Vatican warned Slovakian leaders that "resettlement" meant perdition for its Jews, but only months later Pius allowed the Germans to "re-settle" the Jews of Rome without uttering a word (see chapter 6). Earlier, before the German occupation of Italy, the Vatican and officials in Mussolini's government had cooperated smoothly to save Jews. When the Germans took control of the country, the Vatican refrained from even approaching them on behalf of Jews.[113]

Pius's assumptions and priorities are clearly set forth in his letters to Bishop Preysing in 1943 and 1944. He wanted his German friend from Weimar years to know that he cared about the Jews, but that his first concern was for the Catholic church, its universality and unity. Pius may have feared that communicating throughout the church word of the murders perpetrated by the Catholic Ustasha, the complicity in genocide of Catholic Slovak priest Tiso, and the crimes of Catholic Austrians and Germans committed against Catholics in Poland would deeply divide the church. But this apprehension does not explain the Vatican's deceleration of information about the murder of the Jews.

Pius XII harbored a personal ambition to play an important role in world diplomacy, and he felt duty bound to shield the visible center of Catholicism from destruction. Standing amid the ruins of the Basilica of San Lorenzo, Pope Pius said, "Almost in the center of Rome . . . is our Vatican City, an independent state and an independent neutral state, which shelters priceless treasures, sacred not only to the Apostolic See but to the whole Catholic world."[114] The Vatican's "priceless treasures" were not worth the lives of millions of Jewish men, women, and children, but in Pius's view what those treasures stood for were worth those lives.

Pius XII's priorities put Jews at mortal risk. Thousands, perhaps tens of thousands, of additional Jews would have eluded Hitler's death camps had the Holy See accelerated rather than decelerated information about genocide. Did Pope Pius think the church so fragile that, should he speak out, it would not survive the war, even though it had survived the fratricidal Great War intact? Should the possible bombardment of Rome have been Pius's primary concern, or, as Bishop Preysing pointed out, should not the moral issue of the murder of the Jews have taken precedence? Were the churches and other structures of Rome and the Vatican really the nerve center of Catholic faith that Pius believed them to be? Was the possible future clash between Christianity and atheistic communism more important than the slaughter of the Jews who were being murdered in eastern Europe, and who would continue to be murdered while Pius hoped for a negotiated settlement to the war that would favor genocidal Germany, the church's defender from Russian communism?

The tunnel vision of Pius XII was broadened somewhat in his efforts to use the church's diplomatic network to save Jews. This cannot be taken from him, but, as we will see in the following three chapters, much more could have been accomplished by working within the church's structure, even without a public condemnation of Nazi Germany's genocide.

5. In the Eye of the Storm
German Bishops and the Holocaust

At the height of the Holocaust, German bishops were challenged by one of their members, Konrad Preysing, to confront the Nazi regime about the murder of the Jews. Had this or that bishop in France, Italy, or elsewhere objected to the Holocaust, it would have had only regional repercussions. But had the German bishops confronted the Holocaust publicly and nationally, the possibility of undermining Hitler's death apparatus might have existed. Admittedly, it is speculative to assert this, but it is certain that many more German Catholics would have sought to save Jews by hiding them if their church leaders had spoken out.[1]

The role of German bishops was critical for a second reason. After the suppression of free speech and of political parties, the churches were the only remaining possible force for influencing public opinion.[2] We know, of course, that the bishops failed to use the pulpits for a national outcry against the Holocaust. But several bishops did speak out. What they said about the Holocaust has obviously not impressed historians, certainly not to the degree that the protest of Bishop Clemens August Graf von Galen against the Nazi "euthanasia" process has. Why were the statements of German bishops opposing the killing of innocent people not effective? We will attempt to understand the reasons for this question by following the experiences of two young Germans of the Nazi era, Christel Beilmann, a Catholic teenager at the time, and Gisbert Kranz, a soldier who was forced to face the murder of the Jews in the course of his military duties.

Historians David Bankier and Hans Mommsen, who have examined whether and to what extent Germans knew about the Holocaust, have concluded that the mass murders were easy to learn about if someone really wanted to know.[3] A number of bishops did want to know, and they succeeded very early on in discovering what their government was doing to the Jews in occupied Poland. They then had to face the crucial question of what to do about what they had learned. A preexisting condition, the Concordat between Nazi Germany and the Holy See, inhibited them, as we saw in the introductory chapter. Once the war began, nationalism—not antisemitism—further disinclined them to act on their knowledge about the Holocaust. Nevertheless, it seems certain that a strong papal assertion would have enabled the bishops to overcome their disinclinations.

Given these circumstances, Bishop Preysing's only hope to spur his colleagues into action lay in Pope Pius XII. From the summer of 1943 to late in the war, with the murder of the Jews in full swing, Preysing sought to tip the balance of the debate among German bishops about what to do about the Nazi persecution of the Jews by invoking papal authority. This effort backfired.

A number of Holocaust-related questions bear on what the German bishops did and did not do, and still others bear on what they thought they had done. Was what they said collectively about murder sufficient? Did individual bishops speak out more forcefully than the entire episcopal group? Would the bishops have said more had the Vatican informed them of the extent of the atrocities against the Jewish people of Europe? Could and should bishops have cooperated more closely than they did with resistance groups?

Tracking Genocide in Germany

Wilhelm Berning, bishop of Osnabrück in northwestern Germany, knew about the plan to murder the Jews of Europe in February 1942.[4] This is remarkable. Although historians disagree about when Hitler decided to kill all of the Jews, they agree that the decision to implement genocide was made in 1941, probably sometime after July. The Wannsee meeting took place in January 1942, at which time Himmler's agents were instructed about how to proceed with building death camps in occupied Poland. Thus, even before total genocide occurred, church leaders knew of the plan to kill the Jews.

The lapse of time of only a few months is amazing, but the bishops had reason to be suspicious. From the beginning of the war to about 1942, the Nazis had killed tens of thousands of people in six "euthanasia" facilities in Germany. Working in Berlin, Margarete Sommer was engaged in protecting as many Catholic patients as possible from the doctors of the Reich Enterprise for Health and Welfare Facilities (Reichsarbeitgemeinschaft für Heil- und Pflegeanstalten, or, in Nazi jargon, "T-4").[5] The protest of von Galen, the bishop of Münster, against the "euthanasia" program is well known.[6]

The "resettlement" of Jews in ghettos "in the east" and the murder of other Jews en masse by mobile killing squads (*Einsatzgruppen*) overlapped with the domestic killing of handicapped Germans. In February 1942, Sommer provided the bishops with an accurate description of the Kovno massacre, which had occurred in the summer and fall of 1941. In October 1941, 20,000 Jews from Vienna, Berlin and several other large cities were deported to the Lodz ghetto. Four months later, church leaders found out what happened to them:

> Housing in unheated rooms. Between 32 and 80 persons to a room. For example, in a room measuring only 20 square meters, 32 people. Every evening there is a fight over sleeping places on the floor; people lie on bare earth. Sustenance: about 200 grams of bread a day (that means about 4 small slices), together with a watery soup once or twice a day at noon or in the evening. Washing only possible outdoors at the well. Indescribable cold. No possibility to change clothes. No flushing toilets; no running water. Huge epidemics. Death rate in the first weeks was 35 a day, and, according to one man, 200 a day in January in Litzmannstadt [Lodz].[7]

Sommer's reports demonstrated Nazi disregard for Jewish life. By February 1942, the bishops already knew that their country was murdering Jews and purposely letting them die of exposure and hunger. Bishop Berning, who got his information from Sommer, would not have been entirely surprised when he wrote in his diary that "it appears likely that a plan exists to murder the Jews."[8]

New information confirmed this. Jews had been deported from Münsterland in northwestern Germany late in 1941, and by mid-1942 reliable reports of their mass murder were circulating.[9] Shortly thereafter, church leaders found out from SS officer Kurt Gerstein how Jews were being killed and the dreadful details of the murder process.[10]

There was no need to take just one man's word about the murder of the Jews. A number of Munich Jesuits had become active in a German resistance movement, the Kreisau Circle. These priests hoped to coordinate Catholic resistance with that of the Kreisau Circle.[11] The Jesuits were in frequent contact with Berlin's Bishop Preysing and with the leader of the Kreisau group, Helmuth von Moltke, who was later executed by the Nazis. In December 1942, Augustin Rösch, one of the Jesuits involved with resistance, learned through a leak in the Jewish Affairs office that the plan to deport and exterminate Jews "is frequently already underway."[12] Since Preysing and von Moltke were in regular contact with each other, information of this sort would certainly have made the rounds in private conversations.

German church leaders knew in some detail about atrocities against the Jews almost as soon as they had begun to be starved to death in ghettos or murdered by gunfire in mass graves or gassed and cremated. Church historians in Germany now commonly hold that church leaders knew about the Holocaust by the end of 1942.[13] Although news of the Holocaust traveled quickly throughout the entire western hemisphere, reaching the United States by August 1942, German bishops were certainly among the first to know and they knew more details than most, although not as many as the Vatican.[14]

A sure sign of certainty about the fate of "transported" Jews on the part of some Catholics of the Greater Reich is that in Berlin and Vienna they began hiding Jews toward the end of 1942. Both they and the Jews in hiding had no illusions about the peril surrounding them. Berliner Gertrud Jaffe, who had converted to Catholicism, decided with great inner resolve to come out of hiding and give herself up for deportation and certain death, because she wished to identify, as a Christian, with the suffering of her people.[15] Preferring to die herself rather than endanger the lives of the family that had been hiding her, Liselotte Neumark asked Margarete Sommer to sneak her onto the next Berlin "transportation." By the end of 1942, potential Holocaust victims and their rescuers knew that "transportation" really meant death.

Knowledge about the Holocaust grew as the process of genocide continued. Hans Globke, a high-ranking bureaucrat in the Ministry of the Interior, kept Margarete Sommer informed through an intermediary of developments concerning Jews. Playing what Sommer called a dangerous double game by writing Nazi antisemitic law by day and divulging state secrets by night, Globke knew that hundreds of thousands of Jews were being murdered "in the east."[16] Contact between Sommer and Globke continued during the worst years of the Holocaust. Since Sommer was the episcopacy's consultant on Jewish affairs, the information that she gained from her "leak" would be funneled to the bishops at large.

During and after the war, some German bishops, including Cardinal Adolf Bertram and Conrad Gröber, said that they did not know about the Holocaust. What they meant by this is either that they were not aware of its extent and details or that they were not absolutely certain about it. What this means, in turn, is that, not wanting to know about the Holocaust, they avoided finding out about it. Bishop Gröber himself provides an example. The Jesuit intermediaries who attempted to enlist him in the Kreisau resistance movement found him a "tough nut" to crack.[17] It was disingenuous for Gröber to disassociate himself during the war from groups that gathered information about the Holocaust and then proclaim after the war that he had kept silent because he did not know. Other bishops, not wanting to be branded as traitors, avoided resistance movements.[18] Adolf Bertram simply cut off contact with Margarete Sommer. In 1944, Bertram notified the diocese of Berlin that in the future Sommer's reports would have to be undersigned by Bishop Preysing to verify their details and correctness, an impossible request because of German surveillance. "Please make this clear to Frau Dr. Sommer," Bertram wrote, "since my warnings don't help. Otherwise I will not schedule anymore appointments for her."[19]

The Church's Intramural Debate about Genocide

Once German church leaders knew about the Holocaust, what did they do about it? What options were open to them? There were actually a number of options. They could have appealed to the Vatican for direction, asked the Vatican to denounce the murder of the Jews, joined in resistance movements in Germany, denounced the Nazi government for its policy of genocide, warned Catholics not to be a party to it, announced simultaneously as a body throughout Germany that genocide must cease, spoken out individually, and, at the very least, attempted to protect converted Jews. Or they could have done nothing and claimed that they did not know enough about the Holocaust to act on their information.

To do absolutely nothing was not their disposition. Unlike many churchmen in Croatia, Hungary, and other east European countries, most German bishops were not mean-spirited toward Jews. It was the Corcordat, not ill will toward Jews, that had kept the bishops from speaking out about Nazi antisemitism before the war. Although they failed to speak out against the national pogrom of November 1938, they opposed it.[20]

Once the war began, patriotism became another factor that kept the bishops from forthright statements about the atrocities committed against Jews. After the debacle of the Great War, German bishops no longer posed the question of whether there was such a thing as a just war, a traditional tenet of Catholic morality. Saying that it was no longer possible to determine whether a war was or was not just, German church leaders abandoned this moral question and left judgment up to the state, at the same time warning the faithful to obey its decision.²¹ Even when Pius XII sympathized with the victims of German aggression in western European countries in 1940, the bishops supported the Führer's foreign policy. Very few followed Bishop Preysing's example by refusing to ring the church bells after victories over Poland and France, and even fewer refused to call the war against Russia a crusade against bolshevism.²²

Catholic newspapers reflected the bishops' nationalistic fervor. After the war, American Catholic Gordon Zahn reviewed the Bavarian Catholic press, which he characterized as "hyper-nationalistic."²³ Blind support of the war unfortunately led to a blending of nationalistic goals with Nazi racist goals. Bamberg's diocesan newspaper, the *St. Heinrichsblatt,* justified a war for Lebensraum. The Passau diocesan newspaper asked on January 26, 1941, "why England should rule two-thirds of the world while Germany, more populous, is constrained to a small part of Europe." The paper concluded emphatically: "Our German people fight today for its growth and its Lebensraum."²⁴ Sometimes ideology and the Hitler cult were the links to Lebensraum. The Augsburg *Katholisches Kirchenblatt* of April 20, 1941, endorsed Hitler's wars for Lebensraum, concluding that "the person of the Führer contains the strength, greatness and future of the German people."

The importance of these references to Lebensraum, and others like them, lies in the fact that Germans knew that Hitler was building a "pure racial community." Only "racially pure Aryans" could inhabit Lebensraum. Historian David Bankier has concluded that driving Jews from Germany's Lebensraum "could not be achieved if [Germans] were unduly sensitive to [the] morality" of antisemitism.²⁵ Since German Catholics were not notably antisemitic, it was difficult for them to inure their consciences to the immorality of what Hitler was doing to the Jews.²⁶ Some Catholic soldiers, feeling guilt for murdering Jews even though they were ordered to do so, went to confession to seek forgiveness.²⁷ In this context, church support of Germany's quest for Lebensraum would have worked as a salve for Catholic consciences. To whatever extent the Nazi racial agenda in eastern Europe disturbed the Catholic conscience, German national goals could ease the burden.

The nationalistic feelings of the bishops also inhibited them from becoming deeply involved with German anti-Nazi movements. Helmuth von Moltke, the leader of the Kreisau resistance movement, wished to establish ties with Catholic church authorities. Moltke believed that the Protestant church was too divided within itself to ever take the lead in opposing Hitler. Although Protestant himself, Moltke felt that Catholic church leaders were capable of inciting popular feeling against the atrocities of the Nazis.[28] Working through Jesuits Augustin Rösch, Alfred Delp, and Lothar Koenig, Moltke attempted to build the infrastructure for a united Catholic stand against the regime. The Jesuits knew what was happening to the Jews, and they felt that they themselves would be Hitler's next victims.[29] Rösch, who drew up a draft statement on human rights, and the other Jesuits acted as couriers for the Kreisau Circle, attempting to bring bishops into the resistance movement in 1942 and 1943. They met with very limited success. Bishops Preysing and Dietz were very active, Berning and Wienken less so.[30] Even Preysing had reservations, and the Jesuits could find no bishop willing to take the lead in rallying episcopal colleagues to the cause.[31]

In the end, nothing concrete resulted from the contacts between the Kreisau Circle and the bishops. Relations between the two groups remained informal and underdeveloped. The bishops, one suspects, did not want to be branded as disloyal Germans or, worse, traitors. Nevertheless, the contact with the Kreisau Circle prompted the bishops, especially Preysing, to consider what they should do as moral leaders. The bishops did not want to advocate murdering Hitler, but they felt that Nazi murders had to be addressed. They preferred doing this as churchmen rather than as resisters.

Indeed, as church leaders the bishops came much closer to opposing the Holocaust. Convinced by 1943 that Jews were actually being murdered after their "transportation," the Berlin Catholic resistance circle drafted a letter regarding deported Jews which they intended to send Hitler and other top Nazis under the signatures of all the bishops. At Preysing's behest, Sommer drew up a "Draft for a Petition Favoring the Jews" in August. The letter was remarkable because of its explicit language, and because it addressed the plight of all Jews, not just individuals who fell under church jurisdiction by virtue of their conversion.[32]

> With deepest sorrow—yes, even with holy indignation—have we German bishops learned of the deportation of non-Aryans in a manner that is scornful of all human rights. It is our holy duty to defend the unalienable rights of all men guaranteed by natural law. . . . The world would not understand if we failed to raise our voice loudly against the deprivation of rights of these innocent people. We would stand guilty before God and man because of our silence. The burden of our responsibility grows correspondingly more pressing as . . . shocking reports reach us regarding the awful, gruesome fate of the deported who have already been subjected in frightfully high numbers to really inhuman conditions of existence.

Margarete Sommer and Bishop (later Cardinal) Konrad Graf von Preysing
rescued Berlin Jews and sought in vain to have Pope Pius XII and
German bishops speak out against the murder of the Jews.
(Preysing photo courtesy of the Morus Verlag, Berlin; Sommer photo courtesy of
the Diocesan archives of the Archdiocese of Berlin and the Morus Verlag, Berlin)

The draft then made specific requests that included (1) humane living
and working conditions for the deported, (2) access to contact with
friends and relatives in Germany, (3) admission of chaplains into the set-
tlements or camps of the "transported," (4) admission of a committee to
visit the camps and meet camp inmates, (5) a list of the whereabouts of
all deported people, and (6) a list of all the people who had been evacuated from a camp or ghetto and an explanation for their evacuation.
The concluding sentence makes reference to the Holocaust itself: "We
would not want to omit to say that meeting these stipulations would be
the most certain way to deflate the crescendo of rumors regarding the
mass death of the deported non-Aryans."[33]

Germany's bishops debated whether they should speak out against
the persecution of the Jews in their 1942 Fulda meeting and deliberated
over Sommer's draft the following year. In 1942 they decided to "give
up heroic action in favor of small successes."[34] By this they meant that
taking public action would only make it more difficult for those who
were hiding Jews. In 1943 they rejected Sommer's draft for a number of
reasons. First, the Concordat had conditioned the bishops to refrain
from speaking about issues not directly related to church matters. In
their minds this stricture blocked them from commenting on what was

happening to Mosaic Jews. Thus, even though Bishop Heinrich Wienken was well informed about the Nazi death machine in eastern Europe and very probably assisted in hiding Jews in Berlin, he did not support Sommer's draft that would have led to a confrontation between Catholicism and Nazism.[35]

Second, Cardinal Adolph Bertram, ex officio titular head of the German episcopacy as the bishop of Breslau (then a German city), was an inveterate accommodationist. Old enough to remember the confrontation between church and state that took place under Bismarck in the 1870s—the Kulturkampf—Bertram wished to avoid conflict with the state. He knew that to challenge the Nazis over the Holocaust would irritate the central nerve of Nazi ideology—antisemitism.[36] Preysing, who pushed confrontation, reacted furiously when Bertram sent Hitler birthday greetings in 1939 in the name of all German Catholic bishops.[37]

Finally, the war itself led bishops to reject Sommer's draft. At the outset of hostilities, most bishops adopted a "fatherland first" attitude. Preaching to a full church in August 1943, at the time of the annual meeting of the bishops in Fulda, Archbishop Gröber said that despite disappointment over concordatory abuses, Catholics would never waver in their loyalty to the Fatherland. No German bishop, he said, thinks thoughts that might be harmful to the "beloved folk and Fatherland." Catholics would remain faithful to the last drop of blood.[38]

But, in fact, there were limits to this loyalty. The bishops were not blind. Most of them wanted to draft a letter to Hitler regarding personal freedom and the protection of life.[39] After the deportations began, Faulhaber wrote to Bertram, comparing them to the English slave trade in early modern times and urging him to protest the action sharply in writing.[40] Bertram refused, saying it would not do any good.[41] The bishops were concerned enough about what was happening to the Jews to have invited Sommer to their 1942 meeting to give them a full report. Had someone other than the faint-hearted Bertram been their titular head, someone such as Cardinal Faulhaber, for example, Sommer's 1943 draft proposal might well have been accepted. But the combination of Bertram's accommodating attitude and the "fatherland first" attitude of many bishops made it impossible for Preysing to win over his colleagues at a time when the war had begun to go badly for Germany.[42] As a result, the bishops decided in 1943 to repeat their statement of November 1942, in which they urged that "other races" be treated humanely. In addition, they wrote a pastoral letter to German Catholics admonishing them not to violate the right of others to life, and they specified hostages, prisoners of war, and "human beings of alien races and origin."[43]

The bishops would certainly have risked a breach with their government had either the pope or, possibly, his nuncio in Berlin, Cesare Orsenigo, pushed or led them in this direction. When deportations first began in southwest Germany in October of 1940, a shocked and dismayed Bishop Gröber immediately looked to the nuncio or papacy to intervene.[44] The absence of such leadership, together with internal discord and the bishops' "fatherland first" mentality, made it impossible for Preysing to win over his colleagues against Bertram's opposition. The bishops, who hungered for internal cohesion, looked for it higher up the hierarchical ladder.[45]

Preysing himself realized that the situation could not be changed without the pope's authority. He and Sommer, who had ready access to Orsenigo's residence, informed the nuncio about Nazi genocide.[46] But this avenue proved to be a blind alley. Rather than act, Orsenigo quibbled. Preysing bitterly attacked Orsenigo's casuistry in a letter to Pope Pius XII, in which he related that with regard to the church and Nazi genocide, the nuncio had told him that "charity is well and good but the greatest charity is not to make problems for the church."[47] Fed up with the nuncio, Preysing turned to the Holy See.

Immediately after the war, Bavarian Josef Müller, who had been active in the resistance against Hitler, told Harold Tittman that the German church preferred that the pope should stand aside while the German hierarchy carried on the struggle against the Nazis inside Germany. The pope, Müller added, had followed this advice.[48] This arrangement contradicts in a crucial Holocaust-related context the picture John Cornwell has presented in *Hitler's Pope* of Pius XII dictating policy from Rome. It cannot be denied that Pius XII left the door to protest open for the bishops, giving them freedom to act autonomously. This arrangement did not, of course, preclude the pope from giving counsel to the German episcopacy, and this is exactly what Preysing encouraged him to do.[49] But instead of following Preysing's course, Pius clearly sided with Bertram by telling the bishops that what they had already said in 1942 would one day earn them the respect of world opinion.[50] With the bishops in a muddle over what to do, it is obvious that the path of least resistance was to accept the pope's prophecy of "world respect" rather than Preysing's prophecy of "guilt before God and man."[51]

Compounding the situation for Preysing was the fact that the Holy See withheld information about the Holocaust from German church leaders—information that would have made Cardinal Bertram's position untenable. We have seen how this occurred in a particular case with the priest-president of Slovakia, Tiso. But this reticence holds true as

well for more general, more damning information about the method—
the deaths in gas chambers—and the enormous numbers of murdered
Jews. Even though Vatican secretary of state Maglione accepted this information as true in the spring of 1943, he wrote evasively to Bertram in
November, concealing the fact that he knew that Jews were being murdered en masse, be they Mosaic Jews or Christians of Jewish heritage.[52]

Vatican policy was also inconsistent when it came to Germany. After the Holy See's nuncio to Slovakia reported in the spring of 1942 that
the country's Jews were not going to work in Poland but were going to
gas chambers, Secretary Maglione informed the Slovak envoy that it
disapproved of the deportations.[53] The Slovak government then told the
Germans that they wanted to send an expedition to the labor camps to
check on conditions. This, of course, is exactly what the Sommer protest
draft had demanded. But the Vatican did not tell the German ambassador what it told the Slovak envoy—that it disapproved of deportations
—and the Holy See undermined the proposed Sommer protest when
Pope Pius predicted that the world would respect the German bishops
for their 1942 plea on behalf of "other races."[54] Thus, when the Vatican
finally offered a limited measure of leadership, it agreed with Bertram's
policy of accommodation.

Efforts to Caution Catholics against Genocide

The fact that the German bishops did not make a unified statement on
the murder of the Jews did not bar them from speaking out individually.
It did, however, inhibit them in terms of how boldly they might express
themselves. It was understood that individual bishops would not depart
very far from the commonly agreed-upon course.[55] Even so, several bishops spoke out rather explicitly. Not surprisingly, Preysing was among
them. In November of 1942, he preached on the right of all people to
life, a sermon that the Gestapo said was an attack on the state. The
following month Bishop Frings wrote a pastoral letter, which was read
at Sunday masses throughout the diocese of Cologne, cautioning the
faithful not to violate the inherent rights of others to life, liberty, and
property even under wartime conditions, and even if they were "not of
our blood."[56] In June 1943, Bishop Frings spoke out in the Cologne
cathedral: "No one may take the property or life of an innocent person
just because he is a member of a foreign race."[57] This and other similar
statements were enough to cause the bishop to be harassed by the Gestapo.[58] No other German bishop spoke as pointedly as Preysing and
Frings.

Should the bishops have spoken more bluntly? Should they have risked incarceration in a concentration camp?[59] Should they have provoked a conflict of conscience among Catholics by providing them with precise examples of immoral actions during wartime? What impression did the prohibitions of the bishops against taking human life have on the German public? What did people think they should do when they heard their church leaders preach against murder and against taking the property and goods of others? Put another way, did German Catholics know that their church opposed what the government was doing to Jews?

Historian Günther Lewy broached these same questions three decades ago.[60] More recently, English historian Ian Kershaw examined Lewy's thesis anew, using Catholic Bavaria as his proving ground. While one priest preached in Munich's cathedral, the Frauenkirche, that Christ's message did not derive from the Jews, a priest in Bamberg told Catholics that Jews were useful citizens.[61] In the face of such mixed messages, most clergy, including the bishops, said nothing at all. The end result, Kershaw believes, was a standoff: the Nazis were unable to bestir the people from their passive antisemitism into vicious racism, and the clergy were unable—indeed, they hardly tried—to immunize the people from the dangers of Nazi racism. This made it possible for Hitler to "transport" some 8,500 Jews out of Bavaria during the war while the public remained indifferent.

Some Catholics who went too far in their criticism of the Nazis or support of Jews paid with their lives. Christel Beilmann, a teenager during the war, recalled afterward that church leaders did not sing the praises of people such as Jesuit Alfred Delp, Berlin canon Bernhard Lichtenberg, or Austrian farmer Franz Jägerstätter. But is this retrospective criticism justified? Could the bishops praise martyrdom in the middle of a disastrous war? Besides placing Catholics in a precarious position, would not the bishops have exposed themselves to accusations of treachery? But to Beilmann it was not simply a matter of the church not praising Nazi victims; it seemed to her that the church actually opposed people like Hans and Sophie Scholl, the Munich university students whom the Nazis executed in 1943.[62] Catholics understood from the church that the Nazi regime was to be accepted as the valid state authority, which was to be obeyed. "Whoever opposed the authority of the state in any way," Beilmann recalled, "acted illegally according to the church."[63]

Catholics like Christel Beilmann would not have known what to make of warnings such as the admonition of Bishop Frings not to kill members of a foreign race. Since she did not know what was going on in the Nazi death camps in Poland, the bishop's sermon would not have seemed relevant to her. When all was said and done, its potential relevance made no difference anyway, because even if she had known about the Holocaust, Beilmann says, she would not have protested, because the church taught obedience to the state.

Helmuth von Moltke, leader of the Kreisau resistance group, formed a similar opinion about an even more explicit sermon given by Bishop Preysing in Berlin. In November of 1942, Preysing preached that "it is never allowed to deprive a person of another race his human rights—the right to freedom, the right of ownership, the right of an undissolvable marriage; it is never allowed to commit atrocities on such a person."[64] Preysing's words addressed occurrences that would have been obvious to German Catholics who were witnessing the forced emigration of German Jews. Even if Catholics did not know about what happened to Jews after their "transportation," what Preysing said could hardly be misunderstood. Nevertheless, von Moltke thought Preysing had not hit the nail on the head. Most people, in von Moltke's opinion, would not have taken the bishop's words to heart. Von Moltke wanted a more detailed and explicit message.

Bishop Preysing, in turn, was highly critical of the statement formulated by the German bishops at their 1943 meeting in Fulda. Preysing and Sommer had attempted at this meeting to have the bishops endorse their strong statement, which would have confronted Hitler with the "rumors regarding the mass death of the deported non-Aryans." After hotly debating the Preysing-Sommer proposal, the bishops adopted a much milder statement that said: "Killing is wrong even when committed, supposedly, for the common good." Further, the bishops specified that it was wrong to kill "hostages, prisoners, the weak and mortally ill, civilians caught in war action, and people of another race." Although this seems explicit, it was much less explicit than Sommer's draft. Returning to Berlin from Fulda, Preysing told von Moltke that Sommer's draft had been rendered toothless (*die letzten Flekken sind heraus, aber die Farbe auch*).[65]

For the most part, of course, only civilians heard the bishops' warnings anyway. Able-bodied men were stationed throughout Nazi-occupied Europe. Young people such as Christel Beilmann and the elderly heard, but probably did not fully grasp, the warnings of church leaders. What would be the reaction of a Catholic soldier doing battle for Lebensraum to news of mass murder? The reminiscences of a conscientious Catholic, Gisbert Kranz, allow us to view the situation from another perspective.

Like many other soldiers of the regular army, Kranz was unaware that the German military had become involved in the murder of the Jews in a number of areas on the eastern front of the war. It was to that theater that Kranz, who had been studying to become a priest before being drafted at age twenty, was posted. In western Russia, he happened to meet with a chaplain who had been his hometown priest before the war. Inviting Kranz to his tent after celebrating mass, the chaplain told the young soldier that Germans were killing Jews en masse in eastern Poland and in the Soviet Union.[66] Stunned by this news, Kranz was speechless.

Soon after this chance meeting, Kranz suffered from serious frostbite to his legs and had to be evacuated. Returning on a train to Germany, Kranz heard the chaplain's information repeated when he overheard a German officer speak with horror about the mass killings of Jews. His confirmation of the chaplain's story forced Kranz to believe it was true. Recalling his experiences later, Kranz was able to date these episodes sometime late in 1941. We know, therefore, that what he had heard about related to the murders of the mobile killing squads, and not to the death camps themselves.

After recovering in Germany, Kranz was returned to the eastern front, where he struggled with his conscience. Should he continue to fight for a country that was committing mass murder? He and some comrades, still debating the issue in 1943, noted that the Apostle Paul's letter to the Romans, in which he admonishes them to obey civil authority, was written at the time of Nero's persecution of Christians. On the strength of this scriptural passage, Kranz concluded that his duty was to fight on.

Still, Kranz wrestled with his conscience. Eventually, he decided in 1944 that he could no longer serve Hitler, even though he still lacked knowledge about the death camps. Kranz had the courage to act on his conviction. At an assembly where foot soldiers were being encouraged to fight on because of the Jewish menace, Kranz got to his feet and spoke out in defense of Jews. His punishment—actually a blessing—was reassignment to the western front in France, where he was soon taken prisoner by the British.[67] As a prisoner of war in England, Kranz first learned about his country's death camps in occupied Poland.

Kranz's experiences allow us to see why most people would not have understood the warnings against murder on the part of German bishops or, much less, the vague words of Pius XII in his 1942 Christmas address. Most Germans knew of the Holocaust only through hearsay, and only imprecisely. In order for them to have considered reacting as Kranz did, they would have had to be informed explicitly and in some detail about what was going on in the death camps in the east. The bishops would have had to reveal some particulars about Hitler's death machine; they would have had to say flatly that it was a sin to kill Jewish civilians. No one said this. Unlike Kranz's hometown priest, most Catholic chaplains serving on the eastern front who knew about executions of civilians avoided making a moral issue out of the atrocities.[68] Although Preysing and a few other bishops had sufficient information, most German bishops at home in Germany did not want to look closely into the rumors about genocide. Had the Vatican provided them with the detailed information at its disposal, these more timid bishops would, in all likelihood, have swung over to Preysing's confrontational stance.

The clear-sighted Bishop Preysing understood that Vatican involvement was critical if the German church was to change course. In Pope Pius's letter to Preysing of April 1943, the pontiff defended his handling of Germany's atrocities, but Preysing was dissatisfied. During 1943 and 1944, when millions of Jews fell victim to Nazi death camps, Preysing apparently continued to press Pius to intervene. Of his letters to the pope—thirteen of them in fifteen months, eight in 1943 and five in 1944 —only two have been included in the Vatican's document collection covering the Holocaust, omissions which suggest that Preysing was pressing Pope Pius to speak out about the Europe-wide murder of the Jews. Only papal words, Preysing correctly concluded, would enable the German episcopacy to overcome the years of passivity resulting from the Concordat and their nationalistic disposition heightened by the Second World War.[69] Pius XII's deceleration of knowledge about genocide was especially critical in the case of the German church, because, of course, Germany was causing the murder of European Jewry.

In the end, German bishops could not be persuaded by Preysing and Sommer to condemn Hitler's genocide. But Germany's Catholic prelates spoke more forcefully about the issue of the murder of the Jews than did Pope Pius XII. It will become clear in the following chapter that German bishops also went further than many eastern European prelates in their opposition to genocide, but were less outspoken than Bishop Stepinac in Croatia or than a half-dozen bishops in France. What German church leaders said was not enough. In the words of German Jesuit historian Ludwig Volk, it was a "genuine and deplorable difference" that the Jews, unlike the mentally retarded and handicapped, found no champion of the likes of Bishop von Galen to attempt to stop their murder through a calculated appeal to the public.[70]

6. European Bishops and the Holocaust

Since neither Pope Pius XII nor the German bishops spoke out emphatically against the Holocaust, church leaders in each European country had to decide for themselves what to do about the persecution of the Jews. The Holy See did not offer bishops any general guidelines or counsel about what to do when the Nazis came, but the pope did intervene, at times decisively, in specific situations in some countries. In Rome itself, Pope Pius chose not to intervene until very late in the war.

The overwhelming majority of Holocaust victims were Polish, Baltic, or western Russian Jews who were either shot by mobile killing squads or gassed and cremated in the six killing centers located in occupied Poland. All of these people were murdered without any papal protest other than the veiled ineffectual reference to genocide in Pope Pius's 1942 Christmas address.

There remained a much smaller Jewish population of slightly more than a million in the Balkans and in western Europe, countries where the Nazis often had to deal with national governments when the time came to seek out their Jews for "resettlement." This situation presented local church leaders with an opportunity to intervene to save Jews. The Holy See could also intervene locally, because in many instances a nuncio or other papal representative interacted with the indigenous hierarchy. To the extent that Pope Pius chose to intervene at all, he did so through his intermediaries, the nuncios, rather than by responding to the Holocaust publicly from Rome. In other words, when the pope chose to deal with the murder of the Jews, he did so through diplomatic channels rather than through a moral pronouncement such as an encyclical.

Two largely Catholic countries, Italy and France, were special cases. After the fall of France in 1940, Germany occupied the northern half of the country, seizing Jews whenever the killing timetable called for it. But in southern France, the Nazis had to deal with officials of the French Vichy government when they wanted to "resettle" Jews. Italy constituted the most curious case of any European country. Allied with Germany, it nevertheless proved notoriously recalcitrant when it came to cooperation with the Nazi persecution of the Jews. The Italian safe haven ended when the Mussolini government was overthrown in the summer of 1943 and Germany occupied the country. With this development, the pope was brought face to face with the Holocaust process, since the papal residence, Vatican City, is located in the center of Rome.

Many of the Jews of the Balkans and western Europe fell victim to the Holocaust in 1943 and 1944. By this time Vatican officials had detailed information about the killing process, which by the end of 1942 had already claimed the lives of nearly 4 million Jews, most of whom were eastern Europeans.[1] When German officials negotiated with national governments to "resettle" their Jews, church leaders of those countries knew generally what destiny awaited Jews, although they lacked the Holy See's detailed knowledge of the genocidal process. Because Germany no longer held the upper hand in the war during the years after 1942, and because it had to negotiate "resettlement," the Jews of the Balkans and of western Europe were not evacuated to Poland all at once. The "resettlement" of these Jews did not come as a surprise to the Vatican. There was time, in other words, for Vatican officials to interact with its nuncios and with local church leaders to prepare for the moment when the Nazis came knocking at the door.

The Latin word *nuntius* means messenger. The nuncio is a person who represents the pope to a local government, and at the same time to the bishops of a national church.[2] The nuncio attempts to influence bishops in whatever way the pope wishes, but he lacks the power to overrule the authority of a bishop in his own diocese. As foreigners and outsiders, nuncios are not necessarily well received by local church leaders. German bishops, especially Bishop Preysing, found Nuncio Orsenigo inept and ineffective. There was no guarantee that local church leaders would follow the counsel of a nuncio. It would be a mistake to imagine that Pope Pius was in a position to dictate church policy regarding the persecution of the Jews to the bishops of a country or, even less, to its civil authorities, be they Catholic or not.

Many of the papal representatives acquitted themselves honorably during the Holocaust: Chargé d'Affaires Burzio in Slovakia, Nuncio Bernardini in Switzerland, Nuncio Rotta in Hungary, Nuncio Cassulo in Romania, and Apostolic Delegate Roncalli in Turkey. Often nuncios tried to influence bishops of a given country to do what they could to stop the murder of the Jews by bringing their influence to bear on the country's hierarchy or directly on its government officials. Opposing the nuncios were the officials of the German foreign office and representatives of Adolf Eichmann himself (deportation chief of the Reich Main Security Office), both of whom had to work through non-German government officials to pry loose a given country's Jews for "resettlement." A tug-of-war developed pitting nuncios against German agents, but the contest was played out on an uneven field because of either the pro-Nazi inclinations of some national governments or the antisemitism of its church leaders.

The principal exception to all of this was Poland, whose nuncio had fled the country at the time of the German invasion. Since the Nazis would not allow the Holy See to appoint a new nuncio, the Vatican lacked a voice in Poland to work against the Holocaust process. The only way the Holy See could oppose the Holocaust at its vortex was by speaking out itself, which, as we have seen, Pius failed to do. In the words of historian John Morley, "The sad conclusion is that the tragic events in Poland were not able to move the Pope or his secretary of state to face the reality of a situation whose cruelty was unparalleled in human history."[3]

Elsewhere the Vatican's diplomatic personnel and the church's hierarchy functioned quite effectively at times. This resulted in many Jews' being rescued, both those who had converted and those who had not. But in other instances church interventions failed dismally. The historical record allows us to review this inconsistency in some detail.

Croatia

In chapter 3 we saw that some converted Croat "Jews" were saved when Vatican secretary of state Maglione got permission from the Italian government to allow these refugees to remain in the Italian occupational zone. It is likely that some of these Jews were furnished with baptismal certificates in the interests of their safety. By 1942, roughly 60 percent of the Jews of Zagreb had "converted." Most of the credit belongs to the Italian government, which showed extraordinary largesse by harboring Jews, even those who were not of Italian nationality.

The church's ability to function internationally is illustrated by the attempt of Croatian rabbi Miroslav Freiberger to rescue Jewish children. In August 1942, the rabbi asked Apostolic Visitor Marcone for help in securing safe passage for the children's trip through Hungary and Romania to Turkey. Marcone relayed the request to Secretary Maglione, who in turn contacted Nuncio Angelo Rotta in Bucharest, who made the necessary arrangements. In this manner a number of Jewish children escaped Croatia.[4]

Since Croatia boasted about being a Catholic country under the Ustasha fascists, the church could bring pressure directly on Pavelic regarding genocide, as we have already seen. Archbishop Alojzije Stepinac acted forcefully in this way. We have it on the authority of SS officer Hans Helm, the German police attaché in Croatia who was responsible for "resettling" Jews there, that Stepinac told Pavelic that "the Croatian government would have to bear full responsibility for the growth of the Communist partisan movement . . . because of severe and unlawful measures employed against Orthodox Serbs, Jews and Gypsies, in imitation of German methods."[5] Both Croatian and German officials viewed Stepinac as *Judenfreundlich*—friendly toward Jews.[6]

In the spring of 1942, Stepinac said publicly that it was "forbidden to exterminate Gypsies and Jews because they are said to belong to an inferior race." A year later, in the spring of 1943, Himmler visited Zagreb, signaling the imminent roundup of the remaining Croatian Jews. Stepinac wrote Pavelic that "if indeed these measures were imposed by the intervention of a foreign power in internal affairs of our state, I will not hesitate and raise my voice even against this power. The Catholic church is not afraid of any secular power, whatever it be, when it has to protect basic human values."[7] When 2,000 Jews were seized and deported to Auschwitz, both Marcone and Stepinac protested to Minister of the Interior Andrija Artukovic.[8] Apparently Rabbi Freiberger was killed at this time, either at Auschwitz or in a gas van that was commonly used in Croatia.

Unfortunately, such warnings had little effect on the Pavelic government, which had actually agreed to pay the German government 30 Reichsmark, or about 7 dollars, for every deported Jew.[9] Unlike Stepinac, the Holy See, well informed about events concerning Jews in Croatia through Abbot Marcone, never spoke out about the cruelty or inhumanity of "resettling" people, even when the sick and elderly were removed.[10] Stepinac himself, notwithstanding his sharp public criticism of the Ustasha and his successful efforts to rescue many potential victims of genocide, never severed his ties with the fascist regime.

Before the death camps in Poland were operative, thousands of Croatian Jews were herded into concentration camps. By the end of 1941, approximately one-third of the Jewish population had died or were murdered in these camps. The most notorious camp, Jasenovac, was run by a Franciscan friar, Miroslav Filipovic-Majstorovic, called Brother Satan. During the fall of 1942, 40,000 inmates of this camp, some of them Jews, died from starvation or mistreatment.[11] We saw in chapter 3 that many other Catholic priests were active antisemites who worked closely with Pavelic and the Ustasha movement.

What did Catholic authorities do to curb murderous priests and religious? Archbishop Alojzije Stepinac suspended a number of priests, among them Ivo Guberina and Zvonko Brekalo.[12] This means that they were barred from priestly duties such as preaching and administering the sacraments. Stepinac lacked authority to suspend priests outside of the diocese of Zagreb. He also lacked authority to suspend bishops who collaborated with the Ustasha, such as Ivan Saric, who publicly supported German persecution of Croatian Jews. Only the Holy See had the power to take such a step. Why the Vatican did not rein in antisemitic church leaders is puzzling, since in the spring of 1943 Secretary Maglione instructed Stepinac to save as many Jews—mostly converts—as possible during an upcoming Nazi roundup.[13]

Angelo Roncalli, the apostolic delegate to Turkey during the Holocaust and Pius XII's successor, saved a number of Croatian, Bulgarian, and Hungarian Jews by assisting their emigration to Palestine.[14] Evidently, Roncalli thought that saving Jewish lives should have priority over the question of who eventually would possess the Holy Land.[15] Although Roncalli always said that all of his work for Jews came at the direction of Pope Pius, it is difficult to take this in a literal sense. Historian Stanford Shaw believes that Roncalli acted without Vatican orders, or possibly even against them, in pursuing rescue work that helped Jews escape to Palestine.[16] Roncalli's willingness to work with Zionists to save Jews demonstrated a discrepancy between his mentality and that of Vatican personnel.[17]

Slovakia

When Hitler incorporated western Czechoslovakia into the Greater German Reich in 1939, he allowed the small rump state of Slovakia to form its own government under his close scrutiny. The new state's northern neighbor was Poland; a journey by train to Auschwitz required only an hour.

Like Croatia, the fascist government of Slovakia wanted to serve two masters—Berlin and Rome. Hitler demanded a price for Slovak independence, its 90,000 Jews. Pius XII wished to save them, or at least the 20,000 of them who had converted to Christianity. In Raul Hilberg's view, the government of Slovakia survived until 1944 by giving up its Mosaic Jews to Auschwitz to please Hitler while holding back its Christian "Jews" to please the Holy See.

The politics of the fascist leaders of Croatia and Slovakia bore similarities, but there were two principal differences between the two puppet states. First, Slovakia's population was overwhelmingly Catholic, in contrast to the mixture of Catholics and Greek Orthodox in Croatia. Second, the Communist insurrectionary, Marshall Tito, threatened the Pavelic government, eventually toppling it, whereas Slovakia, under its priest-president Jozef Tiso and prime minister Bela Tuka (who was a daily communicant), remained intact until Russia forced Germany's retreat from east-central Europe late in the war.

Slovakia's Catholicity and its internal security explain why the Holy See would have reacted more forthrightly to genocide there than to genocide in Croatia. Since President Tiso had proudly boasted of Slovakia's Catholic principles, the Vatican and the church in general were embarrassed by the severely antisemitic Codex Judaicum of 1941, the contents of which were given detailed coverage by newspapers as far away as the *Chicago Daily News*.[18] The German government smugly applauded the new Jewish Code with "undisguised gratification," pointing out that it "had been enacted in a state headed by a member of the Catholic clergy."[19] To bring its influence to bear on the Catholic government of the new state, the Vatican appointed a diplomat of considerable mettle, Giuseppe Burzio, a thirty-nine-year-old Italian, as its chargé d'affaires. Acting like a nuncio, Burzio would end up in the middle of the tug-of-war between Berlin and Rome over the Jews of Slovakia.

The first news of a genocide came in October 1941, when Slovak army chaplains reported to Burzio that Jews at the war's eastern front were being shot wherever they were found. This triggered no response from the Vatican, but in 1942 there were more detailed reports of genocide from three sources.[20] Burzio told Secretary Maglione in early 1942 that Slovakia was going to deport 80,000 Jews to Poland, regardless of their age, sex, or religion. This, Burzio added, was "equivalent to condemning a great part of them to death." The nuncio in Hungary, Angelo Rotta, reported in words much like Burzio's that the victims, among whom were "many women and children, were destined in large part to a certain death."[21] Finally, Filippo Bernardini, nuncio in Switzerland, was warned by Gerhard Riegner in Bern of the planned slaughter of Slovak Jews and passed on the information to the Holy See.

The Vatican reacted immediately to Giuseppe Burzio's March message of impending doom. The Holy See protested the deportations to the

Slovak legate to the Vatican, Karl Sidor, pointing out the dislocation of people and the separation of families. The protest specifically mentioned the destination of the Slovak Jews as the region around Lublin, Poland, but did not mention the atrocities that Burzio and others said awaited them there.[22] Again in April the Vatican protested to Sidor, asking why the Slovak government continued to send its people to their deaths. Although these protests were prompt and were judged worrisome by SS agents in Slovakia, they were obviously ineffectual.[23] The protests, after all, were not made in public. The "resettlements" continued into the summer and fall of 1942.

By the end of 1942, a little more than 57,000 Slovak Jews had been deported, most of them during the spring and summer.[24] News concerning the destiny of these people reached the Vatican from yet another source. In June the Polish government in exile in London learned of the murder of some 700,000 Polish Jews in gas chambers and, at the same time, of the deportation of Slovak Jews to Poland. This provided confirmation of what Burzio and others had predicted just three months earlier. In an effort to protect the Slovak Jews, the Poles got word of the situation to Cardinal Hinsley, the Archbishop of Westminster, asking him to see if the pope could use his "influence with the Catholic ruler of the Slovak state."[25]

Curiously, the Holy See reacted more strongly against the use of Jewish girls and young women as prostitutes than against deportation. How can this be explained, since the information coming to the Vatican from all corners of Europe indicated that deportation would mean death for most of the "resettled"? The records indicate only Pope Pius's revulsion, not the reasons for it.[26]

The initiative behind the deportation of the Slovak Jews came from within the government itself. Of course, Germany applied some pressure. In November 1941, the president and prime minister were summoned to meet with Hitler and Himmler in Germany, where they learned of the necessity to build large detention camps for Jews. In the spring of the following year, the Slovak government readily complied with a German request for 20,000 able-bodied Jewish laborers who were needed "in the east." Shortly thereafter, Himmler requested the "resettlement" of all Slovak Jews.[27] The Germans anticipated no problem. Eichmann said at his trial in 1961, "The Slovak officials offered their Jews to us like someone throwing away sour beer."[28] The Slovak government actually paid Germany the equivalent of about $125 for each deported Jew.

Within the Slovak government, Prime Minister Tuka and Foreign Minister Mach, both German-favored rivals of President Tiso, coordinated the deportation while the president pretended to look the other way. But he too was involved in a number of ways. When Jewish leaders appealed to him as a priest to protect their community from deportation, his response was to have them investigated to determine how they had gotten their information. Slovaks themselves, not Germans, rounded up the Jews destined for "resettlement" in the spring of 1942. Fascist Hlinka Guards and ethnic Slovak Germans of the Freiwillige Schutzstaffel tore families apart and, as Burzio reported to the Vatican, beat and kicked Jews as they loaded them onto cattle cars.[29]

How did the Catholic bishops of Slovakia react to these events? Even as the deportations were under way in April 1942, the bishops issued a pastoral letter which showed no sympathy for the Jews. The letter insisted that treatment of Jews should not breach civil or natural law, but also disparaged the Jews for rejecting their redeemer and for preparing an "ignominious death for Him on the cross."[30] In other words, the Jews were getting their due. The Lutherans, a small minority of the population, issued a stronger statement, appealing for Christians to honor "the Jews as human beings, so that not one of them should feel deprived because of his national, religious or racial attachment."[31]

Attitudes toward Jews within the Catholic Slovak hierarchy were mixed. Burzio reported to the Vatican that some of the bishops were indifferent about what was happening. But German intelligence agents reported that some bishops were actively engaged on behalf of Jews.[32] Bishop Pavol Jantausch reportedly "saved the lives of a rabbi and his wife by driving them around in his car until the deportation train" had departed.[33] Given these different attitudes, the Holy See would have had to act with determination to bring about forceful intervention by Slovak church leaders.

Hungarian Margit Slachta recognized this. Slachta, a political and religious activist, traveled to Bratislava at Easter time in 1942, where she witnessed firsthand the treatment being meted out to Jews, which she described as hellish and satanic.[34] Humanitarian and Christian instincts motivated Slachta, but on a practical level she felt that if Hungarian civil or church leaders did not intervene on behalf of Jews in neighboring Slovakia, genocide would spill over into Hungary. "Surely," she argued, "there are no political frontiers before God." Slachta urged the Hungarian bishops to encourage their episcopal colleagues in Slovakia to act decisively. "Could they not be persuaded to excommunicate the weekly communicant, Bela Tuka, . . . the churchman Tiso, . . . and his fellow churchman and Lord Mayor Bela Kovács if they refuse to stop this trade in human beings, this killing and defilement?"[35] These pleas made no impression on the Hungarian hierarchy. This is hardly surprising, as Slachta was appealing to prelates such as Bishop Gyula Glattfelder and Cardinal Justinian Serédi, who, as parliamentarians, had voted for the Anti-Jewish Act in the Hungarian Upper House.

The lack of a forceful intervention from the church, be it from Rome, from Hungary, or from within Slovakia itself, proved unfortunate, because the Slovak public sympathized with the persecuted Jews. Traditional antisemitism proved too weak to suppress empathy for the persecuted Jews who were torn from their families and brutalized by the Hlinka Guard. Even pious antisemites were repelled.[36] This suggests that had church leaders spoken out at the beginning of the deportations, expressing their sympathy for the Jews, the Slovak people would have taken up the cry for ending the deportations—if not for all Jews, then at least for those of Slovakian nationality.

Popular outrage against the brutality of the "resettlements" worked against Prime Minister Tuka and Foreign Minister Mach, the German-favored politicians pushing for deportations, and favored President Tiso. The 30,000 Jews who had escaped "resettlement" in 1942 could now be protected. Those who had converted to Christianity before Slovak statehood and their families were declared not subject to deportation.[37] Other Jews were exempted by presidential decree, which Tiso granted liberally (if often venally). German intelligence agents reported that priests frequently furnished Jews with baptismal certificates, antedating them, and never gave support from the pulpit for deportations.[38] Thus, for a period lasting about a year and a half, from the beginning of 1943 to August 1944, Jews in Slovakia enjoyed safety. The country was even viewed as a refuge by fleeing Polish Jews.

During the period of respite, Germany continued to pressure Slovakia to make its Jews available for "resettlement." President Tiso was summoned to Salzburg, where Hitler personally berated him. Unlike the previous year, however, Tiso now had the advantage of strong support from the hierarchy. In April, Burzio, newly informed about the exact operation of Auschwitz, tried to apprise Tuka of the "sad" destiny of "resettled" Jews, "known all over the world." When Tuka replied that he was a daily communicant with a clear conscience, Burzio rhetorically asked Maglione whether it was "worth the trouble to continue to explain to Your Eminence the rest of my conversation with this demented man."[39] Slovak bishops also brought pressure on the government, speaking out more pointedly and effectively than in their cold statement of 1942. They opposed deportations for both converted "Jews" and "other fellow citizens."[40]

The Holy See also brought effective pressure to bear on the Slovak government. The secretary of state's note of May 5, 1943, was more explicit than previous admonitions. It asserted that the Slovak Catholic population opposed the deportation of Jews at a time when it was being rumored that the remaining Jews, including women and children, were to be "resettled." "The Holy See would fail in its Divine Mandate if it would not deplore these measures . . . which gravely hurt men in their natural human rights."[41]

Margit Slachta played a role, perhaps an important one, in the Vatican's adoption of a stronger tone in its May note. Giving up on Hungarian bishops, Slachta decided to try to see Pope Pius himself when she heard early in 1943 that the remaining Slovak Jews were to be deported. Slachta met with the pope on March 13 and told him that 20,000 Slovak Jews faced untimely deaths. Pius, Slachta later recorded, "listened to me all the way through [and] expressed his shock. . . . He listened to me but said very little."[42] Thinking that the remaining Jews of Slovakia would be put in detention camps prior to their deportation, Slachta asked if the Holy See could supply provisions for them, in the hope that the government would then decide against deportation. President Tiso did in fact agree to place the Jews in detention camps when German foreign minister Ribbentrop pressured him in December 1943, but then reneged on his word. The lull in the persecution of Slovak Jews occurred, we may conclude, as a result of pressure from the Catholic hierarchy and popular opinion in Slovakia.

In August 1944, when the Russians drove the German army westward in close proximity to Slovakia, the German genocide machine pushed aside their puppet Slovak government and "resettled" about 14,000 of the remaining Jews. "All told, about 70,000 Jews had been deported from Slovakia; 65,000 did not return."[43] At no time had the Holy See publicly protested the murder of the Jews of Catholic Slovakia, who were among the first and the last victims of the Holocaust. Nor did the Slovak episcopacy protest this final "resettlement."

France and the Low Countries

In western Europe, the German death machine faced obstacles that had not been a problem in the east. The antisemitism of the populace, of either a religious or secular variety, was less pronounced, and the governments of Holland, Belgium, and France were arguably less racist than the fascists in Croatia and Slovakia.[44] After overrunning western Europe in the spring of 1940, Germany partially solved these difficulties by the simple expedient of appointing *Reichkommissare,* military generals, or ambassadors over the northern half of western Europe. In the southern half, which included Vichy France but not the Iberian peninsula, the Nazis had to deal with the nationalistic regime of Marshal Pétain to pry loose Jews for "resettlement." In western Europe, Jews were often thought of as indigenous nationals rather than as an unassimilated and unassimilable ethnic minority as in the east. As a consequence, post–World War I immigrants to western Europe, roughly 25 percent of all Jews, were in greater jeopardy.[45]

The Frenchman in charge of Vichy's bureaucratic offices for "resettlement" was Pierre Laval, a fervent Catholic and antisemite. He cooperated smoothly with Nazi bureaucratic deportation offices under Eichmann, disappointing him only in that during the initial deportations of 1942 he held back indigenous Jews. Laval compensated for this, however, by throwing in the children of immigrant Jews under sixteen years of age, who were among Eichmann's targeted group.[46] These actions provoked the first objections on the part of the French hierarchy, which said in July,

> Profoundly moved by the reports of massive arrests of Jews . . . and of the harsh treatment inflicted on them, . . . we are unable to suppress the cry of our conscience. . . . In the name of humanity and of Christian principles we lift our voice to protest in favor of the inalienable right of the human conscience.[47]

This appeal, which went on to speak of the suffering of mothers with babies, was clearly humane, but it remained in the private sphere of church and state—the church leaders sent their protest to the government of Marshal Pétain.

In the following month, however, church leaders in southern France protested vigorously and publicly against the deportation of Jews: Archbishop Jules-Gérard Saliège of the diocese of Toulouse on August 23; Bishop Pierre Théas of Montauban on August 30; Archbishop Pierre Gerlier of Marseilles on September 6; and Bishop Moussaron of the diocese of Albi on September 20. The statements of these prelates were not couched in the evasive diplomatic language of the Vatican secretariat or papacy. Bishop Théas said, "I say that all men, Aryan or non-Aryan, are brothers because they are created by God."[48] Saliège said, "That children, women and men, fathers and mothers, should be treated like a vile herd of cattle, that members of the same family should be separated from each other and sent to an unknown destination—it was reserved for our time to witness this tragic spectacle."[49] Historian Lawrence Baron, who specializes in rescue research, calls these statements "impassioned denunciations."[50] Cardinal Saliège and Bishop Théas's statements circulated throughout southern France and were even broadcast by France Libre on BBC.[51] The bishops who made these courageous statements assumed leadership roles, belatedly and temporarily.

In November, the hierarchy of the United States, affirming their agreement with their French colleagues, said,

> Since the murderous assault on Poland, utterly devoid of every semblance of humanity, there has been a premeditated and systematic extermination of the people of this nation. The same satanic technique is being applied to indignities heaped upon the Jews in conquered countries and upon defenseless peoples not of our faith.[52]

In neighboring Belgium, no bishop made a statement condemning the deportation of the Jews.[53] Nor did the French bishops get any public support from Rome for their strong words. When the Archbishop of Toulouse instructed his clergy to protest the deportation of the Jews from the pulpit, Laval requested that the nuncio tell the pope and the secretary of state that France would not tolerate interference in this matter. He added threats: priests who protested would be arrested; cloisters that hid Jews would be violated, and those harbored would be dragged out.[54] From time to time there were rumors that the nuncio would protest the treatment of the Jews, but the German and Vichy governments ascertained that he had taken "no formal steps with the French government in the matter of the recent intensification of the measures against the Jews."[55]

The statements of the French bishops in 1942 were valiant and honorable. Their moral authority aroused public opinion against the Vichy government's cooperation with Nazi deportation authorities. This is remarkable, because the Jews in question were immigrants, not French Jews. The inspiration of the bishops to speak out came not from Rome but from the *Cahiers du Témoignage Chrétien,* the underground newsletter of a mostly Catholic resistance group. Had the French hierarchy continued to speak out in the spirit of the *Cahiers* in 1943 and 1944 when indigenous Jews were being "resettled," there would have been a greater response from the French people than there was in 1942, when the bishops spoke of the plight of France's foreign Jews.[56] Only a minority of French bishops had the courage or conviction to speak out in favor of human rights for Jews. In 1945, General Charles de Gaulle sought to have no fewer than twenty-seven bishops relieved of their duties for not resisting or for collaborating with the Pétain government.[57] After 1942, the few protesting bishops found themselves isolated. If they had opposed Pétain's antisemitic government, they would have done so without the support of the Holy See.[58]

The protests of the French bishops were repeated in 1942 by Cardinal Hinsley in England, who spoke out against the mass murder of the Jews. In the cardinal's last public address, to the 1943 World Jewish Congress, he denounced "with utmost vigor the persecution of the Jews by the Nazi oppressors," and called for retribution against the Nazis.[59] The cardinal's word backed up the English Catholic newspaper *The Tablet*, which, unlike other Catholic publications, maintained that the atrocities were really taking place.[60]

The Jews of the Netherlands and of Italy had the advantage of a sympathetic national response to Nazi persecution. But in the Netherlands this paid no dividend, because the country was governed by a Reichkommissar. Beginning in 1940, Jews were despoiled of their wealth, their property, and their jobs.[61] To be able to pursue this systematically, Reichkommissar Seyss-Inquart directed that the Dutch people register with the government if they had one grandparent who was Jewish. The Protestant Reformed church protested this antisemitic step. Johannes de Jong, the Archbishop of Utrecht, intended to do so also but did not.[62]

When deportations from Holland began in July 1942, the archbishop acted promptly. De Jong pleaded twice with Seyss-Inquart to stop the deportations and then issued a public letter, read in all parishes, asking God to "strengthen the people of Israel so sorely tested in these days."[63] This time some of the Reformed churches did not protest, and the Reichkommissar retaliated in August against Catholics by arresting converted "Jews," including Carmelite nun Edith Stein. Apologists for Pius XII would later refer to this development to argue that the Holy See was correct in affirming that to speak out in defense of the Jews would only lead to harsher persecution; but as we have seen, this argument rings hollow. The archbishop's protest was simply an excuse the Nazis used to seize these Jewish converts prematurely.

Italy

As Hitler's ally, Mussolini succeeded in expanding Italy's national boundaries westward into France and eastward across the Adriatic Sea into the former Yugoslavia. In both areas, the Italian people and their government sought to protect Jews. This is remarkable and significant, because in other parts of Europe "foreign" Jews were expendable. The Vatican became involved in several efforts to provide a safe harbor for these Jews. After Mussolini's fall from power, however, the Vatican had to deal with the Germans themselves, who proceeded to "resettle" all of the Jews—even native Italians who, up until that time, had not been threatened. Although many priests and nuns continued during the German occupation to hide Jews, as did some members of the hierarchy, the Holy See refused to confront Hitler about the Holocaust.

In November 1942, Italian army officers in the Yugoslav zone realized that their German allies were systematically murdering Jews. They began to impede genocide by harboring Jews who fled from Croatia into Dalmatia, the Italian-occupied zone of Yugoslavia. When German SS officers or diplomatic agents asked their Italian allies to return these Jews, Secretary of State Maglione urged the Italian ambassador to the Vatican to dissuade his government from doing so.[64] When in the spring of 1943 German foreign minister Ribbentrop pressured a vacillating Mussolini to surrender the Croatian Jews, the Holy See again tried to dissuade the Italian government from doing so. Cardinal Maglione asked Jesuit Tacchi Venturi, a relentless opponent of the Holocaust, to take charge of the matter.[65]

The Vatican also acted to save a large number of Jews, perhaps several thousand, who had fled to Italy in 1942 to avoid "resettlement." Because a small minority of these Jews had converted to Catholicism, they appealed to the Holy See for assistance. Their daily bread ration had dwindled to 150 grams. The Vatican assigned a Franciscan (Capuchin) priest, Callistus Lopinot, to ease their journey southward toward the large camp for Jews in Calabria, Ferramonti-Tarsia. Begging for money, food, and clothing, Lopinot took care of the entire contingent of Jews, not just the few who had converted, and remained with them at the camp during the war.[66] During their internment, the Vatican contributed funds for their care and had the nuncio to Italy check on their condition on several occasions.[67]

The Italians who ran the Ferramonti camp turned it into a model facility, "the largest kibbutz on the European continent." The refugees were treated respectfully by the camp personnel, some of whom learned a little Yiddish in order to communicate with them.[68] The camp commander "risked his life in 1943" to get permission for the Jews to leave the camp before they were endangered by the German army, which was retreating northward from Sicily. Thus, many Italians besides the pope assisted the Ferramonti Jews. After the war, they wrote to Pius XII expressing their eternal gratitude.

Meanwhile, a replay of the events in Yugoslavia took place in Italy's western zone of occupation in the furthermost corner of southeastern France. In March 1942, the German foreign office asked Mussolini to surrender the 20,000 Jews in this area. The fascist dictator agreed. Somehow the Vatican knew that Ribbentrop had ordered his ambassador to Italy, Hans Georg von Mackensen, to have these Jews "resettled."[69] When the Holy See found out that Mussolini had given in to this request, it instructed the nuncio to Italy to immediately set up an emergency meeting between Deputy Secretary of State Monsignor Montini and Italian Undersecretary of State Giuseppe Bastianini in order to dissuade the Italians from complying with the request for the Jews. When the meeting took place, Montini was told that Mussolini had already been talked into reversing himself. Greatly relieved, Montini told Bastianini that the pope blessed Mussolini's government.[70]

But the drama continued on. In the spring of the following year, von Mackensen was once again demanding that steps be taken to sequester Jews in the Italian occupation zone in preparation for their "resettlement." Once again Mussolini consented, and once again the Italians intentionally frustrated the Germans. Persuaded by Italian Jew Angelo Donati and French priest Father Marie-Benoit Peteul to counter Mussolini's orders, Inspector General Lospinoso simply dropped out of sight, making it impossible for his German counterparts to proceed.[71] Nevertheless, it was a time of uncertainty and jeopardy for the Jews. Donati later conceived a plan to safeguard the Jews by deporting them from occupied France to Italy proper. When the Italian government showed no interest in the plan just after Mussolini's fall from power, Donati turned to Marseilles priest Marie-Benoit for help.

The Vatican would certainly have known who Benoit was, since he corresponded with the Holy See about the predicament of the Jews and because his activities on their behalf had become notorious, but his request for an audience with Pope Pius was not granted. (A Vatican official informed him that Pius no longer gave private audiences, but in March he had given one to Margit Slachta, who was on a similar mission.) On July 16, Benoit, accompanied by his religious superior, finally saw the pope. Benoit gave Pius a written report on the Jews in France, which included those of the Italian-occupied zone who were being pursued by the Germans. (This document is not contained in the Vatican collection *Actes et Documents du Saint Siège pendant le IIe Guere Mondiale*.) A few days later, Deputy Secretary of State Tardini reported that his office would bring the matter up with the Italian government, but a rescue plan failed to materialize.

The situation of the Jews in southeastern France became perilous when the Italian government fell and the Germans established a puppet government under Mussolini. No longer did the German foreign office have to dicker with the Italians over their Jews. Desperate, Donati formulated a new plan to have the Jews picked up by Italian boats and taken to safety in northern Africa, newly occupied by the Allies. To do this, the Americans and British would have to give consent, since they now controlled the Mediterranean Sea. Donati hoped that the Vatican would allow him to speak to the American and English diplomats to the Holy See, but permission to do this was refused, as we saw in chapter 4. Donati then secreted Marie-Benoit Peteul into Vatican City, where he made the necessary contacts. Unfortunately, this plan, like Donati's first one, failed.

In September 1943, Italy surrendered to the Allies. With that, Germany took complete control over the Italian zone of occupation in southeastern France. The German Holocaust machine made short work of the Jews. Thousands were caught in Nice.[72] Others were caught as they tried to escape into Switzerland or Italy. These Jews were then "resettled"—most of them were killed in Auschwitz. In the opinion of Donati, the Vatican deserved some of the blame. Vatican officials, he later wrote, "never did anything to alleviate the situation of the Jews."[73] But Jews recognized individual efforts by Catholics on their behalf. In 1957, the Jewish community of Rome held a reception to honor the "Jewish priest," Father Marie-Benoit.[74]

Pius XII and the Jews of Rome

A consideration of the hierarchy and the Holocaust must include a discussion of the reaction of the bishop of Rome, Pius XII, to the "resettlement" of over one thousand Roman Jews. For many, this incident has become the litmus test of the pope's response to genocide during the war. According to the report of the Reich Security Main Office, the biggest roundup of Jews in Italy took place in Rome on October 16, 1943. More than 1,200 Jews were temporarily incarcerated in the military college 600 feet from the Vatican. Of this group, about 1,000, including 896 women and children, were taken after two days to Rome's main railroad station, where they were packed and locked in freight cars without food, water, or toilet facilities. Five days later the train arrived in Auschwitz, too late in the day for unloading. After another night, the Jews detrained in the morning at Birkenau and passed immediately through Mengele's selection process. About 200 were sent to work; the rest were immediately gassed and cremated.[75]

No events placed Pope Pius in greater physical proximity to the Holocaust than those that occurred in October in Rome. Not surprisingly, the judgment of many historians against the pontiff has revolved around the drama of the Roman Jews. There are three reasons for this: well before the roundup of the Jews, the pope knew that they were going to be seized but failed to warn them; the incident occurred in the immediate vicinity of Vatican City; and after the Jews had been deported, the pope failed to condemn Germany for its barbarity.

The initiative to ward off the impending "resettlement" of Rome's Jews actually came from several Germans working in various capacities in Rome, not from the Vatican. About one week before the October roundup, the acting German ambassador to Italy, Eitel Friedrich Möllhausen, learned of Berlin's orders to "resettle" the Jews of Rome. The arrival in Rome of Theodore Dannecker, Eichmann's SS captain who had seized the Jews of Paris, further alarmed the German embassy staffs in Rome and Vatican City. Horrified at the thought of the massacre of thousands of people, Möllhausen and several associates consulted with the commander of the German army in Rome, Rainer Stahel. Möllhausen then cabled Foreign Minister Ribbentrop in Berlin to ask if it would not be better to put the Jews to work fortifying Rome against the expected Allied invasion than to "liquidate" them. A second telegram informed Ribbentrop that any action against the Jews had been temporarily postponed. Himmler and Ribbentrop, furious at the interventions of their underlings in Rome, told Möllhausen to mind his own business and severely reprimanded him for having used the word "liquidate" in reference to the Jews.[76]

Still hoping to forestall the seizure of the Roman Jews, the embassy personnel informed the German ambassador to the Vatican, Ernst von Weizsäcker, of the planned action. Earlier, Weizsäcker had been instructed by Berlin to elicit a public statement from the Vatican that the behavior of the German army in Rome toward the Vatican had been proper. With this statement still pending, it appeared to the German diplomats that quiet pressure from the Vatican behind the scenes could delay or prevent the scheduled SS roundup of Jews. About a week before the sixteenth of the month, Weizsäcker brought the news of the impending seizure to the attention of the Holy See.[77]

The Jews of Rome also knew that their situation was precarious, but not that "resettlement" meant the Auschwitz gas chambers. Many fled from Rome to reach the safety of the Allies in southern Italy. But most remained in the city, where conditions made it difficult for them to seek refuge. There were at that time more than 200,000 anti-fascist Gentile refugees in Rome. Deprivations of all sorts beleaguered Romans. Under the circumstances, Jews were unlikely to give up their homes. Had they known that it was a matter of life or death, most would have gone into hiding.[78] Realizing by this time rather precisely what the extent of the Nazi genocide was, and that the "resettlement" of the Jews of Rome was imminent, the Vatican could have, but did not, inform the leaders of the Jewish community of their mortal danger. Instead, Ambassador Weizsäcker's deputy, Albrecht von Kessel, took on this task. The diplomat attempted to warn Rome's Jews about what "resettlement" actually entailed. Most, unfortunately, simply did not believe that they would be exterminated.[79] Thus, it was the Germans, not the Vatican, who undertook to ward off the roundup of October 16.

Having failed to stop the roundup of more than one thousand Jews, the German embassies set about to rescue them from "resettlement" and protect those in hiding.[80] On the very day of the roundup, Ambassador Weizsäcker met with Secretary Maglione at the latter's request.[81] Maglione's minutes of the discussion skew the question of who took the initiative: the minutes record that the cardinal secretary asked the German ambassador to intervene, rather than that Weizsäcker asked if the Vatican could put "pressure behind the scenes" to stop the "resettlement." Maglione appealed to Weizsäcker's humanity and Christian charity to do what he could for "so many people [who] have been made to suffer only because they belong to a particular race."[82]

According to Maglione, Weizsäcker then asked, "What will the Holy See do if the events continue?" The cardinal replied that "the Holy See would not want to be put into the necessity of uttering a word of disapproval."[83] This threat of a public protest was considerably mitigated, however, by the fact that Maglione left it up to the German ambassador whether or not their conversation would be reported to Berlin. Clearly, the cardinal wanted the German diplomatic personnel to deal with the crisis, thereby relieving the Vatican of the need to do anything.

The German diplomats found a way to attempt to leverage Berlin by having German sympathizer Bishop Hudal, rector of the Collegia del Anima, write a letter to the commander of the German forces in occupied Rome that suggested the Vatican would intervene if the roundups continued. Vatican personnel neither composed the letter nor directed Hudal to do so.[84] In fact, its contents were dictated to Hudal by the Germans: "In the interests of the good relations which have existed until now between the Vatican and the German High Command . . . I earnestly request that you order the immediate suspension of these arrests both in Rome and its vicinity. Otherwise, I fear that the Pope will take a public stand against this action."[85] Confirming the Hundal letter, Ambassador Weizsäcker tried to put further pressure on Berlin by sending his own message to inform Foreign Minister Ribbentrop of his concern that because the roundup had taken place at the pope's very doorstep, he might be forced to protest. By comparing Pius XII positively to his predecessor and to French bishops, Weizsäcker indicated that Germany had a friend in the pope. Enemies of the Reich, Weizsäcker warned, would use the persecution of the Jews to shake Pius out of his reserve, forcing him to condemn Nazi genocide.

The Vatican's response to the October 16 catastrophe, muted and delayed, was couched in several considerations. Since thousands of Jews remained at large in Rome after the roundup, Ambassador Weizsäcker advised the Vatican not to protest the detention of the Jews, for fear that this might trigger a second, more intensive hunt. But such a protest would have had other, potentially dire consequences for the Vatican and for the Holy Father himself. The possibility that Hitler would take the pope captive was taken seriously by the German diplomatic staff in Rome; a July 1943 diary entry of Propaganda Minister Joseph Goebbels makes it clear that Hitler considered such an action.[86] According to Pope Pius's housekeeper, Sister Pasqualina Lehnert, this threat was taken seriously by Pius himself.[87] Two other possibilities probably seemed more likely, and were of greater importance to the pope. A strong protest against the seizure of the Jews would have irritated Hitler to such an extent that recriminations most likely would have followed. These probably would have taken the form of the Germans' using the city of Rome as a base for military operations against the approaching Allied armies (which no doubt would have meant heavy aerial and artillery bombardment of the city), or of a German attack on Vatican City itself. We have seen in an earlier chapter just how concerned Pope Pius was to preserve Rome physically intact. We have also noted earlier that Pius looked to German occupational forces to control Communist brigands in and around Rome. Clearly, a protest against the October roundup would have had serious consequences both for the Vatican and for the Jews in hiding.

While it would be speculative to affirm which consequence weighed more heavily in the pope's considerations, we know what action the Vatican took after the roundup. On October 19, one day after the freight train packed with Jews left Rome for Auschwitz, the Vatican publicly acknowledged, as Hitler's foreign minister, Ribbentrop, wished, that German military behavior in occupied Rome toward the Vatican had been correct and civil. The Vatican requested additional German forces in Rome to control Communists.[88] Thus, in spite of the roundup of the Jews, Ambassador Weizsäcker could report to Berlin that Germany was winning the propaganda war in the Vatican against the Allies.[89] And, still on the nineteenth, the Holy Father pressed American Chargé d'Affaires Tittman to give assurances that the Allied forces would not attack Rome (earlier, in July, Pius had written President Roosevelt an emotional letter of complaint on account of a recent bombing), and expressed concern about possible violence by Italian Communist bands in the vicinity of Rome.[90] Pius held up Germany's good conduct in Rome to Tittman and contrasted it with Allied bombings. As the Roman Jews were en route to Auschwitz, Pope Pius gave his attention to the protection of the city of Rome.

On October 25–26, ten days after the roundup of the Jews, the following veiled statement appeared in *L'Osservatore Romano,* the voice of the Holy See: "With the augmentation of so much evil, the universal and paternal charity of the Supreme Pontiff has become, it might be said, ever more active; it knows neither boundaries nor nationality, neither religion nor race."[91] Ernst von Weizsäcker told his home office not to fret about the statement, because only a few "people will recognize in it a special allusion to the Jewish question." Even if the cagey Weizsäcker did word his communiqué to shed what Berlin would interpret as a favorable light on Pope Pius, this evaluation seems correct. An American Catholic religious and close observer of the Vatican during the Nazi occupation of Rome, Jane Scrivener, did not recognize a protest in *L'Osservatore Romano*'s statement.[92] On the same day that the article appeared in the Vatican paper, Tittman notified the State Department that the Holy See's anxiety over German violation of its neutrality had given way to optimism.[93]

What pleased Weizsäcker displeased other members of the diplomatic corps assigned to the Vatican. British minister Osborne told Pius that many people thought "he underestimated his own moral authority," and said that he tended to agree. Osborne urged the pope to take a strong line.[94] Tacchi-Venturi, the Jesuit rescuer, was also displeased. He repeatedly asked his high-ranking contacts in the secretariat of state to see if the pope would not speak out about the Roman Jews, "transported barbarously like beasts for slaughter."[95] Venturi knew some of the "resettled" Jews and their families personally. He appealed to the secretariat to find out what fate they endured. In early November, Maglione wrote to Ambassador Weizsäcker—later convicted at Nuremberg of signing papers in France dooming people to "resettlement"—asking whether out of the "nobility of soul of Your Excellency" he would find out the whereabouts of the deported Jews.

Nothing came of this tentative request. In the end, nothing came of anything the Holy See said about the fateful days beginning on October 16, 1943. Having known in advance what would befall the Roman Jews, the pope said nothing to forestall it. Afterward, he said nothing to condemn it.

The Vatican did, however, play an active role in harboring those Jews who escaped the October 16 *razzia* (roundup). Terrorized, many Jews found refuge in church properties. Ambassador Weizsäcker had foreseen this need, and he provided German military authorities with maps that clearly displayed buildings that enjoyed extraterritorial status. Between 4,000 and 5,000 Jews—perhaps most of the remaining Jewish population in Rome—found refuge in these properties or in houses of men and women religious.[96] Although it is possible that a small number of Jews found refuge within Vatican City itself, recent scholarship has not been able to verify this.[97]

There is disagreement about what role Pius XII played in the rescue effort. Robert Leiber, S.J., an eyewitness to the events, affirmed in 1961 that Pope Pius personally ordered the superiors of church properties to open their doors to the Jews.[98] But written instructions to this effect have never surfaced.[99] The claim that Pius saved thousands of Roman Jews by opening monasteries and convents to them is an exaggeration. In fact, like other Italians, many monks and nuns sheltered Jews independently, without the Vatican's instructions.[100] Much of the credit for saving Jewish refugees in Rome goes to French priest Marie-Benoit. After the October 16 roundup, the number of Jews under his care rose to about 4,000, a number that would account for most of the remaining Jews in Rome. Father Marie-Benoit, who found food and shelter for these Jews day after day, did not receive money from the Vatican for this work.[101] Of course, Pius deserves credit for saving the lives of those relatively few Jews who found shelter within Vatican City, if, indeed, any did.[102] Pope Pius also supplied food from time to time for Jews hiding in convents or monasteries in Rome.[103]

The efforts of Pope Pius to save Jews by helping to hide them demonstrates clearly enough his concern for them. Why, then, did he not warn them before the October *razzia*, and why did he not protest afterward? A review of the Holy See's action regarding Jews during the months after October provides a plausible answer to this question. In December, Italy's fascist puppet regime issued a directive to provincial administrators ordering that all Jews be sent to concentration camps. *L'Osservatore Romano* protested, calling the order un-Christian and inhuman with regard to both Mosaic and converted "Jews." To expose women, children, the lame, and the elderly to the harsh conditions of a concentration camp was a violation of the laws of God, it said.[104] Jane Scrivener, who had taken no note at all of the Vatican's veiled demur of October 26, characterized the December 3 article as a "strong protest."[105]

The following day, the fascist press responded, asserting that Jews were alien foreigners, and as such were subject to concentration camp detention. *L'Osservatore Romano* did not back off. On December 5, the Vatican paper objected that the fascists had offered no satisfactory answers to the criticisms the Vatican had made earlier. Why, *L'Osservatore Romano* asked, did fascists consider Jews born in Italy to be national enemies and aliens? What legal right did the state have to confiscate their property? Rather, *L'Osservatore Romano* insisted, the fascists must obey public law, according to which the state lacked the jurisdiction to change the status of an Italian-born citizen. Again, the Vatican asserted that in no event should the elderly, women, children, and the ill be subject to detention.[106]

Why would the Vatican protest strongly in December of 1943 against a detention order but not have done so a few months earlier, in October, when the Jews were not only rounded up and incarcerated but straightaway shipped off to Auschwitz in boxcars? The explanation lies most likely in the fact that Germany was directly involved in the former incident but not in the latter.

A subsequent development in the summer of 1944 throws further light on the matter of the Jews and the Vatican. When Jews in northern Italy faced possible "resettlement," the papacy was asked to intervene. Pius, now "eager to co-operate in the endeavor to save Jewish lives," told Myron Taylor that he would urge Ambassador Weizsäcker to press his government to desist from further deportations. "The pope declared that neither history nor his conscience would forgive him if he made no effort to save at this psychological juncture further threatened lives."[107] Why would Pope Pius be "eager" to oppose Germany on behalf of Jews in August 1944, but not in 1943? Why would his conscience bother him in August 1944, but not in October 1943? The explanation lies again in the fact that in June of 1944 the Germans had evacuated Rome, so they no longer posed a physical threat to the city or to the Vatican itself.[108]

Thus, the Vatican's handling of the Roman October crisis and of subsequent Holocaust-related incidents in Italy follows closely the pattern that we observed in chapter 4. At various times, the Holy See did intervene diplomatically with several governments to save Jews, but not with Germany itself. For Pius XII, Christian Germany was a bulwark against communism, both internationally and locally in Rome, but the Germany of the Third Reich was a bully that, if challenged about genocide, could easily turn on Christendom itself, even at its heart in the Eternal City.

Because of this constraint, Pope Pius, the bishop of Rome, actually involved himself less than other Italian bishops in rescue work. The assertion that he directed the Italian hierarchy to engage in hiding Jews has simply not been substantiated.[109] Among the prominent rescuers in Italy were Cardinal Pietro Boetto of Genoa, Cardinal Elia Dalla Costa of Florence, and Cardinal Ildefonso Schuster of Milan.[110] These church leaders actively solicited parish priests and men and women religious to hide Jews. To denounce from the pulpit the murder of the Jews would probably have resulted in martyrdom or the concentration camp. No Italian bishop was prepared to pay a price this high, although many of the lower clergy did. For an Italian bishop to speak out more forthrightly against the Holocaust than the bishop of Rome himself would have been awkward.

Hungary

The last Jews of Europe to fall victim to the Holocaust lived in Hungary. Although antisemitic legislation had been passed between 1941 and 1943, Jews living in isolated communities felt unmolested. Elie Wiesel's village, Sighet, disregarded stories about the Holocaust told to them by the village "madman." In larger mixed communities Jews had been deeply affected by Admiral Miklós Horthy's antisemitic policies. These had pauperized many Jews, creating a problem for which there was but one solution, the German one.[111]

First affected were the 300,000 "foreign" Jews who had become Hungarian as a result of forced territorial concessions ordered by Hitler that returned areas taken from Hungary by the Peace of Paris at the end of the Great War. This had already begun in 1942, when more than

10,000 "foreign" Jews were pushed out of Hungary into the fire of German mobile killing squads.[112] But the great majority of the Jews in Hungary lived, while those who had inhabited European countries in every other direction perished. Between 1942 and 1944, Prime Minister Kállay resisted German pressure to relinquish the country's Jews.

The Hungarian sea of tranquility came to a ferocious end in March 1944, when Germany occupied the country. For historian Raul Hilberg, what took place in Hungary over the next few months provides a perfect yardstick for measuring everyone's conduct vis-à-vis the Holocaust: that of the Hungarian Jews, the Hungarian government, world Jewish leaders, and leaders of the free world. The murder of Hungary's Jews also sheds light and shadow on the leaders of the Catholic church.

Beginning in mid-May 1944, more than 400,000 Jews were "resettled" over a period of just two months. To dispose of so many corpses, the Auschwitz crematoria had to burn day and night.[113] The deportation of a half million Hungarian Jews to that death camp in the spring and summer of 1944 was accomplished with terrible efficiency. Historian Leni Yahil attributes this to three factors: the highly experienced team put together and led by Adolf Eichmann, the connivance or apathy of the Hungarian government, and poor leadership within the badly organized Hungarian Jewish community.[114] Other historians, chiefly Randolph L. Braham, would add a fourth factor: the failure of the church to protest openly, which led to "the climate that made the unhindered implementation of the Final Solution possible."[115]

The attitude of the Hungarian hierarchy toward Jews undoubtedly contributed to the complacency of the people regarding the fate of the Jews. Since the bishops did not protest against the Holocaust, priests did not make use of their pulpits to counteract it. Some of the lower clergy opposed atrocities openly, but a few, including Ignác László and András Kun, advocated annihilation of the Jews. Most clergy were just passive.[116] A principal reason for the callousness of the hierarchy toward the Jews was that more than anywhere else, they constituted the middle class in Hungary—the driving force behind industrialization and modernization, whose materialistic values the church opposed. Fear and complacency among the Catholic population contributed in turn to the unprecedented swiftness and thoroughness of the "resettlement" process.[117]

Adolf Eichmann, who was personally on the scene, masterfully organizing the deportation process, said at his trial that the Hungarians encouraged the Germans in their work and celebrated when their areas became *Judenfrei,* free of Jews.[118] Members of the fascist Hungarian vigilante organization Arrow Cross assisted the Germans; indeed, they probably supplied most of the manpower needed to carry out the deportations, German manpower having been exhausted by the final months of the war. Without the Hungarians, Eichmann testified, the deportations could not have taken place. But the cooperation of local officials, such as mayors and bishops, was also necessary. The silence of the church, Braham contends, "made the unhindered implementation of the Final Solution possible."[119]

Because of the Auschwitz Protocol, a document detailing the extermination process as told by two escapees, Rudolf Vrba and Alfred Wetzler, the hierarchy in Hungary knew exactly what "resettlement" meant for the deported Jews. Yet this key fact was omitted when Cardinal Justinian Serédi issued a much-delayed letter of protest about the treatment of the Jews. Why? In late May, Serédi was pushed by Bishop Apor to protest the deportation of the Jews, whereupon the cardinal wrote a draft of the proposed protest. After reviewing the draft, Gyula Czapik, who as the Archbishop of Eger was the second-highest-ranking member of the Hungarian hierarchy, advised that Serédi "not make public what is happening to the Jews; what is happening to the Jews at the present time is nothing but appropriate punishment for their misdeeds in the past."[120] The cardinal's letter said in so many words that the bishops would be glad to see the Jewish influence in Hungary eliminated, but not by unlawful deportations.[121] By the time that the pastoral letter was delivered to the parishes, to be read in July, nearly half of the Jews of Hungary had already been murdered.

The contrast of Cardinal Serédi to Papal Nuncio Angelo Rotta is striking. On the very first day of the deportations, the nuncio wrote the government that "the whole world knows what deportation means in practice. . . . The Apostolic Nuntiature considers it to be its duty to protest against such measures."[122] When the deportations continued, Rotta asked Cardinal Serédi on June 8 why bishops were not confronting the government. Angered, Serédi questioned "the utility of the Apostolic Nunciature in Budapest," which "does nothing and nobody knows if it ever did anything; and it is deceitful for the Apostolic Holy See to maintain diplomatic relations with that German government which carries out the atrocities."[123]

A few courageous Hungarian bishops sided with the nuncio. Aron Marton, whose diocese was in Transylvania, where the family of Elie Wiesel and over 100,000 "foreign" Jews lived, delivered a timely sermon on May 18 that "condemned the ghettoization of the Jews and warned the Hungarians not to abandon the Jews to annihilation. He openly called on the Hungarian government to frustrate the intended deportation of the Jews."[124] Baron Vilmos Apor, bishop of Györ, preached frequently that it was un-Christian to hate particular groups such as Negroes and Jews. Bishop Hamvas of Csanád protested on June 25 against the deportation of hundreds and hundreds of thousands of people, among whom were "innocent children, defenseless women, helpless old people and pitifully sick persons. . . . God's laws protect the right of every man, even the Negro and the Jew, and defend their right to property, liberty, dignity, and health and life. We do not say this as friends of Jews but as friends of truth."[125]

With the hierarchy divided in Hungary and the dissenting minority siding with the papal nuncio, it is important to review the position of the Holy See. The papal nuncio to Switzerland, Filippo Bernardini, sent a copy of the Auschwitz Protocol to the Vatican. On June 25, 1944, Pope Pius responded by sending Regent Horthy an open (public) cable—"the first of its kind during the Holocaust period."[126] The pope urged Horthy to "do everything in your power to save as many unfortunate people [as possible] from further pain and sorrow."[127] After the pope's open message to Horthy, the regent was inundated with telegrams from around the world urging his intervention. In contrast to Pius's diplomatically worded message, the responses of President Franklin D. Roosevelt and other leaders took a threatening tone, promising retaliation if Hungarian Jews were not protected.[128]

At last the Vatican took the lead. But its intervention raises two questions bearing on possible Holocaust prevention. The Holy See had an accurate picture of the murder of the Jews in the spring of 1943, if not earlier. If at that point in time the pope had sent open messages to the leaders of European countries, where no Jews, or at least not all Jews, had been molested yet, would they have been pressured by world opinion to protect Jews, as Horthy was? If the pope had sent his cablegram to Horthy a few weeks earlier, when the majority of Hungarian Jews were still alive, would he have saved them from Eichmann's murderous grasp?

These questions are not as hypothetical as they may seem. In April 1944, one week before the first Hungarians were deported to Auschwitz, Rudolf Vrba and Alfred Wetzler escaped from the death camp with the intention of telling the world how Jews were being killed by the thousands there. Vrba and Wetzler made their way to nearby Slovakia, where the chargé d'affaires, Giuseppe Burzio, heard their account, which he forwarded to Rome by courier in a twenty-nine-page document.[129] Because Allied forces had blocked entry into Rome, it is possible that the messages were not delivered to the Vatican until October, but one of the Auschwitz escapees, Vrba, seems to doubt this.[130] In any event, months earlier, in June of the previous year, the U.S. State Department had instructed Harold Tittman to ask the Vatican to intervene on behalf of Hungarian Jews.[131]

Why, then, did the Vatican wait? The answer to this question reveals that, although the Holy See had broken from previous policy in openly objecting to the persecution of Hungarian Jews, in doing so it did not depart from its customary passivity. The impetus behind world reaction to the Auschwitz Protocol came from four Protestant theologians, including Karl Barth and the head of the Swiss Ecumenical Council of Churches, Visser t'Hooft. The weight of their authority, together with the enormous clamor of the Swiss daily press about the Auschwitz atrocity, forced the hand of the pope and other world leaders.[132] Since Pius refrained from going public with the atrocity information in early June, it may be reasonably assumed that Swiss pressure led him to cable Regent Horthy in late June. Gerhard Riegner, then the director of the Geneva office of the World Jewish Congress, supports this view.[133]

The pressure that world leaders put on Regent Horthy was effective, but in October 1944 a new Hungarian government came to power under Ferenc Szalisi, leader of the fascist Arrow Cross party. Jews immediately began to be deported to Auschwitz once again. It was at this time, the winter of 1944–45, that Nuncio Rotta distinguished himself by working with representatives of other neutral countries, including Raoul Wallenberg, to pressure the Hungarians to stop deporting Jews, and by providing Jews, mostly converts, with letters of protection, which the government had promised to respect. Nuncio Rotta, who also hid Jews, acted in this regard on his own authority, that is, without instructions from the Holy See.[134]

Probably as a result of the nuncio's influence, Cardinal Serédi declared that October 29 would be a day of national prayer for refugees, and that a special collection would be taken up at masses to help them. Pope Pius commended Serédi for this and, in marked contrast to previous Vatican policy during the Holocaust, saw to it that his encouragement of proactive measures would receive widespread publicity. But, although Nuncio Rotta continued to provide him with ghastly information regarding the treatment of Jews and their deportation, Pius declined to condemn publicly the collaboration of the Hungarian government. As in the past, he confined his efforts to diplomatic channels, which amounted to little more than pro forma gestures, such as urging Nuncio Orsenigo in Berlin to approach the Nazi regime about the Hungarian Jews.[135]

The response of the Catholic church to the murder of the Hungarian Jews late in the Second World War presents a picture of an organization in disarray. A lethargic pope, a zealous nuncio, a callously antisemitic Hungarian cardinal, a diversity of opinion about Jews among other bishops, and messages to people in the pews that either conflicted or spoke volumes by their absence—all amounted to organizational chaos.

The record of the rest of the church's European hierarchy during the Holocaust is not altogether dissimilar: it was a patchwork quilt. Italian bishops actively saved Jews. The Vatican worked diplomatically at times on their behalf but at other crucial times did not, or did so lethargically. Cardinal Hinsley in England and Archbishop Stepinac in Croatia spoke out forcefully against the Holocaust. Most of the Vatican's nuncios worked conscientiously, sometimes courageously, to save Jews. Southern French bishops objected to the inhumane treatment of Jews by Nazis and by their own countrymen. But most French bishops failed to speak out. German bishops, debating what to do, decided to plead feebly for "non-Aryans," but they did not do so insistently. The Slovakian hierarchy hesitated for too long before voicing objections to their puppet government's cooperation in genocide. Some Croatian bishops supported genocide; others were equivocal. Most Hungarian bishops, including the leaders of the hierarchy, disregarded the plight of that country's Jews, in spite of Nuncio Rotta's emphatic promptings and personal intervention on behalf of Jews. In all of Europe, only one member of the hierarchy, Poland's Archbishop Twardowski, forfeited his life for hiding Jews.[136]

The church's inconsistency resulted from Pope Pius's failure to exercise leadership regarding genocide. Ever since the First Vatican Council, which proclaimed papal infallibility in 1870, the Catholic hierarchy had been accustomed to a dominant papacy and a centralized church authority. Because Pius XII neither spoke out himself in any significant manner on behalf of Jews nor circulated the courageous statements of bishops who did speak out among the church hierarchy, other bishops, who lacked concern for Jews, felt no pressure from Rome to change their ways. Had Pope Pius chosen to make a public statement about the roundup of Roman Jews, or had he made some gesture on their behalf, his example would undoubtedly have been emulated by at least some other European bishops, and by many priests and laypersons. Since this did not happen, church leaders, unless explicitly informed to the contrary, would have assumed that the fate of the Jews was not important in Rome. The Catholic church could not have halted the Holocaust, but it could have, and did, save Jews. Unfortunately, the opportunity to rescue many thousands more was not taken advantage of.

7. Catholic Rescue Efforts during the Holocaust

Is it a mistake to discuss Catholic rescue? Were not many Catholics among the killers and collaborators? Neither Adolf Hitler nor Heinrich Himmler, the two Germans most responsible for the Holocaust, considered himself to be Catholic, although both were Catholic by birth and education. Although Joseph Goebbels abandoned the strong faith of his Rhenish parents, he retained his Catholic mentality, asking himself, "Who is this man [Hitler], the real Christ or only John [the Baptist]?"[1] Rudolf Höss, who ran Auschwitz, grew up in a thoroughly religious Catholic household. As a young man, he renounced his religion in favor of National Socialism. Höss's Auschwitz villa was a hundred yards from the crematoria. There, in the sweet stink of the chimneys, he and his wife raised their five children and fertilized their strawberry plants with human ashes. In his autobiography, Höss wrote that "even while I was carrying out the task of extermination I lived a normal life."[2] Nevertheless, Höss retained at Auschwitz something of his religious background in the form of a guilty conscience. At the end of his life, awaiting execution, Höss renounced Nazism and reverted to Catholicism.[3]

Other Catholics, such as Hans Globke, attempted to serve two masters, Hitler and their conscience. Globke worked for the Ministry for Internal Affairs, where he produced the manuals that instructed bureaucrats in Germany, and later in nazified Europe, how to apply the Nuremberg Laws. Feeling uncomfortable about his contributions to Nazism, Globke leaked information about the Holocaust to the Berlin resistance circle, but did not resign his government position as did his Protestant colleague Erich Loesener.[4] On the other hand, SS doctor Hans Eisele

Heinrich Himmler (*left*), Joseph Goebbels (*center*), and Rudolf Höss
(Kommandant of Auschwitz) were three of a number of top Nazis who
apostasized from the church. Before being hanged, Höss reconverted to the
faith of his youth. Excommunication from the church was automatic
for apostates such as Adolf Hitler.
(Courtesy of the United States Holocaust Memorial Museum Photo Archives)

made a clean break from his thoroughly Catholic upbringing when he
became a Nazi, but retained a charitable Christian attitude toward imprisoned priests and ministers while murdering Jews with his own hands.

In France, the right-wing Catholic Paul Touvier, working with Klaus
Barbie, sent Jews to their deaths at Auschwitz and had others executed
as hostages. The outstanding French Franciscan rescuer, Father Marie-
Benoit Peteul, had his opposite in the murderous Croat Franciscan,
Miroslav Filipovic-Majstorovic. In contrast to the Belgian clergy, many
priests in the Baltic countries, in Hungary, and in the Balkans told their
parishioners not to interfere with Nazi atrocities, and some priests even
encouraged cooperation with them. In Poland, many Catholics joined in
"rabbit hunts," beating the bushes in the countryside and shooting fleeing Jews, for whom the Germans paid them a bounty, as if they were
rabbits.[5]

To be sure, Catholics were both killers and rescuers. The question
why members of the same religious group would react to Nazism in
such extreme ways has been posed by Holocaust survivor and scholar
Nechama Tec. Why, Tec asked, would some Poles act courageously, others savagely? All were believing Catholics. Tec searched for a solution
to the riddle. Catholics, Tec ultimately decided, were morally ambiguous because on the one hand their church taught contempt for Jews as

Christ-killers, while on the other hand it taught that murder was sinful. Moral ambiguity led Catholics to respond to the Holocaust in extreme ways—some as rescuers, but many others as Nazi collaborators.[6]

Catholic rescuers could not overshadow Catholic killers in number or deed, but they planted the seeds from which new attitudes and teaching about Jews would one day grow. After the Holocaust, whether the killers disappeared behind monastic walls (Touvier), fled Europe (Eisele), or met their executioner (Höss), their day was over. But rescuers lived on to become the link between the Holocaust and the church's renunciation of antisemitism. Rescuers are important for our study because the future belonged to them.

How many Catholics became involved in rescuing Jews? We will attempt to understand in this chapter why the number of rescuers was small. The Holocaust itself followed a long sequence of antisemitic policies, first within Germany and then, during the Second World War, throughout nazified Europe. At various times, knowledge about what was being done to Jews triggered a response among Europeans—Catholics, Protestants, and those without any religious affiliation. A great number of people became rescuers, although in terms of the total population they constituted a very small percentage. One writer estimates that only 1 to 3 percent of the Polish population participated in rescue work.[7]

Proximity to the Holocaust was a factor that related to involvement in rescue. Many antisemitic Poles were shocked by Nazi brutality and came to the rescue of Jews. Historian Lawrence Baron states that thousands of Poles were executed, such as the priest Maximilian Kolbe, or died in concentration camps for trying to help Jews.[8] More Poles by far have been honored as Righteous Gentiles by the Yad Vashem memorial in Israel than any other nationality. Since all of the death camps were located in occupied Poland, other Europeans did not witness the full extent of Nazi brutality. Furthermore, their information about what was happening to the Jews, who were being transported from their countries to "the east," was less immediate and complete than it was for Poles.

Organizationally and institutionally, the Catholic church possessed qualities that made the rescue of Jews more possible and, sometimes, more probable than was the case for other churches or institutions. Monasteries, convents, and orphanages functioned well as refuges. Another factor was the international character of the church. A Jew residing in a convent outside his homeland would not necessarily cause suspicion. Rescuers such as Matylda Getter and Margit Slachta had traveled throughout Europe before the Holocaust, staying in religious houses wherever they went. Because religious orders often had no national boundaries, this behavior was taken for granted.

A third factor setting the Catholic church apart from the Protestant church was its hierarchical structure, which created the potential for organized rescue. Rescue work at this level had the advantage of being regional, as we have seen in our discussion of the Italian hierarchy. But heroic rescue by Protestant groups, such as the Friesians in Holland and the citizens of Le Chambon-sur-Lignon in France, usually remained local. In this chapter we will assess to what degree the Catholic church realized its potential as a vehicle for rescue.

Because of this focus, we will review the efforts of a number of European Catholics who, like Matylda Getter in Poland, organized rescue work within some sort of network, in contrast to people who, like Suzanne Witte in Berlin or Josef Meyer in the General Government, worked in isolation.[9] There is, of course, no thought of belittling the work of hundreds of individual rescuers who have been remembered by Mordecai Paldiel and other authors.[10] But by reviewing the work of "team" rescuers, rather than these individuals, we will be able to place them in an institutional context. This, in turn, will allow us to judge whether or not the church functioned well as a rescue organization during the Holocaust.

The Caritas Organization—Gertrud Luckner

Because Nazi Germany initiated antisemitic policy in Europe, the earliest reaction to it began there. When the Nazis came to power, an extraordinary German citizen of English birth was living in Freiburg, a city in southwestern Germany. Gertrud Luckner sensed the murderous inclinations of Hitler as early as 1933. After the signing of the Concordat between Germany and the Vatican in April, Catholic bishops told their flocks that they could and should try to get along with the Nazi regime. But Luckner disregarded this dictum; she told her Jewish acquaintances to get out of the country before it was too late. It is remarkable that Luckner, in spite of the church's position, had the sense to warn Jews to get out of Germany. Everyone knew that the Nazis were antisemitic, but Luckner grasped their dangerous genocidal potential from the beginning.

After receiving her doctorate in social work from the University of Freiburg in 1938, Luckner took a position with Caritas, the national Catholic charity organization. No doubt Caritas appealed to Luckner because of its potential to help Jews. Increasingly after the passage of the Nuremberg Laws in 1935, Hitler's party and regime isolated Jews from other Germans. The process went from social isolation to physical isolation, from proscribing marriages between "Aryans" and Jews to branding them with the Star of David, from barring them from public schools to confiscating their property. Because Caritas had parish branches throughout the country, the possibility existed that its members could work against Nazi antisemitic tactics.

Defying her government, Luckner worked for Jews both locally and nationally. She was roughed up by Nazi youths for visiting the homes of Jewish acquaintances in her native city. Nationally, Luckner won the confidence of the outstanding leader of German Jewry, Rabbi Leo Baeck, who gave Luckner a secret password so that she could visit Jewish circles in cities throughout the country. Luckner often visited Berlin, where more Jews lived than anywhere else (190,000), and Munich, where the Gauleiter was a notorious Jew-baiter. In the capital of Germany, Luckner worked with Baeck and with the group that formed around the priest Bernhard Lichtenberg, and in Munich, Bavaria, she worked with Jesuit Alfred Delp (later executed by Hitler), who was actively helping Jews.

After emigration became impossible because of the war, Luckner continued her work for Jews through Caritas's war relief office. Luckner traveled around Germany secretly trying to organize an underground support network through local Caritas cells. At the same time, she continued her work in Freiburg, smuggling Jews across the nearby borders of Switzerland and France and providing for those who were unable to emigrate. Luckner's national efforts for Jews through Caritas suffered as a result of time and energy spent locally. In addition, her volatile personality limited her ability to organize a national movement. In Berlin, Margarete Sommer, a close associate of Luckner, complained after the war that her national efforts lacked rhyme and reason and seemed unintelligible.[11] "She pops up suddenly and whenever, asks a few questions, gives a few vague answers about everything that concerns her work, and then vanishes like a comet again."[12] Luckner's work, partially illegal and wholly displeasing to the Nazis, came to an abrupt end with her arrest in the spring of 1943.

On several occasions before her imprisonment, Luckner visited Breslau, near the Polish border, and crossed over to find out for herself what was happening to the Jews who were being "transported." She succeeded in getting to Kattowitz, a city located in the immediate vicinity of Auschwitz.[13] There she made contact with Polish personnel of Caritas. We may assume that the Poles informed Luckner of German brutality against Polish Catholics and Jews. Luckner's last visit to Kattowitz took place early in 1943, at which time the new modernized gas chamber–cremation complexes were just being constructed at Berkenau (also known as Auschwitz II).[14] The Kattowitz Caritas people were in touch with other Poles who were knowledgeable about other death camps (Treblinka, Sobibor, and Belzec) within occupied Poland that were already operational.[15] Clearly Caritas, as an international organization, held potential for a Catholic response to the Holocaust.

Luckner was engaged in promoting her national rescue mission when she was arrested on March 24, 1943, by the Gestapo while she was on a train bound for Berlin. She was carrying 5,000RM on her person, which she intended for distribution among Jews of that city.[16] But the actual reason for Luckner's arrest may have been her trip to Kattowitz, of which the Gestapo had taken note.[17]

With her arrest, a two-year-long life-threatening ordeal began for Luckner. Initially she was taken to Berlin, her interrogation beginning en route on the train. Afterward she was questioned daily for nine straight weeks; at one point she was grilled every night from six in the evening to eight in the morning for three weeks. The purpose of this was to discover what she and her bishop, Conrad Gröber of Freiburg, were doing on behalf of Jews. Ernst Kaltenbrunner, chief of the Reich Security Main Office, personally signed her arrest papers, sending her permanently to prison, because "if she were released she'd work against the Reich again," on behalf of the Jews.[18]

The Ravensbrück concentration camp for women proved to be a frightful place. The camp was supposed to accommodate about 7,000 prisoners, but the actual number exceeded capacity by several thousand. In Luckner's words, "the place was overflowing day and night." As in other concentration camps, living conditions and sanitation were atrocious, causing a high death rate. Between 1939 and the end of the war, around 90,000 women died in Ravensbrück. Although it was not a death camp like Treblinka or Sobibor, there were "selections"; those who appeared weak or seriously sick were gassed and cremated.

Luckner arrived at the camp in early November 1943. She had to undress immediately and stand naked outdoors, along with the others in her group, for hours on end in the cold. Eventually, they were given filthy clothes to put on in place of their own. Luckner's were bloodstained. After several months, Luckner developed severe intestinal influenza and a large painful abscess on her neck, which constantly drained blood and pus. She was transferred to the barracks for the sick and dying, where she lay, literally, between dead people amid lice and filth. The camp doctor treated her brutally, and in July of 1944 he put her on a "death transport" to Bergen-Belsen, where she would have been gassed had her female Communist cellmates not rescued her.[19]

In hindsight we can see that Luckner's work was timely but limited. Before the war, Caritas had functioned well enough to enable converted German "Jews" to emigrate between 1935 and 1941. This is important, because it means that Caritas assisted in saving hundreds of lives. But Luckner was not successful in getting Caritas parish affiliates throughout Germany to defy Hitler by hiding Jews once it became clear what "transportation" really meant. There can be no talk of a systematic saving of life. The Caritas cells, which Luckner said she contacted "in almost every German city," that might have functioned in this manner failed to do so.[20] Sommer reported after the war that the parish Caritas cells in Berlin refrained from challenging Nazi racial policy.[21] Some Caritas women did hide Jews, as did members of the Catholic women's Elizabeth Society, but most affiliates "were not up to the test."[22]

The reasons for this failure have to do with Luckner's lack of organizational skills, her division of her time and energy between local and national work, and her early arrest. In the final analysis, however, fear and apathy restrained Caritas members from mounting a systematic national challenge to the murder of the Jews.[23] What did Luckner accomplish? In terms of saving life, very little. Only a few survivors of the Holocaust owed their good fortune to her personally or to her endeavors.[24] By no means should her efforts be belittled, but the fact is that Luckner remained a lonely crusader.

Convent Rescue: Matylda Getter and Margit Slachta

Rescue work by organized religious members of the church was similar to the work of Caritas in that it was often national in scope, but it was altogether dissimilar in terms of its effectiveness. Among those who mounted rescue efforts were the members of the Sisters of the Family of Mary in Poland and the Hungarian Social Service Sisterhood. Two extraordinary women, both of whom had already distinguished themselves for social and civil accomplishments before the war, headed these sisterhoods. Poland awarded Matylda Getter two distinguished national awards in 1925 and 1931, and in 1920 Margit Slachta became the first Hungarian woman to be elected to parliament.[25]

Getter came face to face with the murder of the Jews earlier than

Matylda Getter, Mother Superior of the Sisters of
the Family of Mary in Poland, organized the rescue
of hundreds of Jews, many of whom were children.
(Courtesy of the archives of the Sisters of the Family of Mary)

Slachta, but both women managed to engage the sisters of their organizations in rescue work in timely fashion. One significant difference between them is that Slachta tried to enlist the hierarchy of the entire church in the rescue of the Jews, whereas Getter, as far as we know, did not. The reason for this difference may be the fact that Poland was an occupied country, whereas Hungary retained its own government throughout the era of the Holocaust.

We saw in the first chapter of this study that antisemitism deeply stained the Catholics of both nations. On this account, the rescue work of the sisters was an arduous and dangerous task. And in neither country did a church authority command or suggest that they engage in rescuing Jews. How, then, did Getter and Slachta coax their sisters into becoming involved in this life-threatening mission? Mother Matylda Getter told her sisters that by saving Jewish children they would be saving their own souls; she also asked the sisters to look into the innocent eyes of any child who arrived at one of their houses and believe that the child had been sent there by God.

Slachta's approach was different. In 1944, when Eichmann's pursuit of Hungarian Jews reached its greatest intensity, Slachta called her sisters to the Budapest mother house and told them that everything they stood for was on the line. If the sisters lived up to the highest precepts of Christianity and showed fraternal love by saving Jews, their organization would survive and flourish even if many of their members were killed in the line of duty. What good, Slachta asked, would their work and property have if in the end they had to hide their face "shamefully before the eyes of God"?[26] Getter and Slachta could ask for and receive a level of commitment from their members that far exceeded what Luckner could have expected or gotten from the average Catholic member of Caritas.

Getter and Slachta reacted early on to brutality inflicted on Jewish people. The mother house of Getter's sisters was situated at the corner of Zelazna and Leszno Streets in Warsaw, directly across from one of the entrances to the Warsaw ghetto that was established in November 1940. Roughly a third of the city's population was forced to live in an extremely small area of just a few square miles (2.5 percent of the city).[27] An extraordinarily high mortality rate resulted from the atrocious conditions imposed on the Jews in the ghetto. Eyewitnesses reported that it was impossible to separate the healthy from the sick and the living from the dead.[28] People dropped in their tracks; corpses littered streets. Even mass graves could not accommodate the dead. Emanuel Ringelblum, historian and archivist of the Warsaw ghetto, estimated that more than 2,000 died in January 1941, and another 2,000 in February.[29] Street children dressed in rags begged by day and wailed all night from hunger and cold. Many froze to death.[30] None of this could have escaped the attention of Getter and her sisters across the street in their convent.

It was also in November 1940 when Slachta first heard about Hungarian brutality against Jews. That month, twenty-four families were taken from their homes in one city, trucked to an isolated mountain region across Hungary's border, and abandoned there without shelter or food. Eventually, these "displaced persons" were allowed to return, but by that time six families were missing, perhaps dead of exposure. Slachta wrote to church and civil authorities at the local, regional, and national levels to demand the return of the families. To hasten the return of the deportees, she offered to pay for their travel expenses.[31]

In 1941, Getter and Slachta and their sisters expanded their efforts against abuses aimed at the Jews. On its own initiative, Hungary deported some 20,000 borderland Jews in July and August to Galicia, where more than half of them were murdered by a mobile killing squad.[32] This spurred Slachta to write to the wife of the regent of Hungary, Ilona Horthy, protesting the atrocity on humanitarian, Christian, and Hungarian national principles.[33] In January of the same year, German occupational authorities decided to clear the Warsaw ghetto of its thousands of begging, sickly street children. Their numbers were so great that the children could not begin to be accommodated in the orphanage of the famous ghetto doctor Janusz Korczak. A Gentile social worker, Jan Dobraczynski, managed to place roughly 2,500 children in cooperating convents of Warsaw.[34] Knowing that these children would die or be killed, Getter took many of them into her convent just outside the ghetto wall, from where they were dispersed to other homes of the Family of Mary in Warsaw and outlying provinces of occupied Poland.[35]

During the last half of 1942, the Nazis transported most of the Jews of the Warsaw ghetto to the gas chambers of Treblinka. The Warsaw ghetto rebellion ensued. The fate of Jewish orphans worried Adam Czerniakow, head of the Warsaw self-government organization, Jewish Council. It is likely that he undertook to get as many of these children out of the ghetto as he could before he himself was overcome by the desperateness of the entire situation and committed suicide in July. As the Jews of Warsaw became convinced of their fate, they did not abandon their orphans. Janusz Korczak himself chose to go the gas chambers with the children of his orphanage rather than escape. During the ghetto uprising, an estimated 8,000 Jews managed to escape, finding refuge on the outside.[36] The number of Jewish orphans in the care of the Family of Mary surged upward.

Since providing identity papers for orphans was routine work for the Family of Mary sisters, they could easily invent new identities for Jewish children. In Catholic Poland, a baptismal certificate served this purpose. Getter followed a policy of not baptizing children whose parents were alive; instead, a fake baptismal certificate was issued. After the children were placed in orphanages throughout Poland, the sisters taught them Catholic prayers and customs to protect their false identities. Children were baptized only occasionally, and then only with the permission of their parents. Neither Getter nor her sisters exploited the situation brought about by the Holocaust to proselytize Jewish children.

The critical hour for Jews in Hungary came in 1944. Within three months of the occupation of Hungary by Germany in March 1944, a half million Jews were deported, most of whom were murdered. The Hungarian government, knowing full well what fate awaited its Jews, cooperated in their deportation. The Catholic church, under the leadership of Justinian Serédi, stood passively by.

The ambivalence of her church did not keep Margit Slachta from acting decisively during the critical months of 1944. The members of her Social Service Sisterhood cooperated with others in organizing mass baptisms of Jews in the hope that it would save their lives.[37] Slachta's sisters responded to the Jews' predicament by offering food and supplies to those in the ghetto, especially those in the overcrowded Budapest ghetto. To do this, they exchanged their religious garb for ordinary street clothes when going in and out of the ghetto. During the deportations, the sisters used their houses, spread throughout Hungary, to hide Jews.

Convent rescue was immensely more successful than anything the lay members of Caritas achieved.[38] Getter and Slachta's sisters rescued about 3,000 Jews (750 in Poland and 2,000 in Hungary). The number is probably much greater, but verification exists for roughly this many. Both Getter and Slachta, and their sisters as well, have been recognized as Righteous Gentiles by the Holocaust Martyrs' and Heroes' Remembrance Authority at Yad Vashem in Jerusalem.

It is obvious that with their many convent houses and orphanages, sisterhoods held a structural advantage over the individual Catholic. It is equally clear that the dedicated sisters operated at a higher level of commitment. The Sisters of the Family of Mary lived in daily fear of the Germans. When an employee of the Pludy orphanage accidentally divulged her Jewish ethnicity, putting everyone at risk, Getter asked herself what right she had to urge her sisters to a level of moral courage that was much higher than the church demanded of other Catholics. Nazis feigned the execution of one of Getter's sisters at the Pludy orphanage, which deeply frightened Getter and the sisters. In Hungary, the fascist Arrow Cross executed one of the sisters of the Social Service Sisterhood. Slachta herself was beaten and narrowly escaped execution.[39]

Getter and Slachta and their sisters undertook rescue work on their own initiative. No one ordered them to save Jews. We know that a number of other sisterhoods also acted on their own initiative to rescue Jews: the Ursulines, the Sisters of Charity, the Servants of Mary, and the Order of the Immaculate Conception.[40] Resistance fighter Aba Kovner was hidden by Benedictine sisters, who also smuggled arms for him and instructed him about how to operate a new kind of grenade with which he was unfamiliar. Other convents also stored caches of weapons. Resistance fighter Jurek Wilner found refuge with Dominican sisters.[41] Many sisters paid with their lives for hiding Jews. Eight Sisters of Charity were shot for refusing to turn over Jews. The Nazis executed Ewa Noyszewska, Mother Superior of the Order of Immaculate Conception, for the same reason.[42]

Diocesan Rescue—Margareta Sommer

Could the usual, day-to-day Catholic chain of command from bishops to priests to parishioners function to save Jews? Such a prospect might seem improbable. Caritas, after all, was also a part of the church's structure, and its members were laypeople, that is, ordinary people in the parish pews. But, in fact, diocesan rescue, like convent rescue, succeeded where Caritas failed.

Diocesan rescue was more common in Italy than in Germany, but Berlin offers the most complete illustration of how and why it took place. In many parts of Germany, Jews had become something of an abstraction for Germans, either because they had lost their ethnic identity or because they constituted only a very negligible portion of the population.[43] But this was hardly the case in the city of Berlin, where there were 190,000 Jewish citizens in 1936, of whom about 40,000 were converts to Christianity.[44] The large Jewish population of Berlin and the great number of marriages between Jews and Catholics provide the sociological explanation for Christian rescue in that city.

As Nazi persecution of Jews escalated in Germany during the 1930s, the famous priest of Berlin's historic St. Hedwigs Cathedral, Bernhard Lichtenberg, organized an office to assist Jews. Its title, Special Relief of the Diocese of Berlin (Hilfswerk beim Ordinariat Berlin), gave no hint of its purpose. Canon Lichtenberg inspired Margarete Sommer and others to join in his cause. After Lichtenberg was arrested and imprisoned for praying publicly (in German; the rest of the mass was in Latin) for Jews after the national pogrom of November 1938, Bishop Preysing appointed Sommer to take over Special Relief.[45]

Because of the way public welfare was organized in Germany, Sommer originally restricted her work to Catholic Jews. Since this ceased to make sense when the Nazi persecution of Jews escalated after the beginning of the war, Sommer's office personnel began helping Jews regardless of their confessional choice. The kind of help provided by the Special Relief office ranged from supporting elderly people (about 37 percent of all adult clients), the sick, and the handicapped, to providing for those who were too indigent to provide for their basic housing and nutritional needs, to obtaining visa papers for those who sought to emigrate (400 succeeded between 1934 and 1939). An analysis of Sommer's notebook discloses that about 20 percent of those whose emigration she assisted had not converted, and that an additional 20 percent had converted to Protestantism. About half of the men who received assistance from Special Relief in 1939–40 were Jews who had not changed their religion.[46]

By the beginning of 1942, Sommer had detailed information about the desperate life in the ghettos to which Berlin Jews were being herded. She knew that Jews who were about to be swallowed up in the Nazi ghettoization process became traumatized when they received notification of deportation.[47] To help people through the moment of crisis, Sommer organized parish support teams that stood ready at a moment's notice to go to the home of a family that was about to be deported. The visitors tried to quiet the nerves of victims by taking care of last-minute household details, by promising to send provisions to wherever the family was resettled, and by giving assurances that they would look after the personal property of the deportees so that restitution could take place when they returned. A coded telephone message was made to the parish priest, who came to administer the sacraments of penance and the Eucharist to Catholic "Jews."[48]

On the last Saturday of February 1943, the operation code-named Aktion Fabrik took place in Berlin. Without warning, 8,000 Jews were taken from their places of work to temporary makeshift detention facilities, and then evacuated within twenty-four to forty-eight hours to concentration camps or ghettos in eastern Europe. Sommer wrote that

> they were loaded onto trucks and taken to large halls or barracks without any opportunity for them, or for others helping them, to pick up suitable clothing. What their families brought to them from home could not be taken. Precisely this circumstance . . . changed our suspicion that they had no future into a certainty.[49]

The realization that deported Jews "had no future" led Sommer and her staff to begin hiding them. This activity probably began even before the February *razzia*. As we have seen, Sommer reported on the Kovno massacre early in 1942. In August, SS officer Kurt Gerstein visited Berlin. His revelations about the Belzec death camp, along with other information that the Berlin resistance circle acquired, led Sommer to organize rescue work, probably around the end of 1942.

There are a number of explicit references in Sommer's papers that establish this activity, but because of constant Gestapo surveillance and the great risk involved, the personnel of Special Relief kept no records about their work and never dealt with it by letter or telephone. Furthermore, to protect themselves from divulging information under duress to the Gestapo, no one working in the Office of Special Relief was told or wanted to know what she did not need to know. Not even Sommer knew how many Jews were being hidden by Special Relief personnel or by parish support groups working with them.[50] Nor did she know about other Berlin Catholics, such as Susanne Witte, who were acting independently to hide Jews.[51]

Rescuing Jews cut across lines of religious preference. This was because the Nazi persecution of the Jews had created a common bond among them. Whether converts to Christianity or practicing or non-practicing Mosaic Jews, the persecuted pondered the meaning of the experience that gripped them. Gertrud Jaffe, a convert to Catholicism, worked in the missions of the Special Relief office to help as many as she could, irrespective of their religious preference, and then decided, with great inner resolve, to give herself up for deportation and certain death in order to identify, as a Christian, with the suffering of her people.[52] It worked the other way as well. Jews who were not Christian, such as Martha Mosse, worked to help and save other Jews regardless of their religion.[53]

The Berlin diocesan effort to rescue Jews was unique in Germany and Austria. Like Bishop Preysing, Cardinal Innitzer was extremely active in Vienna, but it appears that he concentrated his efforts on behalf of converted "Jews." In need of funds to assist emigrating "non-Aryan" Catholics, Innitzer drew on resources from the entire church, from Pius XII to monasteries to parishes. Vienna's cathedral parish handed out fake baptismal certificates liberally before the Nazis began deporting converted "Jews." At some point, the diocesan office called Charitable Assistance for Non-Aryan Christians (Hilfstelle der Caritas für nichtarische Christen), directed by Ludwig Born, S.J., began hiding Jews, who were referred to as *U-Boote*, the German word for submarines.[54] One Viennese Austrian, Peter Lorenz, hid sixteen Hungarian Jews, probably with the assistance of the diocesan office.[55] It is not known whether the dioceses of other German cities organized assistance for Jews.

Rescue in Italy appears to be distinguished from efforts in every other country because of the extent of involvement of the institutional church at the diocesan level. Pope Pius himself must be included in this regard, even though he seems not to have been as active as other Italian bishops. Two nuns of the Sisters of Zion, Virginia and Emilia Badetti, who rescued more than 150 Jews, got provisions from the Vatican through Monsignor Montini and Sister Pasqualini. Generally speaking, cooperative efforts between church leaders, priests or nuns, and the ordinary laity were common in Italy, and they often were instigated by and carried out within the diocesan organizational structure of the church.

In northern and central Italy, diocesan priests such as Francesco Repetto (Genoa), Vincenzo Barale (Turin), Aldo Brunacci (Assisi), Paolo Liggeri (Milan), and Cipriano Ricotti (Florence) worked under the direction of their bishops to provide Jewish refugees "with shelter, food, documents, and money, helping hundreds to reach Switzerland."[56] Having the authority of the local bishop behind them meant that these priests could appeal to laypeople, including those in outlying rural parishes and convents, to find shelters. The very successful Assisi Underground was a cooperative venture of the bishop, priests, and lay men and women. Thousands of lives were saved by these and other rescuers.

The most famous priest-rescuer in Italy was Father Maria Benedetto, whom we have met previously under his French name, Marie-Benoit Peteul. In his rescue work, Benedetto, unlike the priests in other large cities, did not have the backing of the local bishop, Pope Pius. Working with DELASEM (the Committee for Aid to Jewish Emigrants), Benedetto found hiding places all over the city of Rome and provided for the necessities of the refugees—as many as 4,000 of them. This effort required considerable resources, which Benedetto obtained through the Joint Distribution Committee, an American Jewish organization. He was not supported by the Vatican.[57]

German occupation forces in northern Italy penalized rescuers brutally. More than 170 priests were executed in less than two years. Others were imprisoned in the notoriously cruel camp of Mauthausen in Austria; others were sent to the concentration camp in Dachau, Germany. As elsewhere, rescue work in Italy had to be kept secret. As a consequence, there is much that we will never find out about its functioning. But rescue work in Italy came closer than in any other country to being an institutional undertaking of the church. As historian Susan Zuccotti wrote, "most men and women of the Church [in Italy] were a credit to their calling."[58]

Italy and Berlin demonstrate that diocesan rescue had the potential to be more successful than any other mode.[59] Belgium also exemplifies organized diocesan rescue to some extent. Encouraged by their parish priests, Belgian Catholics responded by joining an effective underground rescue operation.[60] Even more comprehensive than convent networks, diocesan rescue saved a great number of potential genocide victims. The obvious question is why diocesan rescue was found so rarely outside of Italy. After all, it required only vigorous leadership on the part of the bishop and collaboration on the part of the parish priests, who as a matter of course accepted his canonical authority. Why, then, did Italy stand virtually alone in effective widespread diocesan rescue? The country's pluralism and centuries-long exposure to various cultures and religions of the Mediterranean basin helps to explain why Italians in high and low stations of life rescued Jews almost as a matter of course. Historian Jonathan Steinberg has demonstrated that officers and soldiers in the Italian army routinely and instinctively sabotaged German "resettlement" efforts, even though the countries were allies during the time of the Holocaust.[61]

Vigorous episcopal leadership was precisely what was lacking outside Italy. In eastern Europe, as we saw in the previous chapter, antisemitic attitudes militated against bishops taking the initiative to defend Jews. In Germany, the presence of the Gestapo and their legion of informers meant that a bishop would have to have been courageous to do what Preysing did in Berlin. Very few were willing to brook the authority of the state. So timid were Bavarian bishops that they did not even urge their priests to disregard Nazi racial policy regarding Catholic Poles doing forced labor in Germany.[62] Ideally, Vichy France, which, like Italy, enjoyed self-government for the greater part of the war years, should have produced diocesan rescue work. Unfortunately, French bishops by and large were an undistinguished group, many of whom were forced to resign after the war because of their collaboration with or lack of resistance to the Nazis. In every European country except Poland, the church's diocesan structure was in place, but it was not infused with the spirit and vigor found in Italy and Berlin.

Zegota and Amitié Chrétienne: Zofia Kossak-Sczcucka and Germaine Ribière

Instead of working through diocesan structures or convents, some Catholics set up their own rescue organizations. Two of these—Zegota in Poland and Amitié Chrétienne in France—shared a number of characteristics. They were founded by Catholics, their members included many non-Catholics, they had no official tie to the church, women were prominent in both organizations, and, measured in terms of the number of people rescued, both enjoyed considerable success. On the other hand, the environment in which the two organizations functioned differed considerably.

Unlike the Vichy French, Poles lived in terror under the Nazi occupation. Jews were less assimilated there than they were in France, and because many spoke Polish with an accent, they were more identifiable than French Jews.[63] In addition, Polish Gentiles tended to be more hostile toward Jews than were the French; most of them were unconcerned about the fate of the Jews.[64] Polish Catholics who protected Jews risked ostracization from Gentile society at best and murder (with their families) by the occupational German forces at worst. This was not the case in France. Thus, Zegota functioned in conditions far more trying than did Amitié Chrétienne.

The attitudes of Ribière and Kossak-Szczucka toward Jews illustrate how conditions in France and Poland differed. Germaine Ribière reacted strongly against the antisemitic decrees of the German occupational forces in northern France and those of the Vichy government in the south. Critical of the church, she noted in her diary in May 1941 that "those who should keep watch are the ones who put others to sleep." A month later, Ribière confided again to her diary: "The church, the hierarchy, remain silent. They allow the truth to be profaned."[65] On the other hand, Zofia Kossak-Szczucka, a self-acknowledged antisemite, would not have objected to the social and economic penalties lodged against Jews in France. But when the issue at hand in Poland escalated to genocide, Kossak-Szczucka urged Poles to come to the rescue of the Jews even if they did not like them. "Whoever remains silent in the face of murder becomes an accomplice of the murder."[66] Her conviction that murder was wrong overcame her cultural prejudice.

In the eyes of the young university student Germaine Ribière, matters were troublesome enough in France even before deportations began. In May 1941, she witnessed the Nazi roundup of Jews from Le Marais, the ancient Jewish quarter of Paris. When Cardinal Suhard failed to protest the forced removal of these families from their homes and their subsequent detention, Ribière attempted, unsuccessfully, to gain support for the Jews by organizing a student prayer rally to protest the Nazi action. Disgusted, Ribière quit Paris for Vichy France, where she became a motivating force behind the protest journal *Cahiers du Témoignage Chrétien* and the organization Amitié Chrétienne. Zofia Kossak-Szczucka, on the other hand, co-founded Zegota herself. Her call to action, clandestinely published and distributed in 1942, became the organization's principal inspiration.

Lack of papal support created an acute problem for both Amitié Chrétienne and Zegota. These rescue organizations, which must be counted among Europe's most important, needed material support and, even more urgently, moral support. Both organizations relied on help from Catholics at large. An underground letter, such as the one Pius wrote to the Polish church during its persecution before the battle of

Stalingrad, would have resulted in more rescuers for Amitié Chrétienne and Zegota, because the Poles were very loyal to the church; the French, somewhat so.

The resistance newspaper *Cahiers du Témoignage Chrétien* unquestionably succeeded in spreading the word about the perilous situation of the Jews.[67] The first issue of *Témoignage* came out in November 1941. It condemned racism and Nazism and said that Vichy's antisemitic policies would lead to perversion; furthermore, it protested the Gurs internment camp and the film *Jüd Süss*.[68]

Later on, the paper gave details of brutality associated with the roundups and divulged that the Vichy government was going to turn over its foreign Jews to the Nazis.[69] In January 1943, *Témoignage* broke the news that Jews from all over Europe were being transported to Poland, where, worked to death, they were starving and freezing.[70] Relying on information from Cardinal Hlond, whose broadcasts from the Vatican radio had been discontinued, *Témoignage* disclosed that more than 700,000 Jews had been killed in specially constructed gas chambers, and that Hitler planned to do away with all Jews in this manner.

The circulation of *Témoignage* grew to about 25,000. An underground journal, it was delivered by volunteers clandestinely. Every French bishop received a copy. Even members of the Vichy administration, whose collaboration with the Nazis *Témoignage* criticized, read the paper.[71] It is doubtful that the statements made by French bishops, which we reviewed in the previous chapter, would have been made or would have been so strongly worded had not *Témoignage Chrétien* managed previously to arouse public awareness.[72]

Circulation was not *Témoignage Chrétien*'s problem; attracting supporters was. In the absence of word from Pius XII, *Témoignage* found itself forced to hark back to Pius XI's "Spiritually, we are Semites" statement in its attempt to attract followers. To enlist support for Jews, the editors of *Témoignage Chrétien* also relied upon Jacques Maritain's British Broadcast Corporation addresses for inspiration. But Maritain did not have the influence of the papacy. Support from the Vatican would have led to protests by more French bishops, and to stronger protests from those who spoke out on their own initiative.

The Vatican did not supply material support for the rescue work of Amitié Chrétienne and Zegota. Pope Pius, as we have seen, wanted the Polish people to believe that he was contributing to their support, but operating funds for Zegota came only from the Polish government in exile. The situation was the same in France. Because Jews as well as Christians were active in Amitié Chrétienne, it attracted funds from

French Jewish organizations and from the American Joint Distribution Committee. This income allowed Amitié to expand its work from Lyons throughout southern France.[73] The Jesuits who associated themselves with Amitié Chrétienne did so in defiance of their general in Rome.[74]

Amitié Chrétienne and Zegota did receive considerable support from the church locally. Laypeople ran Zegota, but priests and nuns were vital to its operation. Priests destroyed death certificates and released false birth certificates matching the age and sex of the deceased with the Jewish recipient. Many nuns, including Matylda Getter, harbored Jewish children.[75] Led by Jesuit priest Pierre Chaillet, Amitié Chrétienne got endorsement from the cardinal of Lyons when the organization ran afoul of the Vichy government.[76] In May 1942, French authorities cooperated with the Nazis to detain eighty-four children in Lyons, from where they were to be deported or "resettled." Claiming that the parents of the children had made them wards of Amitié, Chaillet took the children from the local social welfare bureau and placed them in hiding. Both the prefect of Lyons and the chief of police attempted to force Amitié into abandoning the children, but Chaillet told them they would not be given up to be "sent to exile and undoubtedly to death."[77] When the prefect confronted Cardinal Gerlier over Amitié's civil disobedience, he was told that the action represented a protest by the church against the surrender of Jews to the Germans. According to Serge Klarsfeld, this interference by the church caused French officials to back off from their commitment to the German deportation schedule, a delay that gave Amitié time to expand its operations.

In the end, what held Zegota and Amitié Chrétienne together, in spite of their ideologically diverse members, was the Nazi genocide. "Obedience to the discipline of the conspiracy" against the Nazi Holocaust brought a limited number of French and Polish Catholics together in an effort to save Jews. The struggle became especially heroic in Poland, where many Zegota members were executed by the Nazis when informants betrayed them (Zegota also executed Polish informants). Kossak was herself captured by the Nazis and imprisoned in Auschwitz. She survived, only to be seized by postwar Polish Communists and sent into exile for the rest of her life. But the members of Zegota accomplished a great deal during their brief history; perhaps as many as 5,000 Jews were saved through their efforts.[78]

In France, the penalty for resistance was less severe. Nevertheless, danger stalked the resisters. Amitié went underground after the Germans broke their word and invaded Vichy France in November of 1942. When it became known that "transportation" actually meant death,

Amitié began illegal resistance work. The members hid Jews, found non-members who were willing to hide the hunted, smuggled people out of France, and printed a variety of false documents to provide new identities for people. When the big roundups of 1942 occurred, Ribière was able to warn some Jews in time for them to avoid detention. According to her biographer, Eva Fleischner, it was also Ribière who assumed the guise of a charwoman and turned away Amitié associates at the door, thereby preventing their arrest when the Gestapo raided Amitié's central office in January 1943.[79] Along with a small clique of Jesuits, Ribière provided much of Amitié's inspiration and was one of its most active members.

Zegota and Amitié Chrétienne shared a characteristic that most other forms of rescue lacked—impassioned, determined men and women. Tenacity in the face of genocide allowed them to cut across religious and political lines to form effective rescue organizations. The absence of official ties with the institutional church meant that the Polish and French could function in large geographical areas of their countries irrespective of diocesan boundaries. In Berlin, Bishop Preysing and Margarete Sommer attempted to make their efforts national by channeling their rescue work to other German dioceses, but they were not successful, as we saw in chapter 5. Similarly, convent rescue remained by and large within the network of the organizations of the sisters rather than becoming a more general movement.

To some extent, Slachta's work in Hungary constitutes an exception to the convent pattern. Slachta asked Hungarian women to encourage their husbands to be compassionate toward "labor servicemen" (Jewish men doing forced labor). When the government criticized her for this and accused her of acting disloyally, Slachta replied that "love obliges us to accept natural laws for our fellow men without any exception."[80] Perhaps it was Slachta's appeals that led hundreds of Hungarians to disregard the hostility of their country toward Jews and become rescuers. (One historian has compiled a list of more than 400 Hungarian rescuers.[81]) Various associations of Catholic and Protestant women attempted to assist Jews who had been crammed into boxcars for transportation from Hungary to concentration camps. Women protested the plight of these deportees who had been left without food, water, or sanitary facilities.[82] When the trains arrived at their destinations in the Reich or in Poland, hundreds of the Jews had died en route.[83]

While Zegota and Amitié Chrétienne had many advantages over other forms of rescue, their organizations could rely on only a limited number of participants. Relatively few people would take the risks involved with their work. There were others who were indeed willing to undertake heroic rescue but preferred to work alone. Along with Pierre Chaillet of Amitié, eighty-four other French clergymen have been recognized by Yad Vashem as Righteous Gentiles.[84] Most of these priests were not involved with Amitié.

Many priests all over Europe opposed the Nazis, but exactly how many of them there were, and precisely what the reason for their opposition was, we often do not know. In France alone, 231 priests were executed by the Nazis.[85] Thousands of Polish priests met the same fate. Before and during the war, the Gestapo questioned or arrested German priests by the thousands. (Only rarely, however, did this occur because a priest had spoken out for Jews.[86]) Belgian Benedictine monk Aimé Lambert, captured by the SS, was badly beaten and held in a cell with others that stank so badly that the SS would not enter it. On the day he died, he witnessed the deaths of six others who were beheaded before it was his turn. As each prepared for his execution, Lambert read the prayers for the dying from his breviary. The German chaplain answered with the responses. When it came Lambert's time to be beheaded, he continued saying the prayers, and the chaplain continued answering—until his head fell.[87] Did Lambert and thousands of other priests sacrifice their lives for their opposition to genocide? We know that many Italian priests did, and that Polish priest Maximillian Kolbe rescued a Jew by taking his place in Auschwitz before a firing squad. For how many other priests was this the case? Or did they give their lives in defense of Christian principles in general and out of loyalty to the church?

Besides priests, many individual sisters and lay men and women helped Jews during the Holocaust. Like Raoul Wallenberg in Hungary, Portuguese diplomat Aristides de Sousa Mendes saved many Jews in western Europe by passing out false visas.[88] Swiss Catholic newspapers, like the French underground paper *Témoignage Chrétien,* tried to rally Catholic support for Jews.[89] Germans Susanne Witte and Josef Meyer saved Jews.[90] There were many hundreds of rescuers in Catholic eastern Europe as well: Ilona Elias in Croatia; Helena Korzeniowska, Maria Babicz, and Dr. Viktoria Strusinska in Poland; Karla Weiss in Czechoslovakia. How many more were there? Rescue work, by nature secret, cannot be analyzed closely. Unlike protesters such as Canon Bernard Lichtenberg in Berlin, who told a Nazi judge that Hitler's deeds were evil because his principles were wrong, rescuers wrapped their work in secrecy for obvious reasons. We have no idea whether more rescuers worked individually than in the forms of organized rescue that we have surveyed. But it is clear that Catholic women played a very significant role in the rescue of Jews.

Because church authorities left Catholics in moral ambiguity by not speaking out, the great majority remained bystanders. Jan Karski, a famous Polish Catholic underground courier, hoped to persuade world leaders to speak out about the Holocaust to inhibit the Germans and to inspire others to rescue activity. Karski risked his life by becoming an eyewitness to murder at Belzec in order to bring news about the Holocaust to the western world. Karski spoke to Winston Churchill, Franklin Roosevelt, and a host of other top government officials of both England and the United States, but he was unable to move them to take any steps to rescue the Jews.[91] His experiences led him to conclude that individuals saved Jews, but governments and churches did not.

With the exception of Italy, Karski's judgment holds true for the Catholic church. Priests, nuns, and laypeople were imprisoned or executed by the Nazis, but only one bishop lost his life for Jews. In the opinion of resistance historian Eva Fogelman, French Catholics accomplished a great deal more to save Jews than did the Vatican.[92] Only in Italy did bishops work energetically to save Jews. No bishop emulated Canon Bernard Lichtenberg's daring words in order to inspire Catholic men and women to save Jews. To do so would not even have occurred to most eastern European bishops. Getter's orphanages in Poland, Slachta's convents in Hungary, the diocese of Berlin, and monastic institutions in Italy all demonstrated the great potential the Catholic church had for the rescue of Jews.

Much of this potential was never realized, because the Holy See and Catholic bishops did not urge, publicly or clandestinely, an institutional response to the Holocaust. Publicly, the Vatican could have achieved this through its radio broadcasts, which were clearly received in France by clergy who could testify to their authenticity.[93] Privately, the Vatican could have transmitted messages clandestinely to occupied countries, and even to Germany, as the circulation of the encyclical *Mit brennender Sorge* and the secret letter to the Polish church in 1942 demonstrated. Had the leaders of the church urged Catholics to save Jews, there would have been more rescuers and fewer victims.

8. Answering for the Holocaust
The United States Confronts Germany

As World War II drew to an end, ghastly scenes of German concentration camps, with their piled corpses and human skeletons, flashed around the world in wire photos and on newsreel screens. People were reminded of these unforgettable images again months later, during the International Military Tribunal, the Nuremberg Trials. One witness told of infants being thrown alive into the ovens at Auschwitz. The world seethed with anger. If it were possible to differentiate the reasons for the wrath against Germany, more of it would be found to stem from what Hitler had done to non-Jewish people than from what he had done to the Jews. Nevertheless, hatred and revulsion nested together easily.

Such was the force of anti-German feeling that it did not spare German Catholics in the eyes of other Catholics.[1] In a rare display of disunity within the Catholic hierarchy, Dutch bishops criticized their German counterparts for not speaking out during the Holocaust.[2] Dutch priests complained that the German people had not and would not acknowledge guilt for what they had done under Hitler. French Catholic novelist Georges Bernanos lashed out in rage: "Would that God will let Germany suffer in body and soul. . . . Would that He will let Germany do penance—completely in excess and more than humans can bear—so that they pay for their guilt."[3] No one was angrier than the Poles, who, as Germany's future chancellor Konrad Adenauer acknowledged, suffered unspeakable atrocities at the hands of German soldiers.[4] In 1942, American bishops had protested Germany's "mass arrests and maltreatment of Jews," and in 1946 they affirmed that "our enemies, with utter disregard for the sacredness of human life, committed brutalities that horrified us."[5] In England the bishop of Chichester urged Germans to admit guilt so that a process of renewal could begin.[6]

How did German church leaders and German Catholics react to the international Catholic chorus of inculpation? Mindful of the atrocities, German Catholics debated their responsibility for them from the summer of 1945 until 1948—the period of Holocaust remembrance. During these years, two influences pulled them in opposite directions: Pope Pius XII said that German Catholics had opposed Hitler with all their hearts, and the American occupational authorities said that all Germans bore some responsibility for their government's atrocities. These two authorities affected Germans more intensely and directly than international opinion.

Even though the German Catholic church had supported Hitler's wars unreservedly, its leaders felt the church had won a victory with the demise of the Führer. The war had presented the bishops with a Hobson's choice: to prove their patriotism, they had to support a regime that, if successful in war, would later destroy the church. Because the Nazis had become increasingly hostile toward the church during their twelve years of rule, it was possible for church leaders to claim victory along with the Allies when they finally defeated Hitler.[7] Did that mean that Catholics and their leaders did not share in German guilt for an unjust war and for wartime atrocities? Most bishops, pointing to the church's persecution, said no. But other German Catholics, aware that their countrymen at large had known about the Holocaust, said yes.

German Catholics Debate Holocaust Guilt

Not without reason did church leaders feel vindicated. Immediately after the war, American occupational authorities believed the Catholic church was particularly well suited to assist in the democratic reconstruction of the country.[8] As German historian Konrad Repgen has pointed out, 92 percent of the clergy in the Dachau concentration camp were Roman Catholic (most of them, however, were Polish, not German).[9] When the German people were subjected to a political cleansing process, less than 1 percent of the 5,500 priests of Catholic Bavaria needed to be denazified. In some other dioceses, not a single priest required the treatment.[10] In contrast, occupational authorities viewed the Protestant church of Bavaria with caution and suspicion; they sought to have 170 Protestant clergymen of that state relieved of their duties.[11]

Some articulate German Catholic laypersons realized that their church's record lacked the luster that it had in the eyes of the country's victors. Right after the war, during the summer of 1945, a group of

Rhineland Catholics drew up a white paper called "German Catholics to the Allied Authorities Submitted through the German Episcopacy," which they presented to the bishops before their all-important annual meeting at Fulda in August of 1945. These Catholics, "convinced that only an honesty before God and a courageous, open recognition of our guilt will make possible an inner renewal," requested that church authorities forward their statement to the occupational authorities through the pope.[12]

That same summer, an even more explicit statement from a second group of concerned Catholics pointedly asked how many Germans through their thoughts, desires, and feelings had anticipated demonic rule long before anyone heard of Adolf Hitler. Speaking directly to the point of the Holocaust, these Catholics admitted that they had failed "to see that the basically violent [Nazi] antisemitism was the beginning of the path that led to the gas chambers of Auschwitz."[13]

The following month, the Catholic hierarchy drew up their own official statement when they met at Fulda in August 1945. In contrast to the statements of lay Catholics, the bishops dealt guardedly with the matter of German guilt.[14] Both the penultimate draft and the final Fulda statement are extant, allowing us to glimpse the thought process that took place among the same bishops who just two years earlier had hotly debated whether they should speak out about the atrocities against the Jews.[15] Bishop Konrad Preysing, leader of the most vocal anti-Nazi episcopal clique during the Third Reich, was dissatisfied with the draft that glossed over the Holocaust, calling it only a "dark chapter" in Germany's history. Preysing's revisions, which were adopted, asserted that many Germans were contaminated by National Socialism, that many had remained unconcerned when crimes against human dignity occurred, and, that many, including Catholics, had become war criminals.[16]

The final draft of the bishops put some teeth into the accusation of guilt, but it stayed within the bounds of individual, as opposed to collective, German accountability. It is instructive to note what was edited out of the penultimate draft. The bishops omitted the section on Nazi suppression of free speech (because this brings up the embarrassing question of why the bishops did not use their pulpits to fill the breach).[17] Cardinal Frings avoided accepting church responsibility for Nazi crimes, saying that the church was not a *Kontrollinstanz* (supervisor) of the state; the bishops were not obligated to "correct" the state when it erred.[18] The section that denied that Germans knew about specifics concerning atrocities was also left out (because, in fact, they did know).[19] Furthermore, the bishops avoided the issues of antisemitism and Catholic enthusiasm for the war, both of which were brought to their attention by the statements forwarded to them in July.

After the bishops published their Fulda statement, some of the glow surrounding the Catholic church dissipated. The Fulda document aimed to clear Catholics at large of Holocaust guilt. As historian Karl-Dietrich Bracher has written, the Protestants admitted their failure, but "others, including the Catholic church, sought to escape their share of the blame."[20] An open rift occurred between heavily Catholic southern Germany and the Occupational Military Government–United States (OMGUS) when the latter censored the Fulda letter. The most controversial paragraph dealt with the Holocaust and the question of individual guilt (favored by the bishops) versus collective guilt.[21] Cardinal Michael Faulhaber refused to publish a censored version of the text in Bavaria.

Although the Catholic Fulda statement did not viscerally bestir the people-in-the-pew as did the Protestant church's Stuttgart attestation of guilt, it caused considerable reaction.[22] Protestants complained that their leaders had gone too far with their Stuttgart admission of guilt. Some Catholics, on the other hand, who felt that "the hierarchy failed the people in the moment of their greatest need," wanted the bishops to make a clean break with the past. The omissions of the Fulda letter meant that the bishops shouldered no responsibility and accepted no share of guilt for failing to exercise their moral authority during the Holocaust. Walter Dirks, whose circle had sent one of the above-mentioned letters to the bishops, later reported that they had wanted to "give the bishops the courage to proclaim Catholic guilt for National Socialism, but as far as I know we didn't even get a formal answer."[23]

Konrad Adenauer also believed that Catholics—flock and shepherds alike—bore responsibility for the Holocaust. "I believe," he wrote before his re-entry into politics,

> that if the bishops altogether had publicly taken a stance from the pulpit a lot could have been avoided. That didn't happen and there's no excuse for it. If the bishops had been taken to the concentration camps or to jail it wouldn't have hurt anything—on the contrary.[24]

Adenauer kept his opinions to himself, but they found expression in modified form in the essays of Jesuit Max Pribilla.

The only way the murder of the Jews might have been stopped, Pribilla wrote in *Stimmen der Zeit* in 1946, was by an open, bold condemnation of Nazi atrocities and illegalities.[25] Many priests and ministers, Pribilla noted, had risked their safety by speaking out, but the church, that is, the bishops, had not. Most historians today agree that a common statement from the bishops would not have forced Hitler to stop the murder of the Jews. He did not stop the euthanasia program when Bishop von Galen and other churchmen objected to it publicly. But the Nazis were forced to go about killing the handicapped with greater secrecy. A statement by the bishops about the Holocaust would likely have had the same effect. Certainly such a statement would have led more Catholics to hide Jews during the war.

The Jesuit also addressed a conspicuous omission of the bishops' Fulda statement—knowledge about the Holocaust. "Many millions of Germans," Pribilla charged, "knew about the atrocities that took place in prisoner of war camps, and in concentration camps to Jews," but "many chose not to see or hear because in this way they could dodge a painful responsibility."[26]

No essay stirred up more interest in the accountability question than the piece by Ida Friederike Görres, "Open Letter On the Church," which appeared in a new journal, the *Frankfurter Hefte*, in 1946.[27] This Catholic laywoman penned a profile of the German church that, while well-intended, was devastating: it portrayed a power-hungry institution full of career-minded prelates and authoritarian clergy that tended toward mediocrity, insensitivity, and triumphalism.

Like dynamite detonating a dam, Görres's open letter occasioned a barrage of criticism. The bishops' Fulda letter, Catholics said, was out of touch with reality. The pastoral letter had failed to make Germans aware of their guilt, or worse, it allowed them to clear their consciences by putting guilt off onto others. Instead of being mealy-mouthed, critics charged, the bishops should have told Catholics not to fight for Hitler's wars.[28] Others complained that the hierarchy's protests to the Nazis had been issued on paper only through bureaucratic channels; the faithful were left to live out the consequences of their words.[29]

Associate editor Walter Dirks of the *Frankfurter Hefte* was inundated with mail. At a time when paper was extremely scarce in Germany, more than 600 pages of letters and publications flowed in from throughout the country.[30] Sorting through the pile of mail, Ida Görres found that 79 percent of the respondents favored her position or were in general agreement.[31] A little more than half of the letters were from the lower clergy, who almost invariably concurred with Görres. German Jesuits also backed up her point of view.[32] The bishops, not surprisingly, did not.[33]

Sharp criticism of church leaders also came from the pages of the conservative journal *Neuen Abendland,* which devoted an entire issue to the guilt question in October of 1946. A German pastor, whom Cardinal Schulte (Frings's predecessor in Cologne) had tried to muzzle during the Nazi era, called for all Catholics—starting with the bishops—to repent. Unfortunately, the priest said, this probably would not happen, because Germans lacked contrition for their atrocities.[34]

No German dealt with the problem of guilt more cogently than Eugen Kogon, an Austrian Catholic survivor of seven years in the Buchenwald concentration camp. The phenomenal success of his book *The Theory and Practice of Hell*, first published in 1946, has had an "intentionalist" impact on Holocaust historiography, and this, in turn, has led to the misconception that Kogon himself was an intentionalist who believed that only a "clearly defined and recognizable small group of persons" were accountable for genocide.[35] Kogon did not limit responsibility to this group. In his 1946 article "Judgment and Conscience," Kogon asked Germans to admit that they knew about concentration camps, about arbitrary deaths, about burning synagogues, about people collapsing from overwork and of starvation. "And how did we react? As a people, not at all. That is a bitter truth but it is the truth."[36]

Lamenting German denial, Kogon urged Germans to have the courage to look at themselves in the mirror and to face the world. Going to the heart of the matter, Kogon bluntly said that it was the gruesome concentration camps that people were afraid to face up to. "Wouldn't it be better," he asked, "if we uncovered them to the naked eye, took a good look at them, and passed judgment on them ourselves" (rather than having judgment passed by non-German courts)?[37] Kogon concluded that "it is senseless now, bloodied and stained, to stand before the European people without guilt and shame." Germany would have to face the reality of the worst disaster of its history in order to begin anew. Clearly, a strong and vocal segment of the Catholic population accepted wider guilt on the part of the German people for the war and its atrocities.

Church Leaders Plead for War Crime Criminals

While the debate over Holocaust guilt and responsibility persisted, the bishops changed their minds about the punishment of individual perpetrators of atrocities. In spite of the fact that in 1945 their Fulda statement had unequivocally said that those who engaged in atrocities must be brought to justice and must pay for their crimes, only months later German Catholic bishops began to plead for leniency for those who had engaged personally in the Holocaust.[38] The reason for their reversal can be traced to Rome. Just months after the Fulda statement, Bishop Clemens August Graf von Galen—the "Lion of Münster" who had dared to challenge the Nazis on euthanasia—published an address in which he sharply attacked the Nuremberg "show trials" (the International Military Tribunal at Nuremberg). The trials, Galen said, were not about justice but about the defamation of the German people.[39] In one passage of Galen's statement, the bishop made the outrageous claim that the prisons of the occupational authority were worse than the Nazi concentration camps in eastern Europe.[40]

As recently as one month before the publication of von Galen's statement, an OMGUS report indicated that the Catholic clergy were "pleased with [Nuremberg prosecutor] Justice Jackson's determination to convict those guilty of crimes against natural law and the law of conscience."[41] Abruptly after church leaders found out about von Galen's attack, they distanced themselves from OMGUS authorities, who would not have allowed Galen to publish in Germany. Of course, the fact that von Galen's tract came out in Rome signaled the bishops that the Holy See opposed punishment of German war criminals.[42] Given the green light from Rome, German bishops began a long and largely successful campaign to free imprisoned criminals and have the sentences of those condemned to death commuted to incarceration.

Catholic bishops, accusing the occupational authority of playing God, did not stand alone in their campaign to free war criminals.[43] The case of convicted murderer Hans Eisele illustrates the extent of involvement of the church on behalf of war criminals. Raised Catholic, Eisele committed himself in his youth and early manhood to church practice. His activity in the St. Vincent de Paul Society, a charitable organization, demonstrated some depth in his belief. Nazism, however, proved to be an even stronger magnet, and when Eisele came to realize the incompatibility of a strong bond to both the church and Hitler, he abandoned his faith while studying to pursue a medical career. Still devoted to his principles, the apostate Catholic joined the SS.

As an SS medical officer, Eisele served his country during the war in a number of concentration camps, including Dachau, Natzweiler, and Buchenwald. The young doctor developed a Jekyll-and-Hyde personality, analyzed more precisely by historian-psychologist Robert Lifton as a "doubling" behavior. Lifton found that SS doctors often worked diligently in some aspects of their professional expertise—seeking cures for malaria, for example—to "make up for" their killing.[44] In Eisele's case, doubling manifested itself in his solicitous and kindly manner toward non-Jewish prisoners while he was ruthlessly murdering Jews. The se-

SS doctor Hans Eisele, a one-time fervent Catholic who became an even
more fervent Nazi, murdered Jews with his own hands. *Abgespritzt,*
"to inject off," was the slang word Nazi doctors used for murdering
Jews by injections directly into the heart with a syringe.
(Courtesy of the United States Holocaust Memorial Museum)

lected victim would come to Eisele's office expecting medical assistance
and would assume a position that thrust his chest forward (one forearm
behind the back and the other covering the eyes with the head tilted
back). Eisele would then jab a syringe directly into the victim's heart,
injecting him with evipan-natrium.[45] Death was instantaneous. A pris-
oner-worker would drag the body out of the office, and the next "pa-
tient" would enter through another door. In this manner, Eisele did away
with as many as sixty Jews a week at the Dachau and Buchenwald concentration camps.[46]

An American army court at Dachau found Eisele guilty of murder and
condemned him to death in 1946, as did a Russian army court at Buchenwald in the Soviet zone. Eisele awaited his execution in the Landsberg
prison, where he wore the red jacket designated for those given death
sentences.

The execution never took place. So-called friends of the court left
no stone unturned, applying every possible appeal for commutation of
Eisele's sentence. Many former concentration camp internees, non-Jews

to be sure, testified to Eisele's humane treatment of prisoners. Thus, in July of 1947, Pastor Wessel's affidavit credited Eisele with saving his life. Wessel had been sentenced to hard labor in Buchenwald, which, at sixty years of age, meant death. Eisele told him to undergo an appendectomy so that he could keep the pastor quietly in the infirmary. Wessel agreed and survived.[47] Dachau prisoner Michael Hoeck, along with Pastor Niemöller and Munich priest Johannes Neuhäusler, reported that Eisele had treated them well. Many others testified that they could not believe Eisele could have committed the crimes of which he was accused. Some said that they would have heard about it if the SS doctor had treated Jews differently than he did political prisoners.

The most damaging testimony against Eisele came from none other than Eugon Kogon. In *The Theory and Practice of Hell,* Kogon accused the former Catholic of horrendous crimes, including performing needless vivisections on Jews without benefit of anesthesia. Kogon could back up his testimony with the testimony of a survivor-victim, Dutch Jew Max Nebig, whom "Eysele [*sic*] used as a guinea pig to perform a stomach resection."[48] Afterward Nebig was supposed to have been injected with evipan-natrium, but the attending Kapo orderly filled the syringe with water. Eisele, Kogon asserted, killed a number of Dutch Jews and acted with greater depravity than any other SS doctor.

Although Eisele still described himself as a Nazi during his trial, after his conviction he learned how to play the prodigal son. This role saved his life. Making appeals all around, Eisele won an important ally, Heinrich Auer, the director of Caritas. Auer had had two contacts with Eisele: once when the young Catholic was a member of the chapter of the St. Vincent de Paul Society, of which Auer was president, and again when Auer was a political prisoner in Dachau, where Eisele treated him well.[49] Believing in his innocence, Auer appealed Eisele's case to the German bishops and to Bishop Aloysius Muench, the American Catholic liaison to OMGUS. Muench, in turn, kept critical offices such as the War Criminals Appeals Board and the Ministry of Foreign Affairs aware of Eisele's protests of innocence. Muench's assistant, Jesuit Ivo Zeiger, even appealed the matter to the Vatican.[50]

By the summer of 1948, time was running out for Eisele. His appeals through church channels and every other avenue proved unsuccessful. His execution was set for June 28, 1948. Shortly before that date, Auer appealed urgently again to Muench, requesting that he ask General Lucius D. Clay, the first U.S. military governor in Germany, to stay Eisele's execution.[51] Clay gave in. Later that year, on Christmas day, possibly after another intervention by Muench, Clay commuted Eisele's sentence to life imprisonment.[52] Subsequent appeals reduced the life sentence to ten years and, finally, to time served. In 1952, the SS murderer Hans Eisele was a free man.[53]

The case provides a clue to the postwar mentality of German Catholics. When theologian Michael Hoeck wrote the appeals board on Eisele's behalf, he ridiculed Kogon's *The Theory and Practice of Hell*, claiming it was a subjective journalistic account. Hoeck recommended that the board instead read a factual and objective book by the recently appointed Munich auxiliary bishop Johannes Neuhäusler, *Cross and Swastika*. The recommendation would not stand the test of time, for Kogon's book became a classic, and Neuhäusler was discovered, years later, to have falsified documents for his study in order to make the church record during the Nazi years look better than it was. But at the time—1947—the word of an apostate-turned-Nazi, Hans Eisele, was preferred over that of a loyal Catholic, Eugon Kogon, who had paid for his convictions by spending the entire war in the Buchenwald concentration camp.

As far as the Catholic church was concerned, the Eisele case constituted the rule, not the exception. Year after year, Catholic bishops peppered General Clay and John J. McCloy, the first high commissioner of occupied Germany, with requests for sentence reductions or outright amnesty for all convicted wartime criminals. The bishops asserted that the trials (both the Nuremberg Trials and the subsequent zonal army trials) were a product of power politics, that they were morally questionable and overly hasty decisions that represented victor's justice, and that they were unfair because when the crimes had been committed by the defendants, there was no law against them.[54] In 1948, the bishops forwarded a collective statement to Clay affirming that the Nuremberg and army trials lacked moral and legal foundations. Their countrymen were being tried for breaking laws "hitherto unknown in Germany."[55] Did the bishops really believe that there was no law against murdering Jews?

In making their appeals, Catholic leaders split hairs and produced unsupportable arguments. The bishops urged, for example, that Victor Brack's death sentence be commuted to a lesser penalty on the grounds that his implementation of the euthanasia program was based on rational, not avaricious, convictions.[56] Brack, they said, demonstrated this when he represented the Nazis in a discussion with church leaders who opposed the euthanasia program. Brack killed purposefully, not capriciously. The argument was specious. Furthermore, the bishops overlooked the fact that Brack was a key figure in bridging the domestic euthanasia program to the gassing of Jews outside Germany.[57] Clay rejected the appeal.

Although Cardinal Josef Frings of Cologne had hoped in 1946 that those who had committed war crimes would be "harshly punished," he subsequently led the crusade to undo the justice meted out to war criminals.[58] Skillfully appealing to public opinion while coordinating his efforts with the Vatican and with the West German federal republic (after 1949), Frings met on several occasions with the highest-ranking occupational authorities to bring pressure on them to relax the sentences of atrocity perpetrators. These efforts led to one review board after another, including one by the U.S. Congress, to investigate the fairness of the trials and their verdicts. By and large, the integrity of the trials stood up. But the convicted benefited from the years of procrastination, because in the meantime the Cold War and its realignment of the Federal Republic of Germany as a western ally became reality. In January of 1951, American occupational authorities reduced significantly the sentences of many war criminals. According to historian Frank Buscher, "The number of prisoners on Landsberg's death row decreased from 28 to 7 due to sentence commutations."[59]

In addition to collective efforts by all of the bishops, individual church leaders appealed to occupational authorities to save the condemned. The bishop of Augsburg, for example, wrote to McCloy to ask for clemency, using the frequently repeated argument that because the condemned had suffered "so long and so greatly in the anxiety of uncertainty" about whether their sentences would be commuted, they deserved compassion.[60] By far the peskiest activist of the Catholic lobby was the auxiliary bishop of Munich, Johannes Neuhäusler, whose incarceration in the Dachau concentration camp testified to his opposition to Nazism. But Neuhäusler equally opposed foreigner's justice. The bishop even pressed for leniency for notorious murderers such as Oswald Pohl, who oversaw the organization of Nazi death camps, and Otto Ohlendorf, the commander of a mobile killing squad. Bishop Muench of the U.S., who recognized that Neuhäusler was a fanatic, warned him in 1948 that "in good [German] Catholic circles [of laypersons] criticism of the intervention of Catholic bishops on behalf of common atrocity perpetrators [has] become loud."[61] Although Cardinal Frings sometimes irritated occupational authorities, and Neuhäusler often did, the pressure of church leaders took its toll on Clay and McCloy, saddled as they were with the heavy responsibility of being the last office of appeal for the condemned war criminals.

In the end, almost all of the sentences of war criminals were commuted to lesser penalties. High Commissioner John J. McCloy let only five death sentences stand. Nevertheless, the execution of these notorious murderers caused an uproar in Germany. McCloy angrily and pointedly told Cardinal Frings that "many of the leaders of German thought, to whom I felt I had the right to look for support and understanding in these decisions, manifested [instead] a tendency to put my words under a microscope for the purposes of detecting flaws which have . . . nothing to do with the main issues involved in these cases."[62]

The Church's New Self-Image

While avoiding the question of society's responsibility for the Holocaust and relentlessly seeking leniency for its actual perpetrators, church authorities pictured the church as the prey of Nazism. Pope Pius XII himself stated immediately after the war that German Catholics were martyrs, and that most Catholics had opposed Nazism with all their hearts.[63] This, of course, was not the case. Historians agree that while the church had undergone persecution, especially during the latter years of the Third Reich, it continued to the end to accommodate itself to Nazism. As German historian Werner Blessing has written, "The picture of intact opposition largely concealed the ambivalence of the basic [church] position in 1933 and its lasting thrust toward compromise."[64]

As a consequence of their position that German Catholics and their leaders were victims of the Nazis, postwar church leaders expressed few words of sorrow for the real victims, the Jews. Instead, they called attention to the persecution of the church itself. Seldom were Catholics thought of as perpetrators or as bystanders who should have intervened. Most outrageous was the statement of the Austrian episcopacy that "no group had to make greater sacrifice in terms of property and wealth, of freedom and health, of life and blood as Christ's church."[65] Cardinal Joseph Frings of Cologne often pictured the church as a victim and sometimes mentioned the church in this regard before mentioning Jews, Poles, and Russians. A frustrated High Commissioner McCloy told Frings that "sympathy should be not so much for the perpetrators of the deeds as for their victims."[66] The exception to this mentality was Bishop Preysing of Berlin, who had pressed the pope and his fellow bishops to speak out about the Holocaust during the war. Each year on the occasion of the anniversary of the great national pogrom of 1938, Preysing publicly remembered the 5 million (his figure) murdered Jews, which included the aged and children. "It was a crime that has no parallel," he said.[67]

Although some bishops (e.g., Gröber) expressed profound shame regarding German atrocities, and others (e.g., Sproll) said that the Germans themselves were responsible for the misery in which they found themselves in the aftermath of the war, here again the view was introspective. The focus was not on the murdered Jews. Similarly, OMGUS reported after the war that popular opinion maintained the preposterous view that twelve Germans had died in bombing raids for each Jew who died in a concentration camp, and that the people had already suffered enough for any crimes the country might have committed.[68] At a dialogue between Christians and Jews held in Munich in 1949, sponsored by the OMGUS-established Society for Christian-Jewish Collaboration, the Christians said that their wartime experiences were similar to the hardships the Jews had to endure during the Holocaust.[69]

One important exception to the Catholic-as-victim syndrome was the statement of the Mainz Katholikentag of 1948, which contritely admitted crimes against "the people of Jewish stock."[70] This singular expression is notable, representing as it does a collective statement of the entire church. But credit for its formulation and eventual declaration goes not so much to the bishops, who merely approved it, as to the Freiburg circle of Gertrud Luckner, which formulated it and lobbied for it. Few other Germans seem to have had the millions of murdered Jews on their minds.

Adopting a posture as victims allowed Catholic bishops to step forward as the defenders of the German people against a "new" menace, the occupational authorities. In the absence of a civilian German authority, the bishops spoke up to defend their country. In the process, their language became increasingly rancorous. For their part, the German people used the churches to plead their case with occupational authorities for deliverance from the severe cold of the first postwar winters and from hunger, both of which were compounded by the influx into western zonal Germany of more than 10 million Volksdeutsch who had been driven out of eastern Europe at the war's end.[71] Not a few of the immigrant Germans starved or died of exposure, since more than 500,000 native Germans were themselves homeless in 1945, the result of wartime bombing. Postwar "victimization" of Germans fit nicely with the theory of Nazi victimization of the church, whose leaders responded by faulting occupational authorities, blaming them for much of the country's ongoing misery.[72]

Cardinal Josef Frings, whose Cologne See fell within the British sector of zonal Germany, was outspoken in this regard. When he interceded for greater allocations of coal for Germans, Frings was informed that German coal was for the French, whose coal mines the Germans had destroyed. The British told Frings to tell his people to be satisfied with their cold and hungry lot. Instead, the cardinal gave his famous "hamster" radio address, in which he told the youth they could steal coal from freight trains to keep their elderly family members from freezing. After that, Cologne Catholics coined a new word for stealing necessities, *fringsen.*[73]

Because the bishops had adopted a confrontational posture vis-à-vis occupational authorities, they reacted heatedly when Eugon Kogon published another critical piece about them. In August of 1947, exactly two years after the Fulda statement, Kogon asserted that the reason the bishops were unable to influence the occupational authorities to provide better living conditions was that they had lost their moral authority through their cowardice during the Nazi era. Had church leaders shown more courage and determination in standing up to Nazi misrule, Kogon said, the occupational authorities would have taken their appeals more seriously. What Kogon said, in other words, was that the bishops had lost their right to speak out as advocates of humanity.[74]

Kogon's assertions cut Catholic bishops to the quick. An interview by an OMGUS official captured their peevish reaction to the article.[75] Cardinal Frings said that to have challenged the brutality and ruthlessness of the Nazis any further would have led to the liquidation of church leaders on the charge of high treason. "Who has the right," the cardinal asked, "to demand that the bishops should have chosen a form of resistance which would have sent them to the gallows with infallible certainty?" A second prelate (Bishop Jaeger) agreed: "It is not easy to demand of another that he risk certain death with a stake the success of which is more than dubious." In fact, not one bishop ever went to prison—much less the gallows—during the Nazi era.[76]

The bishops thought of themselves as having put up passive rather than active resistance to Hitler. Their pastoral disposition was derived "from the higher example set by Jesus when he was brought before the High Priests, before King Herod, and Pilate." This posture was not cowardly, Frings asserted. "Of the soldiers fighting on a battlefield not only those who are wounded are looked upon as heroes but also those who come through the shower of bullets unharmed and can carry on the fight." With these odd analogies, the bishops struggled to put a good face on their behavior under Hitler's rule.

Becoming assertive, the bishops had nothing good to say about Germans who, like Kogon himself, had suffered imprisonment or even death, such as Jesuit Alfred Delp, or Austrian peasant Franz Jägerstätter, or the Scholl student circle in Munich. "Too often former concentration camp inmates wrongfully refer to their own experiences with the purpose of setting themselves as examples of the past. Actually, they were not more courageous than the bishops who are so lightly criticized today." One bishop asserted that these people haplessly ended up dead or in concentration camps without having served any good purpose.[77] No one disagreed.

Bishop Stohr inadvertently contradicted himself and the other church leaders when he responded to a question about the Holocaust by saying that to have spoken out would have meant death. Fear of martyrdom kept them from confronting Hitler about the murder of the Jews. Stohr maintained that within any nation there are only a very few people who are willing to become death-defying heroes. A Catholic laywoman later recalled that the bishops never encouraged Catholics to resist; on the contrary, they gave the impression that they were opposed to people like pacifist Franz Jägerstätter or activists Hans and Sophie Scholl or Swabian Catholic Claus Stauffenberg, who attempted to assassinate Hitler in July of 1944 because, among other things, he objected to Nazi cruelty toward Jews.[78] The bishops certainly never identified these victims of Nazis as martyrs.[79]

There was a second reason, the Catholic church leaders asserted, for their supposed timidity during the Nazi years. They did not wish to force Catholics to choose between loyalty to the church and loyalty to Hitler. They had to be careful, Bishop Jaeger said, because a "political split had affected the entire German people. . . . Many members of our church, who had been blinded and misled by a deceitful propaganda, would have been driven all the more into the arms of National Socialism by too sharp a language." Cardinal Frings agreed with this point and accused Kogon of speaking out of ignorance "about decisions [we] reached to avoid a greater evil. In order not to overburden the faithful we had to choose the 'minus malum.'" By making these statements, the bishops inadvertently and flatly contradicted Pope Pius's assertion that German Catholics had opposed Hitler wholeheartedly.

But Nazi contamination of Catholics did not mean, said the bishops, that they should now be held responsible for the Holocaust. The Nazis, Bishop Stohr incorrectly asserted, exterminated the Jews on the grounds of their collective guilt for crucifying Christ. Now the occupational authorities wanted to punish all Germans on the grounds of their collective guilt for what in reality was the responsibility of only a relative few. Because they did not know about Nazi crimes, "the German people," Cardinal Frings said, "are more the victims than the perpetrators of [SS] atrocities."[80] Because of the charge of collective guilt, Germans were now being oppressed by their victors just as they had formerly been oppressed by the Nazis.[81]

The OMGUS interview, never published, shows how much the attitude of the bishops had changed since the time of the Holocaust. In 1943, Bishop Preysing had told them that they, the bishops, would stand guilty before God and man if they did not speak out. Right after the war, in their 1945 statement, the bishops did not admit to this guilt, and in 1947 they took the offensive by maintaining that they had acted correctly by not addressing the murder of the Jews during the war. (Bishop Preysing was not among the bishops who were interviewed.) This frame of mind led them to exonerate German people from Holocaust guilt, to charge that war crimes trials were unjust, and to urge leniency for Holocaust perpetrators.

Holocaust research in recent years shows that the assumption of the bishops was incorrect. A very representative group of Germans assisted in the murder of the Jews, and did so for a variety of reasons, including peer pressure, careerism, war propaganda, and, in the case of a few, neurotic antisemitism. Although there is evidence that Catholics were underrepresented in the Nazi party and the SS, no one could possibly discount the involvement of a considerable number of Catholics in war crimes.[82] But the bishops wished to step forward as the defenders of the German people; they sought pardons for those convicted of major wartime atrocities and asserted that the occupational authorities were treating Germans as brutally and undeservedly as Nazis had treated Jews.[83]

Antisemitism and Restitution in Postwar Germany

A principal reason for this absurd assertion lay in the denazification process. This procedure was predicated on the idea that guilt was diffuse, and that Nazism had infected broad segments of the population. Denazification had the immediate effect of creating solidarity among Germans, even between former Nazis and non-Nazis.[84] During the Nazi years, lower-echelon party members often protected non-Nazis from arbitrary harassment; after the war, those who had been shielded returned the favor for party members. Complaining that the long process of denazification kept German society from stabilizing by barring employment for heads of families, both the Protestant and Catholic churches objected to it and refused to cooperate with the process.[85] Clergymen routinely issued *Persilscheine* that claimed, like the Ivory Soap commercial, that former Nazis were 99 percent pure of ideological contamination.[86] Clergymen also provided occupational authorities with "white

After the war and the Holocaust, Generals Dwight Eisenhower (*left foreground*) and Lucius Clay (*right foreground*) carried out policies to execute President Harry Truman's directive that "we must make clear to the German people that we thoroughly abhor the Nazi policies of hatred and persecution." Clay was the U.S. Military Governor of postwar Germany.
(Courtesy of the Harry S. Truman Library)

lists" of people who should not be considered strong Nazis, but failed to provide the authorities with "black lists."[87]

OMGUS pressed on with denazification in the belief that Germans had to be cleansed before the country's successful democratic reconstruction could take place. In the minds of the Americans, antisemitism was a central issue of denazification and democratization. President Harry Truman assigned the matter great importance. After Earl Harrison, the president's special emissary, delivered his report in the summer of 1945 on the condition of the survivors of the Holocaust in German-guarded displaced persons camps surrounded by barbed wire, Truman wrote to General Dwight Eisenhower saying, "we must make clear to the German people that we thoroughly abhor the Nazi policies of hatred and persecution."[88] Occupational authorities hoped to access this matter directly through the question of guilt for the Holocaust. The German people at large, they asserted, should accept guilt or responsibility, because their antisemitism kept them from defending the rights of fellow citizens.

President Truman's proconsuls in zonal Germany and the Federal

Republic, General Clay and John McCloy, remained very concerned about human rights. Clay and McCloy involved themselves on a regular basis in questions bearing on German attitudes toward Holocaust survivors. Clay worked hard to establish working Societies for Christian-Jewish Collaboration (Gesellschaft für christlich-jüdische Zusammenarbeit); affiliates were set up initially in Munich, Berlin, Frankfurt, and other large cities.[89] In 1947, when the new Munich synagogue was consecrated, replacing the one destroyed during the November pogrom of 1938, the highest American authorities, General Clay and Ambassador Robert Murphy, took part in the ceremony. McCloy was especially active in pressing for restitution for survivors.[90] The concern about antisemitism by top occupational authorities led to efforts by OMGUS to keep close tabs on Germany's progress. Again and again, OMGUS personnel polled the German people to discover their attitudes toward Jews.

The results were anything but encouraging. Postwar German antisemitism festered in nestled interactive layers. In addition to traditional antisemitism, many Germans had drunk in the antisemitic propaganda of the Nazis, as attested by the continued use of jargon such as "Aryan" and "mixed breed." As in the past—even the pre-Nazi past—many Germans blamed Jews for their misery, which was admittedly abject in the immediate postwar years. Some Germans believed that President Truman, General Clay, and Commissioner McCloy were Jews or Jewish pawns.[91] Angry Germans most frequently fingered Henry Morgenthau, President Roosevelt's finance minister, because he was Jewish and the author of the plan that called for the most severe policy for postwar Germany.[92]

New forms of antisemitism grew out of postwar conditions. In 1946 there were only 28,000 Jews in the American zone, but two years later this number had grown ten times, to about 250,000, almost all of whom were eastern European Jews. Once international Jewish relief organizations and the United Nations Relief and Rehabilitation Agency (UNRRA) began delivering foodstuffs and dry goods to Holocaust survivors, disgruntled, hungry Germans looked on resentfully.[93] Germans resented UNRRA because the agency took very good care of Jewish displaced persons while largely ignoring and even aggravating German suffering.[94] Extra rations meant that the Jews could play a big role in the black market. This caused additional ill will, since Germans saw themselves being despoiled of non-perishable valuables for Jewish goods such as cigarettes and chocolate and other perishable supplies. Some of the survivors, now better off than their former tormentors, made use of the opportunity to get even with the Germans who had murdered their loved ones. A Munich streetcar conductor told of Jews taunting other passengers by giving their poodles chocolate to eat.[95]

It was after the Kielce pogrom occurred in Poland in July 1946 that wave after wave of additional Jewish displaced persons found their way into occupied Germany. This influx brought about additional antisemitic feelings among Germans, who, like other Europeans, had a special dislike of eastern European Jews. Most of these Jews found accommodations in the UNRRA camps ringing Munich. Culturally they were quite distinct from German Jews. As historian Michael Marrus has pointed out, even some sympathetic American Jews working for OMGUS found these eastern European Holocaust survivors an offensive, "infernal nuisance."[96] GIs, who also found them to be culturally weird, preferred to hobnob with Germans, with whom they shared their dislike of the Jewish immigrants.[97]

Occupational authorities kept measuring antisemitism in Germany, hoping to use its abatement as a sign of democratization. But to their dismay, they found it was only increasing. Early in 1947, a three-day conference of the congress of the Council of Liberated Jews of Germany met in Bad Reichenhall, Bavaria, where they were greeted with signs reading "Get out of here, Jews, before we put you in gas chambers."[98] A national Jewish organization notified General Clay that "at present two years after the end of the war, antisemitism has not only regained its old intensity, but infected even those parts of the German population which not so long ago rejected the National Socialist ideology."[99] Hans Lukaschek, a nationally known German political figure and a prominent member of Gertrud Luckner's philo-Semitic Freiburg circle, reported that antisemitism spread like wildfire in the postwar years.[100] OMGUS surveys confirm that these assertions were by no means impressionistic.

OMGUS authorities expected to enlist the church in the fight against antisemitism. They had reason to hope for cooperation. Cardinal Faulhaber had said openly that German Jews should be welcomed back to the country, where, he asserted, they belonged just as much as did other Germans. He even offered to pay for their transportation from Theresienstadt back to Germany.[101] The Jewish Community Center wrote to Faulhaber expressing gratitude for the friendly and well-meaning attitude he showed Munich Jews during the Nazi persecution.[102] Calling antisemitism a scourge of humankind, the cardinal promised an Anglo-American delegation that "I will do all that stands in my power to convince the Roman Catholics of Bavaria that they must tear out all remaining antisemitism from their hearts."[103] As we have seen, Cardinal Preysing in Berlin, alone among all German churchmen, remembered

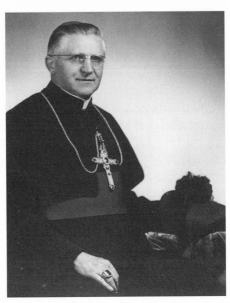

Bishop, later Cardinal, Aloysius Muench was Pius XII's
Apostolic Visitator to postwar zonal Germany and Liaison
Officer between the U.S. Military Government and the German
Catholic Church. In these capacities, Muench opposed many of
General Lucius Clay's attempted reforms of German society.
(Photograph courtesy of the Archdiocese of Milwaukee Archives)

the tragedy of the Holocaust each year on the anniversary of the November 1938 pogrom. Thus, two great leaders of the German Catholic
church were prepared to fight antisemitism, but the third, the ex officio
head of the church as bishop of Cologne, Josef Frings, had little interest
in the cause. Frings, who had spoken out so heatedly in the OMGUS
interview discussed earlier, prevented the Freiburg circle from keeping
the Holocaust issue alive via the church and its channels during the
1950s.[104]

The deaths of Preysing and Faulhaber in 1952 left a void, but even
during the five years after the war, they accomplished little or nothing of
national significance in attacking antisemitism. This had more to do
with the Vatican's priorities and Pope Pius's envoy to zonal Germany,
Bishop Aloysius Muench, than with Cardinal Frings.

Muench's position was extraordinary. At one and the same time,
he was President Truman's Catholic liaison to OMGUS and Pius XII's
personal envoy to zonal Germany.[105] Serving two masters, he listened to
Rome, not Washington, from the moment of his arrival in Germany in
the summer of 1946, although he assured General Clay during their first

meeting that he was not a Vatican representative.[106] Had the pope instructed Muench to induce the German church to fight antisemitism, he certainly would have done so. But these were not his orders, and he had absolutely no inclination to move in this direction on his own initiative. On the contrary, the German-speaking first-generation son of immigrants from Bavaria sympathized with Germans, not the survivors of the Holocaust, and was certain that German Catholics had had nothing to do with Adolf Hitler.[107]

In fact, Muench exhibited some prejudice against Jews, and no understanding of the horrors of the Holocaust or Germany's responsibility for it. Muench viewed the Holocaust as a wartime catastrophe no different from others, such as the atomic bombing of Japan and the saturation bombing of German cities. Like Germans, he disliked the fact that Jewish displaced persons were better off than ethnic Germans.[108] He did not think of Jews as Holocaust survivors but simply as immigrants. Unlike other American Catholic occupational authorities—John Riedl of Marquette University and George Shuster of Notre Dame, for example—Muench did not believe the German people should be obliged to bear any responsibility for the Holocaust.[109]

Muench disliked occupational authorities, who appeared to him to be overly critical of Germans. He especially disliked the Jewish refugees who returned from the United States to Germany after the war to help with the country's democratization. Muench consistently referred to these Jews as "alien émigrés," or "alien Americans," who, he confided to his diary, "do not know our history, traditions, [and have] no spirit of fair play." Even though many of these Jews were highly regarded social scientists or historians, such as Hajo Holborn, Muench felt that they had no talent or qualifications for their work except that they spoke German.

Seeking rationalizations to exonerate the German people of Nazism, Muench somehow convinced himself that the governments that had maintained diplomatic relations with Hitler's Germany had collaborated with Nazism in the same sense as the German people themselves.[110] It did not seem to dawn on him that by such a standard the Vatican would be the chief foreign collaborator, since it had rushed to sign a Concordat with Hitler in 1933 and never severed diplomatic relations with Nazi Germany.

Muench blamed German antisemitism on the Jews. It stemmed from Jewish black marketeers or from Jewish *Treuhändler*, individuals who had been awarded the property of a German as a result of the denazification process.[111] But Muench reserved most of the blame for

German antisemitism for American Jews, the "alien émigrés." In his diary, Muench railed against these Jews over and over again, fingering them for everything that ailed Germany—overly strict denazification processes, trials for war crimes perpetrators, a flagging economy, and the slow pace of school reform. Decrying an American army trial in a letter to Frings, Muench referred to the Jewish names of the prosecutors and allowed that "real Americans" were not responsible for the miscarriage of justice.[112] "Alien" American Jews also bore the blame for Catholic antisemitism, because they allocated paper to scurrilous publications such as *Simplicimus* that made fun of the churches while denying paper to religious publications. Muench asked "if it was made unlawful to vilify democracy and Jews, why should it not be declared unlawful also by OMGUS to vilify religion and Catholics."[113] Not understanding the European anticlerical tradition, Muench blamed the "alien émigrés" for the fact that the secular German press lacked the respect for religion shown by the American press.

Germans often complained to Muench about the Jews. Princess Elizabeth von Isenberg, who had frequently contacted Muench to plead for the life of SS doctor Hans Eisele, also wrote to him to blame Jews for the lack of Latvian visa papers, presumably for ethnic Germans who wished to return there. Judging from the number of entries in his diary on this theme, the American envoy lent a sympathetic ear to complaints regarding Jews.

Under the extraordinary circumstances—survivors temporarily housed in the very midst of the people who had murdered their families—it seems doubtful that the crusade against German antisemitism could have succeeded. Nevertheless, it was a high priority of OMGUS, and the fact that two of Germany's highest churchmen, Faulhaber and Preysing, were sympathetic to it indicated that some progress might have been achieved. But given Muench's coolness toward Jews and his lack of sympathy for those who suffered in the Holocaust, not to mention the fact that he was the pope's voice in Germany, there was little chance that OMGUS could enlist the Catholic church in its fight against antisemitism.

OMGUS hoped to achieve this through school reform, but its attempt to democratize schools in Catholic Bavaria through deconfessionalization provoked a furor. Bishop Muench, who sincerely, if naively, believed in German Catholic innocence, chose to accommodate Rome rather than Washington, and effectively obstructed the work of OMGUS.[114] However, the Milwaukeean of German heritage made the mistake of annoying French occupational authorities at the same time that he was irritating OMGUS over school reform. France's ambassador to the Vatican, Jacques Maritain, had made the issue of German and European antisemitism the highest priority of his mission in Rome. Muench's disregard of this issue and his philo-Teutonic attitude sickened Maritain. The United States, which lacked formal diplomatic relations with the Vatican, could not easily intervene in the matter, but France instructed Jacques Maritain to lodge a formal complaint against Muench, the pope's emissary.[115]

The Americans and the French decided to take matters into their own hands and rid themselves of the bothersome papal envoy. In October 1947, General Clay invited Muench to fly with him back to the United States for the Christmas holidays. Airborne, Muench dined with the Murphies, the Clays, and the Bedell-Smiths, not knowing that General Clay carried with him the French complaint against the American bishop, which Clay intended to use to strand him stateside.[116] Just as Muench was being ushered back to the United States, Jacques Maritain met with OMGUS educational official John Riedl in Rome. Maritain complained openly about Vatican policy regarding Germany, and put the blame on German bishops and on Muench, who, he said, not sensing the need for a spiritual revival of the country, had provided the Holy See with one-sided, anti-French, pro-German information.[117]

The ploy against Muench did not work. The charges against him proved to be not significant enough for President Truman to replace him, and Pope Pius had absolutely no thought of doing so. Muench returned to Germany, albeit not in Clay's airplane. Understandably, relations between the two Americans remained strained for a time. Muench's unrepentance meant that OMGUS would have no cooperation from the principal American Catholic player in occupied Germany in combating antisemitism, the prevalence of which prompted most German survivors to emigrate to Israel. A German Jesuit wrote of the emigration that "with terrible sorrow I must point out that [this] very comprehensible decision signifies a last triumph for Hitler."[118]

Muench's disposition in the matter of antisemitism closely resembled his attitude toward restitution for survivors and victims of the Holocaust. Here again, the American bishop stood at cross-purposes with other occupational authorities. In the absence of a federal government OMGUS put pressure on German states and on the German public by insisting on the duty of restitution. Unwilling to leave this matter to German bureaucratic goodwill, General Clay made restitution Military Law Number 59 late in 1947.[119] Falling in step behind Clay, Commissioner McCloy supported Jewish demands and "repeatedly exerted strong and direct pressure on the German [state] governments . . . to speed up and complete the restitution program."[120] Bishop Muench thought otherwise. Sympathizing with a distant relative who had been fined 2,000 marks and whose business had been taken from him by a military court, Muench complained that the business was now in the hands of a Warsaw Jew. In a letter to his mother, Muench asserted that "a lot of hardship and injustice comes about because of [restitution resulting from] denazification."[121]

As with antisemitism, Muench's attitude toward restitution held in check the very real possibility that the church might take effective leadership. After the war, three main areas were operative where restitution or, failing that, a support system for survivors until restitution would be made available. These were in Freiburg, where Gertrud Luckner attempted to organize a national effort through her office with Caritas; in Frankfurt, where Jesuit Ludwig Born headed the effort; and in Berlin, where Margarete Sommer continued to direct the diocesan office that had been established under the Nazis to help Jews.[122] Within months after the war's end, Berlin Catholics donated money to provide relief for returning Jews. They collected 3,000 marks (more than $900) on Christmas 1945.[123] Luckner received $5,000 in relief money from U.S. bishops and CARE packages.[124] Practical assistance of all three centers was focused on former "Jews" who had converted to Catholicism, because assistance for Jews from international agencies generally excluded these people, whom the Nazis had targeted just as viciously as others.

These local efforts became national in 1948, when the German bishops asked all Catholics to contribute to restitution efforts. At their Mainz Katholikentag meeting, the bishops asserted that Holocaust injustices had to be made good as far as possible by restitution, and that Catholics could free themselves of antisemitism by participating.[125] Unquestionably, the Mainz statement indicates a correct attitude on the part of the church, since making restitution has always been a fixed principle of Christian teaching. It is consistent with the 1945 warning of Cardinal Frings not to "acquire property of others who, after all, hopefully will return to claim it."[126]

It cannot be asserted, however, that church leaders pursued restitution intently. Their statements in 1948, 1949, and 1950 urging restitution was a result of the initiative of Gertrud Luckner's Freiburg circle, which lobbied to have restitution included in the annual pastoral letter of the bishops to their flock. As in the case of antisemitism, German church leaders got no encouragement from Rome to pursue this matter. Neither, of course, did they receive encouragement from Bishop Muench. As time passed, German bishops found that they led an increasingly chary flock when it came to the obligation of restitution.

The passage of time and growing antisemitism eroded the initial support that Germans gave for the restitution effort. German people were increasingly reluctant to comply with the request of occupational and religious authorities to make restitution. Granted, the country lived in extreme poverty during the initial postwar years, but the people seemed unable to empathize with survivors of the Holocaust. In the words of Alexander and Margarete Mitcherlich, a German simply did not know what it felt like for a sixteen-year-old girl to have both her parents murdered in the same concentration camp in which she was held captive.[127] Some Germans lacked goodwill. Historian Frank Stern tells of one city which asked its survivors to pay back taxes on the property where their temple had stood until Germans destroyed it on the Night of Broken Glass.[128] While most Germans were not this inconceivably coarse, Eugon Kogon noted in 1946 that the prevailing attitude left much to be desired. People, he wrote, should have had endless patience with the anger of the Jews, but instead there was indifference far and wide.[129]

Margarete Sommer admitted privately that even within the church, an understanding of what the Jews had suffered—"the frightful tracking down, the cold-blooded murder, the herding into ghettos and concentration camps, the mistreatment, [and] the destruction of homes and businesses in connection with 'Kristallnacht'"—was absent.[130] Empathy of this sort, sustained over a number of years, would have ensured justice for the survivors. But only Germans such as Sommer, who had actively helped and rescued Jews during the Holocaust, operated at this level of motivation.[131]

In February 1947, Bishop Muench met with General Clay. More insightful in personal relationships than in matters of policy, Muench thought he noticed a slight shift in the general's attitude toward Germans—perhaps a softening. The perceptive Muench picked up an early indication of the chill that was developing between the United States and Russia, the consequence of which was the tendency to see a greater danger to the world in communism than in nazism.[132] By no means did this situation cause Clay to abruptly curtail his occupation policies. But in April Muench noted that Clay feared the Communists would exploit denazification to woo Germans away from the west.[133] By the fall, Clay wanted to end denazification processes altogether.[134] When Muench suggested that suitable German churchmen, such as Cardinal Preysing, be allowed to undertake goodwill tours to the United States, Clay consented.[135]

In the last half of 1947, Germans in western bizonia began to acquire a new identity as participants in the dawning Cold War struggle for freedom dramatized daily by the Berlin airlift. Newspapers around the world began running pictures of cheering Berliners welcoming American planes with their relief provisions as they flew low over the city approaching Templehof Airport. Soon forgotten were the pictures of corpses in concentration camps. The Cold War, along with German hatred of denazification processes, snuffed out public discussion of the Holocaust. Most Catholic church leaders had no objection to this. The Fulda statement of 1945 and the unpublished OMGUS interview of 1947 indicate that the bishops had long since wanted to close the books on the discussion about the Holocaust and Holocaust guilt. International feeling, so overwhelmingly anti-German at the end of the war, stifled itself as soon as various European countries became aware of the extent of the collaborationist activity of their own citizens and governments.[136] By 1948 the period of remembrance had ended, and Holocaust amnesia had set in.

9. The Holocaust and the Priorities of Pius XII during the Cold War

The end of the Second World War gave rise to a number of Holocaust-related issues, which, as we have seen, related mostly to Germans: restitution, the question of guilt, punishment of the guilty, and antisemitism. Soon another matter arose that was of great concern to 250,000 displaced persons who had survived the Holocaust—the question of a Jewish homeland. The Vatican took an interest in some of these issues while ignoring others. Unknown to most of the world at the time was yet another Holocaust-related matter that involved the Vatican—fugitive war criminals. By allowing the Vatican to become engaged in providing refuge for Holocaust perpetrators, Pius XII committed the greatest impropriety of his pontificate.

Just as during the war itself, Pius continued afterward to view Holocaust-related questions in the contexts of international politics and church affairs. For Pius, the Cold War did not begin in 1948 but in 1945. He had predicted in 1943 that if the war ended with Russia on western Germany's doorstep, the Communists would threaten western Europe.[1] Communist guerrillas murdered fifty-two priests in northern Italy between 1944 and 1946.[2] The success of the Communist party in Italy, as well as in other western European countries, alarmed the pope.[3] Extremely pessimistic about the 1948 Italian elections, Pius told a visiting American that he would not leave Vatican City if the Communist party won.[4] (Together with the Socialists, the Communists got 31 percent of the vote.) It would be a mistake to imagine that Pius assigned great importance to questions surrounding the aftermath of the Holocaust.

But because these questions concerned Germany, Pius would not have overlooked them under any circumstances. Neither the war nor the Holocaust had diminished Pius's esteem for the land where he had once lived, whose churches and language he knew, and with whom he had negotiated the concordats that established his career. When Pius learned that Cardinal Hlond had banned the use of German in liturgical services in Poland, where Volksdeutsch Catholics still lived, he wept.[5] The pope had wanted a negotiated conclusion to the war; when that failed to materialize, he wanted to see Germany's power restored. Pius also wished to maintain the validity of the Concordat to the last iota with a restored Germany. It is not surprising that the pope's attitude toward Germany bore no resemblance to the wholly negative disposition of the country's occupational authorities.

We know a great deal about the degree of attention that Pius paid to Germany and his feelings regarding Germans through his American envoy to that land, Bishop Aloysius Muench. After his very first meeting with Pius in July 1946, Muench noted the pope's concerns: the Concordat, displaced persons (eastern European Volksdeutsch, not the survivors), and his love of Germany. Muench visited the Vatican every year, usually in October. His meetings with Pius lasted more than an hour, sometimes several hours. In addition, he spent entire days being briefed by Undersecretaries of State Montini and Tardini. Muench confided the essentials of these Vatican conferences as well as his daily affairs in Germany to his diary, which has somehow eluded the obscurity of the Vatican archives.[6]

In discussing Pope Pius in the Cold War era, we must remember that the nimbus surrounding his relation to the Holocaust did not break down until soon after his death in 1958. Immediately after the war, the secretary general of the World Jewish Congress, the director of the American Joint Distribution Committee, and the chief rabbi of Palestine all called on Pope Pius to thank him for the assistance rendered by the Holy See for the relief of Jews during the war.[7] Pius's high repute first began to fall into eclipse in 1960, not with German playwright Rolf Hochhuth's famous play *The Deputy*, but with statements by German Catholic bishops at the time of the sensational Adolf Eichmann trial in Jerusalem and on the eve of the Second Vatican Council. Julius Döpfner, the cardinal of Munich, spoke of regrettable decisions that had been made by church leaders during the Nazi era, and collectively German bishops apologized for the "inhumane extermination of the Jewish people."[8]

During the first decade of the Cold War, however, Pope Pius's reputation soared to lofty heights. Two years—from the summer of 1945 to the summer of 1947—were required for the United States to reverse completely its punitive economic policy in order to enlist Germany in the fight against communism. Then in short order came the Truman Doctrine, the Marshall Plan, the Berlin Airlift, and the North Atlantic Treaty Organization. The onset of the Cold War must have made Pope Pius seem uncannily wise to western statesmen.[9] Only he had followed a pro-German course consistently.

Actually, it never occurred to Pius to do otherwise. His early reaction to the question of German guilt for the Holocaust makes this evident.[10] The Americans and English, who had been urging Pope Pius to speak out against genocide since 1942, tried in April 1945 to disabuse Pius of his ideas about German innocence by submitting photos of the Nazi death camps for him to review. The pictures indicated that not only the SS but also German civilians in general "found nothing reprehensible about such crimes" as had occurred there.[11] Immediately after the war, the Holy See did not oppose punishment of individuals for war crimes, but Pius shunned the English minister's suggestion that the Holy See send representatives to the concentration camps so that they could judge the breadth of German guilt firsthand.

Pius would have none of it. Instead of asking for a statement of guilt, as the World Council of Churches did of the German Protestant church, he defended the integrity of the German church and of its members. Pius's inaccurate characterization of Catholics as "wholeheartedly" opposed to Hitler's regime demonstrated his full acceptance of the German bishops' rejection of collective guilt in their Fulda statement of 1945.[12] As the allied victors convened an international tribunal at Nuremberg to put Nazism and its leaders on trial, and as they instituted an elaborate denazification process to determine the complicity of the German people in the crimes of the Nazis, Pope Pius publicly defended Germany and its Catholic citizens, calling them heroes and martyrs in August 1945, and saying later that year that most of them had opposed Nazism with their whole heart.[13] In 1946, the Vatican objected to denazification, affirming that there were "literally thousands of teachers in Germany . . . who were forced into the Nazi party but who openly sabotaged the Nazi doctrine in the classroom." The U.S. political adviser for Germany, Robert D. Murphy, disagreed pointedly, and notified the Vatican that "the greatest hopefulness and the most diligent efforts of the Allied authorities have failed to uncover any such open saboteurs."[14]

In contrast to the punitive policies of the occupational authorities before the Cold War, Pope Pius sought to relieve the suffering of the Germans immediately after the war. Former president Herbert Hoover, who disagreed with his country's harsh treatment of Germans, praised Pius's success in getting South American Catholics to ship more than 17,000 tons of provisions to Germany, four or five times what was expected.[15] The efforts of Pius's envoy to Germany, Bishop Muench, to ease living conditions won the praise of the pope. His longtime personal secretary, the German sister Pasqualina Lehnert, wrote Muench in 1947, telling him "how much the dear Holy Father rejoices that his representative dedicates himself with so much love and goodness to the poor Germans."[16] The pope also showed concern for Jewish refugees in Italy, but he ignored the question of restitution. Pius did not discuss Germany's obligation to make good for Jewish assets and property with his envoy Muench, even though restitution has always been a tenet of Catholic morality and was a high priority of General Clay and Commissioner McCloy.

Pope Pius's attitude toward the Holocaust allowed the German church to set off on a triumphal path immediately after the war by denying collective guilt for German crimes.[17] Pius's position on the matter opposed that of the Allies, who charged Germans with collective responsibility, if not guilt.[18] Since Pius's own reputation was totally unspotted at the time, his pronouncements regarding the innocence of the German people at large had great impact, most of all on the Germans themselves. As German historian Werner Blessing has pointed out, the papacy became for the first time the focal point of German Catholicism. By exonerating the "good Germans" in a June 1945 radio address, Pius made it possible for German Catholics to believe their claim of innocence, or *Selbstfreispruch*.[19]

Pius XII and Convicted War Criminals

It was not only ordinary Germans whom Pius wished to exonerate. The pope was also anxious to see that convicted war criminals be given clemency, and in all likelihood he opposed the Nuremberg Trials. This became evident in the spring of 1946, when Bishop von Galen penned a diatribe against the trials that was published in Rome.[20] Von Galen's tract illustrates the Vatican's postwar strategy. The bishop's objection that the Allies had agreed to Germany's postwar boundaries without any German input echoed Pius's wartime efforts for a negotiated peace that would leave Germany intact and vigorous. Since that did not happen, von Galen warned that Europe was falling prey to socialism, as Italy was demonstrating. Von Galen implied that a restored, strong Germany could stop the socialist erosion.

As we have seen, von Galen's tract initiated the reversal of the policy of the German bishops toward war criminals. Not coincidentally, it also marked the beginning of Vatican efforts on behalf of German war criminals, including the perpetrators of the Holocaust. Bishop Muench found himself under increasing pressure from Rome and from German bishops to intercede on behalf of war criminals during the years 1947 to 1952. The Vatican also used its nuncio to the United States to apply pressure on top occupational authorities to commute the sentences of convicted Germans.[21] In October 1948, when General Clay lifted the ban on executions of war criminals after a special committee found their trials to have been substantially just, Cardinal Frings sent the military governor a telegram protesting his decision. Coordinating his action with that of Frings, Pope Pius urged President Harry Truman to show leniency toward the condemned.[22] Later, the Vatican pressed General Clay himself to extend a blanket pardon to all war criminals who had received death sentences, something that Clay refused to do, arguing that those individuals had been found guilty of specific, heinous crimes.[23] Polish authorities also refused Pius's plea to spare the condemned Nazi Arthur Greiser, who had obliged Himmler with more than 100,000 murders during the early months of the Holocaust.[24]

The Vatican persisted, asking Muench to intervene in 1951 on behalf of the few remaining war criminals awaiting execution. These included the infamous Otto Ohlendorf, who had commanded a mobile killing squad, and Oswald Pohl, who was in charge of death camp organization. These interventions caused Envoy Muench to write to Undersecretary Montini, warning him that Rome was on dangerously thin ice. Trying to dampen the Vatican's eagerness, Muench pointed out that General Clay, High Commissioner McCloy, and General Thomas T. Handy, commander in chief of the U.S. Army-European Command, had all acted reasonably and conscientiously in reviewing the sentences of convicted war criminals. Fearing that the Vatican would breach correct diplomatic good form in trying to intervene for the Holocaust perpetrators, Muench assured Montini that German church leaders had done all they could on behalf of the prisoners, and that, with the exception of Auxiliary Bishop Neuhäusler, they had conducted themselves appropriately and with "reserve." Muench reported that the people who had been urging the Vatican to intercede—Princess von Isenberg and others—were well-intentioned dupes of former Nazis.[25]

Although Muench addressed his concerns to Undersecretary of State Montini, it was Pope Pius who wanted to intervene on behalf of the convicted war criminals. Just as before and during the war, the pope continued to micromanage German affairs. A Vatican diplomat, Cardinal Filippo Bernardini of Italy, told Muench at the time of his appointment as papal envoy to occupied Germany that the pope still thought he was the nuncio to Germany and that he loved Germans too much.[26] Myron Taylor, the American president's personal representative to the Vatican, complained to the U.S. State Department that Pope Pius's failure to appoint a successor to the deceased secretary of state, Cardinal Maglione, had caused confusion in diplomatic dealings, because people did not know whether to address matters to the pope or to the undersecretaries of state. "There is no doubt," Taylor asserted, "that being his own secretary of state is not distasteful to him and that [the pope] welcomes the opportunity personally to supervise even the minutest details of administration." To accommodate Pius's micromanagement of foreign issues, it was necessary for Undersecretary of State Montini, and probably his counterpart Tardini as well, to meet with the pope twice a day, every day.[27]

In the matter of the convicted war criminals, Muench performed his greatest service to the papacy, although it was not recognized as such. His intervention saved the Vatican from becoming publicly associated with former Nazis, whose organization, the Association for Truth and Justice (Bund für Wahrheit und Gerechtigkeit), also lobbied on behalf of those imprisoned for German war crimes. The pope's concern for the convicted perpetrators of atrocities was actually an effort to engage in Cold War power politics. By 1951, the Federal Republic of Germany, under Chancellor Konrad Adenauer, was committed to joining in the defense of the west against the Communist east. Before his return to politics, Adenauer believed that the Allies were doing Germany a favor by taking care of the country's dirty laundry at Nuremberg. But as chancellor, he completely reversed himself and brought heavy pressure to bear on the United States to release war criminals.[28] Any treaty committing the republic to confrontation with communism would have to be ratified by the German Parliament, whose three major parties all intended to use the issue as a bargaining chip to free the country's war criminals.[29] German politicians argued that their country could not effectively join in the defense of the west with many of its former military personnel in prison. Thus, the Cold War had an exacerbating effect on the question of the convicted war criminals.[30] Muench reported to Montini that the sentences and executions of the convicted individuals had stirred up German public opinion because of the new international situation. He cautioned that any statement the Holy See might make in favor of the condemned men would be interpreted by OMGUS personnel as abetting a nationalistic movement with Nazi connotations. "This is why," Muench explained, "I have not dared to advise the Holy See to intervene, especially if such intervention would eventually become public."[31]

Of course, Pope Pius was sorely tempted to intervene in the war criminals issue, because a strong Germany had always been the bedrock of his diplomatic chessboard. Had Muench not had his guard up, the Vatican might well have embarrassed itself over the war criminals question. Muench's handling of this long-drawn-out issue was deft. On the one hand he managed to dampen Vatican aspirations and those of the hot-headed Bishop Neuhäusler, while on the other he evenhandedly nudged Clay, McCloy, and Handy in the direction of clemency. Although Muench had considerable reservations about the war crimes trials of the Allies, his feelings about the criminals probably came close to those of George Shuster, commissioner of Bavaria, who was quoted in the Frankfurter *Allgemeine Zeitung* as saying, "certain atrocities should not be forgotten by mankind. It is ridiculous when a person like Ohlendorf tries to excuse himself with the [Nazi] reason of state."[32] Whatever his precise feelings on the matter, Muench kept them to himself in his dealings with the top American personnel in Germany.

The Holy See and Fugitives from Justice

The eagerness of the Vatican to intervene across the board for convicted German war criminals relates closely to the question of its harboring and abetting fugitives from justice during the late war and early postwar era. Interviewing a number of clerical and non-clerical operatives in Rome, historian Gitta Sereny found that Vatican money was used to pay for the escape of war crimes fugitives.[33] Gertrude Depuis, who worked for the Red Cross in Rome, recalled that her personnel took it for granted that Vatican funds were being used for refugees, including fugitives from justice.[34] British and American secret service agents routinely reported the same thing. Sereny, who did not use archival files of intelligence agents, found some confirmation of her suspicions about the Vatican through interviews, and asked whether the Holy See actually knew it was abetting the escape of war crimes fugitives.

More recently, other writers, working independently of each other and using different archival source material, have asserted that the innermost and highest circles of the Vatican (Montini, and thus probably the pope himself) knew that their appointees, Bishop Alois Hudal and Father Krunoslav Dragonovic, were helping notorious fugitives from justice such as Franz Stangl, Adolf Eichmann, and Ante Pavelic.[35]

Did Undersecretary of State Montini and the pope himself assist the .escape of atrocity perpetrators to South America and other lands beyond the reach of the Allies? American Jesuit Robert Graham, a longtime Vatican operative, has denied this, maintaining that the two key personalities engaged in secreting war criminals out of Europe, Bishop Hudal and Father Dragonovic, acted independently of the Vatican.[36] It is a known fact that Hudal helped notorious Holocaust perpetrators such as Franz Stangl (commandant of the Treblinka death camp), Walter Rauff (who organized gas-van murders), Adolf Eichmann (deportation chief of the Reich Main Security Office), and many other Nazis escape from Europe. Otto Wächter, a high-ranking SS officer widely sought by the occupational authorities and Jewish intelligence because of his direct implication in the Holocaust, died in Rome in Hudal's arms.[37] Hudal assisted fugitive Nazis by procuring passports and visas, buying passenger tickets for voyages, and providing pocket money for the refugees. Did the pope know this? Historians Weisbord and Sillanpoa assert that if the rescue of Roman Jews could not have been accomplished without Pope Pius's "knowledge and encouragement, tacit or explicit," as his apologists would have it, then neither could the harboring of Nazis and Ustashi.[38]

Where did Hudal get the funds to carry on such an operation? Robert Graham and German Burkard Schneider, a second Jesuit stationed in Rome, have insisted that it was not from the Vatican, but a third operative, Silesian priest Karl Bayer, told historian Gitta Sereny that "the Pope did provide money for [Hudal's work]; in driblets sometimes, but it did come."[39] To what extent, then, can we view Hudal as a Vatican operative engaged in secreting war crimes fugitives out of Europe?

Hudal won an important appointment as rector of the Collegia del Anima in Rome in spite of his well-publicized antisemitism and support of Nazism. According to Hudal's successor at the Anima, the rector enjoyed a close friendship with Pope Pius, who, when he was the papal nuncio to Germany, had himself officiated at the bishop's consecration.[40] During the war, Hudal was in touch with the Vatican on a number of occasions. He also corresponded with Robert Leiber, the Jesuit confidant of the pope. Contact with the Vatican continued after the war, when Hudal harbored fleeing Nazis. In fact, the Holy See appointed Hudal, whom they knew to be a Nazi sympathizer, to be the "Spiritual Head of the German People Resident in Italy," a position that guaranteed that he would come into contact with Nazis.[41] From among the many German-speaking priests residing in Rome, why did the Vatican choose the most notorious pro-Nazi for this position? Furthermore, on at least one occasion Hudal received money from the Holy See. In April 1949, Montini forwarded 30,000 Lire (about $1,800 in 1945 dollars) to Hudal, a "special grant from the Holy Father for the benefit of Austrians."[42] Since Hudal did not have to account for this money, he may well have used it for Nazi fugitives instead of for the benefit of Austrian seminarians at the Anima.

In 1952 the Holy See, fearing that the outspoken Bishop Hudal, who made no secret of his work for Nazi fugitives, would become an embarrassment, forced him to resign his position as rector of the Austrian seminary. Gitta Sereny has speculated that the Vatican might have used Hudal as a scapegoat for its own efforts on behalf of fugitive Nazis.[43] Hudal became embittered, at any rate, and is said to have provided Rolf Hochhuth with the image of Pope Pius as the heartless, money-grasping pontiff that the playwright portrayed in *The Deputy*.[44]

The United States became suspicious of the activities of people who, like Bishop Hudal, worked in Rome to spirit former Nazis out of the country. In January of 1946, the State Department appealed to all countries that had been neutral in wartime to provide a list of Germans residing within their borders for the purpose of their repatriation to occupied Germany. The records of the State Department report that Vatican cooperation with the request was "negligible" (even though they had promised in 1943 to abide by international law in such matters).[45] Vincent La Vista, a Strategic Services Unit (SSU) agent, investigated the matter. His report, dated July 14, 1947, explained why the Holy See was not cooperating with the State Department's request for repatriation of Nazis. The Vatican, knowing them to be ideologically anti-Communist, preferred to plant them in South America and elsewhere to negate the spread of Marxism there rather than repatriate them to authorities in occupied Germany, where they would have to stand trial for accusations of wartime atrocities.[46]

La Vista found that the Vatican's involvement in illegal emigration was more extensive than that of any other agency. Second only to the Vatican was the Jewish organization the American Joint Distribution

Committee (AJDC), which placed refugee Jews in Palestine. La Vista counted as many as twenty-two Catholic agents or agencies, such as Hudal and the Dalmatian Ecclesiastical Institute, that engaged in placing refugees in foreign lands, and he assumed that the Vatican knew the nature of their work. But the intelligence agent actually found closer links between the AJDC and Jewish placement agencies than between the Vatican and the twenty-two Catholic agencies—with several important exceptions: Bishop Hudal and a German priest, Father Karl Bayer, who actually operated out of the offices of the former German embassy to the Holy See. Bayer used his Vatican contacts to obtain credential letters for illegal emigrants—letters that have been of "tremendous help in this chain."[47] The most concrete case linking the Vatican to shady refugee work concerned a Dr. Willy Nix, who, like Bishop Hudal, placed refugees he knew to be wanted war criminals in foreign countries. When the Italian government was about to arrest Nix, he sought and found refuge inside the Vatican state.[48]

The evidence unquestionably points to the Holy See's assistance to fleeing Nazis. Why would the Vatican abet their escape by providing money and credentials for them and by pressuring South American states to accept them? First of all, being a Nazi did not make one a criminal in Pope Pius's eyes. As the war drew to its close and the occupation of Germany became a certainty, American intelligence agents reported that they believed that the Vatican planned to tell German priests not to point out Nazis to Allied personnel.[49] As far as the Holy See was concerned, the positive qualifications of these refugees as anti-Communists outweighed any possible negatives connected with membership in the Nazi party. In addition, although Bishop Hudal knew that any number of the refugees he assisted had been, like Franz Stangl and Adolf Eichmann, central figures in carrying out the Holocaust, we cannot say that the pope himself or his Undersecretaries Montini and Tardini knew this, but they had every reason to suspect it with Hudal as their agent. Refugees by the thousands and tens of thousands flooded postwar Italy, the overwhelming majority of whom, like the Catholics from Slovakia and Jewish survivors, were perfectly legitimate. Ferreting out the few fugitives from justice proved impossible. As La Vista himself put it, "anyone can show up, tell a sad story, and get a visa."[50]

But did Pius XII really care to know which specific Germans were fugitives from justice? Probably not. In the summer of 1944, during the period of transition from German to American occupation of Rome, a few Georgian priests, some of whom were Nazi collaborators, purchased property in Rome and asked the Holy See's permission to establish a seminary, such as many other nationals like Bishop Hudal ran in the Eternal City.[51] Permission was granted, and the Holy Father gave the Georgian priests his apostolic blessing. Months later, when the "seminarians" turned out to be SS officers with girlfriends, U.S. occupational forces raided the "seminary," where they found sophisticated radio transmission facilities operating in the basement. The Georgian "rector of the seminary" had the telephone number in his wallet of SS Lt. Colonel Herbert Kappler, the Nazi who had carried out the arrest and deportation of Rome's Jews.[52] The Holy See claimed to be greatly embarrassed by the exposure of the Nazi-collaborating priests, but the incident did not keep Pope Pius from appointing Nazi sympathizers, such as Bishop Hudal, to positions where they would be in touch with fugitives. We may conclude that at the very least the Holy See allowed an environment to exist in Rome through which fugitives from justice could escape to foreign lands.

The case of Croatian war criminals presents an even more damaging indictment against the Holy See. The Vatican's response to Croatia's genocidal policies—which was only a diplomatic response—and its first-hand contact with Ustasha officials, including members of the clergy, make it likely that the Holy See knew the identity of some of the Croatians it harbored after the war, and for whom it provided false identity papers. During the war, Pope Pius and his top personnel, Monsignors Montini and Tardini, had met with Croatian government officials, including the Croat fascist leader Ante Pavelic. As we have seen, in 1941 Pavelic sought Vatican recognition of his Nazi-favored fascist government of Catholic Croatia. Pavelic had himself been received by the pope, an audience that the English minister to the Vatican warned would put the papacy's moral authority at risk.[53] During the war, Pavelic's unofficial diplomatic emissaries to the Holy See were scolded by Tardini and Montini, who were aware of the Ustasha's atrocities against Jews and Orthodox Christians. Naturally, the Holy See also met clerical supporters of the Ustasha. These included Bishop Stepinac, who brought with him to Rome in 1943 Father Krunoslav Dragonovic, the personal secretary of Bishop Ivan Saric. Unlike Stepinac, Bishop Saric never denounced the genocide committed by Pavelic's regime.

As the Second World War ended, Croat refugees, many of them fugitives from justice, flooded western Europe. U.S. military personnel had a list of some 475 Ustasha Croatians living in Italy who were wanted in Yugoslavia for war crimes. Nests of former members of the fascist

Ustasha congregated in Vienna and Paris. In Rome, more than thirty of them boarded in the seminary of St. Jerome (San Girolamo degli Illirici), five of whom, including one priest, were on the list of wanted war criminals. Additional Ustashi found shelter in other Catholic institutions, such as the Oriental Institute, some of which belonged to the Vatican, although not all of them were situated inside Vatican City. Bishop Ivan Saric, a passionate supporter of Pavelic during the Ustasha bloodletting in Yugoslavia, resided at the Oriental, according to intelligence reports.[54]

During the Croatian genocide, the Vatican had compiled a list of Croatian priests who participated in atrocities, whom they intended to discipline in peacetime.[55] Why then were these fugitive clerics not arrested? Why were they allowed to take up housing on Vatican property? The list of aberrant clergy was drawn up at a time when the Holy See expected a Catholic Croatia to emerge in postwar Europe. The reality turned out to be a re-created Yugoslavia under Communist leadership. For the ascetic but pragmatic Pope Pius, 1945 was not a time for discipline but a time to harness all fascists in the effort against communism.

The United States thought otherwise. Immediately after the war, U.S. intelligence agents kept close track of Ustashi, hoping, since the Cold War had not yet begun, to seize fugitives and return them to Yugoslavia for trial for war crimes. Above all, the Americans wished to capture the leader of the Ustasha fascists, Ante Pavelic, who at one time was thought to be boarding at the North American College (the seminary in Rome for U.S. seminarians). In the spring and summer of the first year after the war, it became clear to a number of Allied intelligence personnel that the Vatican was in close touch with the Ustasha refugees and fugitives, many of whom lived in the large complex known as St. Jerome's. For some months after the war, there was a plan, Operation Krizari, calling for the Ustashi to return to Yugoslavia and overturn the Tito regime. The Holy See appointed a Croatian priest, Father Ante Golik, to be their contact person at St. Jerome's. Golik's job was to take care of former Ustasha fascists and to supply them with "false identification papers and other documents, as well as with visas or passports, also largely spurious, for emigration to South America" after the Cold War eliminated the option of a return to Croatia.[56]

How were the superiors of St. Jerome's able to support so many Ustashi living in Rome and elsewhere in Italy? When the fascist government under Pavelic collapsed in 1944, Ustashi fled the country, taking with them about 350 million Swiss francs, mostly in the form of gold coins. The money had been plundered from murdered Jews and Serbs.

British authorities seized 150 million francs' worth of the looted money from the fleeing Croatians at the Austrian-Swiss border, but the remaining 200 million—$857,265 in 1945 U.S. dollars—the fugitives were able to bring with them to Rome. While experts consider the figure of $857,265, about $8 million in today's money, to be preposterously high, they do not doubt that some money reached Rome and, possibly, the Vatican.[57] In October of 1946, American Emerson Bigelow, an SSU agent who earlier had funneled funds to the Office of Strategic Services (OSS) and later to the Central Intelligence Agency (CIA) for their operations, notified Harold Glasser, the director of monetary research of the U.S. Treasury, that the looted gold was held by the Vatican, presumably in the Vatican bank.[58] According to the 1998 report of William Slany, the historian of the U.S. State Department, this looted gold has never been accounted for.[59] We cannot say for certain that looted gold reached the Vatican, because, unlike the Swiss, the Holy See has not disclosed its bank records.

If the money did reach the Vatican, does this mean that the Holy See knowingly accepted looted gold that was stolen from Croatian genocide victims? Not necessarily. Although more than three-quarters of a million dollars was a princely sum in postwar Italy, the actual amount may have been much less, and in any event, it is hardly likely that the fugitive Ustashi would have divulged its squalid provenance. In his report to Glasser, Bigelow said that the looted money had been brought to Rome by members of the "former Independent Croat State where Jews and Serbs were plundered to support the Ustascha [sic] organization in exile."[60] If Bigelow knew the money was looted, would Vatican bank personnel also have known? The fact that the gold brought to Rome was in the form of coins, rather than bricks bearing a stamp of the Croatian (or former Yugoslavian) treasury, should have signaled to the Vatican that they were dealing with dirty money. As a guard against inflation and monetary debasement, Europeans often collected gold coins that had been minted down through the centuries to commemorate great events or rulers. Sovereign states, on the other hand, stored their gold in brick form.[61] Given the fact of a variety of coins coming from a country that had just witnessed an extensive genocide, Vatican personnel should have been more than a little suspicious about its origins. The Vatican may not have known that the Ustasha money was looted, but if, as reported by Bigelow, the Holy See accepted assets from fugitive Ustashi, they knew that they were dealing with people who had committed genocide.

Was the looted money used to help fugitives from justice? If so, was the Vatican aware of this? Yes; whether or not it knew that the money was looted, the Holy See would certainly have known that among the Croatian refugees there were many fugitives from justice. If the looted money was indeed deposited in the Vatican bank, it is probable that it was placed in the account of the Office of Pontifical Assistance, since the money was to help Croat refugees. In fact, the very people who took charge of dispensing Vatican-held funds were the supervisors of St. Jerome's, the refuge of leading Ustashi. For several years after the war, the complex of buildings at St. Jerome's resembled a fortress more than a seminary. The Ustashi had to be constantly vigilant, because Tito's "hit men" were prowling about the place. As a consequence, St. Jerome's became notorious in the minds of Romans. American intelligence officers, like everyone else, were quite aware of this; in the fall of 1946, a month before Bigelow's report, they reported that Vatican funds were being used to finance the Ustasha movement in exile.[62] Separate intelligence reports link the priests Golik and Dragonovic—both of whom were identified with St. Jerome's—to the Vatican as the conduit for the funds being used to support the exiled Ustashi.[63]

Which Vatican officials knew about the funding for the Ustashi? Pius XII had established the Office of Pontifical Assistance to take care of the hundreds of thousands of refugees flooding into Rome just before and after the end of the war. When Secretary of State Maglione died in 1944, the pope's close confidant, Undersecretary of State Montini, took over Pontifical Assistance. Montini chose various nationals to be his liaison with refugees and prisoners of war held by the Allies. For contact with the Croatians, Montini chose none other than Father Krunoslav Dragonovic. Obviously, this is why intelligence agents fingered this priest as the money link between the Vatican and St. Jerome's. Just as the Nazi sympathizer Hudal was appointed in a slightly different capacity to look after German refugees, a Ustasha fascist, Dragonovic, was chosen to be the Vatican's liaison to Croatians. Dragonovic was not just any run-of-the-mill Ustasha member. Montini knew him because of his association with Bishop Stepinac, who in 1941 had set up the audience for Pavelic and Pius XII. He also knew him because he was the confidant and personal secretary of Bishop Ivan Saric, the most prominent clerical advocate of Pavelic after Stepinac's enthusiasm for him cooled as a result of the Ustasha atrocities.[64] It was Bishop Saric, it will be recalled, who denounced the Jews while they were being murdered in his diocese. The bishop stood accused of being a party to looting, and was a fugitive in Rome at the time of Dragonovic's appointment. Given Dragonovic's position as visitor of Pontifical Assistance and as the unofficial superior of St. Jerome's, Montini had to know that the person he had chosen as his liaison would use relief funds for fugitives from justice. Among the latter was the notorious Klaus Barbie, whose visa bore Dragonovic's signature.[65]

Would Pope Pius himself have known? There are, of course, no records of the conversations that took place between Montini and the pope, but the undersecretary reported to the pontiff at length twice a day. Did Pius and other Vatican officials know that Montini was involving the Holy See in the protection of war criminals? A straightforward affirmative answer to this question would fail to reflect the historical context of postwar Rome and Europe. The British could have arrested the leader of the Ustashi, Ante Pavelic, when he fled Croatia, but chose not to. It was widely known that Dragonovic kept in close contact with Pavelic—that he was, in fact, Pavelic's alter ego.[66] This did not keep U.S. army personnel from assisting Dragonovic in various ways; nor did it keep the CIA from paying him handsomely for feeding fugitives—including Holocaust perpetrator Klaus Barbie—into its "rat line."[67] In truth, one could put any face that one liked on the mercurial, venal Father Dragonovic, and the Vatican preferred to see him as an enemy of communism. Even before the U.S. government found it convenient to overlook the background of war criminals for the sake of enlisting them to fight communism, the Vatican did so. The Holy See simply avoided the question of the uglier side of Dragonovic's work.[68] Fighting communism was, after all, Pope Pius's highest priority. Did the Holy See know, then, that they were assisting war criminals? Certainly; just days after Pius XII's death, the Vatican ordered Krunoslav Dragonovic to leave St. Jerome's.[69]

Until the Cold War began in the latter part of 1947, Ustasha dictator Ante Pavelic was one of the most wanted fugitives in all of Europe. Sought for the murder of King Alexander of Yugoslavia before World War II, and for being principally responsible for the Croatian genocide during war, Pavelic was at the top of lists of most-wanted fugitives. Marshal Josip Tito's agents, American intelligence personnel, and the Italian police all sought to capture him. Everyone believed that Pavelic was hiding in Rome, but where? The Yugoslavs suspected that the Holy See was concealing him somewhere within the confines of Vatican City. Some historians accept this as fact.[70] A former American military intelligence agent, William E. W. Gowen, believes otherwise. Gowen, assigned to the 428th U.S. Army Counter Intelligence Corps (CIC), searched the streets of Rome for Pavelic for months on end from March to October

1947.[71] Although, of course, Gowen could not search Vatican City, he considered the area much too small to conceal a person as notorious and recognizable as Pavelic. (CIC agent Gowen's father, Franklyn C. Gowen, also served in Rome at this time, in fact, in Vatican City, as Myron Taylor's assistant.)

As a counterintelligence agent, William Gowen had routine and close contact with other Secret Service personnel, many of whom had reported that Krunoslav Dragonovic knew the whereabouts of Pavelic and sponsored him and his wife in Rome. Gowen, who suspected that Pavelic hid in and around the city's famous Aventine Hill on Vatican properties that enjoy extraterritorial status, also knew that Dragonovic reported regularly to Montini in his capacity as a visitator of Pontifical Assistance, and to the English minister to the Holy See, D'Arcy Osborne, because Croat prisoners of war were in English custody. Gowen was also aware that Montini was especially cordial and friendly toward D'Arcy Osborne. Later, when the Cold War began, Gowen came to realize that Pavelic's escape from Croatia had resulted from British collusion with Dragonovic. It is distinctly possible, therefore, that Pavelic's ultimate escape from Italy to Argentina in 1947 took place through the complicity of the Holy See and the British, for both of whom Pavelic's capture and public trial would have been an embarrassment.

In 1946, a Yugoslav diplomat on the trail of the fugitive Ante Pavelic visited the Vatican. Meeting with Cardinal Tisserant, he asked how the pope could have given an audience to the murderer Pavelic and shaken his hand. The cardinal, embarrassed, changed the subject but assured the Yugoslav that "neither I nor the Vatican knows the whereabouts of Pavelic; if we did, we should denounce him to the Allied police."[72] One year later, the United States intercepted a telegram en route from Argentina to Germany which said that the Italian liner *Andrea Grille* had arrived from Genoa, Italy, with Ante Pavelic on board, dressed as a priest. The telegram reported further that Pavelic had been able to get his passport through the Dalmatian Ecclesiastical Institute in Rome, which supplies refugees with new identity papers and testimonials that are confirmed by the Vatican.[73]

The intercepted telegram would seem to compromise Cardinal Tisserant badly, but circumstances suggest otherwise. During the early months of World War II, before the Holocaust, Tisserant had urged Pope Pius to write an encyclical on genocide. Pius declined. Tisserant also became disillusioned with Pius's conduct of diplomacy. In a letter to Cardinal Suhard of Paris, which was seized by the Gestapo during the war, Tisserant voiced his feelings: "I fear that history will reproach the Holy See with having practiced a policy of selfish convenience and not much else."[74]

Not surprisingly, Tisserant was left out of the loop as far as the Vatican's conduct of diplomacy was concerned. Monsignors Tardini and Montini, undersecretaries of state, dealt with Holocaust matters and with the genocide perpetrated by Pavelic's Ustasha. Thus, when the Yugoslav diplomat came to Rome on the trail of the war criminal Pavelic, the Vatican set him up by arranging for him to interview the widely respected but rather uninformed Cardinal Tisserant.

The record of the Holy See from the end of the Second World War to the beginning of the Cold War reveals that the Vatican consistently neglected issues surrounding the perpetrators of the Nazi and Ustasha genocides. Soon after the war, a number of European countries and the occupational forces of zonal Germany established courts of law to conduct legal procedures against suspected war criminals. On the other hand, the Vatican, out of step with the times,

- sought clemency for convicted war criminals;
- was uncooperative in extraditing potential German war criminals;
- may have accepted funds from the criminal Ustasha regime;
- should have suspected that Ustasha funds had been looted;
- abetted the escape of fugitives by appointing Nazi and Ustasha sympathizers (Hudal and Dragonovic) to key positions;
- and allowed fugitives from justice to hide on Vatican properties.

The Vatican's actions, if not in violation of international law, were far from its spirit. Later on, when the Cold War began, other countries, including the United States, began abetting the escape of those fugitives from justice from whose scientific expertise they stood to benefit. The Vatican initiated this activity immediately after the war to thwart communism. For the sake of expediency, the Vatican acted unethically; the end justified the means.

Pius XII and a Jewish Homeland

A second matter of high priority for Pope Pius during the war and the Holocaust was, as we have seen, the unity and welfare of his church. This continued after the war. When the question arose of the emigration of Holocaust survivors from displaced person camps to Palestine, it was Catholics and their rights that Pius thought about.[75] After the war, the

Holy See continued to insist, as it had during the Holocaust, on the "right" of Christians to the holy places in Palestine. This reflected traditional church teaching toward Jews that denied them the Holy Land. A Catholic authority who opposed this teaching, Cardinal Johannes Willebrands, has summarized it in these words: Because Jews as a people are guilty of Christ's death, they have been condemned "to eternal pilgrimage across the world outside the land of Israel."[76] The Holy See's policy left stranded the quarter of a million Holocaust survivors, now displaced persons, who huddled in occupied Germany, where they clamored for a Jewish homeland. Pius preferred emigration to the United States rather than Palestine. When Rabbi Philip S. Bernstein reminded him that the survivors wished to settle in Palestine, Pius replied, "Yes, I recognize that as their desire."[77]

By no means did Rabbi Bernstein come away from the audience feeling that Pope Pius was unconcerned about Holocaust survivor refugees. Many of them were in fact being housed virtually at no cost, he reported, on Vatican property.[78] Furthermore, the pope promised to urge the Italian government to move ahead on its pledge to accept 10,000 Jewish displaced persons. Bernstein concluded his report on the audience by saying that Pope Pius had made "a deep and thoroughly favorable impression on me." Thus, while Pius cared—sincerely cared—about the Jewish predicament, he did not intend to alter his Holy Land policy.

After Israeli statehood, Pope Pius continued to be negative about the situation both diplomatically and theologically. Israel would jeopardize Christian "rights" to Holy Places and would lead to too many conflicts in the land where Christ died, fighting that might possibly damage church property or even the Holy Places themselves.[79] James G. McDonald, special representative of the United States to the Provisional Government of Israel, reported that the pontiff opposed Israeli control of the city of Jerusalem because he did not trust Israelis to keep their promises regarding the religious rights of Christian churches.[80] Cardinal Tisserant advised Pope Pius to be conciliatory and seek a compromise with the Israelis, but to no avail. Rabbi Jacob Herzog of the Israeli Ministry for Religious Affairs visited the Vatican in 1948, hoping to register assurances regarding the protection of church property, but he did not even get to speak with Undersecretaries of State Montini and Tardini, let alone Pope Pius.[81] Some observers think it likely that traditional Catholic teaching about Jews explains why the Vatican refused to extend diplomatic recognition to Israel.[82]

In connection with the Holy Land, Pope Pius launched an investigation of Gertrud Luckner's pioneer German Catholic movement, which was philo-Semitic and pro-Israel. In 1948, Luckner and her Freiburg circle in southwest Germany joined with international Protestants in affirming that neither "theological considerations nor biblical teachings would justify a negative position among Christians toward the establishment of a Jewish state in Palestine."[83] Luckner had innocently sought the pope's support for her work, but discovered instead that the Holy See intended to investigate her. In June of 1948, the Holy Office issued a *monitum* (warning) to the German church charging that efforts of religious groups to attack antisemitism were encouraging religious indifferentism (the belief that one religion is as good as the next). Since Luckner's group was the only Catholic group promoting Christian-Jewish reconciliation, everyone assumed that the *monitum* intended to single out her circle.[84] In April of 1950, Pius sent two of his closest advisers, Jesuits Leiber and Bea, to Germany to look into the work of the Freiburg circle. The emissaries found nothing theologically wrong with their work (Bea actually affirmed it).

Post-Holocaust Antisemitism and the Holy See

After the Second World War, Gertrud Luckner thought that civilization and Christianity were threatened more by the evil that had already befallen European Jewry than by the communism that might overcome it at some future point in time. Having been saved on several occasions from a trip to the gas chamber by her Communist cellmates in the Ravensbrück concentration camp, Luckner lacked Pope Pius's visceral fear of communism. Similarly, Jacques Maritain, accustomed to pluralistic France, feared antisemitism more than Marxism. Luckner and Maritain, each in their own way, sought to bring the Holy See around to their worldview. As we will see in the following chapter, Luckner worked slowly and methodically to win her church's leaders over to her point of view regarding antisemitism and the Holocaust. Maritain, on the other hand, worked impulsively and impatiently to sway the Holy See.

Jacques Maritain became the French ambassador to the Vatican in the spring of 1945. There was speculation in diplomatic circles about why General Charles de Gaulle chose Maritain for the Vatican post. Was it because of the general's dependence on French Christian Democrats? Or was it because he and Maritain held in common a view of Europe's future in terms of federalized states under French leadership? Whatever motivated de Gaulle, it is certain that Maritain's views on the danger of antisemitism motivated him to accept the position.

Even before the Holocaust, Maritain had written presciently about

As France's postwar ambassador to the Vatican, Jacques Maritain
(*right foreground*) sought unsuccessfully to urge Pope Pius XII to lead
a crusade against antisemitism. Even before the Hitler era, Maritain's
attitude toward Jews was decades ahead of his time. Pope Pius XII's
confidant Giovanni Montini (later Pope Paul VI, as seen here with
Maritain) worked closely with the pope during the Holocaust years.
(Courtesy of the University of Notre Dame Maritain Center)

the peril of antisemitism, although he too had been washed by the waters of French Catholic antisemitism.[85] During the war, Maritain came
to understand what other Christians did not grasp, that "Nazi antisemitism is at the very core of the present ordeal of civilization."[86] Toward the end of the war, the well-known French intellectual begged the
world not to be blind to "the most appalling mystery of contemporary
history—the mass crucifixion of the Jewish people, . . . the new passion
which Christ is now undergoing in His people and race."[87]

As the French ambassador to the Vatican, Maritain was a man with
a cause. Deeply appreciative of American society, he wanted to establish
a federation of European states, including Germany, that would be pluralistic and free. But he believed strongly that this could not be built on
the moral morass of the Holocaust. Justice demanded that Germany be
dealt with severely. Only then could a spiritual rebirth in Germany and
in Europe take place. German repentance would restore the moral order,
without which there could be no new beginning in Europe.[88]

This was the context—not hatred of Germans—of Maritain's efforts to persuade Pius XII to take the lead in eradicating antisemitism in Europe and in restoring moral order. In an intense, passionate letter to his friend Undersecretary Giovanni Montini, one of Pius XII's closest advisers, Maritain spoke openly of the Holocaust, pointing out that hundreds of thousands of its victims were innocent children and infants. The Holy See must speak out about this unprecedented rupture of natural law, Maritain urged, in order to show the pope's compassion for the Jewish people.[89]

Maritain followed this letter up with a second, which appealed more to reason than to emotion. Discerningly, he spoke of collective responsibility for genocide rather than of collective guilt. He argued that in modern society, individual freedom is tied to collective responsibility. From this it followed that even though many Germans were not themselves guilty of the crimes of the Gestapo and of the SS, all must answer for them, because these organizations were prominent agents of the community. Collective responsibility rested as well on the shoulders of German Catholics, or, perhaps, especially on them. Who, Maritain asked, would engage in the process of repentance and renewal if believers did not?[90]

What kind of a hearing Montini was able to get for Maritain's thoughts is unknown. It appears, however, that the pontiff rejected them explicitly when he raised the bishops of Berlin, Cologne, and Münster to the cardinalate early in 1946, to indicate to the world his high esteem for the German church. On this occasion he told Frings that "it is unjust to treat someone as guilty . . . only because he belongs to a certain organization."[91] Pius obviously did not agree with Maritain's thoughts about the SS and Gestapo mirroring the German community. Pius never addressed the question of civil responsibility on the part of those who were not personally guilty of a crime.

As France's ambassador to the Vatican, Jacques Maritain tried to break through the papal mindset. The real danger, he sought to point out, was not what might develop—the spread of communism—but in the present and continuing evil of antisemitism. The French ambassador, surely unaware of German and Croatian murderers virtually under his nose, wanted Pius "to awaken the consciousness of people regarding the horror of racism" by holding up the example of the "extermination of millions of Jews in gas chambers and their torture in death camps."[92] Maritain pointed out that Catholics were playing a part in the rise of postwar antisemitism in occupied Germany.[93]

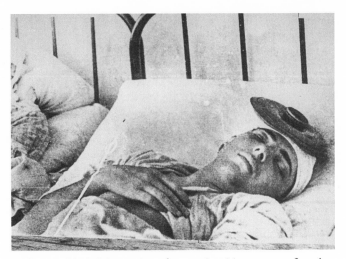

Jacques Maritain's warnings about antisemitism were confirmed
when the Kielce pogrom occurred in Poland in July 1946. More
than forty Jews were killed in Kielce; others were severely injured.
(Courtesy of the United States Holocaust Memorial Museum Photo Archives)

In the midst of Maritain's efforts to enlighten the Holy See about
contemporary antisemitism, the Kielce pogrom occurred in Catholic Poland. As if to punctuate Maritain's thoughts and warnings about antisemitism, forty-one Jews were massacred on July 4, 1946.[94] The incident
was provoked when a Polish boy who had run away from home returned three days later and said, in order to protect himself, that he had
been kidnapped by Jews.[95] But Kielce was not an isolated event. Attacks
on Jews between November 1944 and October 1945 were frequent,
leading to the death of 351 Jews in Poland.[96] Postwar pogroms in other
Catholic countries of eastern Europe took the lives of hundreds more.[97]

As a result of Kielce, the church was pressed to call upon the faithful
to rid themselves of antisemitism. After visiting Poland, Rabbi Philip
Bernstein, adviser to the U.S. European theater commander on Jewish
affairs, discussed the Kielce pogrom in September with Pope Pius during
a private audience. Bernstein believed that the Polish hierarchy bore responsibility for the country's antisemitism.[98] He took the position during his conversation with the pope that only the church in Poland could
mitigate antisemitism. Bernstein urged Pius to direct the Polish hierarchy to condemn the Kielce massacre specifically. Pius responded by saying that he found the pogrom "dreadful." The pope was somewhat evasive about pressuring church leaders in Poland, referring to the Iron

Curtain and consequent limitations on freedom. Pius laid responsibility for Kielce on Russian nationalism and communism.[99]

But Pope Pius promised Rabbi Bernstein that he would direct church leaders in Poland to work against antisemitism. If the pope carried out his pledge, it did not have much effect on Cardinal Hlond, primate of the Polish church, who found a way to blame Jews for Kielce. Calling the pogrom a tragedy that he sincerely regretted, Hlond denied that its cause was racial. Rather, it was a reaction against Jewish bureaucrats serving the Communist regime's attempts to restructure Polish life.[100] The local bishop of Kielce said that "no Catholic can refrain from expressing genuine and sincere regret" over the pogrom, but he avoided attributing the massacre specifically to racism. It was the result of a "combination of events which built on each other as rapidly as an avalanche."[101] Shortly after Kielce, a newspaper correspondent asked Cardinal Hlond whether the Polish bishops had considered issuing a statement condemning antisemitism and decided against it. Hlond replied that this was true, but now that Kielce had happened, they would have to rethink the matter. But the annual pastoral letter of 1947 of the Polish bishops to the faithful contains no condemnation in general or in particular of Kielce or of antisemitism.[102]

Non-Polish ad hoc committees disagreed in part with the analysis of Pope Pius and Hlond. A group called the Research Committee of Deported Jews pointed out that traditional Christian antisemitism conditioned Poles to hate Jews. They called the attention of Cardinals Sapieha and Hlond to religious pictures at a popular pilgrimage place that depicted the murder of a young Christian woman being perpetrated by Jews, one of whom was armed with a large knife, while the others were intent on gathering the blood of the butchered girl in a basin.[103] A second group, the International Emergency Conference to Combat Antisemitism, found that the Kielce murders had been perpetrated by a gang that associated Jews with Communists. Nevertheless, the investigators were certain that incidents such as Kielce had "something of a religious character about them."[104]

Like Ambassador Maritain, Munich's Cardinal Michael Faulhaber saw antisemitism as a great threat to western civilization. Five months before the Kielce pogrom, Faulhaber told a visiting Anglo-Saxon delegation that he hoped the pope would work to stamp out antisemitism in Germany and all of Europe, adding that he would ask the pope to issue a pastoral letter on this matter to all European Catholics.[105] After Kielce, American Jews pleaded with Ambassador Maritain to intercede with the pope so that "the survivors of the gas chambers and crematoria shall not again face death after the defeat of Hitlerism."[106] Maritain immediately appealed to the pope through his friend Montini. Writing, he said, as a Catholic rather than as a diplomat, Maritain declared that for a number of years he had been struck by the savage hatred of Hitler for Jews. The Nazis had intended to eliminate them as a people from the face of the earth, and had succeeded in murdering some 6 million, among whom were many thousands of infants. This crime, Maritain asserted, was beyond nature; it had a supernatural significance. Now was the time for the pope to speak out. "When I think of the part Catholicism has played in the development of antisemitism in Germany, in Europe and in places like Argentina, I see how appropriate a word from the pope would be."[107] Maritain clearly wanted the pope to seize the moment and take up world leadership in the fight against antisemitism, but neither in Germany nor in Poland did this happen. Maritain failed to convince the Holy See of the importance of the Holocaust.

Fearful that Nazism would rise again like a phoenix, American presidential advisers and their postwar proconsuls in Germany, General Clay and John J. McCloy, remained concerned about human rights and antisemitism in Germany. While they were well aware of the post–World War I circumstances that caused the demise of the Weimar Republic and the rise of Nazism, neither was an eyewitness to these events, as was Pius XII, the Vatican's onetime nuncio to Germany, who had stared down an intruding gun-toting Communist revolutionary in his Munich residence in 1919. Soon the Americans themselves became alarmed about the growth of communism in Italy and France, and they reversed their German policy in order to reinvigorate the economy of all of western Europe. The Cold War began. Realizing that his arguments for a papal-led spiritual reawakening in Europe would come to naught, Jacques Maritain resigned his ambassadorship in 1948.

Maritain saw that emotionally and mentally, Pius XII was fixated on communism, and that he would be unable to divert the pope from the realm of politics and the practical. Having saved Rome from the immediate threat of bombardment during the war, Pius reverted thereafter to his foremost fear—communism. The war's end heightened this anxiety. Russia controlled much of eastern Europe and half of Germany itself. Communist Yugoslavia supplanted Catholic Croatia. Italian Communists gained momentum. The sensational trial in 1946 under Yugoslav Communist auspices of the Catholic Croat nationalist Archbishop Alojzije Stepinac presaged the Cold War, and further unnerved the Holy See.

Always the diplomat, Pope Pius preoccupied himself during the postwar era with the great questions of European politics. Hoping desperately to shore up the postwar situation of the church against communism, Pius XII met with Generals Dwight Eisenhower and Mark Clark in September of 1945, just a few months after the war's end. Believing that a groundswell of support would emerge for the restoration of the Hapsburg monarchy in Austria and for the creation of an entirely new, great monarchical state in Catholic central Europe that might also include Croatia, Pius pressed the generals to let the voice of the people be heard.[108] Moral questions relating to antisemitism, restitution, and strict justice for war criminals fell outside the pontiff's concerns. Indeed, under the watch of Pope Pius XII, the Vatican was quite prepared to press fugitives from justice into service for the coming anti-Communist campaign.

10. Catholics and Jews after the Holocaust

While still deep in the shadow of the Holocaust, a few Christians in western Europe and North America began in the 1950s to deal with the age-old problem of church antisemitism. On the Catholic side, Augustin Bea, S.J., at the Vatican, Paul Démann in France and Belgium, Johannes Willebrands in the Netherlands, Charles Boyer, S.J., at the Gregorian University in Rome, and Gregory Baum and John Oesterreicher in North America were pioneers. In Germany itself, Gertrud Luckner established a center for Catholic-Jewish reconciliation in Freiburg. For both Protestants and Catholics, the book *Jesus and Israel,* by French educator and survivor Jules Isaac, provided seminal thought and focus.

Because Germany had perpetrated the Holocaust, changing Christian-Jewish relations could not happen there as easily or in the same manner as elsewhere in the west. The mood of the country in the 1950s did not support a topic, such as Christian-Jewish relations, that would unavoidably remind the public of the Holocaust. Helmut Gollwitzer recalled that "at the time of my return from Russia in 1950 unrepentance was definitely a characteristic of our society."[1] At mid-century, the Federal Republic of Germany had settled comfortably into its new democratic, anti-Communist posture. The past was past. This held for the Catholic church as well, which, in the absence of American reformers, could finally celebrate its "triumph" over Hitler in peace while salvaging the benefits of the Concordat from the Nazi era.[2] The Christian Democrats led the Federal Republic under the widely respected Catholic politician Konrad Adenauer, in whose power and influence the church shared.[3] In the prevailing atmosphere, most Germans, not surprisingly, found the conciliatory work of Gertrud Luckner's Freiburg circle contretemps.

Having risked her life for Jews and spent the last two years of the war in the Ravensbrück concentration camp, Luckner had found it impossible to abandon the remnant of Jewish humanity that survived the Holocaust. Already forty-five years old at the war's end and in poor physical condition, the irrepressible Luckner decided to dedicate herself anew to fighting German antisemitism and promoting Christian-Jewish reconciliation. We saw in chapter 8 that in the short term this took the form of providing relief for survivors. Christian-Jewish reconciliation, Luckner knew, would be a long-term process, simply because it meant confronting German and Christian antisemitism.

To address Christian-Jewish relations successfully, Luckner saw that she would have to function in and through her church. Unfortunately, the Vatican appeared to be suspicious of any movement that brought Catholics into contact with non-Catholics. Early in the 1950s, Pius XII suppressed the priest-worker movement in France, forced an English cardinal to end his participation in the ecumenical movement, and treated the ecumenical work of future cardinal Johannes Willebrands of the Netherlands with suspicion.[4] Earlier, Rome had refused permission for the Jesuit Pierre Chaillet to travel to New York, where he was to be honored by B'nai B'rith for his wartime rescue work.[5] Luckner fared no better. It is difficult to imagine circumstances more trying than those of the 1950s church for a Catholic activist who was a woman, a layperson, and a convert. To make matters worse, the leader of the German church, Cardinal Frings, mistrusted the Freiburg circle. Luckner managed to deflect this hostility somewhat by reminding authorities over and over again, long after the death of her bishop, Conrad Gröber, that he had commissioned her work.

Although most Germans found the Freiburg circle to be an embarrassment at best, certain national and international factors favored Luckner's cause, or at least made its pursuit possible. Luckner and her associate Karl Thieme found encouragement in the fact that their contacts in other countries were making some progress with Christian-Jewish reconciliation. At home in Germany, antisemitic or Holocaust-related events cropped up with enough regularity to give the Freiburg circle's work a grudging credibility. Incidents that made national headlines were reparations for Israel, the *Norbert Wollheim v. I. G. Farben* trial, the firing of state reparations specialist Otto Küster, and, of particular relevance to the church, an antisemitic textbook in a Catholic primary school. The past was not really past after all. In Germany, the Holocaust and the rethinking of Christian-Jewish relations were linked together much more closely than in other western lands.

Reviving Christian-Jewish Relations in Germany

Luckner's Freiburg circle, which consisted of a handful of men with solid anti-Nazi credentials such as Karl Thieme, Franz Böhm, and Hans Lukaschek, founded a journal, the *Freiburger Rundbrief,* to keep the memory of the Holocaust alive and counter antisemitism.[6] The circle stated that their objective was "to awaken in our consciousness our duties and responsibilities toward our Jewish brothers."[7] Over the years, the *Rundbrief* reestablished German-Jewish relations at a cultural level.[8] Since many of Germany's leading Jewish intellectuals had fallen victim to the Holocaust or had fled the country, very few Jews remained with whom Germans could enter into dialogue. Conversely, there were few Germans with whom Jews would want to enter into dialogue. Luckner's wartime suffering with Jews at Ravensbrück (she narrowly escaped being gassed) provided the *Freiburger Rundbrief* with a credibility that allowed it to attract Jewish readers and correspondents of international reputation, such as Martin Buber, Rabbi Leo Baeck, Ernst Ludwig Ehrlich, and Alfred Wiener.

Catholics who interested themselves in Christian-Jewish relations in the 1950s were like sixteenth-century scientists who suspected that the sun did not revolve around the earth but could not explain heliocentrism. If Jews were not to be disparaged for rejecting their Messiah, just what relation did they have to Christianity, and how should they be treated? The Holocaust had not altered the Protestant and Catholic assumption that Jews existed to be converted.[9] In fact, even the most well-intentioned Catholics, such as Jacques Maritain, thought that the enormity of the Holocaust would be so overwhelming and bewildering for Jews that they would be psychologically disposed to accept Christianity.[10]

Luckner also initially thought in terms of Jewish conversion. Since her doctorate was in social work, Luckner contacted a theologian, Karl Thieme, inviting him to join her in the work of Jewish-Catholic reconciliation.[11] Although Thieme held strong credentials for dialoguing with Jews, their conversion was initially his hidden agenda as well. Writing to Luckner in 1948, he mentioned that their missionary mission was *pro foro interno* more than "for public consumption."[12] But there was a difference between Luckner and Thieme's approach to Jews and that of other Catholics, who continued to hold that only conversion would release the individual Jew from the curse on his race. The Freiburg group urged Catholics not to utter racial slurs, and to acknowledge that Jesus

Gertrud Luckner rescued Jews during the Holocaust
and pioneered Jewish-Catholic relations after the war.
(Courtesy of the Caritas Archives)

was proud of his Jewishness. It gave preference to Jews, and lamented that they did not recognize the Messiah.[13]

Good intentions notwithstanding, Karl Thieme's preoccupation with converting Jews soon got him into hot water with Jewish correspondents. Hans Ornstein, who published two books on antisemitism shortly after the Holocaust, reacted angrily to the first edition of the Freiburg journal. How, he asked, could Thieme speak of Christian patience being tested by Jewish irreligion after all that the Jews had gone through over the last ten years? How could he speak of the Holocaust as God's warning to the Jewish people?[14] Martin Buber became similarly outraged by Thieme's reference to spiritually dead Jews in the second issue of the *Rundbrief*.[15] Thieme, attempting to get his foot out of his mouth, gamely sought to address their protests, but only Luckner's proven record of genuine concern for Jews kept them in dialogue with German Catholics. Rabbi Leo Baeck had himself survived the Holocaust, and he never forgot that Luckner was on a mission to give him relief money when she was arrested. The very first letter that Luckner received after the liberation of the Ravensbrück concentration camp was from Rabbi Baeck. Later he wrote to Luckner, "I can imagine how difficult

Rabbi Leo Baeck (*right*), who was president of the National
Representation of German Jews during the Third Reich,
helped Luckner with her rescue work during the Holocaust and
promoted her postwar work. Martin Buber (*left*) encouraged
Luckner's efforts to end antisemitism in the post-Nazi era
by sending correspondence to her newspaper.
(Courtesy of the United States Holocaust Memorial Museum Photo Archives)

[your] work is and how you meet not only with resistance and opposition but also with enemies."[16] Thus, in spite of Thieme's awkwardness
in dialogue, Jews fundamentally trusted Luckner's enterprise.

Fortunately, Thieme did not hold rigidly to his ideas about Jews.
The Freiburg circle underwent a continuous theological evolution, leading them away from viewing Jews as potential converts toward accepting Judaism's permanent validity.[17] Referring to a radio address by Jules
Isaac, during which the French survivor made mention of the inability of
Christians to abdicate their missionary effort, Thieme wrote to Martin
Buber in 1949 to say that he believed Christians should appeal to Jews
only through their example of love. By the following year, Thieme had
come to view Jews as brothers in the Word of God.[18] In 1952, Thieme
asserted that Jews are still called to the priesthood of God and are still
in the house of God.[19] That same year, he came to the conclusion that
Jews remained the People of God, and therefore they stood in an ecumenical rather than missionary relationship to Christians.[20] Thus, in less
than a decade after the publication in 1945 of his *Church and Synagogue,* which Jews roundly rejected, Thieme's thinking changed radi-

cally. The pages of the *Freiburger Rundbrief* reflected this theological journey, which was an important learning experience—dotted with controversy, to be sure—for the Freiburg circle and for the Christian readers of the *Rundbrief.*

Cardinal Frings Opposes Luckner's Work

The theological evolution and the Freiburg circle's dialogue with Jews aroused the suspicion of church authorities both in Rome and in Germany. In 1948, the Freiburg circle had gotten the bishops to admit contritely that crimes against "the people of Jewish stock" had been committed.[21] Although not nearly as strongly worded as the circle had advised, the statement won praise from Jews.[22] Thereafter the influence of the circle on the bishops declined.[23] In October of 1950, Karl Thieme wrote discouragingly to Gertrud Luckner that the bishops had become passive regarding their work.[24] His perception was on the mark; in the late 1940s, Cardinal Frings became suspicious of the Freiburg circle's philo-Semitic efforts. Then, in 1950, the Vatican issued a *monitum,* or warning, regarding indifferentism (the belief that religions are of equal value) resulting from Christian-Jewish dialogue.[25] The *monitum* was clearly intended for the Freiburg activists, because no other German Catholics were engaged in dialogue. The Vatican sent a team of investigators to check into Luckner's work. The emissaries, as we have seen, found nothing objectionable. Cardinal Frings, nevertheless, remained suspicious. In 1952, Frings sent a circular letter to German bishops that referred back to the *monitum* and warned again about indifferentism, thereby renewing the doubt and mistrust that had fallen on the Freiburg group.[26]

The cardinal's position of leadership and negative attitude adversely affected the Freiburg circle's battle against antisemitism, which had not abated during the 1950s, when Germans found a new identity as the west's first line of defense against communism.[27] As a result of the cardinal's disposition, the Freiburg circle found that it could not confront the issue of antisemitism head on. In 1950, the Freiburg circle had fashioned a strategy for a concerted attack on antisemitism, envisioning a three-pronged approach. They asked that on the first Sunday of November there be a prayer said in all churches for those who had suffered unjust assaults during the Nazi years (obviously, a commemoration of the November pogrom of 1938); secondly, that the older youth—namely, those old enough to have been tainted by Nazi antisemitism—be given more intensive instruction on the importance of the Hebrew

Scriptures; and, finally, that in catechistic work, all parishes make use of certain recommended literature against antisemitism.[28] Thieme feared that Cardinal Frings might not back the plan at the church's all-important annual meeting, the *Katholikentag*.[29] His premonition was correct; although the cardinal conceded that the effort was a "Christian concern," he blocked it from the national agenda, thereby forcing the Freiburg group to lay their plan piecemeal before each individual bishop.[30]

Clearly, Cardinal Frings did not assign antisemitism the importance the Freiburg circle gave it. Yet indications of antisemitism abounded. In September of 1949, the liberal Munich newspaper *Süddeutsche Zeitung* printed an article on German society's Holocaust awareness, titled "The Jewish Question as Test Case"; the response to the article overwhelmed the editors. The newspaper made the mistake of printing, without comment, a letter of one "Adolf Bleibtreu" (meaning "faithful to Adolf"). A riot ensued in downtown Munich, provoked by survivors living in displaced persons camps around Munich, but involving antisemitic Germans as well. The combined efforts of the German police and U.S. military police were required to quiet the disturbance. The newspaper editor later confided to Luckner that some of the letters to the editor sided with "Bleibtreu," whom he described as a genocidal antisemite.[31]

The "Bleibtreu" incident was not an isolated one. The experience of having their country occupied for an extended period of time after the Nazi era and the lost war triggered new varieties of antisemitism throughout the land. A widowed pensioner from Lower Saxony believed that eastern European Jews climbed the social ladder in Germany through dishonest dealings (the black market) and then "messed" with German girls; a Schwäbian woman and a middle Rhenish bureaucrat thought that the Morgenthau Plan was Jewish revenge; and a Bavarian widow held that the restitution claims of Holocaust survivors were unjustified.[32]

Antisemitism also found expression in the frequent and unrelenting desecration of Jewish cemeteries.[33] The *Wiener Library Journal* reported twenty-one such incidents in a seven-month period in 1947, and thirty desecrations in the British and American zones of occupation in 1949.[34] "The Nazi poison lives on," Solomon Heinemann wrote in 1950 in reference to continued desecrations.[35] Antisemitic slurs persisted in schools and public pageants such as the *Oberammergau Passion Play*, all of whose actors were former Nazis, with the exception of the one who played Judas.[36] This irritated John J. McCloy, who admitted in 1949 to the leaders of German Jewish community agencies that antisemitism was still rife on the eve of the country's return to sovereignty.[37]

An experiment by Ernst Ludwig Ehrlich, the most regular Jewish contributor to the *Freiburger Rundbrief,* illustrated an instinctive anti-semitism and vast ignorance on the part of German youth regarding the Holocaust. Ehrlich visited a Berlin Gymnasium in 1952, where he played a simulated radio drama of the Warsaw Ghetto Uprising for the purpose of stimulating the class of nineteen-year-olds to discuss Nazi racism. Ehrlich was concerned that the students would react only with plati-tudes. What instead came forth from the mouths of the students, who had been twelve years old at the war's end, was pure racist jargon. "It was frightful," Ehrlich recalled, to hear "the entire awful terminology of the Nazi period expressed in full authentic [Nazi] language."[38] Further inquiry disclosed that the students supposed that there were no Jews in their school because they were attending some other school. It had not occurred to them that Jews of their generation had been murdered dur-ing the Holocaust.

At mid-century, the interest of German church leaders in the prob-lem of antisemitism flagged. Two examples pertain to Cardinal Joseph Frings, the longtime postwar leader of the German church. The OM-GUS religious affairs office had appointed an American, Carl F. Zeit-low, to head its Society for Christian-Jewish Collaboration (Gesellschaft für christlich-jüdische Zusammenarbeit). Zeitlow hired a German, Karl Thieme—Luckner's close associate—to be his field agent. Shortly after the Vatican *monitum,* Thieme and Zeitlow sought the help of Frings in getting Catholics to protect Jewish cemeteries. Zeitlow and Thieme felt that under the leadership of Frings, the Catholic church was not re-sponding to this problem as well as the Protestant churches.[39]

An incident that arose in a Catholic elementary school in the Rhine-land illustrated that antisemitism remained a rather formidable knot within Christianity and its leaders. In 1950 it was discovered that a Catholic grade school in the state of Hesse was using a textbook that contained blatant antisemitic copy. There were flagrant slurs in a chap-ter entitled "Volk und Vaterland," and a long story in another chapter that recounted a totally fictitious incident in which Christ cursed the Jew Ahasuerus and the Jewish people. The antisemitic material dated back to the last century, but the textbook had been published in 1950.

Outraged, the president of the Society for Christian-Jewish Collabo-ration wrote to the Minister of Culture:

> We must point out that after the Hitler years disgraced the German name, anything about Jews in our school books must be positive, not negative. With regard to The Eternal Jew . . . we point out that the murder, violence,

and so on, of this piece is hardly suitable for eleven-year-old kids. It is a
disgrace that these children are exposed to the idea of the Eternal Jew who
is painted as the refuse of the world. The outcome of this for the youth
will be withdrawal from Jews and the inclination to think that what Hitler
did was correct because the eleven-year-old child will replace the millions
that died [during the Holocaust] with the "eternal jew."[40]

In an article in the journal *Michael,* Karl Thieme pointed out that the
antisemitic piece had been inserted in the text through the efforts of the
principal of the Catholic school. Borrowing words from Walter Dirks,
Thieme wrote that such "good Christians" as the principal were the
"tactless, stupid, spiritually dead, indolent" *Mitläufer* (fellow travelers)
of the Holocaust era. The German Jewish newspaper *Allgemeine Wochenzeitung der Juden in Deutschland* wrote that it was regrettable and
most thought-provoking that it required the Society for Christian-Jewish Collaboration to blow the whistle on this case, which was, after all,
an incident of twice-over institutionalized antisemitism.[41] Where were
the church and state authorities?

The leader of German Catholicism was minimally concerned by the
textbook incident. Instead of using it to speak out publicly against antisemitism, Cardinal Frings privately accused the Society for Christian-Jewish Collaboration of having used the Catholic school case as an
opportunity to attack the Christian Democratic minister of education.
Frings's reaction was indicative of the complacent milieu into which
church leaders had settled during the decade of the 1950s.

Although Americans such as High Commissioner John J. McCloy
associated antisemitism with Auschwitz, most Germans did not. By publishing facts relating to the Holocaust and postwar antisemitic occurrences, Luckner's *Freiburger Rundbrief* continually reminded Germans
of the connection. Even as a wall of silence grew up around the Holocaust elsewhere in the land, readers of the *Rundbrief* were exposed to
precise factual information: 200 Jews had committed suicide in one day
in Frankfurt; 1,400,000 Jewish children under the age of fourteen had
been murdered; and so on.[42] This kind of copy did little to bolster subscription, which hovered between 3,000 and 4,000, but it preserved a
minimal memory of the Holocaust in the Christian conscience.

Luckner Presses for Restitution for Survivors

The Freiburg circle was also outspoken regarding restitution and indemnification for survivors, an issue that was unavoidably linked to
the Holocaust. Luckner realized that there was a psychological as well

as material aspect to restitution, for which reason the Freiburg circle wanted to tie compensation to the work of eradicating antisemitism.[43] But a growing opposition among Germans stalled progress on restitution and indemnification matters.[44] Immediately after the war, virtually all Germans agreed that restitution and compensation were national obligations, but by the time the denazification ordeal wound down in 1948, German opinion had lost this focus.[45] In 1949 about 54 percent of the people favored indemnifying Holocaust survivors, but by 1952 only 33 percent did. Those most in favor of compensation were church-going Christians.[46] Reactions on the part of other Germans varied. Some thought that indemnification was all right, but that Jews should have to wait until after German war casualties were taken care of, while others thought that it was purely an administrative task, and that persons in possession of formerly Jewish property had no obligation to return it.[47] In contrast, the *Rundbrief* asserted that holders of "Aryanized" property had a subjective and objective moral obligation to make restitution.[48]

Compensation and indemnification were matters of justice, not charity. The morality of the issue was obvious, but so was the fact that the more dilatory the Germans were, the less they would end up paying. The *Freiburger Rundbrief* took note in 1949 that indemnification was still outstanding four years after the Holocaust; in the meantime, old age and sickness had increased among survivors. Their mortality rate made this clear; in the state of Nordrhein-Westfalen 35 died in 1945, 142 in 1946, 275 in 1947, 297 in 1948, and 364 in 1949.[49] As of 1955, about 25,000 survivors who had rights to compensation had died without receiving anything. Of those remaining, 40 percent were over 60 years of age, and 33 percent were between 60 and 70. Those who had succeeded in getting compensation had gotten only a fraction of it.[50] Luckner told Thieme in 1952 that her Jewish acquaintances were "completely dejected" over the indemnification issue.[51]

Immediately after the war, Germans had little ability to pay, saddled as they were with the problem of wave after wave of ethnic German immigration numbering in the millions. But by 1952 a degree of prosperity had taken root, in the opinion of Commissioner John J. McCloy.[52] Economic improvement did not bring about a change of heart about restitution and indemnification. In July of 1963, a Bundestag report maintained that the only group in Germany whose standard of living had continually fallen since the end of the war was the formerly racially persecuted.[53]

The Catholic church had made it clear that restitution and compensation constituted a moral obligation on the part of both individuals and the country.[54] As a result of the Freiburg circle's lobbying, this was affirmed by the church at its annual meetings in 1948 in Mainz, in 1949 in Bochum, and in 1950 in Passau. By the beginning of the 1950s, however, almost nothing had been accomplished at the state or federal level. Unfortunately, the church did not maintain its call for indemnification. Thieme and Luckner wanted to make compensation a major theme of the 1950 Katholikentag, but their proposal was rejected.[55] Compensation for Holocaust victims had ceased to be a high priority among Catholic church leaders; nor, as we have seen, were they even minimally pressed on this matter by Rome. Commissioner McCloy's observation that German solicitude extended more to the perpetrators of the Holocaust than to its victims and survivors applies to church leaders as well.[56]

During the 1950s, Catholic bishops left it to others to remind the German public that indemnification and restitution were moral obligations. It fell to political rather than church leaders to get out the message about the morality of the question. In urging a very reluctant German public to accept his efforts to pay reparations to the state of Israel, Konrad Adenauer said that "unspeakable crimes were committed in the name of the German people, crimes which oblige us to moral and material restitution."[57] The U.S. High Commissioner frequently reminded German politicians and the public alike that the county had a "strong moral obligation" to make restitution to Jews.[58] In the middle of the decade, when the federal government had still not passed compensatory legislation and the will to do so had flagged, the Society for Christian-Jewish Collaboration wrote to Chancellor Adenauer urging that a "law that will measure up to the debt of conscience of the German people" be passed. Yet another public official, Minister of Justice H. Wilden, reminded the public in 1955 that "compensation for the state's injustices is a primary moral obligation."[59]

Luckner soon recognized that at least in the matter of restitution, her energies would be better spent urging state and federal, rather than church, authorities to do the right thing. Unlike most other Germans, Luckner knew what it meant to have been in a Nazi concentration camp. She understood that those who had been incarcerated for political reasons came out strengthened, whereas the racially persecuted came out psychologically damaged—"lacking stability and judgment."[60] In 1950 she had been deeply hurt by the refusal of Cardinal Frings to appoint her to a restitution committee, even though she was recognized as a national leader in this effort and was one of the handful of German Christians who enjoyed the implicit trust of Jews. Luckner pleaded with the president of her organization: "In the interests of Caritas, I'd like to ask if I am to continue to be shut out."[61] Not being allowed to make restitution a major topic of the annual Catholic meeting in Passau that same year was a second rebuff. Consequently, Luckner turned her efforts toward secular authorities. In July she was appointed to the commission for restitution and compensation for the state of Baden.[62]

Early in the 1950s, Luckner traveled to Israel. She understood that since most of the Holocaust survivors had emigrated to that country, Germany should compensate the State of Israel, which had become responsible for caring for survivors, not a few of whom required psychological and economic assistance. Luckner became involved with discussions at The Hague and the Parliament of the Federal Republic about compensation for survivors that eventually led to an agreement on the sum of 500 million deutsche marks, most of which would be paid to the Israeli government. One of the negotiators credited Luckner for the success of the negotiations: "Because of your moral and national motivations you have supported compensation unreservedly. . . . Your contribution toward what is right and just has won an important struggle."[63]

The agreement had to be ratified by the Federal Republic's Parliament, and the procedure for the distribution of the indemnification money had to be defined and enacted. This still had not been accomplished in 1955, some ten years after the Holocaust. Trying to apply pressure, Luckner wrote a pamphlet disclosing that because the German states and the federal government had passed responsibility for compensation back and forth to each other, nothing had been accomplished to help the victims of the "unlawful and illegal proceedings of the Nazi state."[64] In 1955, a group of U.S. Jews wrote to Chancellor Adenauer bitterly complaining about Germany's sloth while Holocaust survivors lived in poverty. Adenauer promised the president of the Jewish World Organization, Nahum Goldmann, that he would try to pick up the pace.

The reason for the foot-dragging was that Germans lacked the will to pay. Two incidents, one involving Otto Küster and the other Norbert Wollheim, both of which attracted widespread national attention, are illustrative. After being fired by the Nazis in 1933, Küster became Germany's leading expert on indemnification and reparations after the war, only to be fired once again in 1954 by the state of Württemberg, essentially for his zealous handling of Jewish claims.[65] The significance of his dismissal extended beyond the south German state, because Küster was also the leader of the German delegation for restitution discussions with Israel.

Luckner's Freiburg circle involved itself heavily in the Küster dismissal. Their letter to the Württemberg Parliament protesting his dismissal infuriated the legislators. Luckner and her associates followed this up with a letter to Chancellor Adenauer, saying that Küster's dismissal threatened the chancellor's previous efforts to come to terms with Israel, and suggesting that he appoint Küster to a national position that would allow the work to be accelerated.[66] In September Luckner dedicated an entire edition of the *Freiburger Rundbrief* to the Küster affair.[67] Doctors, lawyers, legislators, professors, priests, and ministers from all over Germany responded positively to the edition. One of the younger bishops, appointed after the Nazi era, wrote that he hoped the issue would promote a climate of wellness and humanity toward Jews. Congratulating Luckner, Rabbi Leo Baeck wrote that the edition of the *Rundbrief* had become an historical document in its own right.[68] Küster himself said that the reason for his troubles lay in the fact that there existed in Germany "a deep inner rejection of the work for restitution."[69] The firing of Küster may have reminded Luckner of the refusal of Cardinal Frings to appoint her to a restitution committee a few years earlier. At any rate, she used the Küster affair to expose German negligence regarding compensation.

But Luckner knew that the situation was anything but encouraging. She reported in 1954 that the states had one-third less money at their disposal for indemnification than they had had the previous year, while the need of survivors had only increased with age. State governments lacked the necessary civil courage to deal with reparations expeditiously, as the firing of Küster clearly demonstrated. Politicians feared that they would be accused by the German public of overcompensating survivors. Lower-level bureaucrats, understaffed and unfamiliar with how to file claims correctly, fumbled around and procrastinated. Judges and court proceedings often made decisions that disfavored survivor-plaintiffs. Worst of all, former Nazis had infiltrated their way back into government positions, where they hampered indemnification and restitution claims.[70]

The issue of compensation remained before the German public throughout the 1950s for a second reason—the sensational case of *Norbert Wollheim v. I. G. Farben,* which dragged on from 1951 to 1957. This trial focused public attention directly and excruciatingly on the Holocaust, since Wollheim had been forced into slave labor at Auschwitz (Monowitz) for I. G. Farben, after being separated from his family, whom he never saw again, at the railroad ramps of Auschwitz-Birkenau.[71] Wollheim sued Farben for the quite reasonable sum of DM10,000 (about $2,500). The court found in favor of the plaintiff in 1953, point-ing out that witnesses for Farben lacked credibility because of their state-ments and memory lapses.

When I. G. Farben appealed the case to a higher court, Otto Küster, now released from his Württemberg position, joined Wollheim's legal team. Küster argued that indemnification was the absolute minimum that could be done in terms of humane treatment. In the meantime, in-demnification had become a national issue. As the legal teams regrouped for the second trial, German-Israeli negotiations led to an agreement in 1957 that allocated $7.5 million to former slave laborers now residing in forty-two countries around the world. Wollheim allowed his individ-ual case to be subsumed by the international agreement. The Wollheim trial provided Luckner with a second issue with which to remind Ger-man Christians, and especially their leaders, of Germany's debt to Jews.

In 1957, federal funds were at last made available for survivors of the Holocaust. Luckner hurried home from Israel to take up her Cari-tas work; she would become responsible for distributing approximate-ly $1 million to German "Jews" who had become Catholics. The final, long-delayed success of the drive for restitution by Germany for the Ho-locaust cannot, of course, be attributed principally to Luckner. Never-theless, her influence made a difference. Chancellor Adenauer took an interest in the work of the Freiburg circle and in their journal. Through intermediaries, he kept abreast of their support of restitution for survi-vors.[72] In the final analysis, the constant pressure of High Commissioner McCloy; the skill and persuasiveness of Nahum Goldmann, president of the World Jewish Congress; the leadership of Konrad Adenauer; and the tactful prompting of the United States made restitution a reality.[73] But behind the scenes, Luckner and the Freiburg circle played an important role by championing an unpopular cause, keeping it before the German public, and pressuring legislators and administrators of the Federal Re-public to fulfill Germany's obligations. Luckner was awarded Germany's highest distinction, the *Bundesverdienstkreutz,* in 1953, and in 1966 the State of Israel awarded her the Medal of the Just.

The Debate about the Holocaust Resurfaces

In the end, the public questions that Germans faced after the Holocaust, such as ongoing antisemitism and the matter of restitution, could be settled or would persist, but in neither case would the consequence be a fundamental change of hearts and minds about Jews. To whatever ex-tent this was at all possible, a theological change had to occur. Because

Germany was a Christian country, a positive characterization of the Chosen People had to replace the myth of collective Jewish guilt for the death of Christ.

Luckner recognized this from the beginning. In the very first edition of the *Freiburger Rundbrief,* she addressed the heart of the matter by reporting on an outstanding statement of the Protestant Confessing Church which affirmed that Christians had been unable to resist Nazism because they had lost their love and respect for Jews. Throughout the 1950s, the *Rundbrief* promoted an exploratory theological learning process regarding the place of Jews in salvific history. A starting point for Catholics concerned the Good Friday liturgy, which included a reference to the "perfidious Jews." Luckner and Thieme urged that a more correct and less offensive translation be adopted, a recommendation that came to pass in 1948.[74]

Theologically, the Freiburg journal plowed new ground. Controversy often resulted. German Catholics even took exception to the *Rundbrief*'s title, with its reference to the "two peoples of God" (Jews and Christians), because it affirmed the permanency of the covenant between God and the Chosen People. In 1951 the Freiburg group published a pamphlet on "Christian Attitudes Regarding the Jewish Question," in which Thieme wrote that not all Jews of the time of Christ were guilty of his crucifixion, and that no Jews of subsequent generations and centuries were.[75] The *Rundbrief* posed these and other questions undogmatically, inviting and maintaining a dialogue on them. Slowly, and not without considerable resistance from within the church, the Freiburg circle effected an attitudinal change among some Catholics toward Jews.

These developments were not peculiar to Germany. The Freiburg circle contributed to and benefited from a small international group of Catholics who were rethinking Christian-Jewish relations during the 1950s. The *Freiburger Rundbrief* closely followed the seminal work of French survivor Jules Isaac, whose book *Jesus and Israel* inspired Paul Démann and Cardinal Jules Saliège to change French catechesis on Jews so that a positive image emerged.[76] The Freiburg journal kept in regular contact with the work of leaders such as Démann, John Oesterreicher, Johannes Willebrands, Jacques Maritain, Ives Congar, Augustin Bea, Charles Boyer, and Jean Daniélou. Before Jewish convert Oesterreicher fled Hitler's Reich, he and Thieme had become close friends. The bond loosened once Oesterreicher established himself in the United States and began editing *The Bridge* at Seton Hall University, but they continued a fruitful exchange of ideas regarding Christian-Jewish relations.[77] Oesterreicher thought that Thieme's work lacked a sympathetic quality and was overly critical of secular Jews; on the other hand, he found Paul Démann overly sympathetic and overly extended—"his heart overrules his head."[78] The ideas of these innovative theologians were debated at international meetings, such as the ones in Switzerland in 1950 and in Holland in 1958, in which Luckner and Thieme played active roles. After falling under a cloud of suspicion in the Vatican at the beginning of the 1950s, Luckner and Thieme made it a point to keep in constant contact with Rome, if not with the pope himself. By the mid-1950s, they had won the support of the very people who had been sent by Pope Pius to investigate their work—Bea, Leiber, and Boyer.[79]

At home in Germany, the Freiburg circle found support among leading Catholic figures as well as Jews. Karl Rahner, himself under suspicion in Rome, and Romano Guardini, the most widely read and influential theologian in Germany in the 1950s, backed Luckner's efforts to rethink Christian-Jewish relations. Rabbi Eschelbacher wrote to Luckner congratulating her for the progress in Catholic attitudes and behavior toward Jews that he recognized had taken place since the war.[80] Luckner and Thieme organized several international conferences on antisemitism in Germany and how it might be combated. Alfred Wiener, a Jewish authority and director of the Wiener library, took part in these conferences.[81]

Amid the cool climate of the 1950s, the Freiburg circle also managed public relations well. As time passed, German bishops became more and more supportive of Luckner's work. Even some of the bishops from the Nazi era came around—Buchberger and Berning, if not Frings. Luckner's strategy was to influence the newly appointed younger bishops.[82] Luckner established contact with them when they took office and maintained it by sending them personal notes along with each new issue of her journal. A case in point was Julius Cardinal Döpfner, who became Europe's youngest bishop in 1948, at the age of thirty-five, and who was a lifelong supporter of the Freiburg circle. Another church leader of the younger generation, Joseph Stimpfle, the bishop of Augsburg, wrote a letter to the city's Jewish community on the occasion of the dedication of their new synagogue. He recalled that as a soldier during the war he had taken a room with the Schillers, a Jewish family with whom he became good friends. After the battle of Stalingrad, the Schillers heard Hitler lash out at the Jews in a radio address. They immediately came to Stimpfle's room—he was shaking, and his wife was crying. Their time, they knew, would now be short. The next day they were sent to Auschwitz. Before departing, Schiller gave Stimpfle a black jacket, which the bishop still was wearing years later in remembrance of the 6 million.[83]

By printing copy of this sort in the *Freiburger Rundbrief,* Luckner won over the younger generation of German bishops.

Beginning in 1959, German bishops made a series of remarkable statements regarding the Holocaust. Taken together, their remarks demonstrate, first, that church leaders now recognized German guilt for the Holocaust; second, that they blamed Catholic Germans, and especially church leaders, for not having spoken out against the murderous Nazi regime; and third, that they felt profoundly sorry for the Jewish people and were able to express empathy publicly and appropriately.[84] Thus, the words that OMGUS personnel had wanted to hear fifteen years earlier were finally being uttered.

The statements of the bishops were not idle words; they backed them with their pocketbook. During the twelve years from the end of the war to the time when federal funds were finally made available for the claims and needs of survivors, Luckner and others had to make do with church funds to support Catholics of Jewish origin. The need of survivors was great, and in most instances they lacked families to fall back on for support. With hundreds of survivors of the Holocaust living in poverty, and additional hundreds dying without receiving any restitution, Gertrud Luckner had pressed for the church to provide more of its own money for "Jewish" converts. She got very little. Funds allocated by the bishops for this purpose grew slowly, from DM8,858 in 1950 to DM23,743 (about $6,000) in 1958. During this period, Germany's economy grew at a record pace. The church could easily have set aside more funds for survivors. In 1959, when the country finally first awoke to feelings of guilt for the Holocaust, the amount allocated for survivors jumped to DM67,946 ($17,000).[85]

Several circumstances surrounding the bishops' change of heart and budgetary allotment deserve mention. Although the bishops spoke out several years before Rudolf Hochhuth's famous play *The Deputy,* which created a sensation because of the shadow it cast over Pius XII, it is no accident that the bishops waited until just after the death of Pius to speak out. Respected and beloved by Germans, Pius in turn never flagged in his loyalty to them. The bishops would not have wanted or dared to sever this bond.

It is also important to realize that the bishops who spoke out in 1959 were all postwar appointees. In other words, those who eventually spoke out were not those who had kept silent in 1943 and 1945. Most of the Third Reich–era bishops had died and been replaced by 1959. Of the older set, only a few remained active (including Frings in Cologne and Jaeger in Paderborn).[86]

Finally, church leaders were not the only public people to speak out in 1959. A number of incidents had suddenly and finally aroused the German public to the horror of the Holocaust. Suspicion was aroused about public officials such as Hans Globke, who had held a number of high positions in government. Although Globke had secretly funneled information about the Holocaust to Margarete Sommer in Berlin, he had also helped implement the racist policies of the Nazis. Since Chancellor Adenauer refused to fire him, cynicism about government officials began to spread in Germany, especially among the youth.[87] Adding to this feeling were the trials of war crimes perpetrators, now taking place in German rather than U.S. courts, that exposed the public to the frightfulness of the Holocaust and demonstrated to them that they rubbed shoulders daily with former murderers.

The case of SS doctor Hans Eisele, a formerly observant Catholic, received national publicity. Eisele, twice condemned to death for his war crimes at Buchenwald, Dachau, and Netzweiler, was saved from the gallows by pleas from German bishops and from Bishop Muench. He subsequently received full amnesty in 1952, and in spite of his SS background and convictions, he received DM3000 from the Bavarian state fund for late-returning veterans and an interest-free loan of DM25,000 with which he developed a very successful medical practice in a posh Munich suburb. In 1956, Jewish survivors gave new testimony against Eisele, accusing him of killing hundreds of Jews with lethal injections. An indictment was issued against the former Nazi doctor, but before he could be arrested he was spirited out of the country by the underground SS organization, the *Ehemaligen*. An unrepentant Eisele reemerged in Egypt, which had no extradition treaty with Germany. All of the circumstances surrounding the Hans Eisele case made front-page national news in Germany week after week. The country was startled to discover that a good burgher such as Eisele was actually a mass murderer.[88]

In 1960, just when public opinion had become aroused over the Holocaust, Adolf Eichmann was put on trial in Israel, charged with masterminding the murder of millions of Jews. More than anything else, it was the Eichmann trial in Jerusalem that electrified Germany. For the first time since the Nuremberg trials, the case provided Germans with an overview of the totality of human slaughter that had come to be known as the Holocaust. With the nation's focus riveted on the Holocaust, Germans heard Eichmann's chief prosecutor, Gideon Hausner, suggest that the Vatican had known about the Holocaust, but that Pope Pius did not speak out about it because of sensitivity to the predicament in which it would have placed German Catholics. With that, the conduct of the church itself during the Nazi era and in connection with the Holocaust became a matter of public debate in Germany.

Gertrud Luckner had always known that Catholics and the church had not reacted vigorously, to say the least, during and after the Holocaust. But she also knew that it would be fatal for her cause to point the accusatory finger. Now, however, with the discussion about the church launched from other quarters, Luckner gave it great play in the *Freiburger Rundbrief*. Almost every German family, Luckner noted, was hotly questioning and discussing their country's past. The stage was set once again for the church's response. It marked a turning point. The church exchanged its garments of triumphalism for those of penance. At the outset of the trial, Bishop—later Cardinal—Julius Döpfner published an open letter in which he told in graphic detail about the murders of a specific group of Romanian children who were exterminated after a cruel period of waiting. It shames us, Döpfner concluded, that this took place in the Christian west. Another bishop, Franz Hengsbach of Essen, said, "clearly or not so clearly, . . . all of us have a share in the sin [of the atrocities]."

In 1961, Luckner's Freiburg circle once again influenced Catholics throughout Germany. The bishops directed that on Sunday, June 11, a prayer for the persecuted Jews, which Luckner's group had provided, should be offered in all of the nation's Catholic churches. It read, in part, "we confess before You that millions of persons in our midst were murdered because they belonged to the race from which the Messiah took on flesh. . . . We beseech You: teach all those among us, who are guilty through deed, omission, or silence, understanding and conversion."[89]

When the German bishops finally spoke out about the Holocaust, their voices joined those of television, radio, and the press.[90] Does this mean that the bishops spoke insincerely—that they had waited until such time as the Holocaust had become *salonfähig* before stepping forward?[91] No; we may suppose that they had been held in check by the dual authority of the pope and of their titular leader, Cardinal Frings. Over the course of a dozen years, Luckner's Freiburg circle made steady inroads on the triumphalism of the post-Nazi Catholic church, winning over the younger generation of bishops. The sincerity of their penitential words regarding the Holocaust and their commitment to reversing antisemitism would be demonstrated in a critical way during the coming years at the Second Vatican Council.

11. The Holocaust Recalled, Antisemitism Renounced
The Second Vatican Council

Led by a new pope, John XXIII, and compelled by the memory of the Holocaust, the Catholic church reversed its 2,000-year tradition of antisemitism during the Second Vatican Council in 1965.

How can this extraordinary turnabout be explained? The title of the Council's revolutionary document—*Nostra Aetate* (*In Our Times*)—offers a clue. At the end of his life, Pope Pius XI had taken strong steps to counter racism and rethink Christian-Jewish relations. By asserting that Christians are spiritual Semites, Pius XI hinted at what was to come in the Second Vatican Council's *Declaration on the Relationship of the Church to Non-Christian Religions*. But the pope died before he could instill his vision in the draft of the encyclical, and his successor, Pius XII, was preoccupied with other concerns. When in 1950 Pope Pius XII declared the doctrine of the Assumption of the Blessed Virgin, ancient traditions in both the eastern Orthodox and western church stood behind the pronouncement. By contrast, the eastern church opposed *Nostra Aetate,* and nothing had transpired theologically in the western church in ancient times to prepare the world for the step taken by Vatican II. Indeed, the pronouncement of the Council ran counter to the teaching of the Fathers of the Church and the practices and beliefs of centuries gone by. The Council's declaration was a product of our times.

The Holocaust, not tradition, was the formative event that occasioned the church's somersault. Two old men, both of whose lives had been touched by the Holocaust, provided the immediate spark that generated *Nostra Aetate*. While stationed in Istanbul as a papal diplomat during the war, the future pope, Angelo Roncalli, observed firsthand the

French survivor Jules Isaac wrote the
groundbreaking work *Jesus and Israel* while
in hiding in France during the Holocaust.
(Courtesy of Dr. Eva Fleischner)

torture of the Jews and personally participated in their rescue. Jules Isaac, a French survivor who lost most of his family to Auschwitz, dedicated his life to dissolving the Christian antisemitic tradition. The pope and the Jewish scholar made history when they met in Rome in 1959.

Isaac's 1949 and 1959 Papal Audiences

Jules Isaac's two visits to Rome make obvious the sudden shift in Vatican policy that papal succession triggered. In 1949, Pius XII gave the French survivor a private audience. His reception, as Isaac himself described it, was typical of the experiences of others with Pope Pius: "I was received with such complete openness and such obvious good will that I felt encouraged to speak my heart freely."[1] Isaac began by telling the pope how he had come to the study of Jewish-Christian relations. He must have related how he completed the manuscript of *Jesus and Israel* during the Holocaust after receiving a secret letter from his wife, who was being transported to Auschwitz, encouraging him to save himself and complete his task. Isaac then explained that his objective was to cleanse Christian teaching of falsehoods about Jews. He went on to say that he had been working with well-intentioned Catholics, and that together they had formulated and agreed upon the Seelisberg theses (de-

Germaine Bocquet, a Catholic member of the
French underground, hid Isaac and brought him
the books he needed to write *Jesus and Israel.*
(Courtesy of Dr. Eva Fleischner)

fined below). Pope Pius, Isaac reported, listened to him attentively and
sympathetically and promised to look over the theses. In fact, the theses
aroused the pope's suspicions.

Isaac's book and the Seelisberg theses might never have become reality had it not been for a French woman, Germaine Bocquet. Bocquet hid
Jules Isaac from the Gestapo in 1943 and provided him with the historical literature and documents he needed to write *Jesus and Israel.* Published shortly after the war, Isaac's study would in time become critically
important for the change in Catholic teaching about Jews that resulted
from the Second Vatican Council. Bocquet and her husband were members of the French underground resistance, though not of Amitié Chrétienne. As resistance-minded Catholics, they undoubtedly read the journal *Témoignage Chrétien.*

Bocquet's rescue of Isaac was accidental in two respects. She and her
husband had been asked to hide him without having any idea that he
was a well-known French educator.[2] As resistance workers, they agreed
simply because he was a Jewish refugee from the Nazis. There was also
the happenstance of Bocquet's unusual religious background. The child
of atheists, she had attended public schools, avoiding the traditional
Catholic antisemitic teaching about the curse that Jews as a people had

acquired for killing Christ. When Bocquet rebelled against her parents and converted to Catholicism, she took instruction from a philo-Semitic woman who had been influenced to teach positively about Jews by Jacques Maritain.

As a result of these circumstances, Bocquet was amazed to learn from Isaac about Christian antisemitism, and Isaac was amazed to meet a Catholic who was free of antisemitism. What the Nazis were doing to Jews convinced Isaac, himself an assimilated Jew and an accomplished historian, that he must dedicate himself to exposing the roots of Christian antisemitism. During the nearly two years that Bocquet hid Isaac, she made trips to various libraries to bring him the research material he needed to write *Jesus and Israel*. Isolated on a rural farm in the Berry region of France, Isaac used Bocquet as a foil for his seminal ideas that were destined to change Christian-Jewish relations. It was not until Isaac had nearly finished his work that he learned that almost all of his family had perished in Auschwitz.

The Seelisberg theses consisted of four positive and six negative assertions. Briefly, they affirmed that both the Old and New Testaments were inspired by one and the same God; that Jesus was Jewish; that the disciples, apostles, and first martyrs were Jewish; and that the command to "love God and neighbor" is found in both testaments. They denied that the Jewish religion ended with Christianity; that the word "Jew" means "enemy of Christ"; that the blame for the death of Christ should be attributed to all Jews; that Jesus, dying on the cross, cursed his crucifiers; that the Jewish people are cursed; and that the first members of the church were not Jewish.

The Catholics who had collaborated with Isaac in formulating the Seelisberg theses included Jacques Maritain, president of the International Council of Christians and Jews, Karl Thieme, and Gertrud Luckner. Maritain, as we have seen, had pressed Rome emphatically to take the lead in condemning the Holocaust atrocities and European antisemitism. He had resigned his ambassadorship one year before Isaac's visit, when he saw that his efforts were to no avail. Luckner and Thieme were enthusiastic about the Vatican's reception of Isaac, hoping it boded well for the work of their Freiburg circle. In the spring of 1950, six months after Isaac's audience with Pius, Thieme visited Rome for the purpose of giving curial officials the opportunity to review the Seelisberg theses. No one would make an official statement, but the theses were given tentative approval. Thieme also visited Robert Leiber, the pope's German Jesuit confidant. Leiber, troubled by the impact that Nazism had had on

German youth, many of whom no longer believed that the God of the Jews was the same as the God of the Christians, expressed interest in the Freiburg circle's work and said that he hoped that the pope himself would someday make a statement on Christian-Jewish reconciliation.

This never occurred. Instead, in October 1950, the Holy Office issued the *monitum,* or warning, and sent Bea, Leiber, and Boyer to investigate the Freiburg circle. What went wrong? A number of possibilities come to mind. The International Council on Christians and Jews, with which the Seelisberg working group was associated, gave high priority to confronting Christian antisemitism, a problem that held little interest for the pope. Second, the same working group that produced the theses had also called for recognition of the State of Israel, to which the Vatican was opposed. Third, besides the International Council there were several other international organizations, which overlapped or interacted with each other, that endorsed the Seelisberg theses and advocated improving Christian-Jewish relations. The approach that some of these organizations took to the problem of antisemitism was rooted in the American experience of religious pluralism, which the Vatican interpreted as indifferentism (the idea that all religions are good, and that the individual should choose which is right for himself). In the mid-1950s, the Vatican silenced American Jesuit theologian John Courtney Murray for his advocacy of religious freedom. Whatever the exact reason for Rome's negative reaction to the Seelisberg theses, it is certain that Pope Pius did not diffuse them. Jules Isaac's mission came to naught.

The pioneers of Jewish-Catholic relations received no direction or encouragement from Pius XII. As we have seen, the Vatican was highly suspicious of their work in the early 1950s. Thieme, Luckner, and Willebrands learned that by keeping in touch with Monsignor Bea and Cardinal Alfredo Ottoviani, they could shield themselves from harassment.[3] Obviously Rome was not taking the lead.

But an archaeological discovery greatly boosted the nascent interest of Christians in Christian-Jewish relations. In the late 1940s and the 1950s, the discovery of the Dead Sea Scrolls disclosed the spiritual vitality of the Jews shortly before the time of Christ. Bea's scholarship on the Sacred Scriptures, made possible by Pius XII's 1943 encyclical *Divino Afflante Spiritu,* also infused the church with an appreciation for Judaism and kindled Bea's enthusiasm for Christian-Jewish relations. But he was not able to found the Secretariat on Religious Relations with the Jews until 1959, when he was named a cardinal by the newly elected Pope John. In short, the 1950s witnessed no groundswell of interest in

Christian-Jewish relations within the church of a magnitude that could account for the Council's deliberations of the early 1960s that produced *Nostra Aetate*.

Isaac's second visit to Rome produced dramatically different results. Probably lured by Pope John's liturgical reforms that eliminated negative depictions of Jews, Isaac decided to risk his luck in Rome a second time, eleven years after his first unproductive attempt. His objective remained exactly what it had been in 1949, to rid Catholic religious teaching of falsehoods about Jews.

Shortly before Isaac's visit, it had been decided that the Council would include a discussion on the relationship of the church to non-Christian religions. But Judaism was not included. During his audience, Isaac suggested to Pope John that the Council appoint a subcommittee to review relations of the church with Jews. The pope responded immediately that he had been thinking the very same thing from the moment Isaac's visit began. John XXIII then did an amazing thing: he sent Isaac himself to see Cardinal Bea, to tell him to include the Jews in the Council's deliberations. The cardinal was stunned to find that the pope had sent an 84-year-old Jewish messenger to confide his wishes to him.[4]

The Holocaust and the Conciliar Debate about Deicide

Once the consideration of the Jews was included in the Council's agenda, it became one of the most controversial issues of the long proceedings, and the one most publicized by the worldwide media. After *Nostra Aetate* was finally adopted by the Council, Cardinal Bea remarked that if he had known how difficult a process it would prove to be, he doubted if he would have had the courage to undertake it. What made the statement on relations with Jews so problematic?

There were three stumbling blocks. First, many Council Fathers did not understand the thinking of the small and isolated seminal groups that had been rethinking Christian-Jewish relations during the previous decade. Second, Pope John, who had initiated the discussion of the Jews, died in 1963, before *Nostra Aetate*'s passage. Finally, international politics swirled around the existence of an Israeli state in Palestine, making any statement on Jews a lighting rod for controversy.

From the beginning of the Council, the word "deicide" was the crux of the debate over the declaration on Jews. Cardinal Bea warned the Council Fathers of world Jewry's high expectations; they would have to decide how to deal with the issue of deicide. This remained the sticking point of the deliberations. How to separate the guilt of some Jews for

Christ's death without assigning collective guilt? Most—probably all—of the Council Fathers had grown up in a Catholic tradition that blamed all Jews of Christ's day for his crucifixion. Many also believed, if vaguely, in the curse on the once Chosen People. Furthermore, the fathers did not wish to put the Council in the position of contradicting scripture, which had always conveyed the idea to Christians that the Jews crucified Christ. Yet, remarkably, during the course of deliberations, the great majority of the fathers ended up wanting the term "deicide" explicitly renounced. In the words of the second draft, "the Chosen People cannot without injustice be termed a deicidal one."

When Pope John died in 1963, world Jewry lost a great friend, and Cardinal Bea lost his most powerful support for a strongly worded conciliar statement on Jews. Soon after his election, John XXIII had interrupted the Good Friday liturgy in St. Peter's when one of the celebrants used the word "perfidious" in reference to Jews. John had the prayer repeated with the word omitted. Subsequently, the pope had all negative attributes about Jews, such as references to their "veiled hearts" and "blindness," supplanted in the official liturgy with positive phrases—"the People to whom God first spoke." By eradicating those negative images of Jews from the liturgy, which had provoked centuries of anti-semitism on the part of Catholics, Pope John fulfilled a promise he had made to Jewish leaders in Turkey during the Holocaust.[5] In 1960, when a group of American Jews representing the United Jewish Appeal came to Rome to thank Pope John for his rescue work during the Holocaust, the pope greeted them with the words "I am Joseph, your brother!" (Joseph was one of the pope's baptismal names). In this simple, direct manner, John XXIII showed that he wanted to remove barriers between Christians and Jews.[6]

Nostra Aetate had not yet been finalized when John XXIII died; thereafter, Cardinal Bea found progress on the declaration slow. The proposal for the declaration had come from Pope John himself, and when it became controversial, Pope John intervened decisively. In order to move action on the declaration along, Bea had written an article in 1962. "Are the Jews Guilty of Deicide and Are They Forever Dammed?" was slated to be published in the Italian Jesuit journal *Civita Cathol-ica,* but Secretary of State Cardinal Tardini, fearing Arab reaction, requested its withdrawal. Bea acceded but published it, using a pen name, in the German Jesuit journal *Stimmen der Zeit.*[7] An Italian Jew then translated the article into several languages, whose versions were distributed among the Council Fathers, causing the issue of the declaration on Jews to resurface abruptly. Acting unilaterally, Pope John wrote a

It was Pope John, not his predecessor Pius XII,
who officially eradicated antisemitism from the
Catholic church.
(Photograph courtesy of the Archdiocese of
Milwaukee Archives)

note to Bea saying that he agreed with the article's position and directing him to proceed with the declaration's development.[8] Had Pope John lived until the Council finished its work in 1965, the declaration on the Jews would, without doubt, have been stronger.

In 1964, by the time the fourth draft of *Nostra Aetate* was ready for deliberation, most Council Fathers wanted a powerful statement that freed Jews of the accusation of deicide. Twenty-one fathers spoke explicitly about this point, and an additional six urged that the declaration should attribute the Lord's death to the sins of all people. Most Council Fathers, knowing that Pope John had wanted an expression of love for the Jewish people, urged the Council to adopt a positive statement that went beyond recanting deicide. These sentiments sparked great adulation for the Council among the press of western Europe and North America. Such praise was counterbalanced by a tidal wave of negative criticism from Israel's Arab neighbors. The intensely nationalist Arab states, many newly created since the Second World War, lobbied intensively against the Council's plan to make a statement favorable to Jews, whose homeland had been placed in their midst in 1948. The militancy that would set off the Six-Day War in 1967 was heating up. The Patriarchs of the Near Eastern church jointly visited Pope Paul VI (Montini) to tell him that the Council's proposed declaration on the Jews constituted a major problem for them because of possible retaliation against Catholics living as minorities in Arab states.[9] These Fathers joined with conservatives at the Council to weaken as much as possible any proposed statement on Jews.

Paul VI lacked his predecessor's firm commitment to Christian-Jewish reconciliation and sensitivity to the Holocaust. As we have seen, Giovanni Montini's experience in the Vatican had been in the Secretariat of State. In that capacity, Montini had a conversation in 1945 with Gerhard Riegner, during which he doubted Riegner's word that 1.5 million Jewish children had actually perished in the Holocaust.[10] During the Council's deliberations, when many Fathers expressed regrets about Christian antisemitism in connection with the Holocaust, Pope Paul remained on the defensive. In fact, while the Council was in session, Paul wrote a justification of Pius XII's response to the Holocaust in answer to Rolf Hochhuth's play *The Deputy*.[11]

As Pope Paul VI, Montini continued to have diplomatic concerns. With the fate of *Nostra Aetate* far from decided, the pope traveled to the Holy Land with the intention of relaxing tension between Arabs and Jews. His trip had the opposite effect. Arab radio and television repeatedly accused the Jews of attacking them just as they had attacked Christ 2,000 years before. A Syrian broadcast asked why the church was speaking on behalf of Jews at a time when Jews were slaughtering Arabs, when it had not spoken up for the Jews when they were being slaughtered by Hitler. The Council Fathers and Bea's secretariat personnel became concerned about Arab retaliation against Christians. Was the declaration on Jews untimely? Should it not be postponed? Could the intent of the declaration not be dealt with bureaucratically by the Secretariat? At this point, the declaration was in jeopardy on purely tactical grounds.

With the Council in a muddle over what action to take, a German bishop, not previously heard from, gave an electrifying address. Making direct reference to the recently released sensational play *The Deputy*, Bishop Josef Stangl told the Council Fathers that a storm of debate had arisen in Germany concerning the conduct of Pope Pius XII and the German church during the Holocaust. Now the moment of truth was upon the Council. Would it choose the way of candor and justice or the way of tactics and diplomacy? Using the same word that Hochhuth had chosen for the title of his play, Stangl declared, "If we speak in the name of God, in the name of Jesus Christ, as the *deputies* of the Lord, then our message must be [a clear] 'Yes, yes!' [or] 'No, no'—the truth, not tactics."[12] Stangl's moving address broke the ice; the Council Fathers moved ahead with deliberations on *Nostra Aetate*. A German bishop had made a significant contribution to reversing the church's antisemitism.[13]

Back in Rome, Pope Paul intervened both positively and negatively on the proposed declaration on Jews. Seeking a watered-down declaration that would not free Jews from the accusation of deicide, and hinting that the pope had authorized them to intervene, a coalition of curial officials and conservative Fathers informed Bea that a newly appointed conciliar committee would assume responsibility for formulating the statement. A brouhaha ensued. Bea did not believe that the declaration's opponents had gotten their marching orders from Pope Paul, who confirmed his suspicions. The leading voices among the Council Fathers also took issue with the curia's obvious attempt to undermine the Council's authority. Cardinal Frings, who had emerged as one of the Council's most articulate spokesmen, convened a meeting at his residence in Rome for the purpose of drafting a protest against the curial interference. Nineteen cardinals signed the letter, a strong enough showing to cause the pope to side with them against the proposed committee. For a second time a German had been decisive in the process that would lead the Council to renounce antisemitism.

That the German in question here was none other than Cardinal Josef Frings is surprising, given his record of lack of support for Christian-Jewish relations since the Holocaust. Had the cardinal undergone a change of heart? As one of the Council's most prominent leaders, Frings would have found it difficult to oppose the majority—including, of course, the great majority of German bishops—who favored a strongly worded statement that was favorable to Jews. As a reformist, Frings fought against curial power, which in the past had often eclipsed the power of the bishops. The attempt to form a committee to draft a watered-down statement on the Jews was clearly a curial design to skirt around the Council's bishops. Fring's protest letter was an effort on his part to confront the curia. That the issue involved Jews may have been of secondary importance to the cardinal. His own statement in support of *Nostra Aetate* was rooted in Scriptural exegesis rather than—as was the case with many of his German colleagues—in compunction over the Holocaust. The cardinal underwent a change of mind more than a change of heart.[14]

In the course of the Council's four years of deliberations, the fathers vacillated about an explicit rejection of the word "deicide." Three times it was inserted in the draft, and three times it was deleted. Those who opposed the Council's plan to make a favorable statement on Jews did so for different reasons. For some, pastoral considerations took precedence; for others, theological considerations; and still others were held back by diplomatic sensitivity. This disparate opposition to *Nostra Aetate* coalesced around the word "deicide." In the end, Bea sought a compromise by proposing a draft of *Nostra Aetate* that omitted the word "deicide" but explicitly rejected the notion that Jews were collectively guilty of Christ's death. The majority of the fathers attributed the omission of deicide from the text to Roman diplomacy—a victory over total frankness.[15]

Any thought among the more liberal-minded Fathers of reinserting "deicide" in the declaration before the Council took its final vote was dealt a crushing blow by Pope Paul when in 1965 he gave a sermon on Passion Sunday that directly accused the Jews of deicide. With everything on the line, Pope Paul sided with the conservatives with his exegesis of a passage in the gospel of St. John that relates the passion and death of Christ.[16] As reported in *L'Osservatore Romano,* Pope Paul said that the Jewish people refused to accept the Messiah whom they had awaited for thousands of years, and that when Christ revealed himself to them they "derided, scorned and ridiculed him, and, finally, killed him."[17] Nothing could have been further from the spirit of the drafts of *Nostra Aetate* that the Council had been reviewing than the pope's words. Nothing could have been more out of touch with the Christian-Jewish dialogue that had been in progress for the previous ten years. Nothing could have been further from the disposition of John XXIII. Understandably, protests from world Jewish leaders were loud. How, Rabbi Elio Toaff asked, could the pope accuse the Jewish people of killing Christ just when the Council seemed to be prepared to abrogate this curse?[18]

Even in its final compromise version, *Nostra Aetate* was a stunning pronouncement. It affirmed that the crucifixion of Christ "cannot be blamed upon all Jews then living, without distinction, nor upon the Jews of today." The Fathers proclaimed that Jews are not "repudiated or cursed by God." With these few words, they renounced centuries of Christian antisemitism, which, as we have seen, was still prevalent in certain areas of Europe on the eve of the Holocaust. Furthermore, the declaration retained in its tenor something of Pope John's positive feelings: "The Jews still remain most dear to God."

Did the decree fulfill Pope John's hope "to counter the boundless and abysmal hate of those times with a enduring word of love"?[19] Yes, but only partially. The Council Fathers knew full well that theirs was a belated work. One after the other, they alluded to the Holocaust. Cardinal Augustin Bea, decrying antisemitism and Nazism, referred directly to the Holocaust and to National Socialism in his first address on Jews to the Council Fathers in November 1963.[20] Above all, the Germans drew their motivation from the calamity that the Christian west had brought upon the Jews. As the Council got under way, the German contingent apologized publicly for the "inhumane extermination of the Jewish people." During deliberations in 1964, the German bishops issued a letter saying that they especially welcomed the Council's statements on the Jews "because we are aware of the awful injustices that were perpetrated against the Jews in the name of our people." The statement created a sense of enormous awe in the Fathers.[21]

Non-German Council Fathers also recalled the tradition of Christian antisemitism and the Holocaust time and again during their protracted debates. "The injustices of the centuries cry out for amends" (Ritter); "How many [Jews] have suffered in our times? How many died because Christians did not care and kept silent?" (Cushing); "A truly Christian declaration cannot omit the fact the Jewish people have been subjected to centuries of injustices and atrocities by Christians" (O'Boyle); "[For the Jews, the last war] was a time of completely gross atrocities" (Elchinger); "We condemn the injustices done to Jews, the outbreaks of hate, the beatings, the murders and the pogroms to which they have been subjected" (Daem); "Without doubt it would be unjust to accuse all European Christians of the murder of six million Jews in Germany and Poland in our times. In the same manner, I emphasize, it is unjust to condemn the entire Jewish people for the death of Christ" (Heenan).[22]

Many of the Fathers would have liked the declaration on Jews to include an explicit apology for centuries of Christian antisemitism. The declaration fell short of this but stated that the church "deplores the hatred, persecutions, and displays of antisemitism directed against the Jews of any time and from any source." Because of the many penitent statements made by the Fathers during the deliberations, it was widely understood that *Nostra Aetate* was an implicit acknowledgment of Christian guilt for the Holocaust, and for Christian antisemitism down through the ages. The condemnation of antisemitism, together with the declaration's positive assertions about Jews, came close to fulfilling John XXIII's vision, but a bolder, more emphatic declaration would doubtless have been forthcoming from the Council had the pope lived until 1965.

When the Council finally voted overwhelmingly to ratify *Nostra Aetate*, Paul VI greeted it warmly. "The Jews must never be the "object of our disdain or mistrust but the object of our respect, love and hope."[23] These words, spoken in the fall of 1965, are difficult to reconcile with Paul's Passion Sunday sermon of the spring of that year.

Although Jews were disappointed over the omission of the word "deicide," they praised the Council's statement. A spokesperson for the American Jewish Committee called it a significant event in the history of Judeo-Christian relations. Despite some weaknesses, "the declaration rejects the myth of the collective responsibility of the Jews for the crucifixion, a myth that has caused so much harm in the past."[24] The president of Amitié Judéo-Chrétienne said, "I see the declaration as a beginning, a point of departure. After so many bloody centuries, the Church has finally renewed authentic dialogue with Judaism."[25]

Even though *Nostra Aetate* has been sorely tested again and again over three decades since the Second Vatican Council, these evaluations have proven correct. During the 1980s, at a time when the Vatican had still not recognized the state of Israel, Pope John Paul II met with Yasir Arafat, leader of the Palestine Liberation Organization, an audience which the Israeli government characterized as "revolting."[26] Later in the same decade, Polish Carmelite nuns provoked international Jewish indignation when they established a convent in the immediate vicinity of Auschwitz. An antisemitic sermon by Cardinal Jozef Glemp, primate of Poland, led to increased acrimony before an international committee of Jewish and Catholic leaders resolved the problem.[27] In 1994, John Paul II once again stirred up outrage among both Jews and Catholics by conferring a papal knighthood on Austria's president Kurt Waldheim, former secretary general of the United Nations, whose carefully concealed past included time served as an intelligence officer with the German army when it committed atrocities in the Balkans. A severe strain lies ahead as Pope John Paul proceeds, against the express request of the Israeli government, with the beatification of Pope Pius XII.

These quite serious disagreements notwithstanding, the Vatican has pressed ahead with *Nostra Aetate*. In 1974, the Holy See gave follow-up instructions to the entire church, "Guidelines for Implementation of *Nostra Aetate*." A further step in implementation came in 1985, when "Notes on the Correct Way to Present the Jews and Judaism in the Preaching and Catechesis of the Catholic Church" was issued.[28] Finally, in 1998 the flawed but basically affirmative statement "We Remember" recalled the Holocaust sorrowfully, and was received by Jews internationally with guarded praise. In addition, Pope John Paul II has stated publicly that *Nostra Aetate* will bind the church forever.[29]

Catholic-Jewish relations, born of the Second Vatican Council just thirty-five years ago, have experienced and will continue to experience very trying and sometimes embarrassing growing pains. The three decades that have passed since the council's deliberations are mere minutes in relation to 2,000 years of Christian antisemitism. Nevertheless, the new disposition of the church toward Jews is alive and appears to be irreversible.[30] We may view *Nostra Aetate* as the Catholic church's answer to Auschwitz. Was it an adequate response? Of course not; nothing could be worth the slaughter of the Holocaust. But if unmerited suffering is redemptive, then 6 million Jewish men, women, and children redeemed the Catholic church and freed it from its sin of antisemitism.

12. Epilogue

Looking back, it may appear to us that two popes, Pius XII and John XXIII, dominated the history of Catholicism and the Holocaust. In view of the church's autocratic character, this can hardly be denied. Pope Pius XII could not have halted the Holocaust, but even without a public protest, he could have communicated with church leaders throughout Europe, admonishing those who disdained the Jewish people and encouraging all of them to urge Catholics to provide shelter for Jews. The consequence would have been fewer Catholic collaborators and bystanders, on the one hand, and more Catholic rescuers and fewer victims, on the other. In contrast to Pius's passivity, Roncalli acted energetically to save Jews and, as John XXIII, publicly showed his love and respect for them. When he incorporated Jews into the agenda of the Second Vatican Council, his positive convictions about them became official church teaching.

Pius XII's record regarding Jews over twenty years in the chair of St. Peter was reversed in the few short years of John XXIII's pontificate (1958–1963). What prevented Pope Pius from at least taking the initial steps toward reconciliation with Jews, if not during the Holocaust, then afterward? Granted, no one perceived a need to do this immediately after the war. As we have seen, Jewish survivors as well as the leaders of major Jewish organizations paid homage to the pope for his efforts on behalf of their people during the Nazi genocide. But why did Pope Pius persist in taking steps that seemed, and indeed were, inimical to the Jews and to the memory of those who had been slaughtered? Why did he ignore antisemitism? Why did he seek amnesty for atrocity perpetrators? Why did he allow Vatican-affiliated organizations to expedite the escape of war crimes fugitives? Why did he disapprove of Catholic efforts to reconcile with Jews?

Three considerations explain these deficiencies. The first is Pius XII's fixation on diplomacy. At the very beginning of the war, Pius decided to separate diplomatic from moral matters. He then denounced German atrocities in Poland while remaining silent about German aggression. The first year of the war, when Catholic countries were on the giving and receiving end of genocide, and when the Nazis had not yet determined the fate of the Jews, presented the ideal window of time for the Vatican to denounce genocide. Unfortunately, just months after the beginning of the war, as soon as the Nazis threatened retaliation, Pius ended the Vatican's denunciations of atrocities. The pope abdicated his right as leader of the Catholic church to make pronouncements based on moral principle.

Having retreated from the ethical sphere, Pope Pius was left with secular matters, that is to say, with diplomacy. During the Holocaust, he confined himself to diplomatic channels in his efforts to save Jews. Probably believing that his wartime record with regard to the Jews was a credible one, Pius continued on a diplomatic track after the war. His absolute highest priority was to win assurance that the occupational authorities in Germany would recognize the validity of the Concordat that he had concluded with the Nazi government in 1933. He was completely preoccupied with this contractual relationship. Before the war had even ended, Pius let the U.S. State Department know that he still considered the Concordat to be valid.[1] When the pope's envoy to Germany reported back to him that the Americans and British found this objectionable, Pius told Bishop Muench to disregard their objections.[2] In 1945, German bishops themselves were unenthusiastic about renewing the Concordat.[3] Pius nevertheless pressed on and succeeded in getting the occupational authorities to recognize it.

The next diplomatic hurdle was to persuade the new government of the Federal Republic of Germany to recognize it as well. Pius told his envoy, Bishop Muench, that he wanted the Concordat preserved to the last detail, and that he was to stand firm—to "talk up to the Germans."[4] When negotiations did not go well at first, Pius sent Cardinal Frings a public telegram in which, calling in a favor, he reminded the German people of his kindness and generosity toward them immediately after the war.[5] Should the federal government refuse to recognize the Concordat, the pope instructed his envoy to protest publicly, citing it as a break with a legal obligation.[6] During Muench's annual visits to Rome, his conversations with Pope Pius always dealt with the Concordat, sometimes exclusively so.

In 1949, when the western allies were ready to return sovereignty to Germany, Pius kept his focus on diplomacy. His absolute highest priority was that his envoy become the very first person to present his diplomatic credentials to the Federal Republic of Germany, in this way becoming the doyen of the diplomatic corps in Bonn, just as he had been thirty-one years earlier.[7] Although being the doyen of the diplomatic corps carried more formal than actual significance, the Holy See treated it as a matter of greatest importance—prestige for the Vatican.[8] Having the honor of being doyen was but a small building block in Pius's dream of a powerful Germany linked to the Vatican legally through a Concordat, but Pius attended unrelentingly to it. Contractual and minute diplomatic matters, not antisemitism or other Holocaust-related issues (such as restitution), absorbed the pope.

Jacques Maritain saw accurately that Pius's field of play after the war remained fixed on diplomacy and contractual relationships.[9] The French ambassador recognized that his arguments for a campaign against antisemitism that would be launched by Pope Pius, and for a papal-led spiritual reawakening in Europe, would not succeed. After only a little more than two years of service at the Vatican, Maritain realized that his efforts to divert Pius's mind away from politics and the practical would fail. "One is tempted to say that this attention to the political is too much considering the essential role of the church."[10]

A second fundamental reason for Pius XII's failure to assist Jews during the war and to seek reconciliation with them afterward was his obsession with the threat of communism. Pope Pius's world vision remained fixed on his church and the Marxist danger. Writing to the department of state to comment on one of Pius's 1948 radio addresses, Graham Parsons reported that "as always, the Pope spoke from a background [of] constant preoccupation with the world-wide struggle between Christian morality and Atheist communism."[11] This drama preyed on Pius's mind to such an extent that he linked Catholic spirituality and church discipline to it in several ways. During the war, when it seemed that Russia might fall to German aggression, Pius eagerly questioned Germany's Ambassador Weizsäcker about the prospects of Russian Orthodox Christians being reunited with Rome. Weizsäcker, who almost certainly knew about the murder of the Jews, was uninformed about the possible conversion of Orthodox Christians to Catholicism, and as a Protestant he could not have been much interested in the matter.

In 1942, the pope committed Catholics the world over to dedication to Our Lady of Fatima, whose apparition had appeared to three illiterate children in Portugal in 1917, the same year as the Bolshevik Revolution in Russia. In 1936, the lone surviving visionary recalled that during the apparition Our Lady had promised that if her request for consecration of the world to her Immaculate Heart was fulfilled, Russia would be converted and there would be peace.[12] On the occasion of the silver jubilee of the apparition, Pope Pius broadcast a radio address to Portugal associating himself with the mission that Our Lady had given the children by consecrating the world, and in particular Russia, to the Immaculate Heart of Mary. Two months later, in December 1942, Pius solemnly reiterated the consecration on the feast of the Immaculate Conception in the presence of the hierarchy, members of the diplomatic corps, and the faithful of Rome, who filled the Basilica of St. Peter. During the early years of the Cold War, popular Catholic anti-Communist devotion to Mary—the "Blue Army of our Lady of Fatima"—spread profusely through the United States and western Europe.[13] Pius believed that world peace hinged on Russia's conversion. In the middle of the Second World War, brought about by Germany, Pius XII sought peace through the conversion of Russia.

Not content to leave matters to the cult of Our Lady of Fatima, Pius formulated new disciplinary strictures against Marxists during the early years of the Cold War. In July of 1949, the Holy See decreed that anyone who knowingly supported Communist teaching could not receive the sacraments, and that those who spread such teachings would be excommunicated from the church.[14] As the English minister to the Holy See pointed out, these weapons could also have been used to thwart Holocaust perpetrators, but Pius neglected to do so. Pius XII linked Catholic spirituality and church discipline to the Cold War rather than, as Maritain had hoped, to the moral issue of antisemitism and the Holocaust.

Having dealt with dictators during his entire career, Pius was slow to come around to the idea that democracy was destined to be the slayer of the Communist dragon.[15] The Vatican had traditionally been suspicious of the total freedom and liberty that American democracy spawned.[16] For Pope Pius, Germany remained the first line of defense against the Marxist threat. Before leaving his post as ambassador at the Vatican, a disenchanted Jacques Maritain noted how Pius indulged the German people, noted his "incessant refusal to consider collective responsibility," and noted the continuation of his foreign policy featuring a strong Germany as a barrier to Russian communism.[17]

The evidence for Pius's preoccupation with Germany during and after the war is compelling. With remarkable consistency, the German and

French ambassadors to the Vatican, Ernst von Weizsäcker and Jacques Maritain; the Italian cardinal Filippo Bernardini; and the American papal nuncio, Bishop Aloysius Muench, perceived Pius's fixation with Germany. At the beginning of his reign, Pius told Vatican officials that he would deal with German affairs personally.[18] The fact that he surrounded himself with Germans as his personal advisers and confidants (Monsignor Ludwig Kaas, Robert Leiber, S.J., Sister Pasqualina Lehnert, and a second Jesuit, Augustin Bea, as his confessor) did not escape the attention of U.S. Department of State historian George O. Kent and a number of other observers besides Maritain.[19] Belgian historian Léon Papeleux has asserted that Pius's fondness for things German impaired his judgment and impartiality during the war.[20]

Pius had hoped that Germany and Croatia would emerge intact from the war. When this failed to develop, he sought amnesty for their wartime criminals—probably even abetting their escape from Europe—for one and the same reason: they opposed communism. Postmortem reflections on the Cold War have suggested that when the 1975 Helsinki agreements replaced the moral ambiguity of Cold War tactics with humane values, authoritarianism collapsed in eastern Europe.[21] Pope Pius's pleas for leniency on the part of convicted perpetrators of atrocities and the Vatican's assistance to fugitives from justice after the Holocaust must certainly be counted among the first and greatest moral ambiguities of the Cold War.[22] Pius XII's failure to emphasize the moral issues that affected survivors, such as antisemitism and restitution, and his reliance on fascist opponents to Marxism, even if they were Holocaust perpetrators, attest to the ethical shallowness of his pontificate.

The third reason for Pius XII's failure to deal constructively with Jewish concerns during and after the war centers on the inflexibility of his personality. Historian Peter Kent has pointed out that although conditions in Europe had changed drastically during the six years of the Second World War, Pius's aims and policies in 1945 were exactly what they had been in 1939.[23] Why did Pius XII remain diplomatically locked onto Germany for two decades through thick and thin? His training and temperament hold clues to this question. Educated theologically in canon law, Pope Pius put stock in contractual relationships. Placed on a career track as a diplomat, Pius found the ambiance suited him. As secretary of state, the future pope cut his professional teeth on the concordatory contracts he negotiated with German states and then with the Third Reich. These experiences created a mindset from which he was not temperamentally equipped to free himself.

A variety of observers took note of this. On the eve of Pius's ascendancy to the papacy, German Jesuit Gustav Gundlach, who was stationed in Rome, predicted that diplomacy, not justice, would thenceforth dictate church affairs. Soon after Pius's elevation to the papacy, the future pope, Angello Roncalli, noted the inability of the new pope to act decisively unless he was absolutely sure of himself (completely "at peace with his conscience").[24] Roncalli contrasted Pacelli to his predecessor, who, he said, could think through questions thoroughly and then follow a course of action without hesitation. At the beginning of the war, when Germans, including of course German Catholics, were murdering Polish Catholics, Pius could not bring himself to speak out, according to American diplomats at the Vatican, "largely because of the indecision in his mind as a result of extreme discouragement and depression."[25] In 1945, Myron Taylor advised the State Department that "by temperament important decisions do not come easy to Pius XII."[26]

Indecisiveness did not characterize Pius when it came to contractual dealings. Jesuit Ivo Zeiger, a Vatican collaborator in concordatory negotiations with the Third Reich, recalled the pope's determination and vigor while burning the midnight oil during Holy Week 1933 to redraft the document, characterizing him as "determined," "self-willed," and "impervious to criticism."[27] During the war, when Germans murdered Polish Catholics, and later Polish Jews, Pius worked relentlessly through Nuncio Orsenigo to get Hitler to honor the Concordat between the Vatican and Poland. In order not to jeopardize his Concordat with Germany, Pius rejected Bishop Preysing's advice to break off diplomatic relations with Hitler. During the Cold War, papal envoy Muench slowly came to realize that Pius was continuing to interpret developments in Germany "according to this or that phrase of the [1933] Concordat."[28] Diplomacy was the instinctive ambience of Pope Pius, but he did not adjust to changing conditions.

Pius XII's limitations as a leader notwithstanding, the image of him projected by Rolf Hochhuth in his play *The Deputy* does not square with the historical record. Far from being reserved and coldhearted, those who came into personal contact with him, be they Jews or Gentiles, found him to be warm and personable, even charming. Pius was in fact an emotional person who wept openly on a number of occasions, at least once about the Holocaust, when he learned that the murder of the Jews included infants and the elderly.[29] There was no deep-seated antisemitism in the man, contrary to John Cornwell's thesis in *Hitler's Pope*. But his personal warmth made no difference when it came to the Holocaust, because by temperament Pius did not know how to react to genocide. He relied on contracts and diplomacy, which, of course, did not help the Jews.

Pius XII's leadership failures inevitably affected how Catholics in high and low stations reacted to the Holocaust. The centuries of pogroms and antisemitism notwithstanding, the murder of the Jews was an unprecedented event that struck Catholics, especially in eastern Europe, as an apocalyptic event in some sense. Germans, hoping not to be held responsible for the Holocaust, did not wish to hear news of it.[30] Elsewhere in Europe, the Nazi terror had the same effect on people to a greater or lesser extent, depending upon the degree of collaboration in each region. Only very strong papal leadership could have broken through these several obstructions to rally more Catholics to the cause of the Jews, who were traditionally regarded as outsiders.

The necessity for incisive leadership was most obvious in Catholic Hungary. Eastern European bishops often held leadership positions in both the church and the state prior to the Holocaust. Acting on cultural animosity toward Jews, they helped to enact antisemitic legislation as parliamentarians during the interwar period. Hungary's Cardinal Serédi played this role, and then turned a blind eye to the murder of the Jews during the course of the Second World War. Were these prelates unable to see or to regret that what they had done before the war led ineluctably to what happened to the Jews during the war? When they persisted in their antisemitic convictions, did they think that the Nazis were the hand of God punishing his Chosen People? Since some eastern European bishops showed a correct and courageous attitude toward the persecuted Jews, we may assume that a sharp Vatican rebuke toward callous members of the Slovakian, Croatian, and Hungarian hierarchy would have had some effect.

Those bishops who harbored no ill will toward Jews—and they were numerous in western Europe, including Germany—tried to rescue them. We have seen that this occurred in Italy, France, Belgium, and Germany, although not uniformly throughout the land. Many bishops believed that in the face of Nazi ruthlessness, Catholics could accomplish more by sheltering a few Jews than by a public protest against their mass slaughter. But the postwar statement of Cardinal Frings to the effect that the passivity of German bishops before the Nazis resembled the passivity of Christ before Pilate is completely lacking in credibility. A number of bishops would very likely have spoken out if Pope Pius himself had done so or had encouraged them to do so. Pius XII's limitations as a church leader register here clearly, because, while claiming that when bishops spoke they spoke for him, he failed to tell them about the death camps in eastern Europe. In the absence of Vatican leadership, no European bishop had the courage to follow the example of Berlin priest Bernhard Lichtenberg and protest publicly.

We must look lower down the hierarchical ladder to find the Catholics who sacrificed the most for the Jewish people. Bearing in mind that they were only a tiny minority of all Catholics, we find that priests, nuns, and laypersons, rather than bishops, were prepared to intervene on behalf of Jews. A walk along the Avenue of the Righteous at the Yad Vashem memorial in Jerusalem gives witness to the number of Polish Catholics who sacrificed themselves, even their lives, for Jews. Operating through convent and monastery networks, within diocesan structures, through individual parish communities, through their own organizations such as Zegota, or, quite simply, as individual believers, hundreds, if not thousands, of Catholics throughout Europe came to the assistance of Jews. On the basis of their efforts, we may speculate that if there had been effective leadership on the part of the Holy See or on the part of bishops, the Catholic church could have organized a much more extensive and effective underground rescue operation.

We must not exaggerate about what might have been accomplished. Regardless of who the pontiff was, the centuries-old tradition of antisemitism, dating back to the Fathers of the Church, if not to the Gospels themselves, could not have been reversed quickly enough either to forestall the Holocaust or to cause the majority of Catholics to come to the rescue of the Jews. In the middle of the war, Pope Pius wrote to Bishop Konrad Preysing that his pontificate was the most difficult of modern times. There can be no doubt about that. No other pope had to deal simultaneously with the problems of communism, world war, and genocide. Nevertheless, it remains lamentable that the murder of the Jews found a low place among Pope Pius's concerns. The pope's Cold War policies, giving precedence to the danger of communism over justice for Holocaust war criminals, speak volumes about his priorities. Had either Pius XII's predecessor or his successor led Catholics during the Second World War, historians would have more words of praise and fewer words of regret for the history of the church during the Holocaust.

Just as there has been a tomorrow for the few survivors of the Holocaust, so the relatively few Catholics who saved Jews left a legacy—a tomorrow for the church. If we attempt to explore the very recent intellectual origins of the epoch-ending *Nostra Aetate,* we are struck once again by the importance of the Holocaust. Several groups submitted white papers to the Vatican Secretariat on Religious Relations with the

Jews prior to the Council's deliberations on *Nostra Aetate*. The most important of these was that of the Apeldoorn working group, which had met annually in the Netherlands for some years prior to Pope John's summoning of a council. Members of the Apeldoorn group included Paul Démann, Anton Ramselaar, John Oesterreicher, Karl Thieme, Gertrud Luckner, and Johannes Willebrands. As a young priest, Willebrands rescued Jews in the Netherlands during the Nazi occupation. Oesterreicher, who lost his parents to Auschwitz, fled Nazi Europe. Thieme sought refuge from Nazism in Switzerland. Luckner rescued Jews before her imprisonment in the Ravensbrück concentration camp. The most important Catholic journals devoted to rethinking Christian-Jewish relations were edited by members of the Apeldoorn working group—the *Freiburger Rundbrief* (Luckner), *Cahiers Sioniens* (Démann), and *The Bridge* (Oesterreicher). The influence of the group or of its individual members should not be exaggerated, even within the church. But together they constituted the prophetic element that prepared the way for the council's *Nostra Aetate*. It was the spirit of Apeldoorn that inspired this revolutionary document.[31]

There is one final link to the past that we must consider to appreciate the legacy of the small group of Catholic rescuers. The Holocaust left the Christian community with a burden of humiliation, but it retained some credibility—thanks to the rescuers, and only to them. While the Christian churches did not stand tall during the Holocaust, the rescuers, proportionately a small group, were sufficient in number to have an impact on the memory of Jews when the catastrophe finally had passed. The unbreakable post-Holocaust bond between Gertrud Luckner and Rabbi Leo Baeck symbolizes the fragment of credibility that Christianity retained, without which no Jew would have wished or dared to risk renewing the relationship or dialogue with a Christian neighbor.[32]

Beyond the few members of the Apeldoorn working group, most rescuers were either anonymous or had no role in the development of *Nostra Aetate*. Their connection to that declaration is historically tenuous. But there is one notable exception— French rescuer Germaine Bocquet. As previously mentioned, Bocquet hid Jules Isaac and gathered materials for him so that he could write the seminal book *Jesus and Israel,* which ultimately reversed Christian thinking about Jews.[33] Years later it was Isaac, of course, who prompted John XXIII to include Jews in the agenda of the Second Vatican Council. There is, then, a direct connection between the rescuer Germaine Bocquet and *Nostra Aetate*. To some this link will seem entirely serendipitous, to others, providential.

NOTES

Introduction

1. "We Remember: A Reflection on the Shoah," Commission for Religious Relations with the Jews (The Vatican, 1998).

2. Michael Phayer and Eva Fleischner, *Cries in the Night: Women Who Challenged the Holocaust* (Kansas City: Sheed and Ward, 1997); see chapter 3 by Jessica Sheetz on Margit Slachta, and chapter 4 on Ribière.

3. Avery Dulles, S.J., *The Reshaping of Catholicism* (San Francisco: Harper and Row, 1988), 164.

1. Catholic Attitudes toward Jews before the Holocaust

1. Studies of antisemitism abound. Those dealing especially with Christian antisemitism include Edward H. Flannery, *The Anguish of the Jews: Twenty-three Centuries of Anti-Semitism* (New York: Paulist Press, 1985), and Friedrich Heer, *God's First Love: Christians and Jews over the 2000 Years* (New York: Weybright and Talley, 1970). More recently, Gavin I. Langmuir has distinguished between Christian anti-Judaism and antisemitism, concluding that it is "morally lazy to ask whether Christianity was responsible for Auschwitz"; see *History, Religion, and Antisemitism* (Berkeley: University of California Press, 1990), 367. Friedrich Heer, on the other hand, links the anti-Judaism of the Protestant German Christian movement closely to the Holocaust. Jakob Katz rejects the notion that Christian antisemitism culminated in the Holocaust. He points to the fact that the church traditionally tolerated Jews based on the belief that they would ultimately convert. See Jakob Katz, *From Prejudice to Destruction: Anti-Semitism, 1700–1933* (Cambridge, Mass.: Harvard University Press, 1980), 321–323. Donald Dietrich thinks likewise; see *God and Humanity in Auschwitz* (New Brunswick, N.J.: Transaction Press, 1995), 263. Eva Fleischner contends that Christian and Nazi antisemitism are distinct but that the former fed the latter; see her introduction to *Judaism in German Christian Theology since 1945* (Metuchen, N.J.: Scarecrow Press, 1975).

2. Karl Thieme, "Die Christen, die Juden und das Heil," *Frankfurter Hefte* 4, no. 2 (February 1949): 113–125. See also François Delpech (Rapport général), "Les

Églises et la Persécution raciale," *Églises et chrétiens dans la IIe guerre mondiale. Actes des Collouqes national tenu à Lyon du 27 au 30 janvier 1978* (Lyon: Presses Universitaires de Lyon, 1982), 260ff.

3. Gerhard L. Weinberg, *The Foreign Policy of Hitler's Germany* (Chicago: University of Chicago Press, 1980), 300–301.

4. Heinz Mussinghoff, *Rassenwahn in Münster. Der Judenpogrom 1938 und Bischof Clemens August Graf von Galen* (Regensberg: Münster, 1989), 84.

5. Georges Passelecq and Bernard Suchecky, *L'encyclique Cachée de Pie XI. Une occasion manquée de l'église face à l'antisémitisme* (Paris: Editions La Découverte, 1995), 155–164.

6. *Rundbrief zur Förderung der Freundschaft zwischen dem alten und dem neuen Gottesvolk—im Geiste der beiden Testamente,* ed. Rupert Giessler, Kuno Joerger, Gertrud Luckner, and Karl Thieme, 1 (August 1948); henceforth cited as *Freiburger Rundbrief.* After the war, Ehrlich became the European director of B'nai B'rith.

7. Ronald Modras, *The Catholic Church and Antisemitism: Poland, 1933–1939* (Chur, Switzerland: Harwood Press, 1994), 354–355.

8. Peter C. Kent, "A Tale of Two Popes: Pius XI, Pius XII and the Rome-Berlin Axis," *Journal of Contemporary History* 23 (1988): 601.

9. Walter Bussmann, "Pius XII an die deutschen Bischöfe," *Hochland* 61 (1969): 61–65.

10. Modras, *The Catholic Church and Antisemitism,* 134; see also Susan Zuccotti, *The Italians and the Holocaust* (New York: Basic Books, 1987), 51.

11. Passelecq and Suchecky, 113ff. and chapter 5.

12. Ibid., 117–120.

13. John T. McGreevy, *Parish Boundaries: The Catholic Encounter with Race in the Twentieth-Century Urban North* (Chicago: University of Chicago Press, 1996), 51.

14. Passelecq and Suchecky, 122.

15. Moshe Y. Herczl, *Christianity and the Holocaust of Hungarian Jewry,* trans. Joel Lerner (New York: New York University Press, 1993), 93.

16. Delpech, "Les Églises et la Persécution raciale," 262–264.

17. Michael R. Marrus and Robert O. Paxton, *Vichy France and the Jews* (New York: Basic Books, 1981), 202.

18. Delpech, "Les Églises et la Persécution raciale," 267.

19. John F. Morley, *Vatican Diplomacy and the Jews during the Holocaust, 1939–1943* (New York: KTAV, 1980), 75.

20. Both men fled the Nazis. Oesterreicher later became a naturalized U.S. citizen, and Thieme became a naturalized Swiss citizen.

21. See the correspondence between Oesterreicher and Thieme in April and May 1939, in the Institut für Zeitgeschichte (henceforth IZG) ED 163/59.

22. Ibid., Oesterreicher to Thieme, Paris, 1 May 1939.

23. Tisserant's letter to Suhard was seized by German occupational forces in France when they searched the cardinal's quarters.

24. Memorandum No. 85, 16 June 1942, Myron C. Taylor Papers, U.S. National Archives and Records Administration (henceforth NARA).

25. Thieme, "Die Christen, die Juden und das Heil," 113–125.

26. Shimon Redlich, "Metropolitan Andrei Sheptyts'kyi, Ukrainians and Jews

during and after the Holocaust," in *Remembering for the Future* (Oxford: Pergamon, 1988), I, 200.

27. Randolph L. Braham, *Genocide and Retribution: The Holocaust in Hungarian-Ruled Northern Transylvania* (Boston: Kluwer Nijhoff, 1983), 6ff.

28. Asher Cohen, "Immigrant Jews, Christians and French Jews," in *Remembering for the Future,* I, 223–232.

29. Zuccotti, *The Italians and the Holocaust,* 47.

30. This theme runs through Modras's discussion of Poland; see *The Catholic Church and Antisemitism.*

31. Modras, *The Catholic Church and Antisemitism,* 138.

32. The Protocols of the Elders of Zion was a completely fabricated publication that claimed that Jews plotted to overthrow the world's governments. Published in 1903 in Russia, it was quickly translated into most western European languages.

33. Ezra Mendelsohn, "Interwar Poland: Good for the Jews or Bad for the Jews?" in *The Jews in Poland,* ed. Chimen Abramsky et al. (Oxford: Oxford University Press, 1988), 130–139.

34. Modras, *The Catholic Church and Antisemitism,* 195.

35. Herczl, *Christianity and the Holocaust of Hungarian Jewry,* 9.

36. "The Great Dilemma," *Civita Catholica* (December 1941): 5; "The Actors in the Trial of Jesus," *Civita Catholica* (March 1942): 394–397.

37. Randolph L. Braham, *The Politics of Genocide,* vol. 2 (New York: Columbia University Press, 1981), 1,171.

38. Himmler to Kaltenbrunner, in *Reichsführer! . . . Briefe an und von Himmler,* ed. Helmut Heiber (Stuttgart: Deutsche Verlags-Anstalt, 1968), 266–269.

39. Erika Weinzerl, "Austrian Catholics and Jews," in *Judaism and Christianity under the Impact of National Socialism,* ed. Otto Dov Kulka and Paul R. Mendes-Flohr (Jerusalem: Historical Society of Israel and Zalman Shazar Center for Jewish History, 1987), 283–303. On the shrine, see Franz Cardinal König and Ernst Ludwig Ehrlich, *Haben Wir eine Zukunft* (Kempten: Pendo, 1988), 50ff.

40. Ian Kershaw, *Popular Opinion and Political Dissent in the Third Reich: Bavaria, 1933–1945* (New York: Oxford, 1983), 244. See also Kershaw's "Antisemitismus und Volksmeinung," in *Bayern in der NS-Zeit,* vol. II, ed. M. Broszat and E. Fröhlich (Munich: Oldenbourg, 1979), 347.

41. Paul R. Mendes-Flohr, "Ambivalent Dialogue: Jewish-Christian Theological Encounter in the Weimar Republic," in *Judaism and Christianity,* 99–132.

42. Erich Przywara, S.J., "Judentum und Christentum," *Stimmen der Zeit* 110 (1926): 81–99.

43. Konrad Repgen, "German Catholicism and the Jews 1933–1945," in *Judaism and Christianity under the Impact of National Socialism.*

44. Walter Hannot, *Die Judenfrage in der katholischen Tagespresse Deutschlands und Osterreichs 1923–1933* (Mainz: Grünewald, 1990), Series B of *Veröffentlichungen der Kommission für Zeitgeschichte* (henceforth VKZ), vol. 51, 282.

45. Ibid, 286ff.

46. Werner Chrobak, "Die Regensburger Kirchenzeitung im Dritten Reich," *Beiträge zur Geschichte des Bistums Regensburg* 15 (1981): 389–430.

47. Weinzerl, "Austrian Catholics and Jews," 284 and 303.

48. Thieme to Oesterreicher, Leufelfingen, Quinquagesimae, 1940, IZG ED 163/69.

49. *Schönere Zukunft* 14, no. 21 (February 19, 1939): 548; and *Schönere Zukunft* 32 (May 7, 1939): 534–535.

50. See Hannot's comments on Austria in *Die Judenfrage*, 292–296.

51. Oesterreicher to Thieme, Wien, September 19, 1935, IZG ED 163/59.

52. Oesterreicher to Thieme, Wien, April 21, 1936, IZG ED 163/59.

53. *VKZ*, Series A, vol. 34, 550.

54. Documents may be found in *VKZ*, Series A, vol. 34, 550–551.

55. Weinzerl, "Austrian Catholics and Jews," 290.

56. *VKZ*, Series A 34, *Entwurf*, 64–65; Erich Klausener, *Miterbauer des Bistums Berlin* (Berlin: Knauft, 1979), 175.

57. Weinzerl, "Austrian Catholics and Jews," 290–292. Maglione's reply was the standard, laconic one: the Holy See has not failed to "employ all means so that many . . . unhappy people will be spared."

58. Modras, *The Catholic Church and Antisemitism*, 139–141.

59. Joseph Hudal, *Europas Religiöse Zukunft* (Rome: pamphlet, 1942).

60. Delpech, "Les Églises et la Persécution raciale," 250ff.

61. Ibid., 259.

62. W. D. Halls, "French Christians and the German Occupation," in *Collaboration in France*, ed. G. Hirschfeld and P. Marsh (New York: Berg, 1989), 87.

63. "Germany," *America* (November 26, 1938), 138.

64. Anthony Bosnick, "*America* and the Jews: 1933–1945," *America* 177, no. 15 (November 15, 1997): 23–26.

65. James V. Schall, "The Mystery of 'The Mystery of Israel,'" in *Jacques Maritain and the Jews*, ed. Robert Royal (Notre Dame, Ind.: University of Notre Dame Press, 1994), 51–71.

66. Bernard Doering, "The Origin and Development of Maritain's Idea of the Chosen People," in *Jacques Maritain and the Jews*, 17–35.

67. Jacques Maritain, *A Christian Looks at the Jewish Question* (Longmans, 1939; reprint, New York: Arno Press, 1973).

68. Braham, *The Politics of Genocide*, vol. 1, 126.

69. Herczl, *Christianity and the Holocaust of Hungarian Jewry*, 72.

70. Ibid., 118.

71. Dov Levin, "On the Relations between the Baltic Peoples and Their Jewish Neighbors before, during and after World War II," in *Remembering for the Future*, I, 174.

72. John Conway, "The Churches, the Slovak State and the Jews, 1939–1945," *Slavonic and East European Review* 52, no. 126 (January 1974): 104.

73. George F. Kennan, *From Prague after Munich: Diplomatic Papers, 1938–1940* (Princeton: Princeton University Press, 1968), 53.

74. Rudolf Mikus, S.J., *Slovák* (February 10, 1939); quoted in Ladislav Lipscher, "The Jews of Slovakia: 1939–1945," in *The Jews of Czechoslovakia*, ed. Avigdor Dagan, vol. 3 of Historical Studies and Surveys (New York: Society for the History of Czechoslovak Jews, 1984), 254.

75. Lipscher, "The Jews of Slovakia: 1939–1945," 166.

76. Maria Schmidt, "Margit Slachta's Activities in Support of Slovakian Jewry, 1942–43," in *Remembering for the Future*, I, 208.

77. *Actes et Documentes du Saint-Siège Relatifs à la Seconde Guerre Mondiale*, vol. VI (hereafter *ADSS*) (Vatican City: Libreria editrice Vaticana, 1972), 408–410.

78. Léon Papeleux, *Les silences de Pie XII* (Brussels: Vokaer, 1980), 221.

79. Yisrael Gutman, "Polish Antisemitism between the Wars: An Overview," in *The Jews in Poland Between the Two Wars,* ed. Y. Gutman, et al. (New York: University Press of New England, 1989), 97–108; David Engel, *In the Shadow of Auschwitz: The Polish Government-in-Exile and the Jews, 1939–1942* (Chapel Hill: University of North Carolina Press, 1987), chapter 1.

80. Andrzej Bryk, "Polish-Jewish Relations during the Holocaust: The Hidden Complex of the Polish Mind" (paper presented at conference History and the Culture of the Polish Jews, Jerusalem, 1988).

81. Ronald Modras, "The Catholic Church in Poland and Antisemitism, 1933–1939: Responses to Violence at the Universities and in the Streets," in *Remembering for the Future,* I, 186.

82. Ibid., 183.

83. Saul Friedländer, *Nazi Germany and the Jews: The Years of Persecution* (New York: HarperCollins, 1997), 47–48. Daniel J. Goldhagen, trying to shoehorn the church into his tunnel vision of Germans, presents a wholly under-researched and one-sided discussion in *Hitler's Willing Executioners: Ordinary Germans and the Holocaust* (New York: Knopf, 1996), 109–110 and passim.

84. Friedländer, *Nazi Germany and the Jews,* 47–48.

85. Ibid., 183–184. Friedländer, following Ernst Klee, tenuously links Faulhaber to Nazi racism. Unfortunately, Klee distorted his account of the Hitler-Faulhaber meeting in *Die SA Jesu Christi* (Frankfurt: Fischer, 1989), 127. The only record of the meeting is in Faulhaber's published papers; see Ludwig Volk, ed., *Akten Kardinal Michael von Faulhabers, 1917–1945* (Mainz: Grünewald, 1978), 184, *VKZ,* Series A, vol. 26.

The three-hour meeting in Hitler's Obersalzburg redoubt was not about Jews but about church-state relations in Nazi Germany. Seeking to establish a common ground of understanding, Hitler began the meeting with a long-winded discourse on international politics. Bolshevism threatened Europe, he warned, because Jewish Communists in Spain were attempting to overthrow the government. If they should succeed, France would then fall. Nazism constituted the only bulwark against Bolshevism, for which reason Hitler charged that the church should back him rather than continually finding opportunities for conflict. During the long meeting, the Jews were mentioned only by Hitler, and only in connection with external affairs.

Faulhaber, responding to Hitler's opening remarks and attempting to meet him halfway, referred to similar remarks that Hitler had made during his great Nuremberg speech, and said that his pessimism (*Schwarzseherei*) about Bolshevism was justified. In his discussion of the meeting, Ernst Klee altogether omits mention of the next line of Faulhaber's notes: "Whereas the *Führer's* Nuremberg speech explained with impressive reasoning the general cultural and economic affects of Bolshevism (can only destroy, led by Jews, ruins the *Volkswirtschaft*), the address of the Holy Father, that was given on the same day, singled out atheism, godlessness and opposition to God as the root and the innermost character of Bolshevism" (Volk, *Akten Kardinal Michael von Faulhabers,* 185). Thus, the cardinal agreed with Hitler that the common enemy was Bolshevism, but by referring to the papal address, he omitted the identification of Communists and Jews.

The Obersalzburg discussion was not about the Nuremberg Laws. After the initial salvo and rejoinder, Jews were never mentioned again. Faulhaber complained that the Nazis did not broadcast the pope's speech in Germany, but instead falsely claimed that the Vatican and Russia were attempting to become allies by signing a Concordat. The dialogue between the cardinal and Hitler then dissolved into further argumentative assertions and counter-assertions about church-state relations in Germany. Nearly all of Faulhaber's notes concern these matters; Jews are not the focus.

86. Theodore S. Hamerow, *On the Road to the Wolf's Lair: German Resistance to Hitler* (Cambridge, Mass.: Harvard University Press, 1997), 140.

87. Ibid., 142.

88. Robert A. Krieg, C.S.C., *Karl Adam: Catholicism in German Culture* (Notre Dame, Ind.: University of Notre Dame Press, 1992).

89. Guenter Lewy, *The Catholic Church and Nazi Germany* (New York: McGraw-Hill, 1964), 131. Lewy presents a static picture of the German hierarchy; attitudes toward Jews changed during the Nazi years.

90. Luckner's work is described below in chapters 7, 8, and 10.

91. Gröber to Praelat [illegible]; n.p., October 24, 1940, Archiv Deutscher Caritas 284.3 (henceforth ADC).

92. In *Nazi Germany and the Jews,* Saul Friedländer, following Ernst Klee, writes that Faulhaber had a three-hour talk with Hitler in 1936 and afterward spoke approvingly of the *Führer's* racist tirades (183ff.). I find this unlikely, since in the following year Faulhaber contributed substantially to the encyclical that condemned racism and infuriated the Nazis. It may be that Faulhaber, an ardent anti-Communist, was agreeing that secular Jews in Russia were the leaders of Bolshevism.

93. Lewy, *The Catholic Church and Nazi Germany,* 281.

94. Mussinghoff, *Rassenwahn in Münster,* 75.

95. Rudolf Lill, "German Catholicism's Attitude towards the Jews in the Weimar Republic," in *Judaism and Christianity,* 167.

96. Wolfgang Knauft, "Bernhard Lichtenberg," in *Christen im Widerstand gegen das Dritte Reich,* ed. Joel Pottier (Stuttgart: Burg, 1988), 198. The prayer is related as remembered by a parishioner.

97. Joachim Remak, ed., *The Nazi Years* (Englewood Cliffs, N.J.: Prentice-Hall, 1969), 9–10.

98. Joachim Fest, *Hitler* (New York: Vintage, 1975), chapter 1.

99. Alan T. Davies, *Antisemitism and the Christian Mind* (New York: Herder, 1969), 59.

100. Leo Baerwald to Faulhaber, Munich, March 4, 1939, Bistumsarchiv München (henceforth BAM) 6281.

101. Mussinghoff, *Rassenwahn in Münster,* 87.

102. *Freiburger Rundbrief 3,* no. 10/11 (January 1951): 32. There was also praise from the Jewish community for Cardinal Frings; see Dieter Froitzheim, ed., *Kardinal Frings* (Cologne: Wienand, 1980), 338.

103. Gerhard Reifferscheid, *Das Bistum Ermland und das Dritte Reich* (Vienna: Böhlau, 1975), 253ff.

104. Werner Blessing, "'Deutschland in Not, Wir im Glauben . . . ': Kirche und Kirchenvolk in einer katholischen Region 1933–1949," in *Von Stalingrad zur Währungsreform,* ed. Martin Broszat, et al. (Munich: Oldenbourg, 1988), 27ff.

105. Kershaw, "Antisemitismus und Volksmeinung," II, 311.

106. Charles R. Gallagher, "Patriot Bishop: The Public Career of Archbishop

Joseph R. Hurley, 1937–1967" (Ph.D. diss., Marquette University, 1997), 140; see also Leonard Dinnerstein, "Antisemitism in the United States, 1918–1945," in *Remembering for the Future,* I, 321.

107. Reifferscheid, *Das Bistum Ermland,* 276.

108. John S. Conway, *The Nazi Persecution of the Churches* (New York: Basic Books, 1968); Donald J. Dietrich, *Catholic Citizens in the Third Reich* (New Brunswick, N.J.: Transaction Books, 1988); and Ernst C. Helmreich, *The German Churches under Hitler* (Detroit: Wayne State University Press, 1977).

109. Heinz Hürten, "Zeugnis und Widerstand. Zur Interpretation des Verhaltens der katholischen Kirche im Deutschland Hitlers," in *Widerstand,* ed. Peter Steinbach (Cologne: Berend von Nottbeck, 1987), 144–162.

110. Walter Bussmann, "Pius XII an die deutsche Bischöfe," 61–65. Tisserant's views were made known by him to Cardinal Suhard in a letter captured by Germans during the war. See Lewy, *The Catholic Church and Nazi Germany,* 306–307. Gerhard Reifferscheid has written in *Das Bistum Ermland* that in 1935 the future Pope Pius XII told an Ermland church official that the Concordat was a mistake (137). Perhaps the remark was taken out of context; it contradicts all other evidence on this point.

111. Konrad Repgen, "Kardinal Frings im Rückblick—Zeitgeschichtliche Kontroverspunkte einer künftigen Biographie," *Historisches Jahrbuch* 100 (1980): 307; Heinz Hürten, "Selbstbehauptung und Widerstand der katholischen Kirche," in *Der deutsche Widerstand 1933–1945,* ed. Klaus-Jürgen Müller (Munich: Schöningh, 1986), 135–156.

112. Heinz Hürten, *Deutsche Katholiken* (Munich: Schöningh, 1992), 233ff.

113. Konrad Repgen, "Kardinal Frings im Rückblick," 307; Heinz Hürten, "Selbstbehauptung und Widerstand der katholischen Kirche," in *Der deutsche Widerstand 1933–1945,* ed. Klaus-Jürgen Müller (München: Schöningh, 1986), 135–156.

114. Raul Hilberg, *Perpetrators, Victims, Bystanders* (New York: HarperCollins, 1992), 260–261.

115. Lucy S. Dawidowicz, *The War against the Jews* (New York: Praeger, 1976), xv. This theme also runs through several of the essays in Jeoffrey Wigoder, ed., *Contemporary Jewry* (Jerusalem: Institute of Contemporary Jewry, 1984), 235–245.

116. Kent, "A Tale of Two Popes," 603; and, for the assertion that Pius XI would have spoken bluntly, see Frank J. Coppa, "The Vatican and the Dictators," in *Catholics, the State, and the European Radical Right,* ed. Richard J. Wolff and Jörg K. Hoensch (Boulder, Colo.: Social Science Monographs, 1987), 216.

117. Gallagher, "Patriot Bishop," 173–174.

118. Friedländer, *Nazi Germany and the Jews,* 223.

2. Genocide before the Holocaust: Poland, 1939

1. Gerhard Weinberg wrote, "The war would be fought to the utter destruction not only of Poland's armed forces but of the country as a whole with the utmost brutality." See Weinberg, *The Foreign Policy of Hitler's Germany,* 611.

2. In *The Forgotten Holocaust: The Poles under German Occupation, 1939–*

1944 (Lexington: University of Kentucky Press, 1986), Richard C. Lukas uses the word "Holocaust" to refer to the genocide of Polish Gentiles and Jews. I use the term only in connection with Jews.

3. Leni Yahil, *The Holocaust* (New York: Oxford University Press, 1991), 128–129.

4. Max Domarus, ed., *Adolf Hilter, Speeches and Proclamations,* vol. 2, trans. Mary Fran Gilbert (Wauconda, Ill.: Bolchazy-Carducci, 1990), 2, 100.

5. E. L. Woodward, ed., *Documents on British Foreign Policy, 1919–1939* (London: Her Majesty's Stationery Office, 1954), 3rd Series, 7, 258.

6. Quoted in Norman Davies, *God's Playground,* vol. II (New York: Columbia University Press, 1982), 445.s

7. Richard C. Lucas, *The Forgotten Holocaust,* 1–3.

8. Raul Hilberg, *The Destruction of the European Jews* (New York: Holmes and Meier, 1985), I, 191.

9. Manfred Clauss, *Die Beziehungen des Vatikans zu Polen während des II Weltkrieges* (Cologne: Böhlau, 1979), 34; Wladyslaw Bartoszewski, "Polish-Jewish Relations in Occupied Poland, 1939–1945," in *The Jews in Poland,* ed. Chimen Abramsky et al., 147–160.

10. *Encyclopedia of the Holocaust,* ed. Israel Gutman (New York: Macmillan, 1990), 1, 670.

11. Ibid., 39.

12. Bohdan Wytwycky, *The Other Holocaust* (Washington, D.C.: Novak Report, 1982), 51.

13. Ibid., 41.

14. Hilarius Breitinger, *Als Deutschenseelsorger in Posen und im Warthegau 1934–1945* (Mainz: Grünewald, 1984), 202–210, *VKZ,* Series A, vol. 36.

15. Clauss, *Die Beziehungen des Vatikans,* 41.

16. Ibid., 180–181.

17. Reichsministerium für den kirchlichen Angelegenheiten, Baatz, Chief of Security Police to the Auswärtige Amt, Berlin, June 13, 1940, Bundesarchiv Abteilung Potsdam.

18. Lucas, *The Forgotten Holocaust,* 13–14.

19. Wytwycky, *The Other Holocaust,* 51.

20. Lucas, *Forgotten Holocaust,* 13.

21. Clauss, *Die Beziehungen des Vatikans,* 59.

22. Ibid., 180–181.

23. Breitinger, *Als Deutschenseelsorger in Posen und im Warthegau,* 208–209.

24. Lukas, *Forgotten Holocaust,* 16.

25. Clauss, *Die Beziehungen des Vatikans,* 179.

26. Ibid., 178.

27. Report by the Polish Ambassador to the Holy See on the Situation in German-occupied Poland, Memorandum No. 79, May 29, 1942, Myron Taylor Papers, NARA.

28. The Position of the Vatican in the Present Conflict, Notes: Polish, Dutch, Belgian, Bohemian, and Moravian people are losing faith in the Pope, Memorandum No. 85, June 16, 1942, Myron Taylor Papers, NARA.

29. Józef Garlinski, *Poland and the Second World War* (New York: Hippocrene Books, 1985), 70–71.

30. Gallagher, "Patriot Bishop," 200–207.

31. Clauss, *Die Beziehungen des Vatikans,* 194–198.

32. Ibid., 172.

33. Owen Chadwick, *Britain and the Vatican during the Second World War* (Cambridge: Cambridge University Press, 1986), 82.

34. Ibid., 72.

35. Kazimierz Papée, ed., *Pius XII A Polska, 1939–1949* (Rome: n.p., 1954), 21.

36. *The Persecution of the Catholic Church in German-Occupied Poland. Reports presented by H.E. Cardinal Hlond, Primate of Poland, to Pope Pius XII, Vatican Broadcasts and other Reliable Evidence. Preface by H.E. A. Cardinal Hinsley, Archbishop of Westminster* (New York: Longmans Green, 1941), 115–117.

37. Ibid., 117–118.

38. Burkart Schneider, *Pius XII* (Musterschmidt: Göttingen, 1968), 46–47.

39. Chadwick, *Britain and the Vatican during the Second World War,* 81.

40. Reichsministerium für den kirchlichen Angelegenheiten, Wühlisch, Amt des Generalgouverneurs, to the Auswärtige Amt, Cracaw, March 14, 1940, Bundesarchiv Abteilung Potsdam. This letter reports that permission for a priest in the General Government was denied because of hostile Vatican press and radio communications. I found no other incidents of retaliation resulting from Vatican news releases.

41. Clauss, *Die Beziehungen des Vatikans,* 176.

42. Papeleux, *Les silences de Pie XII,* 165.

43. Gallagher, "Patriot Bishop," 192.

44. Klemens von Klemperer, *German Resistance against Hitler: The Search for Allies Abroad, 1938–1945* (Oxford: Clarendon, 1992), 171ff.

45. Papeleux, *Les silences de Pie XII,* 66 and passim.

46. von Klemperer, *German Resistance against Hitler,* 179; Chadwick, *Britain and the Vatican,* 86–87.

47. von Klemperer, *German Resistance against Hitler,* 174ff.

48. David Alvarez and Robert A. Graham, S.J., *Nothing Sacred: Nazi Espionage against the Vatican, 1939–1945* (London, 1997), 24ff.

49. Papée, *Pius XII A Polska,* 43.

50. Clauss, *Die Beziehungen des Vatikans,* 83.

51. Lucas, *The Forgotten Holocaust,* 16.

52. Clauss, *Die Beziehungen des Vatikans,* 177.

53. Memorandum No. 86, June 23, 1942, Myron C. Taylor Papers, NARA.

54. Tittman to the U.S. State Department, Memorandum No. 114, September 15, 1942, Myron C. Taylor Papers, NARA. Peru and Cuba joined shortly thereafter with their own démarches.

55. Memorandum No. 113, September 14, 1942, Myron C. Taylor Papers, NARA.

56. Clauss, *Die Beziehungen des Vatikans,* 189.

57. Tittman to the Secretary of State, Memorandum No. 87, June 26, 1942, Myron C. Taylor Papers, NARA.

58. Clauss, *Die Beziehungen des Vatikans,* 182.

59. Papée, *Pius XII A Polska,* 58.

60. Breitinger, *Als Deutschenseelsorger in Posen und im Warthegau,* 211.

61. Lucas, *The Forgotten Holocaust,* 14.
62. Jan Sziling, "Die Kirchen im Generalgouvernement," *Miscellanea Historiae Ecclesiasticae* 9 (1984): 282.
63. Morley, *Vatican Diplomacy and the Jews during the Holocaust,* 139.
64. Lucas, *The Forgotten Holocaust,* 25.

3. Genocide before the Holocaust: Croatia, 1941

1. Christopher R. Browning, *Fateful Months: Essays on the Emergence of the Final Solution* (New York: Holmes and Meier, 1985), passim.
2. Jonathan Steinberg, *All or Nothing: The Axis and the Holocaust, 1941–1943* (New York: Routledge, 1990), 39.
3. Aleksa Djilas, *The Contested Country: Yugoslav Unity and Communist Revolution, 1919–1953* (Cambridge, Mass.: Harvard University Press, 1991), chapter 4.
4. Leni Yahil, *The Holocaust* (New York: Oxford, 1991), 349ff.
5. Martin Broszat and Ladislaus Hory, *Der kroatische Ustascha-Staat, 1941–1945* (Stuttgart: dva, 1964), 70–71.
6. Papeleux, *Les silences de Pie XII,* 160ff.
7. Morley, *Vatican Diplomacy and the Jews during the Holocaust,* 148ff.
8. Djilas, *The Contested Country,* 116.
9. Social scientists define genocide variously. Most definitions would include the killing of the Serbs. The Ustasha murders would certainly be included under the United Nations Genocide Convention of 1951, which defines genocide as "acts committed with the intent to destroy, in whole or in part, a national, ethnical, racial or religious group, as such."
10. Yahil, *The Holocaust,* 351.
11. Steinberg, *All or Nothing,* 30.
12. Djilas, *The Contested Country,* 120, 125.
13. Ibid.
14. Karl Pfeifer, "Die Ermordung der kroatischen Juden," *Tribüne* 31, no. 121 (1992): 120.
15. Stella Alexander, *The Triple Myth: A Life of Archbishop Alojzije Stepinac* (Boulder, Colo.: East European Monographs, 1987), 76–79.
16. From the *Katolicki Tjednik,* May 25, 1941; quoted in M. Shelah, "The Catholic Church in Croatia, the Vatican and the Murder of the Croatian Jews," in *Remembering for the Future,* I, 266–280.
17. Alexander, *The Triple Myth,* 69.
18. Shelah, "The Catholic Church in Croatia," 270.
19. Alexander, *The Triple Myth,* 85.
20. Morley, *Vatican Diplomacy and the Jews during the Holocaust,* 151.
21. Shelah, "The Catholic Church in Croatia," 271–272.
22. *ADSS,* 8, 271.
23. Alexander, *The Triple Myth,* 78.
24. Djilas, *The Contested Country,* 126.
25. Peter Heblethwaite, *Paul VI* (New York: Paulist, 1993), 156–158.
26. Pfeifer, "Die Ermordung der kroatischen Juden," 121.
27. Shelah, "The Catholic Church in Croatia," 274ff. The source for the Tardini

quote is *Tajni Dokumenti o odnosima Vatikana: Ustaske N.O.H.* (Zagreb, 1946), 62–63. The source for the Montini quote is *ADSS*, 8, 710. Tardini's words are omitted from the Vatican collection of documents.

28. Shelah, "The Catholic Church in Croatia," 272.
29. Ibid., 273.
30. Steinberg, *All or Nothing*, 39.
31. Yahil, *The Holocaust*, 431. Filipovic-Majstorovic was expelled from the Franciscan order in 1943, but not, evidently, excommunicated; see Frances Hetherington, "Biographical Index," in *Catholics, the State, and the European Radical Right, 1919–1945*, ed. R. J. Wolff and J. K. Hoensch (Boulder: Social Science Monographs, 1987), 235.
32. RG 59, Box 28, NARA. Cardinal Tisserant was the spokesperson.
33. Shelah, "The Catholic Church in Croatia," 276.
34. Yahil, *The Holocaust*, 431.
35. Morley, *Vatican Diplomacy and the Jews during the Holocaust*, 150–151.
36. Ibid., 164.
37. Papeleux, *Les silences de Pie XII*, 89.
38. Djilas, *The Contested Country*, 121.

4. The Holocaust and the Priorities of Pope Pius XII

1. Hilberg, *The Destruction of the European Jews*, 1, 219.
2. Walter Laqueur, *The Terrible Secret: Suppression of the Truth about Hitler's "Final Solution"* (Boston: Little, Brown Press, 1980), passim.
3. Laqueur, *The Terrible Secret*, 237.
4. Ibid.
5. Yahil, *The Holocaust*, 282–283.
6. Avraham Tory, *Surviving the Holocaust: The Kovno Ghetto Diary*, trans. Jerzy Michalowicz (Cambridge, Mass.: Harvard University Press, 1990), 56.
7. *VKZ*, Series A, vol. 34, 675–678.
8. Schneider, *Pius XII*, 32; see also Papeleux, *Les silences de Pie XII*, 58.
9. A memo that Orsenigo sent to the Vatican secretariat on the eve of World War II makes his antisemitism apparent: "The 4 million Jews will certainly do their utmost to excite and to help the others fight against Germany, but they . . . will not fight because the Jew is selfish and does not like fighting." *ADSS*, I, 141.
10. Leiber to Preysing, Rome, October 28, 1945, Diözesanarchiv Berlin (henceforth DAB) V/16-4, Nachlass Preysing. It is not known whether Orsenigo knew of his assistant's party membership. Fr. Leiber found out about it from Ernst von Weizsäcker, the German ambassador to the Vatican.
11. Reifferscheid, *Das Bistum Ermland*, 270–276.
12. Papeleux, *Les silences de Pie XII*, 72.
13. Rolf Steininger, "Katholische Kirche und NS-Judenpolitik," *Zeitschrift für katholische Theologie* 114 (1992): 164.
14. John Morley writes that he *never* intervened on behalf of Jews; Morley, *Vatican Diplomacy and the Jews during the Holocaust*, 178. The German scholar Martin Höllen says that the nuncio helped in arranging visas for emigrating Jews; *Heinrich Wienken. Der 'Unpolitische' Kirchenpolitiker* (Mainz: Grünewald, 1981), 105, *VKZ*, Series B, vol. 33.

15. Morley, *Vatican Diplomacy and the Jews during the Holocaust,* 115. Orsenigo's concern was probably sparked by Margarete Sommer.

16. Friedländer, *Pie XII et le IIIe Reich* (Paris: Editions de Seuil, 1964), see the conclusion.

17. Yahil, *The Holocaust,* 357.

18. Höllen, *Heinrich Wienken,* 108–109.

19. Zuccotti, *The Italians and the Holocaust,* 127–128. Pages 129–135 of *Freiburger Rundbrief* 30 (1978) give the full Gerstein report.

20. Lipscher, "The Jews of Slovakia," 206.

21. *ADSS,* 8, 598 (July 13, 1942).

22. Faulhaber to the Military Administration, Munich, June 9, 1945, BAM File 7500.

23. Lipscher, "The Jews of Slovakia," 256.

24. Shelah, "The Catholic Church in Croatia," 272–276.

25. Morley, *Vatican Diplomacy and the Jews during the Holocaust,* 78.

26. John S. Conway, "Catholicism and the Jews," in *Judaism and Christianity,* 441.

27. *Freiburger Rundbrief* 37 (1980): 124. Subsequent scrutiny of Riegner's famous telegram of August 8, 1942, in which he outlines the intent to kill all Jews, indicates that it was amazingly accurate; see C. R. Browning, "A Final Hitler Decision for the 'Final Solution'? The Riegner Telegram Reconsidered," *Holocaust and Genocide Studies* 10, no. 1 (Spring 1996): 3–10.

28. *ADSS,* 8, 534.

29. *ADSS,* 8, 431; Morley, *Vatican Diplomacy and the Jews during the Holocaust,* 153–154.

30. Morley, *Vatican Diplomacy and the Jews during the Holocaust,* 136.

31. *Foreign Relations of the United States* (hereafter *FRUS*), 1939 (Washington, D.C.: Government Printing Office, 1961), III, 772.

32. *ADSS,* 8, 497.

33. Tittman Report of November 23, 1942, on illegal and inhumane warfare, RG 59, Box 39, NARA.

34. Morley, *Vatican Diplomacy and the Jews during the Holocaust,* 137.

35. See chapter 6.

36. *FRUS,* III, 777.

37. Morley, *Vatican Diplomacy and the Jews during the Holocaust,* 87.

38. Chadwick, *Britain and the Vatican,* 199.

39. Ibid., 213.

40. Richard Breitman, *Official Secrets: What the Nazis Planned, What the British and Americans Knew* (New York, 1998), 145.

41. Friedländer, *Nazi Germany and the Jews,* 75.

42. *ADSS,* 7, 180.

43. See chapter 7.

44. See chapter 6.

45. *ADSS,* 10, 328.

46. *ADSS,* 9, 274; the date was May 5, 1943. In the passage, Maglione incorrectly places the Treblinka death camp near Lublin.

47. Dan Kurzman, *The Race for Rome* (New York: Doubleday, 1975), 64.

48. Godfrey to Maglione, March 13, 1943, *ADSS,* 9, 104.

49. Ludwig Volk, "Der Fuldauer Bischofskonferenz von der Enzyklika 'Mit

Brennender Sorge' bis zum Ende der NS Herrschaft," in *Katholische Kirche im Dritten Reich*, ed. Dieter Albrecht (Mainz: Grünewald, 1976), 79.

50. Höllen, *Heinrich Wienken*, 107.

51. Burkhart Schneider, ed., *Die Briefe Pius' XII. an die deutschen Bischöfe 1939–1944* (Mainz: Grünewald, 1966), VKZ, Series A, vol. 4.

52. Schneider, *Pius XII*, 237–240.

53. Ibid., 242.

54. *Akten Deutscher Bishöfe über die Lage der Kirche 1933–1945*, ed. Ludwig Volk and Bernhard Stasiewski (Mainz: Grünewald Press, 1972), 902, *VKZ*, Series A, vol. 38, 269–272. Maglione's reply is in the footnote.

55. *ADSS*. See vols. 8 through 11.

56. Gerhard L. Weinberg, *Germany, Hitler, and World War II* (New York: Cambridge University Press, 1995), 243.

57. Susan Zuccotti, *The Holocaust, the French, and the Jews* (New York: Basic Books, 1993), 141–142.

58. Elie Wiesel, *Memoirs* (New York: Knopf, 1996), 69.

59. Foreign Funds Control Subject Files, RG 131, Box 487, NARA. See file marked Vatican City Funds in the U.S.

60. Tittman Memorandum no. 109, September 8, 1942, RG 59, 740.00119, NARA.

61. *ADSS*, I, 423.

62. Jacob Presser, *The Destruction of the Dutch Jews*, trans. Arnold Pomerans (New York: Dutton, 1969), 148.

63. Sister M. Pasqualina Lehnert, *Ich dürfte Ihm Dienen* (Würzburg: n.p., 1983), 117–118.

64. This theme comes up frequently in the notes of Ernst von Weizsäcker, Germany's ambassador to the Vatican; see Leonidas E. Hill, *Die Weizsäcker Papiere 1933–1950* (Frankfurt: Allstein, 1974), passim.

65. Hansjakob Stehle, generally critical of Pope Pius, notes this; see Hansjakob Stehle, *Geheimdiplomatie im Vatikan. Die Päpste und die Kommunisten* (Zurich: Benzinger, 1993), 194. Regarding Pius's decision to send only messages of condolence, see Coppa, "The Vatican and the Dictators," 215.

66. Lewy, *The Catholic Church and Nazi Germany*, 32.

67. Tittman to Hull, October 6, 1942, *FRUS*, 1942, III, 777.

68. See chapter 4.

69. George O. Kent, "Pope Pius XII and Germany: Some Aspects of German-Vatican Relations, 1933–1943," *American Historical Review* 70, no. 1 (October 1964): 74–75.

70. Confided to the author by Ger van Roon at the 21st Annual Scholars Conference on the Holocaust and the Churches at Stockton State College, Pomona, New Jersey, in March 1991.

71. Leiber also confided to van Roon that he destroyed his own papers. Since this is a remarkable thing for an historian to do, one assumes that Leiber feared this material would cast Pius in an unfavorable light.

72. Osborne's 1945 Annual Report, Rome, February 22, 1946; reproduced in *Akten Deutscher Bishöfe*, 902.

73. Papeleux, *Les silences de Pie XII*, 68–69.

74. von Klemperer, *German Resistance against Hitler*, 170ff. When the American Jesuit Vincent A. McCormick and the General of the Jesuit order, Wladimir

Lédochowski, attempted to restrain their fellow Jesuit, Robert Leiber, from becoming involved in these negotiations, Pius told them to mind their own business. See James Hennesey, "American Jesuit in Wartime Rome: The Diary of Vincent A. McCormick, S.J., 1942–1945," *Mid-America* 56, no. 1 (January 1974): 32–33.

75. Volker Berghahn points out that even those involved in the July 20 attempt on Hitler intended to roll the Allied invaders back to the beaches of Normandy after taking control of Germany. See Volker Berghahn, "Resisting the Pax Americana?" in *America and the Shaping of German Society, 1945–1955,* ed. Michael Ermarth (Providence, R.I.: Berg, 1993), 95–96.

76. Conway, "Catholicism and the Jews," 439–440.

77. Stehle, *Geheimdiplomatie im Vatikan,* 200ff. Although Stehle's analysis of Vatican diplomacy seems realistic, it is surely speculative to conclude that the Holy See's position of neutrality was nothing but a facade hiding "weakness, indecisiveness and undiluted fear." See p. 202.

78. Saul Friedländer, *Pius XII and the Third Reich: A Documentation* (New York: Knopf, 1966), 175ff.

79. Ibid., 195.

80. Zuccotti, *The Italians and the Holocaust,* 133. The arrest and deportation of Roman Jews, and the relation of the Vatican to these events is taken up in detail in chapter 6.

81. Friedländer, *Pius XII and the Third Reich,* 211ff.

82. Historian Peter Hoffmann writes that Roosevelt's personal envoy to the Vatican, Myron Taylor, was primarily concerned with preventing Pius from making proposals for a compromise peace after the Allies had made unconditional surrender their announced objective in 1942. See "Roncalli in the Second World War: Peace Initiatives, the Greek Famine and the Persecution of the Jews," *Journal of Ecclesiastical History* 40, no. 1 (January 1989): 77.

83. Hill, *Die Weizsäcker Papiere,* 398.

84. José M. Sánchez, "The Popes and Nazi Germany: The View from Madrid" (paper presented at the 1995 spring meeting of the American Catholic Historical Association), 17.

85. See Hill, *Die Weizsäcker Papiere,* 343, 365, 369, 375, 383–385, and 398.

86. Friedländer, *Pius XII and the Third Reich,* 237.

87. For the Vatican's involvement in this effort, see below.

88. Hill, *Die Weizsäcker Papiere,* 392.

89. Chadwick, *Britain and the Vatican,* 265–266.

90. Daniel Carpi, *Between Mussolini and Hitler* (Hanover, N.H.: Brandeis University Press, 1994), 175–178.

91. Gitta Sereny, *Into That Darkness* (New York: Vintage Press, 1983), 333.

92. Boxes 2433–2435, 2439, 2441, 2448–2449, 2451–2454, 2457–2458, 2461–2463, 2465, 2467, 2469, 2470–2477, RG 59 740.0011, NARA. These citations do not include other Vatican communications, also very numerous, about aerial attacks in other parts of Italy.

93. Papeleux, *Les silences de Pie XII,* 58–65.

94. Informal Notes of Taylor for September 27, 1942 of discussion with Mgr. Montini, Myron C. Taylor Papers, 121.866A/302, RG 59. Complete Taylor collection is in Boxes 2433–2477, NARA.

95. RG 982, microfilm reel 165, NARA.

96. FDR to Secretary of State, June 28, 1943, RG 982, microfilm reel 164, NARA.

97. Apostolic Delegate to Myron C. Taylor, Washington, D.C., June 15, 1943, RG 982, microfilm reel 164, NARA.

98. Clauss, *Die Bezeihungen des Vatikans,* 172.

99. Informal Notes of Taylor for 27 September 27, 1942.

100. Chadwick, *Britain and the Vatican,* 216.

101. *ADSS, 9,* 127.

102. For details, see chapter 6.

103. Pius XII to FDR, July 20, 1943, RG 982, microfilm reel 170, NARA.

104. Tittman to State Department, December 29, 1943, Myron C. Taylor Papers, 121.866A/302, NARA. A plenary indulgence was one that dispensed all punishment in purgatory for sins that a person had confessed.

105. Lehnert, *Ich durfter Ihm Dienen,* 116.

106. Tittmann telegram to the U.S. Department of State, Bern, January 3, 1944, RG 982, microfilm reel 178, NARA.

107. Hill, *Die Weizsäcker Papiere,* 352.

108. Friedländer, *Pie XII et le IIIe Reich,* 238.

109. Pius XII to Preysing, Vatican City, March 21, 1944, Korrespondenz 1944–1945, DAB V/16-4.

110. Pius XII to Preysing, Vatican City, April 30, 1943, Korrespondenz 1944–1945, DAB V/16-4.

111. See chapter 6.

112. Regarding Pius's fixation with communism, see Coppa, "The Vatican and the Dictators," 199–203.

113. The one exception to this statement came when the Vatican hinted that it might break its silence if Rome's Jews were deported. This episode is taken up in chapter 6.

114. Reginald F. Walker, ed., *Pius of Peace* (Dublin: Gill and Sons, 1945), 58.

5. In the Eye of the Storm

1. Eugen Kogon's opinion. See Heiner Lichtenstein, "Krummstab und Davidstern, Die katholische Kirche und der Holocaust," in *Katholische Kirche und NS-Staat,* ed. Monika Kringels-Kemen and Ludwig Lemhöfer (Frankfurt: Knecht, 1981), 78.

2. Kershaw, "Antisemitismus und Volksmeinung," 281–348.

3. David Bankier, *The Germans and the Final Solution* (Cambridge: Blackwell, 1992), 206; Hans Mommsen, "Was haben die Deutschen vom Völkermord an den Juden gewusst?" in *From Reichskristallnacht to Genocide,* ed. Walter Pehle (Oxford: Oxford University Press, 1990).

4. Heinz Hürten, *Deutsche Katholiken* (Munich: Schöningh, 1992), 510–511.

5. Sommer Nachlass, DAB. See *Lebenslauf* and correspondence with Zentrale des Katholischen Fürsorgevereins für Mädchen, Frauen und Kinder; for additional details see Phayer, *Protestant and Catholic Women,* chapter 8.

6. There was a direct link between the domestic "euthanasia" program and the gas chambers of the Holocaust in occupied Poland. See Henry Friedlander, *The*

Origin of Nazi Genocide: from Euthanasia to the Final Solution (Chapel Hill, N.C.: University of North Carolina Press, 1995). Euthanasia is placed in quotation marks because the Nazis killed people for racial purposes, not to save them from suffering.

7. *VKZ,* Series A, vol. 34, 550–551.

8. Hürten, *Duetsche Katholiken,* 510–511.

9. Mussinghoff, *Rassenwahn in Münster,* passim.

10. See above, pp. 45–46.

11. Roman Bleistein, *Alfred Delp* (Frankfurt: Knecht, 1989), 532.

12. Augustin Rösch, *Kampf Gegen den Nationalsozialismus,* ed. Roman Bleistein (Frankfurt: Knecht, 1985), 206.

13. Hürten, *Deutsche Katholiken,* 510–512; Höllen, *Heinrich Wienken,* 109.

14. David Wyman, *The Abandonment of the Jews* (New York: Pantheon, 1985), 41.

15. "Zum Gedächtniss Frau Jaffe," Sommer Nachlass, DAB. This was written by her parish priest.

16. Sommer to Gertrud Luckner, Berlin-Dahlem, November 21, 1953, DAB I/1-103.

17. Bleistein, *Alfred Delp,* 264–265; see also Ger van Roon, *Neuordnung im Widerstand* (Munich: Oldenbourg, 1967), 209. For details see Michael Phayer, "The Catholic Resistance Circle in Berlin and German Catholic Bishops during the Holocaust," *Holocaust and Genocide Studies* 7, no. 2 (1993): 216–229.

18. Höllen, *Heinrich Wienken,* 98–99.

19. Quote is from Bertram to Prange, the Vicar General of the diocese of Berlin, written on April 17, 1944, *VKZ,* Series A, vol. 38, 350, footnote 2. For details, see Frank Buscher and Michael Phayer, "German Catholic Bishops and the Holocaust, 1940–1953," *German Studies Review* 11, 3 (October 1988): 163–185. It is obvious that it would have been suicidal for Sommer to put her reports in writing and have Bishop Preysing sign them.

20. Mussinghoff, *Rassenwahn in Münster,* 75.

21. Ludwig Lemhöfer, "Zur Tapferen Pflichterfüllung Gerufen. Die katholiken in Adolf Hitler Krieg," in *Katholische Kirche und NS-Staat,* ed. Monika Kringels-Kemen and Ludwig Lemhöfer (Frankfurt: Knecht, 1981), 83–99.

22. Ibid., 90.

23. Friedrich Ebert Stiftung, Dirks Nachlass; 1960 R-Z.

24. August Brecher points out that the Nazi propaganda office had either taken over many church publications or brought such pressure on them that they had to publish material on the war effort whether they liked it or not. See *Die katholishe Kirchenzeitung für das Bistum Aachen im Dritten Reich* (Aachen: Einhard, 1988), 64–120.

After the war, the editor of the Regensburg church paper, under investigation by OMGUS, testified that he had to print material that the propaganda ministry dictated, and, further, that the Catholic reader could discern which material was coerced and which was not (see Riedl Papers, Box 2, Marquette University Archives). But this was all part of the accommodation mentality. The propaganda ministry informed Bishop Wienken that the Regensburg paper was not measuring up and Wienken then informed the bishop of Regensburg, Michael Buchberger. The editor then published the material that OMGUS found incriminating. Thus, the Gestapo worked through church channels to achieve what they wanted.

25. Bankier, *The Germans and the Final Solution,* 156.

26. Ibid., chapters 2, 4 and 5; especially 129.

27. Hilberg, *The Destruction of the European Jews,* 2, 519.

28. Roon, *Neuordnung im Widerstand,* 236.

29. Roman Bleistein, S.J., "Lothar Koenig," *Stimmen der Zeit* 204 (1986): 313–320.

30. Roman Bleistein, S.J., "Katholische Bischöfe und der Widerstand gegen den Nationalsozialismus," *Stimmen der Zeit* 207 (1989): 579–590.

31. Bleistein, *Alfred Delp,* 265.

32. *VKZ,* Series A, vol. 38, 99–100.

33. Ibid., 220–221. The draft in its entirety reads as follows:

Draft of a Petition of the Germany Episcopacy

Berlin, 22–23 August, 1943.

With deepest sorrow—yes, even with holy indignation—have we German bishops learned of the deportation of non-Aryans in a manner that is scornful of all human rights. It is our holy duty to defend the unalienable rights of all men guaranteed by natural law. We recognize it as our special duty to take a protective stance on behalf of the many thousands of non-Aryans who have become members of our holy Catholic church through holy baptism. The world would not understand if we failed to raise our voice loudly against the deprivation of rights of these innocent people. We would stand guilty before God and man because of our silence. The burden of our responsibility grows correspondingly more pressing as the rather infrequent, but unavoidably urgent, shocking reports reach us regarding the awful, gruesome fate of the deported who have already been subjected in frightfully high numbers to really inhumane conditions of existence. We urge therefore:

1. Reverence for life and protection for the health of camp prisoners— hence, humane living conditions, sufficient nutrition and tolerable working conditions.

2. The possibility of a regular exchange of letters with relatives and friends in Germany, also the possibility of contact in writing with their pastors in Germany.

3. With great urgency we urge above all the admittance of Catholic priests into the displaced persons camps, who would be named by the German bishops in concert with the competent bureaucrat, so that a regularized program for pastoral care will be assured.

4. Notification of all camps (or ghettos) in which deportees are presently living, and notification of the camps (or ghettos) which have been evacuated in the meantime; in addition, information regarding the destination of these people along with an explanation for the reasons for the evacuation.

5. The assurance that a commission could visit the camps and meet personally with the displaced persons.

We would not want to omit to say that meeting these stipulations would be the most certain way to deflate the crescendo of rumors regarding the mass death of the deported non-Aryans.

34. Hürten, *Deutsche Katholiken,* 512.

35. Besides wishing to limit his work to baptized "Jews," Wienken wanted to be in a position to intercede with Nazi officials regarding the great number of imprisoned Catholic priests; see Höllen, *Heinrich Wienken,* 105ff. Luckner hints at Wienken's involvement in concealing Jews; see *Freiburger Rundbrief* 34 (1982): 90–91.

36. Mussinghoff, *Rassenwahn in Münster,* 90.

37. Ulrich von Hehl, ed., *Walter Adolph. Geheime Aufzeichnungen aus dem nationalsozialistischen Kirchenkampf, 1933–1943* (Grünewald: Mainz, 1982).

38. A gestapo agent reported on the bishop's sermon; see Reichsministerium für den kirchlichen Angelegenheiten, 21793, Bundesarchiv Abteilung Potsdam.

39. Repgen, "German Catholicism and the Jews," 223.

40. Steininger, "Katholische Kirche und NS-Judenpolitik," 175.

41. Repgen, "German Catholicism and the Jews," 224–225.

42. Volk, "Die Fuldaer Bischofskonferenz," 79.

43. W. Corsten, ed., *Kölner Aktenstücke zur Lage der Katholischen Kirche in Deutschland 1933–1945* (Cologne: Bachem, 1949), 255. See also Hamerow, *On the Road to the Wolf's Lair,* 305.

44. Letter of Gröber to Praelat [illegible], n.p., October 24, 1940, ADC 284.3.

45. Volk, "Die Fuldaer Bischofskonferenz," 79.

46. *Freiburger Rundbrief* 35 (1983), 103–105.

47. *Freiburger Rundbrief* 28 (1976), 93.

48. Konrad Repgen, "Kardinal Frings im Rückblick," 307; Heinz Hürten, "Selbstbehauptung und Widerstand der katholischen Kirche," *Der deutsche Widerstand 1933–1945,* ed. Klaus-Jürgen Müller (München: Schöningh, 1986), 135–156.

49. RG 59, Box 28, NARA.

50. Augustin Rösch also asked his German Jesuit colleague, Robert Leiber, Pius XII's personal secretary, to urge the pope to speak out; see Roman Bleistein, *Augustinus Rösch: Leben im Widerstand: Biographie und Dokumente* (Frankfurt am Main: Verlag J. Knecht, 1998), 206–207.

51. Friedlander, *Pius XII and the Third Reich*; see the pope's letter to Cardinal Preysing, 135–145.

52. Konrad Repgen leaves the impression that the Vatican preferred Preysing's confrontational attitude to Bertram's accommodationist posture; see "German Catholicism," 210–211. My reading of the documents is just the opposite.

53. Affadavit of Gmelin, June 15, 1948, in Friedländer, *Pius XII and the Third Reich,* 104; *ADSS,* VIII, 459.

54. Friedländer, *Pius XII and the Third Reich,* 135–145. See also Bussman, "Pius XII an die deutschen Bischöfe," 63.

55. File 1304, Geschäftsordnung für die Konferenzen des deutschen Episkopats, BAM.

56. Hamerow, *On the Road to the Wolf's Lair,* 304.

57. Robert Hürtgen, "Untergang und Neubeginn, Köln in den Jahren 1942–1946," in *Kardinal Frings,* ed. Dieter Froitzheim (Cologne: Wienand, 1980), 238ff.

58. Ibid., 36ff.

59. Reifferscheid, *Das Bistum Ermland,* 256ff. No German bishop was sent to a concentration camp, but three had to flee from their dioceses.

60. Lewy, *The Catholic Church and Nazi Germany.*

61. Kershaw, "Antisemitismus und Volksmeinung," 314ff.

62. Heinz Hürten, "Zeugnis und Widerstand," 147. On the Scholls, see Hans

Scholl, *At the Heart of the White Rose: Letters and Diaries of Hans and Sophie Scholl,* ed. I. Jens (New York: Harper and Row, 1987).

63. Christel Beilmann, "Eine Jugend im katholischen Milieu. Zum Verhältnis von Glaube und Widerstand," in *Pirten, Swings und Junge Garde,* ed. Wilfried Breyvogel (Bonn: Dietz, 1991), 64.

64. Roman Bleistein, S.J., "Katholische Bischöfe und der Widerstand gegen den Nationalsozialismus," *Stimmen der Zeit* 207 (1989): 582.

65. Ibid.

66. This particular chaplain may not be representative of other Catholic priests serving the military. See Doris Bergen, "Witnesses to Atrocity: German Military Chaplains and the Holocaust," in *In God's Name: Religion and Genocide in the Twentieth Century,* ed. Omer Bartov and Phyllis Mack (forthcoming).

67. Gisbert Kranz, *Eine katholische Jugend im Dritten Reich. Erinnerungen, 1921–1947* (Freiburg: Herder, 1990).

68. Lichtenstein, "Krummstab und Davidstern," 73.

69. In January 1993, Cardinal Johannes Willebrands graciously acted on my request to seek permission for me to review the unpublished letters. Permission was denied.

70. Repgen, "German Catholicism and the Jews," 224.

6. European Bishops and the Holocaust

1. Hilberg, *The Destruction of the European Jews,* 3, 1220.

2. Richard McBrien, ed., *Encyclopedia of Catholicism* (New York: Harper-Collins, 1995).

3. Morley, *Vatican Diplomacy and the Jews during the Holocaust,* 146.

4. Ibid., 153–154.

5. Shelah, "The Catholic Church in Croatia," 274.

6. Steinberg, *All or Nothing,* 80.

7. Ibid., 272–275; see also *ADSS,* 9, 187.

8. Morley, *Vatican Diplomacy and the Jews during the Holocaust,* 161.

9. Hilberg, *The Destruction of the European Jews,* 2, 717.

10. Morley, *Vatican Diplomacy and the Jews during the Holocaust,* 164–165.

11. Yahil, *The Holocaust,* 431 and Hilberg, 2, 712–713.

12. Alexander, *The Triple Myth,* 102. Shelah says that no priests or religious were reprimanded; "The Catholic Church in Croatia," 275–277.

13. Morley, *Vatican Diplomacy and the Jews during the Holocaust,* 157.

14. Ibid., 161; Sereny, *Into That Darkness,* 319; and, Stanford J. Shaw, *Turkey and the Holocaust* (New York: New York University Press, 1993), 277 and 390.

15. Hoffmann, "Roncalli in the Second World War," 83.

16. Shaw, *Turkey and the Holocaust,* 277 and 390; see the footnote.

17. *Freiburger Rundbrief* 28 (1976). Ernst Ludwig Ehrlich points this out in his review of the Vatican's documentary series, *ADSS,* 126.

18. *Chicago Daily News* (November 6, 1941).

19. Lipscher, "The Jews of Slovakia," 3, 184.

20. Burzio reported the October 1941 murders to the Vatican; see Morley, *Vatican Diplomacy and the Jews during the Holocaust,* 78.

21. Ibid., 79–81.

22. *ADSS*, 8, 459.

23. Morley, *Vatican Diplomacy and the Jews during the Holocaust,* 84; on the Sicherheitsdienst, see Conway, "The Churches, the Slovak State and the Jews 1939–1945," 102.

24. Hilberg, *The Destruction of the European Jews,* 2, 725.

25. Avigdor Dagan, "The Czechoslovak Government in Exile and the Jews," 465.

26. Morley, *Vatican Diplomacy and the Jews during the Holocaust,* 82.

27. Hilberg, *The Destruction of the European Jews,* 2, 728.

28. Livia Rothkirchen, *The Destruction of Slovak Jewry: The Documentary History* (Haifa: Yad Vashem Martyrs' and Heroes Memorial Authority, 1965), xxiv.

29. *ADSS* 8, 486–489. The Schutzstaffel was a volunteer vigilante group.

30. Morley, *Vatican Diplomacy and the Jews during the Holocaust,* 85.

31. Conway, "The Churches, the Slovak State and the Jews, 1939–1945," *Slavonic and East European Review* 52, no. 126 (January 1974): 105.

32. Ibid., 106.

33. Morley, *Vatican Diplomacy and the Jews during the Holocaust,* 85.

34. Maria Schmidt, "Margit Slachta's Activities in Support of Slovakian Jewry," 208.

35. Ibid., 208.

36. Yeshayahu Jelinek, "Stormtroopers in Slovakia: The Rodobrana and the Hlinka Guard," *Journal of Contemporary History* 6, no. 3 (1971): 97–119.

37. Hilberg, *The Destruction of the European Jews,* 2, 733.

38. Conway, "The Churches and the Slovak State," 98–99.

39. Morley, *Vatican Diplomacy and the Jews during the Holocaust,* 239–243.

40. Conway, "The Churches and the Slovak State," 106.

41. Ibid., 108.

42. Schmidt, "Margit Slachta's Activities in Support of Slovakian Jewry," 209. It is difficult to understand how, at that point in time, Pope Pius could be "shocked" by Slachta's account, unless she provided details that others had not known about or had omitted.

43. Hilberg, *The Destruction of the European Jews,* 2, 742.

44. For useful background on Catholics in Vichy France, see W. D. Halls, "French Christians and the German Occupation," 72–92.

45. Hilberg, *The Destruction of the European Jews,* 2, 569.

46. Ibid., 637–638.

47. Delpech, "Les Églises et la Persécution raciale," 269–270.

48. Ibid., 271.

49. Eva Fleischner, "Can the Few Become the Many? Some Catholics in France who Saved Jews during the Holocaust," in *Remembering for the Future* (Oxford: Pergamon, 1988), 1, 234.

50. Lawrence Baron, "The Historical Context of Rescue," in *The Altruistic Personality: Rescuers of Jews in Nazi Europe,* ed. Samuel P. and Pearl M. Oliner (New York: Free Press, 1988), 42.

51. Renée Poznanski, *Etre Juif en France pendant la Seconde Guerre mondiale* (Paris: Hachette, 1994), 435.

52. Raphael M. Huber, ed., *Our Bishops Speak* (Milwaukee: Bruce, 1952), 113.

53. Maxime Steinberg, "Faced with the Final Solution in Occupied Belgium:

The Church's Silence and Christian Action," in *Remembering for the Future* (Oxford: Pergamon, 1988), Supp. vol., 466.

54. Hilberg, *The Destruction of the European Jews*, II, 641.

55. Carpi, *Between Mussolini and Hitler*, 76.

56. Henri de Lubac, *Résistance chrétienne à l'antisémitisme, souvenirs 1940–1944* (Paris: Fayard, 1988), 137. On the situation of foreign Jews, see Morley, *Vatican Diplomacy and the Jews during the Holocaust*, 69; and Carpi, *Between Mussolini and Hitler*, 75.

57. Erich Klausener, *Von Pius XII zu Johannes XXIII* (Berlin: Morus Verlag, 1958), 79.

58. Morley, *Vatican Diplomacy and the Jews during the Holocaust*, 69; and Carpi, *Between Mussolini and Hitler*, 75.

59. Richard Gutterage, "Some Christian Responses in Britain to the Jewish Catastrophe," in *Remembering for the Future* (Oxford: Pergamon, 1988), 1, 358–359.

60. Tony Kushner, "Ambivalence or Antisemitism? Christian Attitudes and Responses in Britain to the Crisis of European Jewry During the Second World War," in *Remembering for the Future* (Oxford: Pergamon, 1988), 1, 404–416.

61. Hilberg, *The Destruction of the European Jews*, 2, 570ff.

62. Presser, *The Destruction of the Dutch Jews*, 23–25.

63. Waltraud Herbstrith, *Edith Stein: A Biography*, trans. Bernard Bonowitz, O.C.S.O. (San Francisco: Harper and Row, 1971), 101.

64. Steinberg, *All or Nothing*, 79–80.

65. Ibid., 123.

66. *Freiburger Rundbrief* 13, nos. 50–52 (June 1961).

67. Morley, *Vatican Diplomacy and the Jews during the Holocaust*, 175.

68. Steinberg, *All or Nothing*, 229.

69. Ibid., 124.

70. Carpi, *Between Mussolini and Hitler*, 131–132.

71. Steinberg, *All or Nothing*, 129, and Zuccotti, *Italians and the Holocaust*, 209.

72. Hilberg, *The Destruction of the European Jews*, 2, 665.

73. Morley, *Vatican Diplomacy and the Jews during the Holocaust*, 66.

74. Karl Thieme Papers, IZG ED 163/50.

75. Susan Zuccotti, "Pope Pius XII and the Holocaust: The Case in Italy," in *The Italian Refuge: Rescue of Jews during the Holocaust*, ed. I. Herzer, K. Voigt, and J. Burgwin (Washington, D.C.: Catholic University of America Press, 1989), 255. Chapter 6 of Zuccotti's book *The Italians and the Holocaust* (New York: Basic Books, 1987) is the best account from the point of view of the victims, many of whom she has interviewed.

76. Robert Katz, *Death in Rome* (New York: Macmillan, 1967), 25.

77. Ibid. According to John Morley the Vatican found out about the planned roundup from another source, Princess Enza Pignatelli Aragona Cortes; Zuccotti concurs that the Vatican could have learned about it from other sources in addition to Weizsäcker. See Susan Zuccotti, "Pope Pius XII and the Holocaust," 259.

78. Meir Michaelis, *Mussolini and the Jews: German-Italian Relations and the Jewish Questions in Italy, 1922–1945* (Oxford: Clarendon Press, 1978), 361.

79. Albrecht von Kessel, "The Pope and the Jews," in *The Storm over "The Deputy,"* ed. Eric Bently (New York: Grove Press, 1964), 74.

80. The Jewish population of Rome was about 12,000. After the German occu-

pation of the city, an unknown number of Jews fled south behind Allied lines. Probably around 5,000, however, remained in Rome.

81. *ADSS,* 9, 506.

82. Morley, *Vatican Diplomacy and the Jews during the Holocaust,* 180.

83. Ibid.

84. Albrecht von Kessel, himself a player in the Roman drama and one who is sympathetic to Pope Pius, affirms that the Hudal letter did not originate in the Vatican; see von Kessel, "The Pope and the Jews," 72. Authors frequently assert that the Vatican was behind Hudal's letter; see Zuccotti, "Pope Pius XII and the Holocaust," 129–130, and Friedländer, *Pie XII et le IIIe Reich,* 206.

85. Kurzman, *The Race for Rome,* 74–75.

86. Goebbels Diary, July 27, 1943. In *The Goebbels Diaries, 1942–1943.* Edited, translated, and with an introduction by Louis P. Lochner (Garden City, N.J.: Doubleday, 1948), 468.

87. von Kessel, "The Pope and the Jews," 75; Leonidas E. Hill III, "The Vatican Embassy of Ernst von Weizsäcker, 1943–1945," *Journal of Modern History* 39, no. 2 (June 1967): 150; and, Lehnert, *Ich dürfte Ihm Dienen,* 121. Mussolini's son-in-law, Count Galeazzo Ciano, noted in his diary in 1940 that the pope would go to a concentration camp before acting against his conscience. Evidently, reference is made here to an Italian, not German, camp. See Michaelis, *Mussolini and the Jews,* 374.

88. Zuccotti, "Pius XII and the Holocaust," 133.

89. Leonidas Hill, ed., *Die Weizsäcker Papiere* (Frankfurt: Allstein, 1974), 352.

90. Tittmann to the State Department, Vatican, October 19, 1943, *FRUS 1943,* 2, Europe, 950.

91. Quoted by Morley, *Vatican Diplomacy and the Jews during the Holocaust,* 184.

92. Jane Scrivener, *Inside Rome with the Germans* (New York: Macmillan, 1945), 204.

93. Kurzman, *The Race for Rome,* 81.

94. Chadwick, *Britain and the Vatican,* 289.

95. Morley, *Vatican Diplomacy and the Jews during the Holocaust,* 183.

96. Statistics given by Robert Katz and by Michaelis agree in large part; Katz, *Death in Rome,* 17, and Michaelis, *Mussolini and the Jews,* 365.

97. Correspondence of Susan Zuccotti with the author, March 28, 1998.

98. Katz, *Death in Rome,* 364.

99. Robert G. Weisbord and Wallace P. Sillanpoa, *The Chief Rabbi, the Pope, and the Holocaust: An Era in Vatican-Jewish Relations* (New Brunswick, N.J., 1992). Confided to me by Robert Weisbord in May 1999.

100. Zuccotti, *Italians and the Holocaust,* 209.

101. Ibid.

102. Baron, "The Historical Context of Rescue," 48.

103. Margherita Marchione, *Yours Is a Precious Witness* (New York: Paulist Press, 1997), 132 and passim.

104. "Carità Civile," *L'Osservatore Romano* (December 3, 1943).

105. Scrivener, *Inside Rome with the Germans,* 65–66.

106. "Motivazioni," *L'Osservatore Romano* (December 5, 1943). For Jane Scrivener's comments, see Scrivener, *Inside Rome with the Germans,* 65–66.

107. Michaelis, *Mussolini and the Jews,* 395. Michaelis's quote is verified by the records of the U.S. Foreign Office; see *FRUS,* 1, 1123: The "Pope told Heathcote-Smith neither history nor his conscience would forgive him if he did not make this effort."

108. The Vatican was still not prepared in the fall of 1944 to condemn mass killings in Auschwitz and Birchenau. The Polish ambassador pleaded with the Holy See to intercede on behalf of those who were still to be murdered there, but he got nothing in reply other than the standard statement that "the Vatican is always ready to alleviate all misery due to war." See Papée, *Pius XII A Polska,* 94.

109. Ibid., 84. Marchione writes that the pope's directive to other Italian bishops to hide Jews was "loud and clear," but she fails to provide documentary evidence for this claim. Like Robert Graham, she avoids discussing the events of October 1943, when Roman Jews were deported without Pius objecting.

110. Zuccotti, *Italians and the Holocaust,* 210ff.

111. Bela Vago, "The Hungarians and the Destruction of the Hungarian Jews," in *The Holocaust in Hungary Forty Years Later,* ed. R. L. Braham and Bela Vago (New York: Social Science Monographs and Institute for Holocaust Studies, 1985), 95.

112. Hilberg, *The Destruction of the European Jews,* 2, 811–812.

113. Yahil, *The Holocaust,* 510.

114. Ibid., 500–520.

115. Braham, *The Politics of Genocide,* 2, 1045. Moshe Y. Herczl emphasizes the failure of the churches to a much greater extent. See *Christianity and the Holocaust of Hungarian Jewry,* trans. Joel Lerner (New York: New York University Press, 1993).

116. Braham, *The Politics of Genocide,* 2, 1047.

117. Yahil, *The Holocaust,* 512.

118. Herczl, *Christianity and the Holocaust of Hungarian Jewry,* 242.

119. Braham, *The Politics of Genocide,* 2, 1045; Herczl, *Christianity and the Holocaust of Hungarian Jewry,* 190.

120. Herczl, *Christianity and the Holocaust of Hungarian Jewry,* 206.

121. Hilberg, *The Destruction of the European Jews,* 2, 838–839.

122. Ibid., 838.

123. Braham, *The Politics of Genocide,* 2, 1035.

124. Randolph L. Braham, *Genocide and Retribution: The Holocaust in Hungarian-Ruled Northern Transylvania* (Boston: Kluwer Nijhoff, 1983), 24.

125. Braham, *The Politics of Genocide,* 1045–1046.

126. Yahil, *The Holocaust,* 640.

127. David H. Kranzler, "The Swiss Press Campaign That Halted Deportations to Auschwitz and the Role of the Vatican, the Swiss and Hungarian Churches," in *Remembering for the Future* (Oxford: Pergamon, 1988), 1, 162.

128. Ibid., 168.

129. See *ADSS,* 9, 50; and Erich Kulka, "The Annihilation of Czechoslovak Jewry," in *The Jews of Czechoslovakia,* ed. Avigdor Dagan, vol. 3 of Historical Studies and Surveys (New York: Society for the History of Czechoslovak Jews, 1984), 262–328.

130. Rudolf Vrba, "Die Missachtete Warnung," *Vierteljahrshefte für Zeitgeschichte* 44, no. 1 (January 1966): 15.

131. *ADSS,* 10, 29.

132. Kranzler, "The Swiss Press Campaign," 168.

133. Gerhard Riegner, address at the Oxford International Scholar's Conference, July 10–13, 1988, Oxford, England.

134. John F. Morley, "Vatican Diplomacy and the Jews of Hungary during the Holocaust: October 15, 1944 to the End" (paper presented at the Second International Holocaust Conference, Berlin, 1994), 13.

135. Ibid., 6–12.

136. Irene Tomaszewski and Tecia Werbowski, *Zegota: The Rescue of Jews in Wartime Poland* (Montreal: Price-Patterson, 1994), 36.

7. Catholic Rescue Efforts during the Holocaust

1. Joseph Goebbels, *The Early Goebbels Diaries, 1925–1929,* trans. O. Weitzson, ed. H. Heiber (New York: Praeger, 1963), October 14, 1925.

2. Quoted in Robert Wistrich, *Who's Who in Nazi Germany* (New York: Macmillan, 1982), 153–154. Höss officially withdrew from the church in 1922.

3. Manfred Deselaers, *"Und Sie hatten nie Gewissenbisse?" Die Biografie von Rudolf Höss, Kommandant von Auschwitz und die Frage nach seiner Verantwortung vor Gott und den Menschen* (Cracow: Benno Press, 1996). On Höss's family life, see 188ff.; on his conscientious regrets, 182ff. and 221ff.

4. Phayer, "The Catholic Resistance Circle in Berlin," 216–229.

5. Nechama Tec, *When Light Pierced the Darkness* (New York: Oxford University Press, 1986), 41. Christopher Browning confirms this activity in *Ordinary Men: Reserve Police Battalion and the Final Solution in Poland* (New York: HarperCollins, 1992).

6. Tec, *When Light Pierced the Darkness,* chapter 9.

7. Wladyslaw T. Bartoszewski, "Polish-Jewish Relations: A Current Debate among Polish Catholics," *Research Report* 7 (October 1987): 1–20.

8. Baron, "The Historical Context of Rescue," 29.

9. Alexander Bronowski, *Es Waren So Wenige. Retter Im Holocaust,* trans. Zeev Eshkolot (Stuttgart: Quell, 1991), 123ff. and 160ff.

10. Mordecai Paldiel, *The Path of the Righteous: Gentile Rescuers of Jews during the Holocaust* (Hoboken, N.J.: Ktav, 1992).

11. Sommer to Ludger Born, S.J., September 15, 1947, DAB I/1-99; and Sommer to Born, Berlin-Dahlem, October 12, 1947.

12. Sommer to Ludger Born, S.J.; n.p. copy; February 21, 1948, DAB I/1-99.

13. Jerzy Myszor, "Stosunki Kościól—Panstwo Okupacyjne W Diecezji Katowickiej, 1939–1945" (unpublished manuscript: Katowice, 1992), 266.

14. Interview of Gertrud Luckner and Marie Schiffer by Dietrich and Ursula Goldschmidt, Barbara Schieb, and Elizabeth von Thadden on October 27, 1988, in Berlin. Many years had passed since the Holocaust when this interview of Luckner was secretly tape-recorded. Although her recollections are extremely valuable, it would be impossible after more than forty years to be perfectly accurate about many details.

15. Myszor, "Stosunki Kościól," 169.

16. Kurt R. Grossmann, "Gertrud Luckner," *Rheinischer Merkur* 46 (November 13, 1970), 4.

17. Myszor, "Stosunki Kościół," 169.

18. Luckner and Schiffer interview.

19. Luckner, in Luckner and Schiffer interview.

20. Ibid.

21. Sommer to Ludger Born, S.J., September 15, 1947, DAB I/1-99.

22. Phayer, *Protestant and Catholic Women,* 222.

23. Ibid., chapter 10.

24. Report on Luckner's 1950 visit to England, ADC R 611 II.

25. Phayer and Fleischner, *Cries in the Night,* 13 and 42.

26. Jessica A. Sheetz, "Margit Slachta's Efforts to Rescue Central European Jews, 1938–1945," in Phayer and Fleischner, *Cries in the Night,* 61.

27. Yahil, *The Holocaust,* 169.

28. Martin Gilbert, *The Holocaust: A History of the Jews of Europe during the Second World War* (New York, 1986), 140. Regarding Nazi brutality, see especially 87ff.

29. Emmanuel Ringelblum, *Notes from the Warsaw Ghetto: The Journal of Emmanuel Ringelblum,* ed. and trans. Jacob Sloan (New York: McGraw-Hill, 1958).

30. Ibid., 81.

31. Sheetz, "Margit Slachta's Efforts to Rescue Central European Jews," 44–54.

32. Randolph L. Braham, "The Kamenets Poldolsk Massacre and Délvidék Massacres: Prelude to the Holocaust," *Yad Vashem Studies on the European Jewish Catastrophe and Resistance* 9 (1973): 133–156.

33. Sheetz, "Margit Slachta's Efforts to Rescue Central European Jews," 50–51.

34. Franciszka Stopniaka, ed., *Materialy I Studia* (Warsaw: Akademia Teologii Katolickiej, 1978), 5, 45ff.

35. Phayer and Fleischner, *Cries in the Night,* 4.

36. Yahil, *The Holocaust,* 380.

37. Historians differ as to whether this was condoned by Cardinal Serédi; Jeno Levai, ed., *Eichmann in Hungary: Documents* (New York: Fertig, 1987), 25, says that it was, but Herczl emphatically denies this in *Christianity and the Holocaust of Hungarian Jewry,* 225.

38. Technically, according to Canon Law sisters are laypeople since they have not been initiated into the lower ranks of Holy Orders.

39. See Sheetz, "Margit Slachta's Efforts to Rescue Central European Jews," 63.

40. Tomaszewski and Werbowski, *Zegota,* 67.

41. Ibid., 99.

42. Ibid., 36.

43. Ian Kershaw, *The Nazi Dictatorship* (New York: Oxford University Press, 1983), 358.

44. Lutz-Eugen Reutter, "Die Hilfstätigkeit Katholischer Organisationen und kirchlicher Stellen für die im nationalsozialistischen Deutschland Verfolgten" (Ph.D. diss., Hamburg University, 1963), 105.

45. For more detailed information about the Berlin circle of Catholics, see Phayer, "The Catholic Resistance Circle in Berlin," 216–229.

46. Whether or not this was because these men were married to Catholics is not clear from Sommer's records in the Berlin church archives.

47. "Kurzer Bericht," Sommer Nachlass, DAB. The mass deportation that took place on February 27, 1943, in Berlin was exceptional; usually Jews were notified

individually. See Leonard Gross, *The Last Jews in Berlin* (New York: Simon and Schuster, 1982).

48. "Kurzer Bericht," Sommer Nachlass, DAB. Since relief was organized by the Berlin diocese and carried out through its parishes, it might appear that Catholics were involved only with Catholics. Such was not the case. Sommer was explicit on this point, saying in her brief postwar memoir that aid was extended to all Jews. For examples of interfaith help, see Phayer, *Protestant and Catholic Women*, pp. 215–216.

49. *VKZ*, Series A, vol. 38, 19–21.

50. "Kurze Bericht." Sommer was aware that another Special Relief employee, Fräulein Joachim, helped ill Jews and hidden Jews "at great personal risk" throughout the period of National Socialist persecution.

51. Interview with the author, June 1985, at the home of Susanne Witte in Berlin.

52. "Zum Gedächtniss an Frau Jaffe," Sommer Nachlass, DAB. This was written by her parish priest.

53. See Sommer's "To Whom It May Concern Letter" about Martha Mosse, Berlin, June 6, 1947, Sommer Nachlass, DAB.

54. Weinzerl, "Austrian Catholics and Jews," 286–288.

55. Ibid., 294.

56. Zuccotti, *The Italians and the Holocaust*, 334.

57. Ibid., 209.

58. Ibid.

59. Roger Gazeau, "Die 'Abtei Liguge,'" in *Christen im Widerstand gegen das Dritte Reich*, ed. Joel Pottier (Stuttgart: Burg, 1988), 89–91.

60. Yahil, *The Holocaust*, 496.

61. Steinberg, *All or Nothing*.

62. John J. Delaney, "Defying Hitler: Clerical Opposition to Religious Apartheid in Nazi Germany" (paper presented at the Spring Meeting of the American Catholic Historical Association, Indianapolis, 1998), 5.

63. The best treatment of Catholic-Jewish relations during the Holocaust is Nechama Tec's *When Light Pierced the Darkness* (New York: Oxford University Press, 1986).

64. Nechama Tec explains this in terms of moral ambiguity. Catholics were taught that, on the one hand, Jews were a cursed people and, on the other, that murder was sinful. Many ordinary people were unable to resolve this conundrum. See Tec, *When Light Pierced the Darkness*.

65. Phayer and Fleischner, *Cries in the Night*, 66.

66. Irene Tomaszeweski and Tecia Werbowski, *Zegota: The Rescue of Jews in Wartime Poland* (Montreal: Price-Patterson, 1994), 43.

67. Maritain made more than 30 broadcasts; they are preserved in the University of Notre Dame Maritain Center, File Broadcasts 16–20.

68. On the journal *Témoignage*, see Susan Zuccotti, *The Holocaust, the French, and the Jews*, 140ff.; and, Delpech, "Les Églises et la Persécution raciale," 268. *Jüd Süss*, like *The Eternal Jew*, was an early World War II antisemitic Nazi propaganda film, described as "nasty" by Victor Klemperer in *I Will Bear Witness, 1933–1941* (New York: Random House, 1998), 343. The Gurs detention camp in France was a main holding facility where Jews were interred before being deported for extermination.

69. Zucotti, *The Holocaust, the French, and the Jews,* 141.

70. Lubac, *Résistance chrétienne à l'antisémitisme,* 166.

71. Zuccotti, *The Holocaust, the French and the Jews,* 149.

72. Poznanski, *Etre Juif en France,* 437.

73. Zuccotti, *The Holocaust, the French and the Jews,* 142.

74. Jean Lacouture, *Jesuits: A Multibiography* (Washington, D.C.: Counterpoint, 1995), 387ff.

75. Tomaszewski and Werbowski, *Zegota,* 65–67.

76. Thomas F. O'Meara, O.P., "The Witness of Pierre Chaillet," *America* 176, no. 18 (May 24, 1997): 12–16; and Renee Bedarida, *Pierre Chaillet. Temoin de la Resistance Spirituelle* (Paris: Fayard, 1988).

77. Serge Klarsfeld, "The Upper Echelons of the Clergy and Public Opinion Force Vichy to Put an End, in September 1942, to Its Broad Participation in the Hunt for Jews," in *Remembering for the Future,* I, 249.

78. Teresa Prekerowa, "The Relief Council for Jews in Poland, 1942–1945," in *The Jews in Poland,* ed. Chimen Abramsky et al., 161–176.

79. Phayer and Fleischner, *Cries in the Night,* 77–78.

80. *A Lelek Szava* 10, no. 5 (March 1, 1943); quoted in Tamás Majsai, "The Deportation of Jews from Csíkszereda and Margit Slachta's Intervention on Their Behalf," in *Studies on the Holocaust in Hungary,* ed. Randolph L. Braham (Boulder, Colo.: Social Science Monographs, 1990), 119.

81. Uri Asaf, "Christian Support for Jews during the Holocaust in Hungary," in *Studies on the Holocaust in Hungary,* ed. Randolph L. Braham (Boulder, Colo.: Social Science Monographs, 1990), 65–113.

82. Braham, *The Politics of Genocide,* 1032.

83. Yahil, *The Holocaust,* 531.

84. Charles Molette, *Prêtres, Religieux et Religieuses dans las Résistance au Nazisme, 1940, 1945* (Paris: Fayard, 1995), 9.

85. Ibid., 14.

86. Ulrich von Hehl, *Priester unter Hitler's Terror: Eine biographische und statistische Erhebung* (Mainz: Grünewald, 1984).

87. Gazeau, "Die 'Abtei Liguge,'" 89–91.

88. At the 1998 Yom Hashoah celebrated in Milwaukee, Wisconsin, Zvi Deutsch recounted how his family was saved by Mendes.

89. Kranzler, "The Swiss Press Campaign," 165.

90. Bronowski, *Es Waren So Wenige,* 123ff. and 160ff. On Witte, see Phayer, *Protestant and Catholic Women,* 220–221.

91. Thomas E. Woods, *Karski: How One Man Tried to Stop the Holocaust,* foreword by Elie Wiesel (New York: Wiley, 1994).

92. Eva Fogelman, *Conscience and Courage: Rescuers of Jews during the Holocaust* (New York: Anchor Books, 1994), 208.

93. Alvarez and Graham, *Nothing Sacred,* 142.

8. Answering for the Holocaust

1. Georges Bernanos, "Bilanz nach 1945," *Dokumente* 18 (1962): 12. Written in November 1945. Bernanos, not known as an ally of the Jews in the prewar era, befriended them because of their persecution by the Nazis.

2. Interview with Cardinal John Willebrands, Rome, February 1, 1993. The oft-repeated papal and German church defense of their silence, based on what happened to Dutch Catholics of Jewish descent, is a poor one—first, because the Gestapo already had the names of those Catholics before the bishops spoke out, and second, because the German bishops and the papacy continued to keep silent *after* European Catholics of Jewish descent were deported to the killing camps.

3. Diary, May 20, 1951, to September 13, 1951, Muench Papers, Catholic University Archives (henceforth CUA).

4. Letter to Bernard Custodis, n.p., February 23, 1946, Hans Peter Mensing, *Konrad Adenauer Briefe Über Deutschland 1945–1951* (Corso: n.p., 1983).

5. See the statements in Hugh J. Nolan, ed., *Pastoral Statements of the United States Catholic Bishops* (Washington, D.C., 1984), 2, 67–73, and in Huber, ed., *Our Bishops Speak*, 113.

6. See the Laros white paper in File 7500, BAM.

It is true that within the church there were right-wing Catholics, especially in Europe, who interpreted the Holocaust in accordance with their antisemitism. On Catholic antisemitism, see Delpech, "Les Églises et la Persécution raciale," 257–304; Gutman, "Polish Antisemitism between the Wars: An Overview," 97–108; Hermann Greive, "Between Christian anti-Judaism and National Socialist Antisemitism: the Case of German Catholicism," in *Judaism and Christianity and the Impact of National Socialism*, ed. Otto Dov Kulka and Paul R. Mendes-Flohr (Jerusalem: Historical Society of Israel and Zalman Shazar Center for Jewish History, 1987), 169–179; and, in the same collection of essays, Rudolf Lill, "German Catholicism's Attitude towards the Jews in the Weimar Republic," 151–168. For them the murder of the Jews was just another demonstration of the curse that Jesus had supposedly laid on the Jewish people. Catholics of this stamp, once vocal in the heyday of fascism, fell silent or, like Paul Touvier, went underground after the war. On Touvier, see the special insert of *Le Monde* (March 24, 1994), and the report on him commissioned by the French Catholic church, *Paul Touvier et l'Eglise* (Fayard: Paris, 1992). Unlike Touvier, the overwhelming majority of French Catholics could not accommodate the gruesome extermination of the Jews within the divine plan.

7. The standard work in English on this subject is John Conway's *The Nazi Persecution of the Churches* (New York: Basic Books, 1968); since the publication of Conway's book, the Catholic commission in Bonn has published a mass of documents, many of which describe the persecution. See Series A of VKZ.

8. Beryl McClaskey, *The History of the U.S. Policy and Program in the Field of Religious Affairs under the Office of the U.S. High Commissioner for Germany* (Historical Division, Office of the Executive Secretary, Office of the U.S. High Commissioner for Germany, 1951); for a good survey of OMGUS and the churches, see Armin Boyens, "Die Kirchenpolitik der amerikanischen Besatzungsmacht in Deutschland von 1944 bis 1946," in *Kirchen in der Nachkriegszeit*, ed. A. Boyens et al. (Göttingen: Vandenhoeck & Ruprecht, 1979), 6–100.

9. Repgen, "German Catholicism and the Jews," 213–214.

10. Hürten, "Selbstbehauptung und Widerstand," 153–54.

11. Heinz Hürten, "Kirchen und amerikanische Besatzungsmacht in Deutschland," in *Kirche, Staat und katholische Wissenschaft in der Neuzeit*, ed. A. Portmann-Tinguely (n.p.: Schöningh, n.d.), 565–581.

12. Dr. Laros to the Archbishops, Kapellen-Stolzenfels, July 11, 1945, File 7500, BAM.

13. Lemhöfer, "Die Katholiken in der Stunde Null. Restauration des Abendlandes oder radikaler Neubeginn?" in *Katholische Kirche und NS-Staat,* ed. M. Kringels-Kemen and L. Lemhöfer (Frankfurt: Knecht, 1981), 101–102.

14. Konrad Repgen, "Die Erfahrung des Dritten Reiches und das Selbstverständniss der deutschen Katholiken nach 1945," in *Die Zeit nach 1945 als Thema kirchlicher Zeitgeschichte,* ed. Victor Conzemius et al. (Göttingen: Vandenhoeck and Ruprecht, 1988), 151–152.

15. Absent was the wartime leader of the Fulda conference, Cardinal Adolf Bertram, who died at the war's end.

16. See *VKZ,* Series A, vol. 38, 654–664, Entwurf eines Hirtenworts des deutschen Episkopats, 21 August, 1945; and, 664–668, Änderungsvorschläge Preysings zum Hirtenwort des deutschen Episkopats, 21–23 August, 1945; and, the final draft, 688–694, Hirtenwort des deutschen Episkopats, Fulda, August, 23, 1945.

17. Buscher and Phayer, "German Catholic Bishops and the Holocaust," 463–485. Subsequently, the German church itself has made this point: the bishops "were the only people who could still speak in public." See "Nach 50 Jahren—die Reden von Schuld, Leid und Versöhnung," Central Committee of German Catholics, February 1988.

18. Denkschrift Frings, August 2, 1945, Köln. *VKZ,* Series A, vol. 38, *Akten deutscher Bischöfe über die Lage der Kirche 1933–45,* ed. Bernhard Stasiewski, 626.

19. The best study of German awareness of the Holocaust is David Bankier, *The Germans and the Final Solution* (Blackwell: Oxford, 1992), and, by the same historian, "The Germans and the Holocaust: What Did They Know?" *Yad Vashem Studies* 20 (1990): 69–98.

20. Karl-Dietrich Bracher, "Problems of the German Resistance," in *The Challenge of the Third Reich,* ed. Hedley Bull (Oxford: Clarendon Press, 1986), 66. Frederic Spotts, although generally critical of Catholic bishops, credits them for being wiser than their Protestant counterparts on the question of German guilt. Spotts, *The Churches and Politics in Germany,* 93.

21. Faulhaber Papers, BAM 7501. The issue was eventually resolved in Faulhaber's favor. The army OMGUS officer who had censored the bishops' text was reassigned stateside.

22. Konrad Repgen is of a different opinion; see "Die Erfahrung des Dritten Reiches," 150ff.; see also Vera Bücker, *Die Schulddiskussion im deutschen Katholizismus nach 1945* (Bochum: Brockmeyer, 1989), 133.

23. Lemhöfer, "Die Katholiken in der Stunde Null," 105; see also Repgen, "Die Erfahrung des Dritten Reiches," 175, fn. 139.

24. Adenauer to Bernard Custodis, February 23, 1946, quoted in Mensing, *Konrad Adenauer Briefe,* 32ff.

25. Max Pribilla, S.J., "Das Schweigen des deutschen Volkes," *Stimmen der Zeit* 139, no. 1 (October 1946): 26.

26. Max Pribilla, S.J., "Wie War Es Möglich?" *Stimmen der Zeit* 139, no. 2 (November 1946): 92.

27. *Frankfurter Hefte* 1, no. 8 (1946): 715–733.

28. Michael Buchberger, "Antwort auf einen 'Brief über die Kirche,'" *Klerusblatt* 27, no. 6 (15 March 1947): 42–45.

29. Bishop Muench, who certainly did not agree with these comments, noted them in his diary; see Muench's diary from April 1947 to November 1947, CUA, 37/1-4.

30. Ibid. Some of the responses and Görres's reply can be found in the *Frankfurter Hefte* 1, no. 3 (March 1947): 275–294.

31. Ida Görres to Dirks, Stuttgart-Degerloch, January 23, 1947, Correspondence, 1946 and 1947, Dirks Nachlaß, Friedrich Ebert Stiftung (henceforth FES).

32. Dirks to Ida Friederike Görres, n.p., March 19, 1947; and Görres to Dirks, Stuttgart-Degerloch, March 24, 1947, ibid.

33. Buchberger, "Antwort auf einen 'Brief über die Kirche,'" 42–45. All of the letters that Görres received from Freiburg in southwest Germany were positive except one, that from Archbishop Conrad Gröber. Other bishops took her to task as well.

34. Konrad Repgen, "Die Erfahrung des Dritten Reiches," 150ff.

35. Alf Lüdtke, "'Coming to Terms with the Past': Illusions of Remembering, Ways of Forgetting Nazism in West Germany," *Journal of Modern History* 65, no. 3 (September 1993): 561. On the impact of the SS state, see Robert Gellately, "Situating the 'SS-State' in a Social-Historical Context: Recent Histories of the SS, the Police, and the Courts in the Third Reich," *Journal of Modern History* 64, no. 2 (June 1992): 338–365. For an analysis of the intentionalist-functionalist debate, see Christopher R. Browning, "Nazi Resettlement Policy and the Search for a Solution to the Jewish Question, 1939–1941," *German Studies Review* 9 (October 1986): 497–520.

36. Hubert Habicht, ed., *Eugen Kogon—ein Politischer Publizist In Hessen* (Frankfurt: Insel, 1982), 169–171.

37. Ibid., 163–164.

38. See Buscher and Phayer, "German Catholic Bishops and the Holocaust," 473ff.; and Buscher, *The U.S. War Crimes Trial Program in Germany, 1946–1955* (New York: Greenwood, 1989), 93–97.

39. Graf von Galen, *Rechtsbewusstsein und Rechtsunsicherheit* (Rome, March 1946). Printed as manuscript.

40. Ibid. To provide an "out" for this assertion, Galen referred to an anonymous English newspaper writer who had made the comparison.

41. Service Center Report of February, 28, 1946, Riedl Papers, Box 3, Bishop Muench File, Marquette University Archives.

42. I found no published copy of Galen's attack on the Nuremberg Trials, only a manuscript copy in the city library of Munich.

43. Werner Schwarz, *Kreuz und Hakenkreuz*, vol. 3 of *Unter der Gewaltherrschaft des Nationalsozialismus 1933–1945* (Oldenburg: University of Oldenburg Press, 1985), 211.

44. Robert Jay Lifton, *The Nazi Doctors: Medical Killing and the Psychology of Genocide* (New York: Basic Books, 1986), 151 and passim.

45. U.S. doctors at Pearl Harbor used evipan as an anesthesia on American personnel who were injured in the Japanese attack, until they discovered that a slight overdose of the drug caused several people to die.

46. "KZ-Arzt Eisele in Kairo gestorben," *Allgemeine Unabhängige Jüdische Wochenzeitung* 22, no. 7 (12 May 1967), 16.

47. Case of Hans Eisele, CUA, 37/131 #111.

48. Ibid., 139.

49. Hans-Josef Wollasch, "Heinrich Auer (1884–1951), Bibliotheksdirektor beim Deutschen Caritasverband, als politischer Schutzhaeftling Nr. 50241 in Konzentrationslager Dachau," *Zeitschrift für die Geschichte des Oberrheins,* 131, Festgabe Gerd Tellenbach (1983), 383–489.

50. Auer files, ADC house archives.

51. Ibid.

52. Case of Hans Eisele; E. Bronberger, Munich, March 19, 1949, to Muench, Kronberg, CUA, 37/131 #111.

53. *Der Spiegel* 12, no. 28 (July 9, 1958): 28–30.

54. CUA, 37/133 #925. Paul Berndorff underplays the extent of Frings's intervention on behalf of wartime criminals in "Oberhirte in den Jahren grosser Not," in *Kardinal Frings,* ed. Dieter Froitzheim (Cologne: Wienand, 1980), 64–77.

55. Ernst Klee, *Persilscheine und falsche Pässe* (Frankfurt: Fischer, 1991), 66.

56. Bishop Wienken to Muench, Berlin, January 19, 1948, Crimes File, CUA.

57. Yahil, *The Holocaust,* 310–311.

58. Froitzheim, *Kardinal Frings,* 268.

59. Buscher and Phayer, "German Catholic Bishops and the Holocaust," 477.

60. CUA, 37/139 #2.

61. Muench to Neuhäusler, Kronberg, November 18, 1948, CUA, 37/133 #4.

62. Hans-Peter Schwartz, *America's Germany: John J. McCloy and the Federal Republic of Germany* (Cambridge, Mass.: Harvard University Press, 1991), 172.

63. Bücker, *Die Schulddiskussion,* 15–18; see also Konrad Repgen, "Die Erfahrung des Dritten Reiches," 134; and Bracher, "Problems of the German Resistance," 57–76.

64. Werner Blessing, "Deutschland in Not, wir im Glauben," 68.

65. Bücker, *Die Schulddiskussion,* 55–57 and chapter 3.

66. Schwartz, *America's Germany,* 172.

67. Ibid., 240.

68. Frank Stern, *The Whitewashing of the Yellow Badge,* trans. William Templer (New York: Pergamon, 1992), 6–7.

69. Ibid., 321.

70. Rolf Rendtorff and Hans Hermann Henrix, eds., *Die Kirchen und das Judentum* (Paderborn: Bonifatius Press, 1988), 239.

71. Michael Marrus, *The Unwanted* (New York: Oxford, 1985), 328ff.

72. See Spotts, *The Churches and Politics in Germany,* chapter 3. Also, Stern, *The Whitewashing of the Yellow Badge,* 333. Bishop Jaeger would be an exception; in 1947 he said the Germans themselves were to blame for their miserable conditions; see Bücker, *Die Schulddiskussion,* 70ff.

73. Hürtgen, "Untergang und Neubeginn," 35–48.

74. Kogon published "Kirchliche Kundgebungen von politischer Bedeutung" in the July 1947 issue of *Frankfurter Hefte* 2, no. 7 (July 1947).

75. OMGUS official Richard G. Akselrad interviewed the bishops on August 23, 1947, during their annual meeting in Fulda. Akselrad evidently used a tape recorder, as large sections of the typed manuscript are direct quotes. Those interviewed were Joseph Frings (Cologne), Albert Stohr (Mainz), Lorenz Jaeger (Paderborn), and Johannes Dietz (Fulda). The transcript is among the John Riedl Papers, Box 2, Catholic Church and Nazism File, Marquette University Archives.

76. Maximilian Kaller, bishop of Ermland, volunteered to be assigned to a concentration camp to work as a priest on behalf of Catholics of Jewish heritage. See

Freiburger Rundbrief 1, no. 1 (August 1948); see also the excellent study of Kaller by Reifferscheid, *Das Bistum Ermland,* 256, fn. 15.

77. Stohr said that he did not include Kogon among the indiscreet. "I know him personally very well and value him highly as a courageous and true Catholic. But I have the impression that this article is the expression of a concentration camp psychosis which has not remained without influence even on such a sharp and analytic mind as Dr. Kogon's."

78. Hoffmann, "Roncalli in the Second World War," 853; see also Heinz Hürten, "Zeugnis und Widerstand," 147.

79. Beilmann, 63. See also Georg Denzler, *Widerstand oder Anpassung?* (Munich: Piper, 1984), 155.

80. Denkschrift Frings, August 2, 1945, Köln, in *Akten deutscher Bischöfe über die Lage der Kirche 1933–45,* ed. Berhard Stasiewski (Mainz: Grünewald, 1968), 625, VKZ, Series A, vol. 38.

81. Bücker, *Die Schulddiskussion,* chapter 2.

82. The best study is Herbert F. Ziegler, *Nazi Germany's New Aristocracy: The SS Leadership, 1925–1939* (Princeton: Princeton University Press, 1989).

83. Bishop Jaeger's contention in the OMGUS interview.

84. Theodor Eschenburg, *Jahre der Besatzung, 1945–1949* (Brockhaus: Wiesbaden, 1983), 115.

85. Spotts, *The Churches and Politics in Germany,* 95ff.

86. Ronald D. E. Webster, "Whither the Mea Culpa of German Protestantism after the Holocaust?" (paper given at the Second International Conference on the Holocaust, Berlin, March 1994). Webster points out that conservative Protestant churchmen criticized Heinrich Grüber and never praised his work for Jews during the Holocaust.

87. Blessing, "Deutschland in Not, wir im Glauben," 64.

88. Stern, *The Whitewashing of the Yellow Badge,* 78–79.

89. Ibid., 317.

90. Erika J. Fischer and Heinz-D. Fischer, *John J. McCloy und die Frühgeschichte der Bundesrepublik Deutschland* (Cologne: Berend von Nottbeck, 1985); see also Stern, *The Whitewashing of the Yellow Badge,* 299.

91. A German wrote to Bishop Muench in 1947 telling him that President Harry Truman was a Jew whose middle name was Solomon. See the Muench Papers in CUA, 37/138 #2.

92. See, for example, *Freiburger Rundbrief* 3, no. 10–11 (1950–51).

93. Clemens Rummel to Faulhaber, Munich, October 12, 1947, BAM 6285.

94. Interview of Saul Sorrin with the author, August 6, 1992, Milwaukee. In October of 1945, General Eisenhower reported to President Truman that the survivors were getting about 2,000 calories a day, and that he would raise this to 2,500 as soon as possible. This was nearly double the amount of German rations of that time. See D. D. Eisenhower to H. S. Truman, October 8, 1945, Myron C. Taylor Papers, Box 1, Truman Library.

95. Clemens Rummel to Faulhaber Munich, October 12, 1947, BAM 6285.

96. Marrus, *The Unwanted,* 308.

97. Stern, *The Whitewashing of the Yellow Badge,* 75ff.

98. Report for Saturday, March 22, 1947, Riedl Papers, Series 5, Box 1, Marquette University Archives.

99. Stern, *The Whitewashing of the Yellow Badge,* 157. The organization was the *Arbeitsgemeinschaft der jüdischen Gemeinden in Deutschland.*

100. Luckner to Thieme, Freiburg, July 26, 1948, IZG FD 163/48.

101. Faulhaber to Allied Military Authority, Munich, June 14, 1945, BAM 6280.

102. President of the Israelitische Kultusgemeinde München to Faulhaber, München, July 25, 1947, BAM 6282.

103. *Aufbau,* no. 7 (February 15, 1946), BAM 6280.

104. Thieme to Gertrud Luckner, June 2, 1955, Karl Thieme Papers, IZG ED 163/50.

105. Muench's official title as a Vatican diplomat was "Apostolic Visitator to Germany and Regent of the Apostolic Nunciature at Bad Godesburg"; see Gallagher, "Patriot Bishop," 314.

106. Muench Diary, June to October 1946, CUA, 37/1-4.

107. Muench's diaries disclose that he frequently pondered whether German Catholics had supported Hitler. He thought not, although the questions would not stop occurring to him. He became a close personal friend of several German bishops, above all Cardinal Faulhaber, but he does not seem to have discussed this question with them, and they evidently did not disturb the papal envoy's thoughts on the matter.

108. Ibid.

109. John Riedl served OMGUS as Chief of Catholic Affairs (1946–1948), Chief of Education Branch (1948–1949), and continued on in this same capacity under the U.S. High Commissioner for Germany until 1952; George Shuster became the Bavarian State Commissioner in 1950. After meeting with Riedl in October of 1946 to discuss the rehabilitation of the German people, Muench confided to his diary that his former Milwaukee altar boy was a "strange character." Muench Diary, June to October 1946, CUA, 37/1-4.

110. Ibid.

111. Ibid.

112. Klee, *Persilscheine und falsche Pässe,* 68.

113. Muench Diary, April to November 1947, CUA, 37/1-4.

114. The OMGUS attempt to reform the Bavarian educational system, and the role that Muench played in thwarting it, is extensively documented in the papers of OMGUS educational official and one-time Marquette University dean John Riedl. See also Frederic Spotts, *The Churches and Politics in Germany,* 84ff.; and Heinz Hürten, "Kirchen und amerikanische Besatzungsmacht," 574.

115. Spotts, *The Churches and Politics in Germany,* 88.

116. Muench Diary, April to November 1947, CUA, 37/1-4; see also Spotts, *The Churches and Politics in Germany,* 88.

117. See John Riedl's account of his trip to Rome, October 15 to November 2, 1947, Reidl Diary, Riedl Papers, Box 2, Catholic Church and Nazism File, Marquette University Archives. Riedl was Chief of Catholic Affairs in the OMGUS Religious and Cultural Affairs Office. A native of Milwaukee, Wisconsin, like Muench, Riedl once served as his altar boy, but the two worked at cross-purposes in Germany. See Muench Diary, October 1946 to April 1947, CUA, 37/1-4.

118. Johann B. Schuster, S.J., "Kollektivschuld," *Frankfurter Hefte* 139 (November 1946): 101–116.

119. Constantin Goschler, "The United States and Wiedergutmachung for Vic-

tims of Nazi Persecution: From Leadership to Disengagement," in *Holocaust and Shilumim: The Policy of Wiedergutmachung in the Early 1950s,* ed. Axel Frohn (Military Law No. 59, Nov, 1947), 9.

120. Ibid., 25.

121. Muench to his mother, Kronberg, October 28, 1946, CUA, 37/30 #6.

122. For background on this office, see my article "The Catholic Resistance Circle in Berlin," 216–229.

123. DAB File I/1-99.

124. Committee to Assist Those Persecuted by Nazis; Notes by Luckner, Freiburg, July 3, 1947, ADC R 611 II.

125. Rendtorff and Henrix, *Die Kirchen und das Judentum,* 239.

126. Quoted in Froitzheim, *Kardinal Frings,* 259.

127. Alexander Mitscherlich and Margerete Mitscherlich, *Die Unfähigkeit zu Trauern* (Munich: Pieper, 1969), 77.

128. Stern, *The Whitewashing of the Yellow Badge,* 97–98.

129. Eugen Kogon, "Christen und Juden," *Frankfurter Hefte* 1, no. 6 (September 1946), 6–8.

130. Sommer put the word Kristallnacht in quotes to indicate her distaste for the euphemistic-sounding Nazi word. File I/1-99, DAB.

131. Sommer is quite critical of the Berlin Caritas personnel who, she said, lacked familiarity with the particulars of the lives of survivors because they had not become involved during the Shoah with the effort to save them; see DAB I/1-99.

132. Muench Diary; see the February 4 entry. CUA, 37/1-4.

133. Ibid., April 9 entry.

134. Ibid., see the entry for September 6, 1947.

135. In her syndicated column Eleanor Roosevelt objected to these tours, writing that the Germans brought their troubles on themselves and were not deserving of sympathy. See the *St. Louis Post Dispatch,* February 21, 1947.

136. David S. Wyman, ed., *The World Reacts to the Holocaust* (Baltimore: Johns Hopkins University Press, 1996), passim.

9. The Holocaust and the Priorities of Pius XII during the Cold War

1. Folder 2, Myron C. Taylor Papers, Truman Archives. See also Stehle, *Geheimdiplomatie im Vatikan,* 201.

2. Owen Chadwick, *The Christian Church in the Cold War* (London: Cambridge University Press, 1992), 15.

3. Anthony Rhodes, *The Vatican in the Age of the Cold War* (Hamshire: Russel, 1992), 231.

4. J. Graham Parsons to "Red" (Walter C. Dowling, Division of Southern European Affairs, Department of State), Rome, March 9, 1948, RG 59, Box 21, NARA.

5. Robert Leiber to Preysing, Rome, October 28, 1945, Cardinal Preysing Papers, DAB V/16-4. See also Clauss, *Die Beziehungen des Vatikans,* 173.

6. Muench's papers are in the archives of the Catholic University of America.

7. Harold H. Tittmann to the Secretary of State, Vatican City, November 30, 1945, RG 59 Box 9, folder marked "Miscellaneous," NARA.

8. Julius Döpfner, *The Questioning Church* (London: Burns and Oates, 1964), 83; see also Papeleux, *Les silences de Pie XII,* 168. The best collection of church statements is in Rolf and Henrix, eds., *Die Kirchen und das Judentum;* see p. 244 for the quoted statement.

9. If statesmen were impressed by Pius's foresight, they paid him little respect in their papers; see, for example, Dean Acheson, *Present at the Creation: My Years in the State Department* (New York: W.W. Norton, 1969), and Kai Bird, *The Chairman: John J. McCloy, the Making of the American Establishment* (New York: Simon and Schuster, 1992).

10. Repgen, "Kardinal Frings im Rückblick," 313.

11. Annual Report of Osborne for 1945; Rome, February 22, 1946, Public Record Office, London, FO 371/60 803; document reprinted in *VKZ,* Series A, vol. 38, 904.

12. For my analysis of this statement, see Buscher and Phayer, "German Catholic Bishops and the Holocaust," 163–185.

13. Bücker, *Die Schulddiskussion,* 15–18; see also Konrad Repgen, "Die Erfahrung des Dritten Reiches," 134; and, Bracher, "Problems of the German Resistance," 57–76.

14. Note to Verbale from Robert D. Murphy, RG 59, Box 13, NARA.

15. Muench Diary, October 1946 to April 1947, CUA, 37/1-4. The goods were sent to Italy and loaded onto 950 boxcars between 1946 and 1949 for shipment over the Alps. See Robert Leiber, "Pius XII," in *The Storm over "The Deputy,"* ed. Eric Bently (New York: Grove Press, 1964), 183.

16. Madre Pascalina (Sister Pasqualina Lehnert) to Muench, Vatican City, March 28, 1948, CUA, 37/37 #7.

17. For an overview of the post-Holocaust German church, see my chapter "Die Katholische Kirche, der Vatikan und der Holocaust," in *Der Umgang mit dem Holocaust nach 1945, Europa-USA-Israel,* ed. Rolf Steininger (Vienna: Böhlau, 1994), 137–146. A more detailed discussion appears in my study "The German Catholic Church after the Holocaust," *Holocaust and Genocide Studies* 10, no. 2 (Fall 1996): 151–167. For a specific discussion of the German church's postwar reaction to the Holocaust, see my article "The Postwar German Catholic Debate over Holocaust Guilt," *Kirchliche Zeitgeschichte* 8, no. 2 (1995): 426–439.

18. Michael Ermarth, ed., *America and the Shaping of German Society, 1945–1955* (Providence, R.I.: Berg, 1993), 9. Pius also recognized the necessity of collective responsibility and he admitted that "not a few even of those who call themselves Christians" were negligent. But Pius did not single out Germany and the murder of the Jews in this regard. See Walker, *Pius of Peace,* 159.

19. Blessing, "Deutschland in Not, wir im Glauben," 68ff.

20. Graf von Galen, *Rechtsbewusstsein und Rechtsunsicherheit* (Rome, March 1946), printed as manuscript.

21. CUA, 37/133 #112.

22. Klee, *Persilscheine und falsche Pässe,* 67.

23. Jean E. Smith, *Lucius D. Clay: An American Life* (New York: Holt, 1990), 301–302.

24. Yahil, *The Holocaust,* 322–323, and Marchione, *Yours Is a Precious Witness,* 159.

25. Muench to Giovanni Battista Montini, Kronberg, February 24, 1951, CUA,

37/133 #2. I am grateful to my brother, Richard Phayer, for translating this letter from the Italian.

26. Muench Diary, June 1946 to October 1946, CUA, 37/1-4.

27. Heblethwaite, *Paul VI,* 155.

28. Buscher, *The U.S. War Crimes Trial Program in Germany,* chapter 5.

29. Ibid., chapter 8.

30. Schwartz, *America's Germany,* 163ff.

31. Muench to Giovanni Battista Montini, Kronberg, February 24, 1951, 37/133 #2.

32. *Frankfurter Allgemeine Zeitung,* January 19, 1951.

33. Sereny, *Into That Darkness,* 315ff. One of the author's interviewees, Burkhardt Schneider, denied that Vatican money was used for this purpose.

34. Sereny, *Into That Darkness,* 315.

35. Klee, *Persilscheine und falsche Pässe*; John Loftus and Mark Aarons, *Unholy Trinity,* 2nd ed. (New York: St. Martins Press, 1992). See page 25, for example, where Bishops Hudal and Montini are linked, and chapter 5, which deals with Croat fugitives: "It is virtually inconceivable that the key officials in the Vatican hierarchy were ignorant of Draganovic's Nazi-smuggling network" (119). Ernst Klee, who specializes in ecclesiastical muckraking for the distinguished German weekly *Die Zeit,* is the only person to have gained access to Hudal's papers in Rome.

36. Sereny, *Into That Darkness,* passim; Loftus and Aarons, *Unholy Trinity,* 30. Unfortunately, Father Graham never discusses the evidence that other historians or journalists have gathered that indicates that, at the least, the Vatican was aware of his activities on behalf of fugitives from justice; see Alvarez and Graham, *Nothing Sacred,* 98.

37. Klee, *Persilscheine und falsche Pässe,* 49.

38. Weisbord and Sillanpoa, *The Chief Rabbi, the Pope, and the Holocaust,* 80.

39. Sereny, *Into That Darkness,* 315.

40. Ibid., 306.

41. Loftus and Aarons, *Unholy Trinity,* 35.

42. Klee, *Persilscheine und falsche Pässe,* 39. Klee simply assumes without comment that this money was used for fugitives.

43. Sereny, *Into That Darkness,* 301.

44. Stehle, *Geheimdiplomatie im Vatikan,* 203.

45. Secretary of State Byrnes to U.S. Political Adviser for Germany Murphy, Jan. 2, 1946, *FRUS,* 1946, 5, 794; for 1943 see *FRUS,* 1943, 1, 468.

46. Vincent La Vista to Herbert J. Cummings, filed at the United States State Department July 14, 1947, under the title "Illegal Emigration Movements in and through Italy," RG 59, Box 4080, NARA. Hereafter cited as the La Vista Report.

47. La Vista Report.

48. Ibid.

49. Records of the Office of Strategic Services, RG 226, Box 427, Entry 14, NARA.

50. La Vista Report.

51. For a complete account of this episode, see Alvarez and Graham, *Nothing Sacred,* chapter 4, "A Convent for Cover."

52. Report of Lt. Col. W. D. Gibson, August 15, 1944, RG 84, Box 47 (General Records. 1944: 840.4–848 Balkans), NARA.

53. Papeleux, *Les silences de Pie XII,* 168.

54. Alexander C. Kirk, U.S. Political Adviser, American Embassy, Rome, to Joseph N. Greene, Jr., Representative of the U.S. Political Adviser, Trieste, Italy, April 22, 1946, RG 84, Box 109 (General Records. 1946: 711.5–711.9), NARA. Included in this file is a letter from D.V. Bendallab of the Office of the British Political Adviser to the Supreme Allied Commander, October 30, 1946, listing the 39 Croats.

55. RG 59, Box 28, NARA.

56. OSS report on Monsignor Ante Golik, alleged Ustasha subsidizer; June 17, 1946, RG 226, Box 29, Folder 170, NARA. This report is rated "reliable," the highest rating for intelligence.

57. Interview with Sidney J. Zabludoff, Symposium on Holocaust-Era Assets, National Archives, December 4, 1998. Mr. Ron Neitzke, U.S. State Department specialist on Croatia, agrees that the sum is much too high.

58. Emerson Bigelow to Harold Glasser, October 21, 1946, RG 226, Box 29, Folder 168, NARA.

59. William Slany, *U.S. and Allied Wartime and Postwar Relations and Negotiations with Argentina, Portugal, Spain, Sweden, and Turkey on Looted Gold and German External Assets and U.S. Concerns about the Fate of the Wartime Ustasha Treasury* (Washington, D.C.: U.S. State Department, 1998), 141–156.

60. Bigelow to Glasser.

61. This question was discussed at the workshop "The Nazi Gold Issue and Jewish Assets" at the November 1998 meeting of the Holocaust Educational Foundation in Boca Raton, Florida.

62. OSS Report, September 20, 1946, "Whereabouts of Former Ustaschi Officials," RG 226, Box 29, Folder 171, NARA.

63. Alexander C. Kirk, U.S. Political Adviser, American Embassy, Rome, to Joseph N. Greene, Jr., Representative of the U.S. Political Adviser, Trieste, Italy, April 22, 1946, RG 84 (General Records. 1946: 711.5–711.9), Box 109, NARA. St. Jerome's (San Girolamo degli Illirici) was located at 123 Via Tomacelli Street in Rome.

64. Shelah, "The Catholic Church in Croatia," 269.

65. Weisbord and Sillanpoa, *The Chief Rabbi, the Pope, and the Holocaust,* 79.

66. Slany, *U.S. and Allied Wartime and Postwar Relations,* 148.

67. Ibid. "Ratlines" was intelligence jargon referring to the Italian escape routes that defectors and war criminals used to flee Europe. A number of governments, including the U.S. government, secretly supported the Ratlines in order to facilitate intelligence gathering. Krunoslav Dragonovic was a main player in the process, for which reason Loftus and Aarons argue that the Ratlines were created by the Vatican.

68. Slany, *U.S. and Allied Wartime and Postwar Relations,* 149.

69. Ibid.

70. Loftus and Aarons, *Unholy Trinity,* 113. My thanks to John Loftus for putting me in touch with Mr. William Gowen.

71. Interview with Mr. William Gowen, New York, October 10, 1988.

72. Interview between Vladimir Stakic and Cardinal Tisserant, April 7, 1946,

Rome RG 59, Box 34, file marked 1947, NARA. It was also Cardinal Tisserant who reported that the Vatican had a list of clerics who had committed war crimes in Croatia. Thus, he would have been unaware of the liaison between the Holy See and St. Jerome's seminary and other places of Croatian refuge.

73. Ibid., folder marked "Political—General 1947"; document entitled U.S. Civil Censorship Submission; Civil Censorship Division, USFET; 6 May 1947; telegram from Antonio E. Vucetich, El Socorro, Argentina, to Olga Vucetich-Radnic, Foderreuthweg 5, Kempten, Allgäu, Bavaria. The telegram does not prove that Pavelic was in Argentina by the spring of 1947. Counter Intelligence Corps Agent Gowen continued to look for him in Rome after this date. Loftus and Aarons state that Pavelic left Italy in September of 1947 and arrived in Argentina in November; see *Unholy Trinity,* 86.

74. Lewy, *The Catholic Church and Nazi Germany,* 307.

75. See chapter 4.

76. Johannes Willebrands, "Vatican II and the Jews: Twenty Years Later," *Christian-Jewish Relations* 18, no. 1 (March 1985): 19.

77. Philip Bernstein to Gen. J. T. McNarney, September 14, 1946, RG 59, Box 28, NARA. Bernstein was the adviser to the Theater Commander on Jewish Affairs.

78. Ibid.

79. *Freiburger Rundbrief* 1, nos. 2, 3, and 4 (March–July 1949).

80. McDonald, Tel Aviv, to AMVAT, October 24, 1949, RG 59, Box 34, NARA.

81. Gowen, Rome, to State Department, November 2, 1948, RG 59, Box 20, NARA.

82. See, for example, Eva Fleischner, "Response to Emil Fackenheim's 'The Holocaust and the State of Israel,'" in *Auschwitz: Beginning of a New Era,* ed. Eva Fleischner (New York: KTAV, 1977), 225–235. The Vatican, the first state to recognize the Federal Republic of Germany, was one of the last to recognize Israel. At the time of the founding of the Jewish state a high Vatican official in the secretariat of state is reputed to have remarked that "it is unthinkable that the Holy Land finds itself in the hands of Christ's murderers." See Kurt Hruby, "Antizionismus, Antijudaismus und christlicher Antizionismus," *Freiburger Rundbrief* 22, no. 81/84 (1970): 11–18.

83. *Freiburger Rundbrief* 1, no. 1 (1948): 13.

84. Copies of the *monitum* are in a number of church archives in Germany; see File I/1-99 in DAB. In the part of the *monitum* dealing with indifferentism someone in the Berlin chancery wrote "Luckner" in the margin.

85. John Hellman, "The Jews in the 'New Middle Ages,'" in *Jacques Maritain and the Jews,* ed. Robert Royal (Notre Dame, Ind.: University of Notre Dame Press, 1994), 89–103. Maritain's wife, Raissa, was a Jewish convert to Catholicism.

86. Jacques Maritain, *Pour la Justice* (New York, n.d.), 196.

87. Ibid., 311.

88. White paper, December 9, 1945, File Ambassade I, Le Centre d'Archives Maritain de Kolbsheim (henceforth CAM).

89. Maritain to Montini, Rome, July 12, 1946, File Ambassade I, CAM.

90. Maritain to Montini, Rome, August 12, 1946, ibid.

91. Froitzheim, *Kardinal Frings,* 263.

92. Maritain to the Conférence Internationale Extraordinaire Pour Combattre l'Antisémitisme; Rome, July 28, 1947, File Ambassade I, CAM.

93. Maritain to Montini, July 12, 1946.

94. Iwona Irwin-Zarecka, "Poland after the Holocaust," in *Remembering for the Future*, I, 143–155. The author points out that Kielce was hardly an isolated event.

95. Jerzy Slawomir Mac, "The Kielce Pogrom 1946," trans. Padraic Kenney, *Studium Papers* 13, no. 2 (April 1989): 46–47.

96. Ibid.; other estimates are considerably higher.

97. Marrus, *The Unwanted*, 325–326.

98. Robert Murphy, Berlin, to the Secretary of State, October 1, 1946, RG 59, Box 28, NARA.

99. Bernstein to Gen. J. T. McNarney, September 14, 1946, RG 54, Box 28, NARA. This report differs substantially from the recollections of Rabbi Herbert A. Friedman, Bernstein's aide, as recorded in *Moment* (October 1996), 16. Friedman asserts that Pope Pius was downright critical of the response of the Polish hierarchy, headed by Cardinal Hlond, to the Kielce massacre. Bernstein's minute does not reflect this.

Furthermore, Friedman writes in *Moment* that Pius promised to issue a letter, to be delivered to all parish pastors in Poland, in which he would "forbid pogroms against Jews." It would be highly unusual for a pope in modern times to bypass the hierarchy of a nation in order to give unilateral instructions regarding a topic as controversial as antisemitism was in Poland. I have found no evidence that Pope Pius actually did this.

The United States Holocaust Memorial Museum's collection of interviews includes an interview with Rabbi Friedman conducted in 1992. Here Friedman relates the indifference of both Cardinal Hlond and the Jewish leader of the Communist Party in Poland to the Kielce massacre. But, in contrast to his strong assertions in *Moment* about Pius XII's dismay over the massacre, Friedman's two-and-a-half-hour taped interview contains no references at all to the pope.

100. Bernstein to McNarney; statement of Cardinal August Hlond of July 11, 1946.

101. S. D. Zagorski, dispatch from the U.S. embassy in Poland, July 12 and 15, 1946, RG 59, Box 28, NARA. On the reaction of Cardinal Hlond to the pogrom, see Michael C. Steinlauf, *Bondage to the Dead: Poland and the Memory of the Holocaust* (Syracuse: Syracuse University Press, 1997), 61.

102. RG 59, box 28, file marked 1947, NARA.

103. Research Committee on Deported Jews; Rome, 15 June 1947, to Cardinal Stefano Sapieha, Archbishop of Cracow, File marked "Son Excellence; M. le Ministre des Affaires Étrangeres," CAM.

104. Ibid.

105. *Aufbau* (a New York newspaper), no. 7 (February 15, 1946).

106. Telegram of the U.S. Jewish Labor Committee to Maritain, July 7, 1946, File Ambassade I, CAM.

107. Maritain to Pope Pius, Rome, July 12, 1946, File marked "Son Excellence; M. le Ministre des Affaires Étrangères," CAM. The letter was actually addressed to Montini but it is clear that it was intended for the pope.

108. Foreign service posts of the Department of State, "Top Secret" file 1944–47, 822–844, RG 84, Box 5, NARA. The audience with Pope Pius took place on September 15, 1945.

10. Catholics and Jews after the Holocaust

1. Helmut Gollwitzer and Gerta Scharffenorth, "Protestanismus, Restauration und Opposition," in *Protestanten in der Demokratie,* ed. Wolfgang Huber (Munich: Kaiser, 1990), 231–247.

2. Ludolf Herbst, "Kontinuität und Diskontinuität in den deutschen Nachkriegsplanungen 1943 bis 1946/7," *Bulletin des Arbeitskreises Zweiter Weltkrieg* 1–4 (1985): 49–69. Frederic Spotts dealt with both churches in *The Churches and Politics in Germany* (Middletown, Conn.: Wesleyan University Press, 1973).

3. Anselm Doering-Manteuffel, "Kirche und Katholizimus in der Bundesrepublik der Fünfziger Jahre," *Historisches Jahrbuch* 102 (1982): 126.

4. Author's interview with Cardinal Johannes Willebrands and Stejphan Schmidt, S.J., Rome, February 1, 1993.

5. Lacouture, *Jesuits: A Multibiography,* 399.

6. Thieme ran afoul of the Nazis and emigrated to Switzerland before the war. Boehm was a member of Gerhard Ritter's anti-Nazi clique in Freiburg. (Saul Friedländer maintains that this group was itself not entirely free of antisemitism; see *Nazi Germany and the Jews,* 297.) Hans Lukaschek resigned his bureaucratic post in Silesia because he refused to implement Nazi directives.

7. *Freiburger Rundbrief* 2/3 (March 1949).

8. Ibid. Although Caritas is listed as the publisher, it did not provide financial support. Luckner had to solicit money from all quarters and could not go to press until costs were covered. Consequently, the early editions of the paper appeared at irregular intervals.

9. Rolf Rendtorff, "Judenmission nach Auschwitz," in *Auschwitz als Herausforderung für Juden und Christen,* ed. Günther Ginzel (Heidelberg: Schneider, 1980), 541–542; see also Stern, *The Whitewashing of the Yellow Badge,* 326.

10. Maritain to Montini, Rome, July 12, 1946, File Ambassade I, CAM.

11. Postcard from Luckner to Thieme, July 8, 1946, IZG FD 163/48.

12. Thieme to Luckner, Loerrach, April 8, 1948, IZG FD 163/48.

13. *Freiburger Rundbrief* 2 and 3 (March 1949): 8–13.

14. Ornstein to Thieme, Zurich, September 16, 1948, IZG ED 163/12.

15. Buber to Thieme, Jerusalem, March 29, 1949, IZG ED 163/10.

16. Luckner to Thieme, Cherbourg, July 11, 1949, IZG ED 163/48.

17. On this, see the valuable study of Eva Fleischner, *Judaism in German Christian Theology since 1945* (Metuchen, N.J.: Scarecrow Press, 1975).

18. Thieme to Oesterreicher, Basel, Easter, 1950, IZG ED 163/60.

19. Thieme to Stegemann, Basel, May 7, 1952, IZG ED 163/83.

20. Thieme to F. Thijssen, Basel, June 23, 1952, IZG ED 163/85. See also Alan T. Davies, *Antisemitism and the Christian Mind* (New York: Herder, 1969), 93ff.

21. Rendtorff and Henrix, *Die Kirchen und das Judentum,* 239.

22. Ralph Giordano praised the statement as a step in the right direction; see the *Jüdische Wochenblatt of Buenos Aires* 9, no. 645 (November 12, 1948).

23. Thieme to Rösen, January 8, 1949, IZG ED 63/113.

24. Thieme to Luckner, Loerrach, October 16, 1950, IZG ED 163/49.

25. "Bericht über Besprechungen mit römischen Kirchenbehörden über die christlich-jüdische Zusammenarbeit," IZG ED 163/116. There were a number of

national and international Jewish-Christian groups that were very loosely affiliated. One was the German Society for Jewish-Christian Cooperation, on whose executive committee Karl Thieme served. Rome made the accusation of indifferentism specifically at the International Council of Christians and Jews, which had held a meeting in Freiburg itself. Thieme was involved minimally with the World Brotherhood, another "suspect" organization. See Vatican Secretariat of State to Muench, the Vatican, October 10, 1950, Sommer Papers, DAB.

26. Sommer to Luckner, February 26, 1952, Sommer Papers, DAB.

27. Ernst Ludwig Ehrlich to author, Riehen, June 22, 1993. Ehrlich recalled that Cardinal Frings had "little understanding for our work before the [Second Vatican] Council."

28. Frings to Thieme, Fulda, August 23, 1950, R 611 II Verfolgtenfürsorge. Solzbacher taught in the Cologne archdiocesan seminary.

29. Thieme to Hoefer, July 7, 1950, IZG ED 163/35.

30. Luckner to Preysing, Freiburg, September 29, 1950, Sommer Papers, DAB.

31. Letter of Schoeningh to Luckner, September 21, 1949, IZG ED 163/48. The article in question had appeared on the 13th of August.

32. *Freiburger Rundbrief,* 3, nos. 10–11 (January 1951), 2.

33. Thieme, "Die Christen, die Juden und das Heil," 113–125.

34. *Wiener Library Bulletin* 2, no. 1 (November 1947): 3; *Wiener Library Bulletin* 3, nos. 3–4 (May–July 1949): 26.

35. Saloman Heinemann to Preysing, Israel, May 14, 1950, DAB I/1-100.

36. Oberammergau is discussed by the Freiburg circle in a section of file R 611 II with the title "Invitation to a meeting on Christianity and Judaism, February 12, 1950," ADC.

37. Stern, *The Whitewashing of the Yellow Badge,* 249.

38. Correspondence between Karl Thieme and Ernst Ludwig Ehrlich, IZG ED 163/17.

39. Zeitlow to Frings, Bad Nauheim, January 4, 1951, Faulhaber Nachlass 6286, BAM.

40. IZG; see the material on this case in file ED 163/115, especially the letters of June 11 and 15, 1950, of the Society for Christian-Jewish Collaboration to the Minister of Culture.

41. "Schuld oder Fahrlässigkeit?" *Allgemeine Wochenzeitung der Juden in Deutschland 5,* 11 (23 June 1950): 1.

42. Information carried in the December 1951 issue.

43. Constantin Goschler, *Wiedergutmachung. Westdeutschland und die Verfolgten des Nationalsozialismus (1945–1954)* (Munich: Oldenburg, 1992), 209.

44. *Freiburger Rundbrief* 3, no. 10/11 (January 1951).

45. *Freiburger Rundbrief* 2, no. 5/6 (December 1949): 4.

46. Thieme Papers, IZG ED/163–116.

47. *Freiburger Rundbrief* 3, no. 10/11(January 1951): 11.

48. *Freiburger Rundbrief* 5, no. 17/18 (August 1952).

49. Ibid., 33.

50. Gertrud Luckner, "Stand und Aufgaben der Wiedergutmachung," *Caritas Sonderdruck,* no. 5 (1955).

51. Luckner to Thieme, Freiburg, August 4, 1952, IZG, Thieme Papers, FD 163/49.

52. Fischer and Fischer, *John J. McCloy.* McCloy's quarterly reports are reprinted here; see p. 154 for McCloy's remarks on the economy in 1952.

53. Luckner report, September 2, 1962, 189.059, ADC.

54. *Freiburger Rundbrief* 5, no. 17/18 (August 1952): 4.

55. Thieme to Landersdorfer, Loerrach, July 10, 1950, IZG, Thieme Papers, ED 163/48.

56. The most notable exception was the Cardinal of Berlin, Konrad Preysing, who died in 1952.

57. Stern, *The Whitewashing of the Yellow Badge,* 367.

58. Goschler, "The United States and Wiedergutmachung," 13.

59. See Luckner's pamphlet, *Stand und Aufgaben der Wiedergutmachung.*

60. Luckner to District Attorney Bader, Freiburg, November 20, 1945, ADC 184.3.

61. J. B. Sandeman, O.S.B. to Mueller, Religious Affairs Adviser's Office, Buende, February 17, 1950, ADC R 611 II; see also in the same file Luckner to President Franz Müller, in house, Freiburg, February 17, 1950. Luckner played a leading role in organizing an English-German effort to help Jewish survivors but was then barred from it. She actually showed up at the initial meeting in 1950 and begged to be allowed to take part but was refused on the grounds that Cardinal Frings had not authorized her membership.

62. Landgerichtspräsident to Luckner, Freiburg, July 3, 1950, ADC R 611 II.

63. Kurt R. Grossmann to Luckner, January 21, 1953, ADC R 611 II, Verfolgtenfürsorge. See also the telegram of March 21 in the same file.

64. A copy of the pamphlet *Stand und Aufgaben der Wiedergutmachung* may be found in ADC 284.3.

65. Wolfgang Benz, *Zwischen Hitler und Adenauer* (Frankfurt: Fischer, 1991), chapter 8. Küster served as the Staatsbeauftragter für die Wiedergutmachung und Leiter der Abteilung Gesetzgebung im Stuttgarter Justizministerium (State Agent for Restitution and Director of the Legal Legislation of the Stuttgart Ministry of Justice).

66. Luckner to Thieme, Freiburg, August 26, 1954, and Luckner, Borgmann, Giessler, Jörger, Schmidtheus, Thieme, and Vögtle to Adenauer, Freiburg, September 1954, IZG, Thieme Papers, ED 163/50.

67. *Freiburger Rundbrief* 7, no. 24/25 (September 1954).

68. See the correspondence in IZG, Thieme Papers, ED 163/50.

69. Verfolgtenfürsorge Kurt Grossmann to Luckner, January 21, 1953, ADC R 611 II.

70. See Luckner's annual report for 1954 in ADC 111.055 Zenralrat.

71. Benz, *Zwischen Hitler und Adenauer,* chapter 8.

72. Thieme Papers Luckner to Thieme, Freiburg, January 13, 1952, IZG FD 163/49.

73. Herbert Blankenhorn, *Verständnis und Verständigung* (Frankfurt: Propyläen, 1980), 138ff. and passim.

74. File FD 163/48 and others in the Thieme Papers (IZG) contain correspondence on this point. See also the *Freiburger Rundbrief* 2 and 3 (March 1949). See the *Acta Apostolicae Sedis* 8/9 (August/September 1948): 342 for the official rewording decree.

75. See the brochure in the Thieme Papers, IZG FD 163/49.

76. *Freiburger Rundbrief* 6 (1954): 24.

77. There is extensive correspondence between Thieme and Oesterreicher among Thieme's papers; see, for example Osterreicher to Thieme, New York, May 1, 1946, IZG ED 163/69.

78. Oesterreicher to Thieme, January 30, 1954, IZG, Thieme Papers, ED 163/60.

79. Thieme to Luckner, October 30, 1954, IZG, Thieme Papers, ED 163/50.

80. Rabbi Dr. M. Eschelbacher to the *Freiburger Rundbrief,* London, February 17, 1958, IZG, Thieme Papers, ED 163/50.

81. One conference was held in 1952 in Bad Godesberg and a second three years later in Bonn. IZG, Thieme Papers, ED 163/12.

82. Thieme to Luckner, June 2, 1955, IZG, Thieme Papers, ED 163/50.

83. *Freiburger Rundbrief* 15, no. 57/60 (January 1964): 80–81.

84. For a collection of all such statements, see Rendtorff and Henrix, *Die Kirchen und das Judentum.* I have commented on selected statements in "Die Katholische Kirche und der Umgang mit dem Holocaust," and in "German Catholic Bishops, the Vatican, and the Holocaust in the Postwar Era," in *The Netherlands and Nazi Genocide,* ed. G. Jan Colijn and Marcia S. Littell (New York: Mellen Press, 1992), 177–189.

85. ADC, Files 101 and 235.9. There were four marks to the dollar at this time.

86. I have not included auxiliary bishops in this count.

87. Hans-Peter Schwarz, *Die Aera Adenauer 1957–1963,* vol. 3 of *Geschichte der Budesrepublik Deutschland,* ed. Karl Dietrich Bracher, et al. (Stuttgart: Deutsche Verlag, 1983), 215ff.

88. The Institut für Zeitgeschichte has a number of files on Eisele in its newspaper collection.

89. Rendtorff and Henrix, *Die Kirchen und das Judentum,* 242.

90. Schwarz, *Die Aera Adenauer,* 204ff.

91. Konrad Repgen has so accused them; see Konrad Repgen, "Die Erfahrung des Dritten Reiches," 151.

11. The Holocaust Recalled, Antisemitism Renounced

1. *Freiburger Rundbrief* 8/9 (August 1950): 3–4.

2. Phayer and Fleischner, *Cries in the Night,* chapter 6.

3. Author's interview with Cardinal John Willebrands and Stjepan Schmidt, S.J., February 1, 1993, in Rome. Willebrands made it a point to travel to Rome once a year to report to Cardinal Ottaviani on his ecumenical work.

4. It is interesting to speculate why Pope John would have sent Isaac rather than use normal Vatican channels of communication. It is possible that he learned that the curia had attempted, and nearly succeeded, in canceling Isaac's audience. Thus, John may have decided to bypass curial offices.

The account I am following here is that of Stjepan Schmidt, *Augustin Bea, Kardinal der Einheit* (Graz: Styria, 1989), 415ff. In footnote 64, Schmidt points out that he and John Oesterreicher disagree on the matter of the importance of Isaac's visit. Schmidt is at pains to show that up until Isaac's visit there had been no discussion about including Jews in the council's agenda. Oesterreicher believes that this would have occurred with or without Isaac's efforts. Schmidt will not concede this, arguing that it is not possible to say what might have occurred had Isaac not visited Rome a second time and affirming that it was precisely his visit that set things in motion.

Both Schmidt and Johannes Willebrands were close associates of Bea in the Secretariat on Religious Relations with Jews at the time of Isaacs's visit and both agree that his visit was decisive.

5. Shaw, *Turkey and the Holocaust,* 278.

6. John M. Oesterreicher, *The New Encounter between Christians and Jews* (New York: Philosophical Library, 1986), 110–112.

7. Schmidt, *Augustin Bea,* 642–643.

8. Schmidt, 645. The note was written on plain paper. This may indicate, once again, that Pope John sought to bypass curial interference and communicate directly with Bea, as he had done through Jules Isaac.

9. Oesterreicher, *New Encounter,* 215.

10. John T. Pawlikowski, "The Vatican and the Holocaust: Unresolved Issues," in *Jewish-Christian Encounters over the Centuries,* ed. Marvin Perry and F. M. Schweitzer (New York: Peter Lang, 1994), 301.

11. Heblethwaite, *Paul VI,* 166.

12. John M. Oesterreicher, "Kommentierende Einleitung zur Erklärung des II. Vatikanischen Konzils über das Verhältnis der Kirche zu den nichtchristlichen Religionen," in *Lexikon für Theologie und Kirche, Das Zweite Vatikanische Konzil,* ed. H. S. Brechter (Freiburg: Herder, 1967), 464.

13. Oesterreicher, "Kommentierende Einleitung," 462–463.

14. After the Council, Cardinal Frings continued to display some lack of sensitivity toward the Jews. In an interview in 1967 with Rabbi Max Nussbaum, formerly of Berlin, Frings made statements that smacked of antisemitism. See the accounts of the interview in *Die Zeit,* "Der Rabbi und der Kardinal," Friday, February 17, 1967, p. 14; and "Kardinal Frings und der Antisemitismus," in the *Allgemeine Unabhängige jüdische Wochenzeitung,* 21, no. 45 (February 3, 1967): 1.

15. Henri Fesquet, *The Drama of Vatican II,* trans. B. Murchland (New York: Random House, 1967), 711.

16. John Oesterreicher, "Erklärung über das Verhältnis der Kirche zu den nichtchristlichen Religionen," *Theologie und Kirche,* supplementary volume on the Second Vatican Council.

17. Oesterreicher, "Kommendierende Einleitung," 466. Pope Paul's biographer, Peter Heblethwaite, fails to mention the pope's sermon.

18. Ibid., 466.

19. Ibid., 409, fn. 12.

20. Fesquet, *The Drama of Vatican II,* 243.

21. Oesterreicher, *The New Encounter between Christians and Jews,* 195.

22. Oesterreicher, "Kommendierende Einleitung," 440–448.

23. Ibid., 474.

24. Fesquet, *The Drama of Vatican II,* 714.

25. Ibid., 713.

26. *New York Times,* September 16, 1982, A14.

27. Rabbi Leon Klenicki, "The Carmelite Convent at Auschwitz—Past and Future," special publication of the Anti-Defamation League of B'nai B'rith, 1989.

28. For a critical review of these documents, see Dietrich, *God and Humanity,* 66–79.

29. Ibid., 86.

30. Not all Catholics, of course, freed themselves of antisemitism just because of the council's pronouncement. When the Fathers were about to adopt *Nostra Aetate*, twenty-eight Catholic groups from around the world circulated a pamphlet accusing the Jews of Christ's death and calling the council the "antipope"; see Fesquet, *The Drama of Vatican II,* 712.

12. Epilogue

1. Clemens Vollnhals, "Das Reichskoncordat als Konfliktfall im Allierten Kontrollrat," *Vierteljahresheft für Zeitgeschichte* 35, no. 4 (1987): 679.

2. Muench Diary, October 1946 to April 1947, Muench Papers, CUA, 37/1-4.

3. Vollnhals, "Das Reichskoncordat," 681–682.

4. Muench Diary, October 1949 to November 1949, Muench Papers, CUA, 37/1-4.

5. Ludwig Volk, "Der Heilige Stuhl und Deutschland 1945–1949," in *Kirche und Katholizismus 1945–1949,* ed. Anton Rauscher (Paderborn: Schöningh, 1977), 78.

6. File 1304, "Visitator Apostolicus in Germania," Kronberg, January 13, 1949, Faulhaber Nachlass, BAM.

7. *Bayerischen Staatszeitung,* March 17, 1951. Pope Pius and Monsignor Tardini put considerable pressure on Muench in this regard, either because they were not sure of the formality that the apostolic nuncio would be ex officio the dean of the corps, or because they were unsure of what status the nuncio would have under the condition of a divided Germany. See Muench's diary notations for October 1950, CUA, 37/1-4.

8. Muench Diary, October 1950 to May 1951, Muench Papers, CUA, 37/1-4.

9. In an unpublished white paper written at the time of his resignation, Maritain noted his impressions of Pius XII. See "Cahiers Jacques Maritain," 4, L'Ambassade au Vatican (1945–1948) in CAM File Ambassade I.

10. Ibid.

11. J. Graham Parsons, Assistant to the Personal Representative of the President to His Holiness Pope Pius XII to the Secretary of State; Vatican City, March 10, 1948, RG 59, Box 21, Folder marked "Political," NARA.

12. Walker, *Pius of Peace,* 112–113.

13. Thomas A. Kselman and Steven Avella, "Marian Piety and the Cold War in the United States," *Catholic Historical Review* 72, no. 3 (July 1986): 407–411. The peak years of devotion to Our Lady of Fatima were 1945 to 1954.

14. Michael O'Carroll, C.S.Sp., *Pius XII, Greatness Dishonored* (Chicago: Franciscan Herald Press, 1980), 159.

15. See the interesting biographical sketch of Pius by the Jesuit Burkart Schneider, *Pius XII* (Göttingen: Musterschmidt, 1968). Schneider was a professor at the Gregorianum in Rome during the war, and helped edit the Vatican's wartime documents in the *ADSS* collection.

16. Gallagher, "Patriot Bishop," 262.

17. White paper "Cahiers Jacques Maritain."

18. Papeleux, *Les silences de Pie XII,* 58. See also Schneider, *Pius XII,* 32.

19. Kent, "Pope Pius and Germany," 65.

20. Papeleux, *Les silences de Pie XII;* see, for example, the German bombing of English churches, 55–65.

21. See, for example, Don Oberdorfer, *The Turn: From the Cold War to the New Era* (New York, 1991), and John Lewis Gaddis, *The United States and the End of the Cold War* (New York: Poseidon Press, 1992).

22. John Lewis Gaddis, *The United States and the End of the Cold War,* 50ff. Moral ambiguities commonly cited in connection with the Cold War are President Truman's 1947 exaggerations regarding communism in Greece and Turkey, the Central Intelligence Agency's postwar interference in the internal affairs of Italy and France, presidential candidate John Kennedy's "missile gap" rhetoric, and, in George F. Kennan's view, nuclear warfare itself.

23. Peter C. Kent, "Toward the Reconstruction of Christian Europe: The War Aims of the Papacy, 1939–1945" (presented at the conference "FDR, the Vatican, and the Roman Catholic Church in America, 1933–1945," at the Roosevelt Library, Hyde Park, New York, October 1988).

24. Memorandum to the State Department, Paris, July 19, 1949, Myron C. Taylor Papers, Truman Library, Box 49.

25. Telegram from the office of Myron Taylor to the president, Rome, March 27, 1941, Welles Papers, Box 151, Folder 4, FDR Library.

26. See the folder marked "Vatican Matters, 1945," RG 59, Box 34, NARA.

27. Muench Diary, October 1946 to April 1947, Muench Papers, CUA, 37/1-4.

28. Muench Diary, October 1948 to May 1949, Muench Papers, CUA, 37/1-4.

29. Stehle, *Geheimdiplomatie im Vatikan,* 205.

30. Bankier, *The Germans and the Final Solution,* 145–149.

31. Oesterreicher, *The New Encounter,* 125.

32. Eva Fleischner and I discuss the context of Christian rescue in the Introduction and chapter 8 of *Cries in the Night: Women Who Challenged the Holocaust* (Kansas City: Sheed and Ward, 1997).

33. Ibid., chapter 6.

REFERENCES

Primary Sources

Archival

Archiv Deutscher Caritas
  Deutscher Caritas Verband File 284/101
  File 111.055 Zenralrat (Annual Reports)
  File 183 Sorge für die ehemals vom Nationalsozialismus Verfolgten
  File 284 Verfolgtenfürsorge
  File R 611 II Committee to assist those persecuted by Nazis
  File 284.3 Luckner's work
  File 189.059 (restitution and Christian-Jewish relations)
  File R 611 II
    All aspects of Luckner's work
    Correspondence to and from Luckner
    Vatican investigation of Freiburg circle
  File of Auer papers (Hans Eisele case)
Diözesanarchiv Berlin
  File I/1–99 Sommer's correspondence and restitution work
  File I/1–100 Jewish-Christian relations
  File on Sommer's papers
  File I/1–103
    papers on Sommer's life work
    Correspondence, especially between Sommer and Luckner
    Sommer's official and unofficial report on Hans Globke
  File V/16–4 Preysing's papers
Bistumsarchiv München
  File 6280 Postwar unsolicited letters on Christians and Jews
  File 6286 Faulhaber's papers (very little in this file; the cardinal's papers are not open to the public)
  File 1303 Faulhaber-Muench correspondence
  File 8423 Efforts to assist Jewish emigration

File 7500 Church-OMGUS matters; guilt question
File 7501 Guilt question
Bundesarchiv Abteilung Potsdam
    File 21793 Reichsministerium für den kirchlichen Angelegenheiten
        Church-state relations; correspondence with Preysing
        Gestapo reports on the church
        Nazi-church relations in occupied Poland
        Correspondence regarding Karl Adam's pro-Nazi brochure
Catholic University of America Archives
    File 37/37 correspondence of Muench
    File 37/138 religious conditions in postwar Germany
    File 37/73 Zeiger-Muench correspondence
    File 37/138 Unsolicited antisemitic letters to Muench
    File 37/139 German Catholics and Nazism
    File 37/1-4 Muench's diaries
    37/131 #111 Case of Hans Eisele
    37/133 #112
        Imprisoned war criminals
        War criminals: German church, Muench, the Vatican
Le Centre d'Archives Maritain de Kolbsheim
    File Ambassade I
        White papers to Montini on postwar antisemitism
        Extensive papers on the Kielce pogrom
    File "Son Excell. Ministre des Affaires Étrangères"
Friedrich Ebert Stiftung
    Walter Dirks papers
        File 1951 Bi-DDr correspondence including Luckner's
        File on 1946 correspondence
Institut für Zeitgeschichte
    File FD 163 Karl Thieme papers (correspondence in this file is voluminous and includes letters to and from Luckner; Thieme kept carbons of his own letters to others.)
    Eisele File (extensive media coverage)
Marquette University Archives
    Riedl papers
        Series 1
        Box 2 Catholic church and Nazisim
        Box 3 Muench-OMGUS File
        Frings File
        Box 4 Denazification
        Series 5
        Box 1 Daily reports
        Box 2 Daily records
        Series 7
        Box 3 Guardini and Kogon File

Truman Archives
    Myron C. Taylor 1940–49
      File 2 Summarized reports
      File 3 FDR's letters to Pius XII
      General File W–Z war crimes
      Boxes marked "Papers of Myron C. Taylor": Correspondence
University of Notre Dame Maritain Center
    File correspondence on antisemitism
    File 24 Maritain's wartime views
    File 16 Maritain's wartime broadcasts to France
U.S. National Archives and Records Administration
    RG 59
      Box 34
      Postwar German church; Yugoslavia; Palestine; Nuremberg Trials
      Box 4012
      Yugoslavia
      Box 13
      Yugoslavia; Muench; denazification
      Box 26
      Palestine and Holocaust survivors
      Box 6
      Maritain's appointment
      Box 20
      Israel and the Vatican
      Vatican and Nuremberg criminals
      Box 21
      German school reforms of OMGUS
      Vatican concern about Italian communism
      Box 9
      Yugoslavia; survivors thank Pius XII
      Box 28
      Communism; Maritain's appointment; Jozsef Mindszenty; German Catholic resistance to Nazism
      Yugoslavia; Kielce pogrom
      Box 17
      Ante Pavelic
      Vatican intercession for Weizsäcker
      Box 30
      Nazi atrocities
    RG 59 740.0011 Boxes 2433–2435, 2439, 2441, 2448–2449, 2451–2454, 2457–2458, 2461–2463, 2465, 2467, 2469, 2470–2477.
      Vatican objections to bombing of Rome
    RG 84
      Box 47

Clerical-Nazi espionage in Rome
Box 5
Eisenhower-Clark audience
Box 109
Ustasha-Vatican links
RG 131
  Box 487
  Transfer of Vatican City Funds to the U.S.
RG 319
  Box 424
  Hudal
  Box 4080
  Vatican and fugitive war criminals
RG 226
  Box 29
  Vatican-Ustasha links
  Box 427
  U.S. intelligence reports on Vatican
  Box 1187
  U.S. intelligence reports on Vatican
  Box 428
  Bombing of Rome
  Box 168a
  Safehaven report on Vatican
RG 982
  Reels 164, 165, 166, 169, 170, 172 174, 178
  Bombing of Rome
  Reel 173
  Communist activity in Rome
  Reel 176
  Possible Nazi kidnapping of pope

Edited Documents

Actes et Documents du Saint Siège relatifs á la Seconde Guerre mondiale. Edited by Pierre Blet, S.J., Angelo Martini, S.J., Burkhart Schneider, S.J., and Robert Graham, S.J. Vatican City: Liberia Editrice Vaticana, 1965–67. 11 vols.

Konrad Adenauer Briefe Über Deutschland, 1945–1951. Edited by Hans Peter Mensing. N.p.: Corso, 1983.

Akten Deutscher Bischöfe über die Lage der Kirche 1933–1945. Edited by Berhard Stasiewki. Mainz: Grünewald, 1968.

Akten Kardinal Michael von Faulhabers, 1917–1945. Edited by Ludwig Volk, S.J. Mainz: Grünewald, 1978. 2 vols.

Ausgaben und Grenzen der Staatsgewalt, eine Stellungnahme der im Jahre 1953 in Fulda versammelten deutschen Bischöfe. Cologne: Bachen, 1953.

Die Briefe Pius XII. an die Deutschen Bischöfe 1939–1944. Edited by Burkhart Schneider. Mainz: Grünewald, 1966.

Dossier: Kreisauer Kreis. Dokumente aus dem Widerstand gegen den National-sozialisten aus dem Nachlass von Lothar König, S.J. Edited by Roman Bleis-tein, S.J. Frankfurt: Knecht, 1987.

Fischer, Erika J., and Heinz-D. Fischer. *John J. McCloy und die Frühgeschichte der Bundesrepublik Deutschland.* Cologne: Nottbeck, 1985. Includes McCloy's quarterly reports.

"Der französische Episkopat während der deutschen Besetzung." Report by the Archbishop-Coadjutor Emile Guerry. *Frankfurter Hefte* 1, no. 5 (August, 1946): 76–78.

Galen, Clemens August Graf von. "Rechtsbewusstsein und Rechtsunsicherheit." Rome, March, 1946. Printed as manuscript.

Grosser katholischer Katechismus. Munich: Kösel, 1948.

Die katholische Kirche und das Judentum, Dokumente von 1945–1982. Edited by Klemens Richter. Freiburg: Herder, 1982.

Katholische Kirche und Nationalsozialismus: Dokumente, 1930–1944. Edited by Hans Müller. Munich: Oldenbourg, 1963.

Die Kirchen und das Judentum. Edited by Rolf Rendtorff and Hans Hermann Hen-rix. Paderborn: Bonifatius Press, 1988.

Kölner Aktenstücke zur Lage der katholischen Kirche in Deutschland, 1933–1945. Edited by Wilhelm Corsten. Cologne: Bachem, 1949.

Phayer, Michael. "Nazism and Some German Bishops." *Continuum* 1, no. 1 (Au-tumn 1990): 143–152. Includes documents translated by the author from Ger-man.

Pius XII a Polska, 1939–1949. Edited by Kazimierz Papée. Rome: n.p., 1954.

Rundbrief zur Förderung der Freundschaft zwischen dem alten und dem neu-en Gottesvolk—im Geiste der beiden Testamente. Edited by Rupert Giessler, Kuno Joerger, Gertrud Luckner, and Karl Thieme. 1948–1968. Title varied sev-eral times over a number of years.

Walter, Adolph. Geheime Aufzeichnungen aus dem nationalsozialistischen Kirchen-kampf, 1933–1943. Edited by Ulrich von Hehl. Mainz: Grünewald, 1982.

Wartime Correspondence between President Roosevelt and Pope Pius XII. Edited by Myron C. Taylor. New York: Macmillan, 1947.

Die Weizsäcker Papiere 1933–1950. Edited by Leonidas E. Hill. Frankfurt: All-stein, 1974.

Memoirs and Interviews

Beilmann, Christel. "Eine Jugend im katholischen Milieu. Zum Verhältnis von Glaube und Widerstand." In *Piroten, Swings und Junge Garde,* ed. Wilfried Breyvogel. Bonn: Dietz, 1991. 57–73.

Ehrlich, Ernst Ludwig, former European Director of B'nai B'rith. Correspondence with the author. 1993.

Gowen, William E. W. Interview. New York, October 10, 1988.

Hudal, Alois C. *Europas Religiöse Zukunft*. Pamphlet. Rome, 1942.

———. *Römische Tagebücher*. Graz: Stocker, 1976.

Kranz, Gisbert. *Eine katholische Jugend im Dritten Reich. Erinnerungen, 1921–1947*. Freiburg: Herder, 1990.

Lehnert, Sr. M. Pascalina. *Ich Dürfte Ihm dienen: Erinnerungen an Papst Pius XII*. Würzburg: n.p., 1982.

Interview of Gertrud Luckner and Marie Schiffer by Dietrich and Ursula Goldschmidt, Barbara Schieb, and Elizabeth von Thadden, October 27, 1988, Berlin.

Scrivener, Jane. *Inside Rome with the Germans*. New York: Macmillan, 1945.

Sorrin, Saul. Director of the United Nations Relief and Rehabilitation Agency in southern Germany from January 1946 to April 1950. Interview with the author, Milwaukee, 1992.

Willebrands, Cardinal John, and Schmidt, Stjepan, S.J. Interview with the author, Rome, 1993.

Secondary Sources

Albrecht, Dieter, ed. *Katholische Kirche und Nationalsozialismus*. Mainz: Grünewald, 1987.

Alexander, Stella. *The Triple Myth: A Life of Archbishop Alojzije Stepinac*. Boulder, Colo.: East European Monographs, 1987.

Almog, Shmuel. *Nationalism and Antisemitism in Modern Europe, 1815–1945*. Jerusalem: Sassoon International Center, 1987.

Altmeyer, Karl Aloys. *Katholische Presse unter NS-Diktature*. Berlin: Morus, 1962.

Alvarez, David. "The Professionalization of the Papal Diplomatic Service, 1909–1967." *The Catholic Historical Review* 72, no. 2 (April 1989): 233–248.

Alvarez, David, and Robert A. Graham, S.J. *Nothing Sacred: Nazi Espionage against the Vatican, 1939–1945*. London: Cass, 1997.

Amery, Carl. *Capitulation*. New York: Herder and Herder, 1967.

Asaf, Uri. "Christian Support for Jews during the Holocaust in Hungary." In *Studies on the Holocaust in Hungary*, ed. Randolph L. Braham. Boulder, Colo.: Social Science Monographs, 1990. 65–113.

Bankier, David. *The Germans and the Final Solution*. Cambridge: Blackwell, 1992.

———. "The Germans and the Holocaust: What Did They Know?" *Yad Vashem Studies* 20 (1990): 69–98.

Baron, Lawrence. "The Historical Context of Rescue." In *The Altruistic Personality: Rescuers of Jews in Nazi Europe*, ed. Samuel P. Oliner and Pearl M. Oliner. New York: Free Press. 13–48.

Barry, Coleman, O.S.B. *American Nuncio: Cardinal Aloisius Muench*. Collegeville, Minn.: St. John's University Press, 1969.

Bartoszewski, Wladyslaw T. "Polish-Jewish Relations: A Current Debate among Polish Catholics." *Research Report* 7 (October 1987): 1–20.

———. "Polish-Jewish Relations in Occupied Poland, 1939–1945." In *The Jews in*

Poland, ed. Chimen Abramsky, Maciej Jachimczyk, and Antony Polansky. Oxford: Oxford University Press, 1988. 147–160.

Bauer, Yehuda, ed. *Present-Day Antisemitism.* Jerusalem: Sassoon International Center, 1988.

Benz, Wolfgang. "Postwar Society and National Socialism: Remembrance, Amnesia, Rejection." *Tel Aviver Jahrbuch für deutsche Geschichte* 19 (1990): 1–12.

———. *Zwischen Hitler und Adenauer.* Frankfurt: Fischer, 1991.

Bergen, Doris. "Witnesses to Atrocity: Germany Military Chaplains and the Holocaust." In *In God's Name: Religion and Genocide in the Twentieth Century,* ed. O. Bartov and P. Mack. Forthcoming.

Berghahn, Volker. "Resisting the Pax Americana?" In *America and the Shaping of German Society, 1945–1955,* ed. Michael Ermarth. Providence, R.I.: Berg, 1993. 85–100.

Bernanos, Georges. "Bilanz nach 1945." *Dokumente* 18 (1962): 7–18.

Berndorff, Paul. "Oberhirte in den Jahren grosser Not." In *Kardinal Frings,* ed. Dieter Froitzheim. Cologne: Wienand, 1980. 64–77.

Blankenhorn, Herbert. *Verständnis und Verständigung.* Frankfurt: Propyläen, 1980.

Bleistein, Roman, S.J. *Alfred Delp.* Frankfurt: Knecht, 1989.

———. "Katholische Bischöfe und der Widerstand gegen den Nationalsozialismus." *Stimmen der Zeit* 207 (1989): 579–590.

———. "Lothar Koenig." *Stimmen der Zeit* 204 (1986). 313–326.

Blessing, Werner. "'Deutschland in Not, wir im Glauben . . . ': Kirche und Kirchenvolk in einer katholischen Region 1933–1949." In *Von Stalingrad zur Währungsreform,* ed. Martin Broszat, K. D. Henke, and H. Woller. Munich: Oldenbourg, 1988. 3–112.

Bloch, Peter André. "Karl Thieme im Briefwechsel mit Jacques Maritain und Karl Barth über den Plan eines Gebetsfeldzugs in Europa gegen die Gefahren des Nationalsozialismus." In *Christen im Widerstand Gegen das Dritte Reich,* ed. Joel Pottier. Stuttgart: Burg, 1988. 19–53.

Boyens, Armin. "Die Kirchenpolitik der amerikanischen Besatzungsmacht in Deutschland von 1944 bis 1946." In *Kirchen in der Nachkriegszeit,* ed. A. Boyens et al. Göttingen: Vandenhoeck and Ruprecht, 1979. 6–100.

Bracher, Karl-Dietrich. "Problems of the German Resistance." In *The Challenge of the Third Reich,* ed. Hedley Bull. Oxford: Clarendon, 1986. 53–76.

Braham, Randolph L. *Genocide and Retribution: The Holocaust in Hungarian-Ruled Northern Transylvania.* Boston: Kluwer Nijhoff, 1983.

———. *The Politics of Genocide.* 2 vols. New York: Columbia University Press, 1981.

Brecher, August. *Die katholische Kirchenzeitung für das Bistum Aachen im Dritten Reich.* Aachen: Einhard, 1988.

Breitinger, Hilarius. *Als Deutscherseelsorger in Posen und im Warthegau 1934–1945.* Mainz: Grünewald, 1984.

Breitman, Richard. *Official Secrets: What the Nazis Planned, What the British and Americans Knew.* New York: Hill and Wang, 1998.

Bronowski, Alexander. *Es Waren So Wenige. Retter Im Holocaust.* Trans. Zeev Eshkolot. Stuttgart: Quell, 1991.

Broszat, Martin, and Ladislaus Hory. *Der kroatische Ustascha-Staat, 1941–1945.* Stuttgart: dva, 1964.

Browning, Christopher R. *Fateful Months: Essays on the Emergence of the Final Solution.* New York: Holmes and Meier, 1985.

———. "A Final Hitler Decision for the 'Final Solution'? The Riegner Telegram Reconsidered." *Holocaust and Genocide Studies* 10, no. 1 (Spring 1996): 3–10.

———. *The Final Solution and the German Foreign Office.* New York: Holmes and Meier, 1978.

Bryk, Andrzej. "Polish-Jewish Relations during the Holocaust: The Hidden Complex of the Polish Mind." Paper presented at the conference History and the Culture of the Polish Jews, Jerusalem, 1988.

———. "Polish Society Today and the Memory of the Holocaust." In *Remembering for the Future.* Oxford: Pergamon, 1988. Supplementary Volume, 55–66.

Buchberger, Michael. "Antwort auf einen 'Brief über die Kirche.'" *Klerusblatt* 27, no. 6 (March 15, 1947): 42–45.

Bücker, Vera. *Die Schulddiskussion im deutschen Katholizismus nach 1945.* Bochum: Studienverlag Brockmeyer, 1989.

Buscher, Frank. *The U.S. War Crimes Trial Program in Germany, 1946–1955.* New York: Greenwood, 1989.

Bussmann, Walter. "Pius XII an die deutschen Bischöfe." *Hochland* 61 (1969): 61–65.

Carpi, Daniel. *Between Mussolini and Hitler.* Hanover, N.H.: Brandeis University Press, 1994.

Chadwick, Owen. *Britain and the Vatican during the Second World War.* Cambridge: Cambridge University Press, 1986.

Chrobak, Werner. "Die Regensburger Kirchenzeitung im Dritten Reich." *Beiträge zur Geschichte des Bistums Regensburg* 15 (1981): 389–430.

Clauss, Manfred. *Die Beziehungen des Vatikans zu Polen während des II Weltkrieges.* Cologne: Böhlau, 1979.

Cohen, Asher. "Immigrant Jews, Christians and French Jews." In *Remembering for the Future.* Oxford: Pergamon, 1988. I, 223–232.

Conway, John S. "Catholicism and the Jews." In *Judaism and Christianity under the Impact of National Socialism,* ed. Otto Dov Kulka and Paul R. Mendes-Flohr. Jerusalem: The Historical Society of Israel and Zalman Shazar Center for Jewish History, 1987. 435–451.

———. "The Churches, the Slovak State and the Jews 1939–1945." *The Slavonic and East European Review* 52, no. 126 (January 1974): 85–112.

———. *The Nazi Persecution of the Churches.* New York: Basic Books, 1968.

Coppa, Frank J. "The Vatican and the Dictators." In *Catholics, the State, and the European Radical Right,* ed. Richard J. Wolff and Jörg K. Hoensch. New York: Columbia University Press, 1987. 199–223.

Dagan, Avigdor. "The Czechoslovak Government in Exile and the Jews." In *The Jews of Czechoslovakia,* ed. Avigdor Dagan. New York: Society for the History of Czechoslovak Jews, 1984. 449–495.

Davies, Alan T. *Antisemitism and the Christian Mind.* New York: Herder, 1969.

Delpech, François. "Les Églises et la Persécution Raciale." In *Églises et Chrétiens dans la IIe Guerre Mondiale.* Lyon: Presses Universitaires de Lyon, 1982. 257–304.

Delzell, Charles F. *Mussolini's Enemies: The Italian Anti-Fascist Resistance.* Princeton, N.J.: Princeton University Press, 1961.

Deselaers, Manfred. *"Und Sie Hatten Nie Gewissensbisse?" Die Biografie von Rudolf Höss, Kommandant von Auschwitz und die Frage nach siener Verantwortung vor Gott und den Menschen.* Cracow: Benno Press, 1997.

Dietrich, Donald J. "Catholic Resistance in the Third Reich." *Holocaust and Genocide Studies* 3, no. 2 (1988): 171–186.

———. *God and Humanity in Auschwitz.* New Brunswick, N.J.: Transaction Press, 1995.

Dinnerstein, Leonard. "Antisemitism in the United States, 1918–1945." In *Remembering for the Future.* Oxford: Pergamon, 1988. I, 315–327.

Dirks, Walter, and Kogon, Eugon. "Verhängnis und Hoffnung im Osten; das Deutsch-Polnische Problem." In *Die Vertreibung der Deutschen aus dem Osten,* ed. Wolfgang Benz. Frankfurt am Main: Fischer, 1985. 125–142.

Djilas, Aleksa. *The Contested Country: Yugoslav Unity and Communist Revolution, 1919–1953.* Cambridge, Mass.: Harvard University Press, 1991.

Doering, Bernard. "The Origin and Development of Maritain's Idea of the Chosen People." In *Jacques Maritain and the Jews,* ed. Robert Royal. Notre Dame, Ind.: Notre Dame University Press, 1994. 17–35.

Doering-Manteuffel, Anselm. "Kirche und Katholizismus in der Bundesrepublik der Fünfziger Jahre." *Historisches Jahrbuch* 102 (1982): 113–134.

Döpfner, Julius. *The Questioning Church.* London: Burns and Oates, 1964.

Dulles, Avery, S.J. *The Reshaping of Catholicism.* San Francisco: HarperCollins, 1988.

Eckert, Willehad Paul. "Zur Geschichte des kirchlichen Widerstands." In *Auschwitz als Herausforderung für Juden und Christen,* ed. Günther Ginzel. Heidelberg: Schneider, 1980. 51–83.

Eggebrecht, Axel, ed. *Die Zornigen Alten Männer.* Hamburg: Rohwolht, 1979.

Endres, Elisabeth. *Edith Stein.* Munich: Piper, 1987.

Engel, David. *In the Shadow of Auschwitz: The Polish Government-in-Exile and the Jews, 1939–1942.* Chapel Hill: University of North Carolina Press, 1987.

Ermarth, Michael, ed. *America and the Shaping of German Society, 1945–1955.* Providence, R.I.: Berg, 1993.

Eschenburg, Theodor. *Jahre der Besatzung, 1945–1949.* Wiesbaden: Brockhaus, 1983.

Fesquet, Henri. *The Drama of Vatican II.* Trans. B. Murchland. New York: Random House, 1967.

Flannery, Edward H. *The Anguish of the Jews: Twenty-three Centuries of Antisem-itism.* New York: Paulist Press, 1985.

Fleischner, Eva. *Judaism in German Christian Theology since 1945.* Metuchen, N.J.: Scarecrow Press, 1975.

———. "Response to Emil Fackenheim's 'The Holocaust and the State of Israel.'" In *Auschwitz: Beginning of a New Era?* ed. Eva Fleischner. New York: KTAV, 1977. 225–235.

Fogelman, Eva. *Conscience and Courage: Rescuers of Jews during the Holocaust.* New York: Anchor Books, 1994.

Fornari, Harry. *Mussolini's Gadfly.* Nashville: Vanderbilt University Press, 1971.

Freeman, Julie D. "German Views of the Holocaust as Reflected in Memoirs." In *Remembering for the Future.* Oxford: Pergamon, 1988. I, 50–61.

Frei, Norbert. "'Vergangenheitsbewältigung' or 'Renazification'? The American Perspective on Germany's Confrontation with the Nazi Past in the Early Years of the Adenauer Era." In *America and the Shaping of German Society, 1945–1955,* ed. Michael Ermarth. Providence, R.I.: Berg, 1993. 47–59.

Freund, Hugo. "Epilog zum Fall Dr. Eisele." *Deutsche Rundschau* 85 (1967). Ed. R. Pechel. Sonderdruck.

Friedländer, Saul. *Nazi Germany and the Jews: The Years of Persecution.* New York: HarperCollins, 1997.

———. *Pie XII et le IIIe Reich.* Paris: Editions du Seuil, 1964.

Froitzheim, Dieter, ed. *Kardinal Frings.* 2nd ed. Cologne: Wienand, 1980.

Gaddis, John Lewis. *The United States and the End of the Cold War.* New York: Oxford University Press, 1992.

Gallagher, Charles R. "Patriot Bishop: The Public Career of Archbishop Joseph R. Hurley, 1937–1967." Ph.D. diss., Marquette University, 1997.

Garlinski, Jozef. *Poland in the Second World War.* New York: Hippocrene Books, 1985.

Gazeau, Roger. "Die 'Abtei Liguge.'" In *Christen im Widerstand gegen das Dritte Reich,* ed. Joel Pottier. Stuttgart: Burg, 1988. 84–94.

Gellately, Robert. "Situating the 'SS-State' in a Social-Historical Context: Recent Histories of the SS, the Police, and the Courts in the Third Reich." *Journal of Modern History* 64, no. 2 (June 1992): 338–365.

Gilbert, Arthur. *The Vatican Council and the Jews.* Cleveland: World Publishing Company, 1968.

Gilbert, Martin. *The Holocaust: A History of the Jews of Europe during the Second World War.* New York: Holt, Rhinehart, and Winston, 1986.

Gollwitzer, Helmut, and Gerta Scharffenorth. "Protestanismus, Restauration und Opposition." In *Protestanten in der Demokratie,* ed. Wolfgang Huber. Munich, 1990. 231–247.

Goschler, Constantin. "The United States and Wiedergutmachung for Victims of Nazi Persecution: From Leadership to Disengagement." In *Holocaust and Shilumim: The Policy of Wiedergutmachung in the Early 1950s,* ed. Axel Frohn. Washington, D.C., 1991. 7–28.

Gottschalk, Alfred. "From the Kingdom of Night to the Kingdom of God: Jewish-Christian Relations and the Search for Religious Authenticity after the Holocaust." In *Contemporary Jewry,* ed. Geoffrey Wigoder. Jerusalem: Institute for Contemporary Judaism, 1984. 235–245.

Graham, Robert A. "Relations of Pius XII and the Catholic Community with Jewish Organizations." In *The Italian Refuge: Rescue of Jews during the Holocaust,* ed. K. Voigt and J. Burgwyn. Washington, D.C.: Catholic University Press of America, 1989. 231–253.

Greive, Hermann. "Between Christian Anti-Judaism and National Socialist Antisemitism: The Case of German Catholicism." In *Judaism and Christianity and the Impact of National Socialism,* ed. O. D. Kulka and Paul R. Mendes-Flohr. Jerusalem: The Historical Society of Israel and Zalman Shazar Center for Jewish History, 1987. 169–179.

Gritschneder, Otto. *Ich predige weiter—Pater Rupert Mayer und das Dritte Reich.* Rosenheim: Rosenheimer Verlag, 1987.

———. *Unbekannte Akten aus der NS-Zeit. Priester vor dem Sondergericht München und die bayerische Justiz.* Munich: Verlag des Historischen Vereins von Oberbayern, 1982.

Gross, Leonard. *The Last Jews of Berlin.* Chapel Hill: University of North Carolina Press, 1983.

Grüber, Heinrich. *Erinnerungen aus sieben Jahrzehten.* Berlin: Kiepenheuer and Witsch, 1968.

Gushee, David P. *The Righteous Gentiles of the Holocaust.* Minneapolis: Fortress Press, 1994.

Gutman, Yisrael. *The Jews of Warsaw, 1939–1943.* Trans. Ina Friedman. Bloomington: Indiana University Press, 1982.

———. "Polish and Jewish Historiography on the Question of Polish-Jewish Relations during World War II." In *The Jews in Poland,* ed. Chimen Abramsky, Maciej Jachimczyk, and Antony Polansky. Oxford: Oxford University Press, 1988. 177–189.

———. "Polish Antisemitism between the Wars: An Overview." In *The Jews in Poland between the Two Wars,* ed. Y. Gutman et al. Hanover, N.H.: University Press of New England, 1989. 97–108.

Gutterage, Richard. "Some Christian Responses in Britain to the Jewish Catastrophe." In *Remembering for the Future.* Oxford: Pergamon, 1988. I, 352–362.

Haar, Carel ter. "P. Friedrich Muckermann, S.J. und 'Der Deutsche Weg': Katholisches Exil im den Niderlanden." In *Christliches Exil und christlicher Widerstand,* ed. W. Frühwald and H. Hürten. Regensburg: Pustet, 1987. 264–275.

Habicht, Hubert, ed. *Eugen Kogon—Ein Politischer Publizist in Hessen.* Frankfurt: Insel, 1982.

Halls, W. D. "French Christians and the German Occupation." In *Collaboration in France,* ed. G. Hirschfeld and P. Marsh. New York: Berg, 1989. 72–92.

Hamerow, Theodore S. *On the Road to the Wolf's Lair: German Resistance to Hitler.* Cambridge, Mass.: Harvard University Press, 1997.

Hannot, Walter. *Die Judenfrage in der katholischen Tagespresse Deutschlands und Oesterreichs 1923–1933.* Mainz: Grünewald, 1990.

Harasko, Alois. *Die Vertreibung der Sudetendeutschen. Sechs Erlebnisberichte in die Vertreibung der Deutschen aus dem Osten.* Edited by Wolfgang Benz. Frankfurt: Fischer, 1985. 105–117.

Heblethwaite, Peter. *Paul VI.* New York: Paulist Press, 1993.

Hehl, Ulrich von. *Priester unter Hitler's Terror: eine biographische und statistische Erhebung.* Mainz: Grünewald, 1984.

Hellman, John. "The Jews in the 'New Middle Ages.'" In *Jacques Maritain and the Jews,* ed. Robert Royal. Notre Dame, Ind.: University of Notre Dame Press, 1994. 89–103.

Hellriegel, Ludwig, ed. *Widerstehen und Verfolgung.* 2 vols. Eltville am Rhein: Walter, 1989.

Helmreich, Ernst C. *The German Churches under Hitler.* Detroit: Wayne State University Press, 1977.

Henke, Josef. "Exodus aus Ostpreussen und Schlesien. Vier Erlebnisberichte." In *Die Vertreibung der Deutschen aus dem Osten,* ed. Wolfgang Benz. Frankfurt: Fischer, 1985. 91–104.

Henningsen, Manfred. "The Politics of Memory." In *Remembering for the Future.* Oxford: Pergamon, 1988. II, 2226–2241.

Herbst, Ludolf. "Kontinuität und Diskontinuität in den deutschen Nachkriegsplanungen 1943 bis 1946/7." *Bulletin des Arbeitskreises Zweiter Weltkrieg* 1–4 (1985): 49–69.

———. *Option für den Westen. Vom Marschallplan bis zum deutsch-französischen Vertrag.* Munich: dtv, 1989.

Herbstrith, Waltraud. *Edith Stein: A Biography.* Trans. Bernard Bonowitz, O.C.S.O. San Francisco: Harper and Row, 1971.

Herczl, Moshe Y. *Christianity and the Holocaust of Hungarian Jewry.* Trans. Joel Lerner. New York: Harper and Row, 1993.

Hessdörfer, Karl. "Die Entschädigungspraxis im Spannungsfeld von Gesetz, Justiz und NS-Opfern." In *Wiedergutmachung in der Bundesrepublik Deutschland,* ed. L. Herbst and C. Goschler. Munich: Oldenbourg, 1989. 231–249.

Hilberg, Raul. *The Destruction of the European Jews.* 3 vols. New York: Holmes and Meier, 1985.

———. *Perpetrators, Victims, Bystanders.* New York: HarperCollins, 1992.

Hill, Leonidas E., III. "The Vatican Embassy of Ernst von Weizsäcker, 1943–1945." *Journal of Modern History* 39, no. 2 (June 1967): 138–159.

Hirschfeld, Gerhard, and Patrick Marsh, eds. *Collaboration in France.* Oxford and New York: Berg, 1989.

Hoffmann, Peter. *Claus Schenk Graf von Stauffenberg und seine Brüder.* Stuttgart: Deutsche Verlagsanstalt, 1992.

———. "Roncalli in the Second World War: Peace Initiatives, the Greek Famine and the Persecution of the Jews." *Journal of Ecclesiastical History* 40, no. 1 (January 1989): 74–99.

Höllen, Martin. *Heinrich Wienken. Der 'Unpolitische' Kirchenpolitiker.* Mainz: Grünewald, 1981.

Huber, Raphael M., ed. *Our Bishops Speak.* Milwaukee: Bruce, 1952.

Hürten, Heinz. *Deutsche Katholiken.* Munich: Schöningh, 1992.

———. "Kirchen und amerikanische Besatzungsmacht in Deutschland." In *Kirche, Staat und katholische Wissenschaft in der Neuzeit,* ed. A. Portmann-Tinguely. N.p.: Schöningh, n.d. Sonderdruck. 565–581.

———. "Selbstbehauptung und Widerstand der katholischen Kirche." In *Der deutsche Widerstand 1933–1945,* ed. Klaus-Jürgen Müller. Munich: Schöningh, 1986. 135–156.

———. *Verfolgung, Widerstand und Zeugnis.* Mainz: Grünewald, 1987.

———. "Zeugnis und Widerstand. Zur Interpretation des Verhaltens der katholischen Kirche im Deutschland Hitlers." In *Widerstand,* ed. Peter Steinbach. Cologne: Berend von Nottbeck, 1987. 144–162.

Hürtgen, Robert. "Untergang und Neubeginn, Köln in den Jahren 1942–1946." In *Kardinal Frings,* ed. Dieter Froitzheim. Cologne: Wienand, 1980. 35–63.

Iranek-Osmecki, Kazimierz. *He Who Saves One Life.* New York: Crown, 1971.

Irwin-Zarecka, Iwona. "Poland after the Holocaust." In *Remembering for the Future.* Oxford: Pergamon, 1988. I, 143–155.

Isaac, Jules. *The Teaching of Contempt.* Trans. Helen Holt. Biographical introduction by Claire Huchet Bishop. New York: Holt, Rhinehart, and Winston, 1964.

Jedin, Herbert. "Pius XII und die Juden." In *Pius XII,* ed. Herbert Schambeck. Kevelaer: Butzon and Bercker, 1986. 185–191.

Juros, Helmut. "Die katholische Kirche im Polen der fünfziger Jahre." *Kirchliche Zeitgeschichte* 3, no. 1 (1990): 59–79. With comments by Henryk Czembor and Zygmunt Zielinski.

Katz, Robert. *Death in Rome.* Cambridge, Mass.: Harvard University Press, 1967.

Keller, Erwin. *Conrad Grüber, 1872–1948.* Freiburg: Herder, 1981.

Kempner, Benedicta Maria. *Priester vor Hitlers Tribunalen.* Munich: Rütten and Loening, 1966.

Kempowski, Walter. *Haben Sie davon gewusst?* Hamburg: Knaurs, 1979.

Kent, Peter C. "A Tale of Two Popes: Pius XI, Pius XII and the Rome-Berlin Axis." *Journal of Contemporary History* 23 (1988): 589–608.

Kershaw, Ian. "Antisemitismus und Volksmeinung." In *Bayern in der NS-Zeit,* ed. M. Broszat and E. Fröhlich. Munich: Oldenbourg, 1979. II, 281–348.

Kessel, Albrecht von. "The Pope and the Jews." In *The Storm over "The Deputy,"* ed. Eric Bently. New York: Grove Press, 1964. 71–75.

Klarsfeld, Serge. "The Upper Echelons of the Clergy and Public Opinion Force Vichy to Put an End in September 1942 to Its Broad Participation in the Hunt for Jews." In *Remembering for the Future.* Oxford: Pergamon, 1988. I, 248–253.

Klausener, Erich. *Von Pius XII zu Johannes XXIII.* Berlin: Morus, 1958.

———. "Zum Widerstand der Katholiken im Dritten Reich." In *Beiträge zum Widerstand 1933–1945,* vol. 22. Berlin: Möller, 1983.

Klee, Ernst. *Persilscheine und falsche Pässe.* Frankfurt: Fischer, 1991.

Klemperer, Klemens von. *German Resistance against Hitler: The Search for Allies Abroad, 1938–1945.* Oxford: Clarendon, 1992.

Knauft, Wolfgang. "Bernhard Lichtenberg." In *Christen im Widerstand Gegen das Dritte Reich,* ed. Joel Pottier. Stuttgart: Burg, 1988. 196–204.

Koch, Peter. *Konrad Adenauer.* Hamburg: Rowohlt, 1985.

Koebner, Thomas. "Die Schuldfrage. Vergangenheitsverweigerung und Lebenslügen in der Diskussion 1945–1949." In *Deutschland nach Hitler,* ed. Thomas Koebner, Gert Sautermeister, and Sigrid Schneider. Opladen: Westdeutscher, 1987. 301–329.

Kogon, Eugon. *Der SS-Staat. Das System der deutschen Konzentrationslager.* Stuttgart: Lizensausgabe des deutschen Bücherbundes, 1974. With appended diagrams and new introduction.

König, Franz Cardinal, and Ehrlich, Ernst Ludwig. *Juden und Christen Haben eine Zukunft.* Kempten: Pendo, 1988.

Korbonski, Stefan. *The Jews and the Poles in World War II.* New York: Hippocrene Books, 1989.

Kranzler, David H. "The Swiss Press Campaign That Halted Deportations to Auschwitz and the Role of the Vatican, the Swiss and Hungarian Churches." In *Remembering for the Future.* Oxford: Pergamon, 1988. I, 156–170.

Krieger, Wolfgang. *General Lucius D. Clay und die amerikanische Deutschlandspolitik, 1945–1949.* Stuttgart: Klett, 1989.

Kulka, Erich. "The Annihilation of Czechoslovak Jewry." In *The Jews of Czechoslovakia,* ed. Avigdor Dagan. New York: Society for the History of Czechoslovak Jews, 1984. 262–328.

Kurzman, Dan. *The Race for Rome.* New York: Doubleday, 1975.

Kushner, Tony. "Ambivalence or Antisemitism? Attitudes and Responses in Britain to the Crisis of European Jewry during the Second World War." In *Remembering for the Future.* Oxford: Pergamon, 1988. I, 404–416.

Lacouture, Jean. *Jesuits: A Multibiography.* Washington, D.C.: Counterpoint, 1995.

Lange-Quassowski, Jutta-B. "Amerikanische Westintegrations Re-education und deutsche Schulpolitik." In *Umerziehung und Wiederaufbau,* ed. Manfred Heinemann. Stuttgart: Nachfolger, 1981. 53–67.

Langmuir, Gavin I. *History, Religion, and Antisemitism.* Berkeley: University of California Press, 1990.

Laqueur, Walter. *The Terrible Secret.* Boston: Little Brown, 1980.

Leffler, Melvyn P. *A Preponderance of Power.* Stanford: Stanford University Press, 1992.

Leiber, Robert. "Pius XII." In *The Storm over "The Deputy,"* ed. Eric Bently. New York: Grove Press, 1964. 173–194.

Lemhöfer, Ludwig. "Zur tapferen Pflichterfüllung Gerufen. Die Katholiken in Adolf Hitler Krieg." In *Katholische Kirche und NS-Staat,* ed. Monika Kringels-Kemen and Ludwig Lemhöfer. Frankfurt: Knecht, 1981. 83–99.

Lewy, Guenter. *The Catholic Church and Nazi Germany.* New York: McGraw-Hill, 1964.

Lichtenstein, Heiner. "Krummstab und Davidstern. Die katholische Kirche und der Holocaust." In *Katholische Kirche und NS-Staat,* ed. Monika Kringels-Kemen and Ludwig Lemhöfer. Frankfurt: Knecht, 1981. 69–81.

Loftus, John, and Mark Aarons. *Unholy Trinity.* New York: St. Martins Press, 1992.

Lubac, Henri de. *Résistance chrétienne á l'antisémitisme, souvenirs 1940–1944.* Paris: Fayard, 1988.

Lucas, Richard C. *The Forgotten Holocaust.* Lexington: University of Kentucky Press, 1986.

———, ed. *Out of the Inferno: Poles Remember the Holocaust.* Lexington: University of Kentucky Press, 1989.

Lüdtke, Alf. "'Coming to Terms with the Past': Illusions of Remembering, Ways of Forgetting Nazism in West Germany." *Journal of Modern History* 65, no. 3 (September 1993): 542–572.

Lustiger, Jean-Marie. *Gotteswahl.* Munich: Piper, 1992.

Mac, Jerzy Slawomir. "The Kielce Pogrom 1946." Trans. Padraic Kenney. *Studium Papers* 13, no. 2 (April 1989): 46–47.

Maier, Hans. "Pius XII—Zukunftsweisender Mahner der Politik." In *Pius XII,* ed. Herbert Schambeck. Kevelaer: Butzon and Bercker, 1986. 29–32.

Majsai, Tamás. "The Deportation of Jews from Csíkszereda and Margit Slachta's Intervention on Their Behalf." In *Studies on the Holocaust in Hungary,* ed. Randolph L. Braham. Boulder, Colo.: Social Science Monographs, 1990. 114–164.

Manoschek, Walter. *Serbien ist Judenfrei: Militärische Besatzungspolitik und Judenvernichtung in Serbien 1941–1942.* Munich: Oldenbourg, 1993.

Marchione, Margherita. *Yours Is a Precious Witness.* New York: Paulist Press, 1997.

Maritain, Jacques. "Europe and the Federal Idea." *Commonweal* 31, no. 26 (April 19, 1940): 544–547.

Marrus, Michael R. "Reflections on the Historiography of the Holocaust." *Journal of Modern History* 66, no. 1 (March 1994): 92–116.

———. *The Unwanted.* New York: Oxford University Press, 1985.

McClaskey, Beryl. *The History of the U.S. Policy and Program in the Field of Religious Affairs under the Office of the U.S. High Commissioner for Germany.* Published by the Historical Division, Office of the Executive Secretary, Office of the U.S. High Commissioner for Germany, 1951. Preface by Harold Zink.

McGreevy, John T. *Parish Boundaries: The Catholic Encounter with Race in the Twentieth-Century Urban North.* Chicago: University of Chicago Press, 1996.

Mendelsohn, Ezra. "Interwar Poland: Good for the Jews or Bad for the Jews?" In *The Jews in Poland,* ed. Chimen Abramsky, Maciej Jachimczyk, and Antony Polansky. Oxford: Oxford University Press, 1988. 130–139.

Mendes-Flohr, Paul R. "Ambivalent Dialogue: Jewish-Christian Theological Encounter in the Weimar Republic." In *Judaism and Christianity under the Impact of National Socialism,* ed. Otto Dov Kulka and Paul R. Mendes-Flohr. Jerusalem: The Historical Society of Israel and Zalman Shazar Center for Jewish History, 1987. 99–132.

Michaelis, Meir. "The Holocaust in Italy and Its Representation in Italian Postwar Literature." In *Remembering for the Future.* Oxford: Pergamon, 1988. I, 254–265.

———. *Mussolini and the Jews: German-Italian Relations and the Jewish Questions in Italy, 1922–1945.* Oxford: Clarendon Press, 1978.

Mitscherlich, Alexander, and Margerete Mitscherlich. *Die Unfähigkeit zu Trauern.* Munich: Piper, 1969.

Modras, Ronald. *The Catholic Church and Antisemitism: Poland, 1933–1939.* Chur, Switzerland: Harwood Press, 1994.

———. "The Catholic Church in Poland and Antisemitism, 1933–1939: Responses to Violence at the Universities and in the Streets." In *Remembering for the Future.* Oxford: Pergamon, 1988. I, 183–196.

Molette, Charles. *Prêtres, Religieux et Religieuses dans la Résistance au Nazisme, 1940–1945.* Paris: Fayard, 1995.

Mommsen, Hans. "Was haben die Deutschen vom Völkermord an den Juden gewusst?" In *From Reichskristallnacht to Genocide,* ed. Walter Pehle. Oxford: Clarendon, 1990.

Morley, John F. *Vatican Diplomacy and the Jews during the Holocaust, 1939–1943.* New York: KTAV, 1980.

———. "Vatican Diplomacy and the Jews of Hungary during the Holocaust: October 15, 1944 to the End." Paper given at the Second International Holocaust Conference, Berlin, 1994.

Mussinghoff, Heinz. *Rassenwahn in Münster. Der Judenpogrom 1938 und Bischof Clemens August Graf von Galen.* Regensberg: Münster, 1989.

Myszor, Jerzy. "Stosunki Kosciol—Panstwo Okupacyjne W Diecezji Katowickiej, 1939–1945." Unpublished manuscript. Katowice, 1992.

Niethammer, Lutz. *Entnazifizierung in Bayern.* Frankfurt: Fischer, 1972.

Oberdorfer, Don. *The Turn: From the Cold War to the New Era.* New York: Poseidon Press, 1991.

Oesterreicher, John. "Cardinal Bea—Paving the Way to a New Relationship between Christians and Jews." In *Simposio Card. Agostino Bea,* ed. Segretariato per l'Unitá die Cristiani. Rome: Pontificia Università Latereuse, 1983. 29–78.

———. *Die Wieder Entdeckung des Judentums Durch die Kirche.* Freiburg: Kyrios, 1971.

———. *The New Encounter between Christians and Jews.* New York: Philosophical Library, 1986.

Oliner, Samuel P., and Pearl M. Oliner. *The Altruistic Personality: Rescuers of Jews in Nazi Europe.* New York: Free Press, 1988.

Olson, David C. "Denazification in the American Zone, 1945–1948: A Study of the Policies and the Effects." N.d. (1954?), n.p. Printed as manuscript.

O'Meara, Thomas F. "A French Resistance Hero." *America* 176, no. 18 (May 24, 1997): 12–16.

———. "'Raid on the Dominicans': The Repression of 1954." *America* 170, no. 4 (February 5, 1994): 8–16.

Papeleux, Léon. *Les Silences de Pie XII.* Brussels: Vokaer, 1980.

Passelecq, Georges, and Bernard Suchecky. *L'encyclique Cachée de Pie XI. Une occasion manquée de l'église face à l'antisémitisme.* Paris: Editions La Découverte, 1995.

Pawlikowski, John T. "The Vatican and the Holocaust: Unresolved Issues." In *Jewish-Christian Encounters over the Centuries,* ed. Marvin Perry and F. M. Schweitzer. New York: Peter Lang, 1994. 294–310.

Paxton, Robert O., and Michael Marrus. *Vichy France and the Jews.* New York: Basic Books, 1981.

Pesch, Otto Hermann. *Das Zweite Vatikanische Konzil.* Würzburg: Echter, 1993.

Peterson, Edward N. *The American Occupation of Germany.* Detroit: Wayne State University Press, 1977.

Pfeifer, Karl. "Die Ermordung der kroatischen Juden." *Tribüne* 31, no. 121 (1992): 117–124.

Phayer, Michael. "The German Catholic Church after the Holocaust." *Holocaust and Genocide Studies* 10, no. 2 (Fall 1996): 151–167.

———. "Die katholische Kirche, der Vatikan und der Holocaust." In *Der Umgang mit dem Holocaust nach 1945, Europa-USA-Israel,* ed. Rolf Steininger. Vienna: Bölau, 1994. 137–146.

———. "Pope Pius XII and the Holocaust during the Cold War." *Holocaust and Genocide Studies* 12, no. 2 (Fall 1998): 233–256.

———. "The Postwar German Catholic Debate over Holocaust Guilt." *Kirchliche Zeitgeschichte* 8, no. 2 (1995): 427–439.

———. *Protestant and Catholic Women in Nazi Germany.* Detroit: Wayne State University Press, 1990.

Phayer, Michael, and Eva Fleischner. *Cries in the Night: Women Who Challenged the Holocaust.* Kansas City: Sheed and Ward, 1997.

Pottier, Joël. *Christen im Widerstand gegen das Dritte Reich.* Stuttgart: Burg, 1988.

Poznanski, Renée. *Etre Juif en France pendant la Seconde Guerre Mondiale.* Paris: Hachette, 1994.

Prekerowa, Teresa. "The Relief Council for Jews in Poland, 1942–1945." In *The Jews in Poland,* ed. Chimen Abramsky, Maciej Jachimczyk, and Antony Polansky. Oxford: Oxford University Press, 1988. 161–176.

Presser, Jacob. *The Destruction of the Dutch Jews.* Trans. Arnold Pomerans. New York: Dutton, 1969.

Pribilla, Max, S.J. "Das Schweigen des deutschen Volkes." *Frankfurter Hefte* 139, no. 1 (October 1946): 15–33.

Recker, Klemens-August. "Wem Wollt Ihr Glauben?" *Bischof Berning im Dritten Reich.* Paderborn: Schöningh, 1968.

Redlich, S. "Metropolitan Andrei Sheptyts'kyi, Ukrainians and Jews during and after the Holocaust." In *Remembering for the Future.* Oxford: Pergamon, 1988. I, 197–206.

Reifferscheid, Gerhard. *Das Bistum Ermland und das Dritte Reich.* Wien: Böhlau, 1975.

Rendtorff, Rolf. "Judenmission nach Auschwitz." In *Auschwitz als Herausforderung für Juden und Christen,* ed. Günther Ginzel. Heidelberg: Schneider, 1980. 539–556.

Repgen, Konrad. "Die Erfahrung des Dritten Reiches und das Selbstverständniss der deutschen Katholiken nach 1945." In *Die Zeit nach 1945 als Thema kirchlicher Zeitgeschichte,* ed. Victor Conzemius, M. Gneschat, and H. Kocher. Göttingen: Vandenhoeck and Ruprecht, 1988. 127–180.

———. "German Catholicism and the Jews, 1933–1945." In *Judaism and Christianity under the Impact of National Socialism,* ed. Otto Dov Kulka and Paul R. Mendes-Flohr. Jerusalem: The Historical Society of Israel and Zalman Shazar Center for Jewish History, 1987. 197–226.

———. "Kardinal Frings im Rückblick—Zeitgeschichtliche Kontroverspunkte einer künftigen Biographie." *Historisches Jahrbuch* 100 (1980): 286–317.

———. "Das Wesen des christlichen Widerstandes." In *Christliches Exil und christlicher Widerstand,* ed. W. Frühwald and H. Hürten. Regensburg: Pustet, 1987. 13–20.

Rhodes, Anthony. *The Vatican in the Age of the Cold War.* Hampshire, Conn.: M. Russell, 1992.

Richter, Klemens, ed. *Die katholische Kirche und das Judentum, Dokumente von 1945–1982.* Freiburg: Herder, 1982.

Roon, Ger van. *Neuordnung im Widerstand.* Munich: Oldenbourg, 1967.

Rossi, Joseph Samuel. "American Catholics and the Formation of the United Nations." Ph.D. diss., Catholic University of America, 1992.

Ruether, Rosemary Radford. "Antisemitism and Christian Theology." In *Auschwitz: Beginning of a New Era?* ed. Eva Fleischner. New York: KTAV, 1977. 79–92.

Sandkühler, Thomas. *Endlösung in Galizien. Der Judenmord in Ostpolen und die Rettungsinitiativen von Berthold Beitz, 1941–1944.* Bonn: J. H. W. Dietz Nachfolger, 1996.

Schaefer, Catherine. *Pius XII and Peace: 1939–1944.* Washington, D.C.: National Catholic Welfare Conference, 1944.

Schall, James V. "The Mystery of 'The Mystery of Israel.'" In *Jacques Maritain and the Jews,* ed. Robert Royal. Notre Dame, Ind.: University of Notre Dame Press, 1994. 51–71.

Schmidt, Maria. "Margit Slachta's Activities in Support of Slovakian Jewry, 1942–43." In *Remembering for the Future.* Oxford: Pergamon, 1988. I, 207–211.

Schmidt, Stjepan. *Augustin Bea, Kardinal der Einheit.* Graz: Styria, 1989.

Schneider, Burkhart. *Pius XII.* Mainz: Grünewald, 1968.

Schuster, Johann B., S.J. "Kollektivschuld." *Frankfurter Hefte* 139 (November 1946): 101–116.

Schwartz, Hans-Peter. *Die Aera Adenauer 1957–1963.* Stuttgart: Deutsche Verlag, 1983.

———. *America's Germany: John J. McCloy and the Federal Republic of Germany.* Cambridge, Mass.: Harvard University Press, 1991.

Schwarz, Werner. *Kreuz und Hakenkreuz*. Oldenburg: University of Oldenburg Press, 1985.

Segev, Tom. *The Seventh Million*. Trans. Haim Watzman. New York: Hill and Wang, 1993.

Sereny, Gitta. *Into That Darkness*. New York: Vintage Press, 1983.

Shaw, Stanford J. *Turkey and the Holocaust*. New York: New York University Press, 1993.

Sheetz, Jessica A. "Margit Slachta's Efforts to Rescue Central European Jews, 1939–1945." In *Cries in the Night: Women Who Challenged the Holocaust*, Michael Phayer and Eva Fleischman. Kansas City: Sheed and Ward, 1997. 42–64.

Shelah, M. "The Catholic Church in Croatia, the Vatican and the Murder of the Croatian Jews." In *Remembering for the Future*. Oxford: Pergamon, 1988. I, 266–280.

Smith, Jean E. *Lucius D. Clay: An American Life*. New York: Holt, 1990.

Spotts, Frederic. *The Churches and Politics in Germany*. Middletown, Conn.: Wesleyan University Press, 1973.

Stehle, Hansjakob. *Geheimdiplomatie im Vatikan. Die Päpste und die Kommunisten*. Zurich: Benzinger, 1993.

Steinberg, Jonathan. *All or Nothing: The Axis and the Holocaust, 1941–1943*. New York: Routledge, 1990.

Steinberg, Maxime. "Faced with the Final Solution in Occupied Belgium: The Church's Silence and Christian Action." In *Remembering for the Future*. Oxford: Pergamon, 1988. Supplementary Volume, 465–478.

Steininger, Rolf. "Katholische Kirche und NS-Judenpolitik." *Zeitschrift fuer katholische Theologie* 114 (1992): 166–179.

Steinlauf, Michael C. *Bondage to the Dead: Poland and the Memory of the Holocaust*. Syracuse: Syracuse University Press, 1997.

Stern, Frank. *The Whitewashing of the Yellow Badge*. Trans. William Templer. New York: Pergamon, 1992.

Stingl, Josef, and Nikolaus von Preradovich, eds. *Gott Segne den Fuehrer!* Starnberger See: Druffel, 1986.

Swiderski, Stanislaw. "Dzialalnosc charytatywna Kosciola Wsród Zydów W Warszawie W Latach Okupacji." In *Materialy I Studia,* ed. Franciszka Stopniaka. Warsaw: Akademia Teologii Katolickiej, 1978. 3, 252–263.

Sziling, Jan. "Die Kirchen im Generalgouvernement." *Miscellanea Historiae Ecclesiasticae* 9 (1984): 277–288.

Tec, Nechama. *When Light Pierced the Darkness*. New York: Oxford University Press, 1986.

Tent, James B. "Education and Religious Affairs Branch, OMGUS." In *Die Entwicklung amerikanischer Bildungspolitik 1944 bis 1949,* ed. Manfred Heinemann. Stuttgart: Burg, 1981. 68–85.

Toaff, Elio. *Perfidi Giudei Fratelli Maggiori*. Milan: Arnoldo Mondadori Press, 1987.

Tomaszewski, Irene, and Tecia Werbowski. *Zegota: The Rescue of Jews in Wartime Poland.* Montreal: Price-Patterson, 1994.

Vago, Bela. "The Hungarians and the Destruction of the Hungarian Jews." In *The Holocaust in Hungary Forty Years Later,* ed. R. L. Braham and Bela Vago. New York: Social Science Monographs and Institute for Holocaust Studies, 1985. 93–106.

Volk, Ludwig. *Der bayerische Episkopat und der Nationalsozialismus, 1930–1934.* Mainz: Grünewald, 1965.

———. "Dir Fuldaer Bischofskonferenz von der Enzyklika 'Mit Brennende Sorge' bis zum Ende der NS Herrschaft." In *Katholische Kirche im Dritten Reich,* ed. Dieter Albrecht. Mainz: Grünewald, 1976. 66–102.

———. "Der Heilige Stuhl und Deutschland 1945–1949." In *Kirche und Katholizismus 1945–1949,* ed. Anton Rauscher. Paderborn: Schöningh, 1977. 53–87.

Vollnhals, Clemens. "Das Reichskondordat als Konfliktfall im Allierten Kontrollrat." *Vierteljahrshefte für Zeitgeschichte* 35, no. 4 (1987): 677–93.

Walker, Reginald F., ed. *Pius of Peace.* Dublin: M. H. Gill and Son, 1945.

Webster, Paul. *Petain's Crime.* London: Macmillan, 1990.

Webster, Ronald D. E. "Whither the Mea Culpa of German Protestantism after the Holocaust." Paper given at the Second International Conference on the Holocaust, Berlin, 1994.

Weinberg, L. Gerhard. *The Foreign Policy of Hitler's Germany.* Chicago: University of Chicago Press, 1980.

———. *Germany, Hitler, and World War II.* New York: Cambridge University Press, 1995.

Weinzerl, Erika. "Austrian Catholics and Jews." In *Judaism and Christianity under the Impact of National Socialism,* ed. Otto Dov Kulka and Paul R. Mendes-Flohr. Jerusalem: The Historical Society of Israel and Zalman Shazar Center for Jewish History, 1987. 283–303.

Weisbord, Robert G., and Wallace P. Sillanpoa. *The Chief Rabbi, the Pope, and the Holocaust: An Era in Vatican-Jewish Relations.* New Brunswick, N.J.: Transaction Press, 1992.

Weiss, Herman. "Die Organisationen der Vertriebenen und ihre Presse." In *Die Vertreibung der Deutschen aus dem Osten,* ed. Wolfgang Benz. Frankfurt: Fischer, 1985. 192–208.

Wigoder, Geoffrey. *Jewish-Christian Relations since the Second World War.* New York: Manchester University Press, 1988.

Wilhelm, Hans-Heinrich. "Zur Haltung der Kirchen während des Ostfeldzuges: Widerstand oder Kollaboration?" *Zeit Geschichte* 13, no. 3 (November 1985): 39–50.

Willebrands, Johannes Cardinal. "Vatican II and the Jews: Twenty Years Later." *Christian-Jewish Relations* 18, no. 1 (March 1985): 16–30.

Wollasch, Hans-Josef. "Heinrich Auer (1884–1951), Bibliotheksdirektor beim Deutschen Caritasverband, als politischer Schutzhäftling Nr. 50241 in Konzentrationslager Dachau." *Zeitschrift für die Geschichte des Oberrheins* 131 (1983): 383–489.

Woods, R. B., and Howard Jones. *Dawning of the Cold War.* Athens and London: University of Georgia Press, 1991.

Wyman, David S., ed. *The World Reacts to the Holocaust.* Baltimore: Johns Hopkins University Press, 1996.

Yahil, Leni. *The Holocaust.* New York: Oxford University Press, 1991.

Zielinski, Zygmunt. "Activities of the Catholic Orders on Behalf of Jews in Nazi-Occupied Poland." In *Judaism and Christianity under the Impact of National Socialism,* ed. Otto Dov Kulka and Paul R. Mendes-Flohr. Jerusalem: The Historical Society of Israel and Zalman Shazar Center for Jewish History, 1987. 381–394.

Zuccotti, Susan. *The Holocaust, the French, and the Jews.* New York: Basic Books, 1993.

———. *The Italians and the Holocaust.* New York: Basic Books, 1987.

———. "Pope Pius XII and the Holocaust: The Case in Italy." In *The Italian Refuge: Rescue of Jews during the Holocaust,* ed. I. Herzer, K. Voigt, and J. Burgwin. Washington, D.C.: Catholic University of America Press, 1989. 254–270.

INDEX

Stern, Frank, historian, 157
Stimmen der Zeit, 9, 136, 209
Stohr, Albert, Bishop, 147
Streicher, Julius, perpetrator, 17
Strusinska, Viktoria, rescuer, 131
Süddeutsche Zeitung, 190
Sudetenland, 58
Suhard, Cardinal of Paris, 6, 127, 174–175
Summi Pontificatus, 24
Szalisi, Ferenc, fascist, 108

T-4. *See* Reich Enterprise for Health and
    Welfare Facilities
The Tablet, British Catholic journal, 94
Tacchi-Venturi, Pietro, S.J., rescuer 39, 95,
    101–102
Tardini, Domenico, Monsignor, 5, 28, 37–
    38, 39, 46, 49, 60, 97, 160, 164, 168–
    169, 175–176, 209
Taylor, Myron C., U.S. foreign service, 23,
    47–49, 61–63, 103, 164, 174, 222
Tec, Nechama, historian, 112–113
Théas, Bishop Pierre, 92–93
Theresienstadt, concentration camp, 151
t'Hooft, Visser, theologian, 108
Tiso, Father Josef, 14, 46–47, 65, 76, 87,
    89, 90–91
Tito, Marshal Josip, 40, 47, 87, 170, 172–
    173
Tittman, Harold H., U.S. foreign service,
    23, 48, 54, 56, 61, 63, 76, 101, 108
Toaff, Elio, Roman rabbi, 213
Touvier, Paul, perpetrator, 112–113
Treblinka, concentration camp, ix, 42, 50,
    116, 120, 166
Truman, Harry, 149–150, 152, 155, 163
Truman Doctrine, 161
Trzeciak, Stanislaw, antisemitic Pole, 8
Tuka, Bela, Slovak prime minister, 87, 89–90

United Nations Relief and Rehabilitation
    Agency (UNRRA), 150–151
Ursuline sisters of Poland, 121

Valeri, Valerio, nuncio, 5, 52
Vatican radio, 25, 46, 49, 128, 132, 162,
    218–220, 235
Vichy France, 5, 7, 13, 52, 64, 83, 92, 126–
    129
Völkische Beobachter, 17
Vrba, Rudolf, 106–108

Wagner, Eduard, German general, 21
Waldheim, Kurt, 215
Wallenberg, Raoul, rescuer, 108, 131
war criminals, xii, xvi, 11, 135, 139, 141,
    143–144, 159, 162–175, 183, 224
Warsaw ghetto, 48, 50, 119–120, 191;
    uprising, 50, 120, 191
Warthegau, Poland, 22–23, 25
Waugh, Evelyn, genocide witness, 35
We Remember: A Reflection on the Shoah,
    Vatican document, xiii, xiv, 215–216
Weinberg, Gerhard, historian, 52
Weiss, Karla, rescuer, 131
Welles, Sumner, U.S. Undersecretary of
    State, 49
Wetmanski, Leon, Bishop, 26
Wetzler, Alfred, Auschwitz escapee, 106–
    108
Wienken, Heinrich, Bishop, 73, 75
Wilner, Jurek, resistance, 121
Wise, Rabbi Stephen S., 49
Witte, Suzanne, rescuer, 114, 124, 131
World Council of Churches, 161
World Jewish Congress, 47, 94, 108, 160,
    197

Yad Vashem (Holocaust Martyrs and
    Heroes Remembrance Authority), 113,
    121, 131, 224
Yahil, Leni, historian, 105

Zahn, Gordon, historian, 72
Zegota, 52–54, 126–131, 224
Zeiger, Ivo, S.J., 141, 222
Zoli, Corrado, genocide witness, 35

MICHAEL PHAYER is Professor of History at Marquette University. In 1992–1993 Phayer held a Senior Fulbright Research Fellowship, which allowed him to do extensive research in Europe for this book. Phayer's two most recent books, *Protestant and Catholic Women in Nazi Germany* and (with Eva Fleischner) *Cries in the Night: Women Who Challenged the Holocaust,* deal extensively with Catholic-Jewish relations before and during the Shoah. The author has also written many articles on aspects of church and Holocaust history.